JAMES THE JUST AND CHRISTIAN ORIGINS

SUPPLEMENTS TO
NOVUM TESTAMENTUM

VOLUME XCVIII

JAMES THE JUST
AND
CHRISTIAN ORIGINS

EDITED BY

BRUCE CHILTON AND CRAIG A. EVANS

BRILL
LEIDEN · BOSTON · KÖLN
1999

This book is printed on acid-free paper.

ISSN   0167-9732
ISBN   90 04 11550 1

PRINTED IN THE NETHERLANDS

CONTENTS

PREFACE

The consultation on James, Jesus' brother, emerged out of interactive scholarship and discussion which has been pursued at Bard College over the past four years. Since 1996, a series of international meetings has focused on the relationship between Judaism and Christianity, especially during their formative periods. A conference at Bard in 1997, entitled "The Missing Jesus — Rabbinic Judaism and the New Testament," found that James was a particularly fruitful focus of inquiry. As a result, Mr. Frank T. Crohn, the principal supporter of our work, suggested that a consultation specifically devoted to James might be productive.

The itinerary and method of the consultation are described in this volume, and the principal contributors have prepared their work for publication. We are indebted to Mr. Crohn, to the contributors, and to Miss Theresa Desmond, our conference officer. Audio and video-tapes of our discussion have also been produced, and are available from Bard College.

The approach and level of our interaction have been developed within the Institute for Advanced Theology at Bard, which is dedicated to comparative study and cooperative scholarship. The Institute sponsored the consultation by means of grants from Mr. Crohn and the Pew Charitable Trusts, and is engaged to pursue this and similar initiatives. As our volume attests, we aim to continue investigating the seam which the study of James has opened up for us.

The authors are grateful to the editorial board of Supplements to Novum Testamentum for accepting this collection of studies for publication, to Dr. Theo Joppe of E. J. Brill for his guidance during the publication process, and to Ginny Evans for preparing the indexes. All of the essays are in English, but contributors were free to follow either British or American style.

Bruce Chilton   June, 1999
Bard College

Craig A. Evans
Trinity Western University

ABBREVIATIONS

AB	Anchor Bible (Commentary)
ABD	D. N. Freedman (ed.), *The Anchor Bible Dictionary* (6 vols., New York: Doubleday, 1992)
ABRL	Anchor Bible Reference Library
AJS Review	*Association for Jewish Studies Review*
ANRW	W. Haase and E. Temporini (eds.), *Aufstieg und Niedergang der römischen Welt* (Berlin: de Gruyter, 1979-)
APOT	R. H. Charles (ed.), *Apocrypha and Pseudepigrapha of the Old Testament* (2 vols., Oxford: Clarendon, 1913)
BAGD	W. Bauer, W. F. Arndt, F. W. Gingrich, and F. W. Danker, *A Greek-English Lexicon of the New Testament* (1979)
BBR	*Bulletin for Biblical Research*
Bib	*Biblica*
BibSem	The Biblical Seminar
BJS	Brown Judaic Studies
BNTC	Black's New Testament Commentary
BTB	*Biblical Theology Bulletin*
BZ	*Biblische Zeitschrift*
BZNW	Beihefte zur *Zeitschrift für die neutestamentliche Wissenschaft*
CBQ	*Catholic Biblical Quarterly*
CBQMS	Catholical Biblical Quarterly Monograph Series
CRINT	Compendia rerum iudaicarum ad novum testamentum
DJD	Discoveries in the Judaean Desert
DSD	*Dead Sea Discoveries*
EKKNT	Evangelisch-katholischer Kommentar zum Neuen Testament
ETR	*Études théologiques et religieuses*
ExpTim	*Expository Times*
FRLANT	Forschungen zur Religion und Literatur des Alten und Neuen Testaments
GNS	Good News Studies
HNT	Handbuch zum Neuen Testament
HTKNT	Herders theologischer Kommentar zum Neuen Testament
HTR	*Harvard Theological Review*
ICC	International Critical Commentary
IEJ	*Israel Exploration Journal*
JBL	*Journal of Biblical Literature*
JJS	*Journal of Jewish Studies*
JSNT	*Journal for the Study of the New Testament*
JSNTSup	*Journal for the Study of the New Testament*, Supplement Series
JSOTSup	*Journal for the Study of the Old Testament*, Supplement Series
JSP	*Journal for the Study of the Pseudepigrapha*
JTS	*Journal of Theological Studies*

LCL	Loeb Classical Library
MNTC	Moffat New Testament Commentary
Mus	*Muséon*
NICNT	New International Commentary on the New Testament
NIGTC	New International Greek Testament Commentary
NovTSup	Novum Tetamentum, Supplements
NTL	New Testament Library
NTOA	Novum Testamentum et Orbis Antiquus
NTS	*New Testament Studies*
NTTS	New Testament Tools and Studies
OTP	James H. Charlesworth (ed.), *Old Testament Pseudepigrapha* (2 vols., New York: Doubleday, 1983-85)
RB	*Revue biblique*
SAJ	Studies in Ancient Judaism
SBLDS	Society of Biblical Literature Dissertation Series
SBLSP	Society of Biblical Literature Seminar Papers
SBT	Studies in Biblical Theology
SEÅ	*Svensk exegetisk årsbok*
SJLA	Studies in Judaism in Late Antiquity
SJT	*Scottish Journal of Theology*
SNTSMS	Society for New Testament Studies Monograph Series
SPB	Studia postbiblica
ST	*Studia theologica*
THKNT	Theologischer Handkommentar zum Neuen Testament
TRu	*Theologische Rundschau*
TSAJ	Texte und Studien zum antiken Judentum
TynBul	*Tyndale Bulletin*
UUÅ	Uppsala universitetsårsskrift
WBC	Word Biblical Commentary
WUNT	Wissenschaftliche Untersuchungen zum Neuen Testament
ZNW	*Zeitschrift für die neutestamentliche Wissenschaft*
ZRGG	*Zeitschrift für Religions- und Geistesgeschichte*

CONTRIBUTORS

Richard Bauckham is Professor of New Testament at St Andrews University, and the author of *Jude and the Relatives of Jesus in the Early Church* (Edinburgh: T. & T. Clark, 1990).

Markus Bockmuehl is Lecturer in New Testament at Cambridge University, and the author of *Revelation and Mystery in Ancient Judaism and Pauline Christianity* (Grand Rapids: Eerdmans, 1997).

Bruce Chilton is Bernard Iddings Bell Professor of Philosophy and Religion at Bard College, and the author of *A Feast of Meanings: Eucharistic Theologies from Jesus through Johannine Circles* (NovTSup 72; Leiden: Brill, 1994).

Peter Davids is Director of Schloss Mittersill, and author of *A Commentary on the Epistle of James* (NIGTC; Grand Rapids: Eerdmans, 1982).

Philip Davies is Professor of Old Testament at Sheffield University, and author of *Scribes and Schools: The Canonization of the Hebrew Scriptures* (Louisville: Westminster, 1998).

Craig Evans is Professor of New Testament at Trinity Western University and Senior Research Fellow at Roehampton Institute London, and author of *Jesus and His Contemporaries: Comparative Studies* (AGJU 25; Leiden: Brill, 1995).

William Farmer is Director of the International Catholic Biblical Commentary, and author of *Peter and Paul in the Church of Rome: The Ecumenical Potential of a Forgotten Perspective* (with Roch Kereszty; New York: Paulist, 1990).

Scot McKnight is Karl A. Olsson Professor in Religious Studies at North Park Theological Seminary, and author of *Light among the Gentiles: Jewish Missionary Activity in the Second Temple Period* (Minneapolis: Fortress, 1991).

Jacob Neusner is Distinguished Professor of Religion at the University of South Florida and Professor of Religion at Bard College, and author of *Judaism: The Evidence of the Mishnah* (Chicago: University of Chicago Press, 1985).

PART ONE

ISSUES OF BACKGROUND AND CONTEXT

INTRODUCTION

Bruce Chilton

Interest in Jesus' brother Ya'aqov, Anglicized as James, has seen a renaissance in recent years. Among contemporary contributions, we might mention the comprehensive presentation of texts and discussion by Wilhelm Pratscher[1] and the semi-popular treatment by Pierre-Antoine Bernheim.[2] Both of those books represent vigorously historical attempts to recover a critical portrait of James. They respond, directly and indirectly, to the controversial thesis of Robert H. Eisenman, who has argued for a number of years that James is to be identified with the righteous teacher of Qumran.[3] Among the vehement responses to that thesis, perhaps the most mature and effective is that of John Painter.[4]

Recovery of interest in James is evidently useful, in that his place within primitive Christianity had been all but eclipsed by the influence of Paulinism in its many forms. The vehemence of response to Eisenman's thesis, quite apart from the specific questions it raises (exegetical, historical, archaeological) might best be explained on theological grounds. A silent James is more easily accommodated to the picture of a smooth transition between Jesus and Paul than a James who substantially contradicts both Paul *and* Jesus. In the dispute which is going on around us, then, we have a good example of how historical and theological questions intersect, and have a tendency to become entangled.

Within this entanglement of history and theology, a well defined

---

[1]   W. Pratscher, *Der Herrenbruder Jakobus und die Jakobustraditionen* (FRLANT 139; Göttingen: Vandenhoeck & Ruprecht, 1987).

[2]   P.-A. Bernheim, *James, Brother of Jesus* (London: SCM Press, 1997); cf. the French original: *Jacques, Frère de Jésus* (Paris: Nôesis, 1996).

[3]   Among his many publications, see *James the Just in the Habakkuk Pesher* (SPB 35; Leiden: Brill, 1986), *James the Brother of Jesus: The Key to Unlocking the Secrets of Early Christianity and the Dead Sea Scrolls* (New York: Viking, 1996).

[4]   J. Painter, *Just James: The Brother of Jesus in History and Tradition* (Columbia: University of South Carolina Press, 1997).

set of issues has been perennially been in play:[5]

- Was James *really* Jesus brother?
- Was James at all sympathetic to Jesus prior to the resurrection?
- Did James require circumcision of males along with baptism by way of initiation into the movement of Jesus?
- Was there any substantial place for non-Jews within James' understanding of the covenant with Abraham, Isaac, and Jacob?
- Did James oppose a Pauline teaching of salvation by grace with an insistence upon obedience to the Torah?
- Was James the most prominent person in Jesus' movement between the resurrection and his own death?

None of the treatments already cited fails to take a stand on each of these issues, and for the most part each issue is also responsibly engaged in those and other discussions. That is both good and bad, because this set of issues is wise and hopeless at one and the same time.

The wisdom of the list resides in its address of a single, systemic concern: in its generative moment, was Christianity in fact *as well as in its self-awareness*, a species of Judaism? That is why the relation between James and Jesus, whether physically or emotionally, is so important. If James self-consciously remained faithful to a received definition of Israel (as Paul did not), and if Jesus and James were indeed brothers of flesh and in their affections, then the grounding conception of Christianity as a separate religion from Judaism, or even as offering a distinct revelation, is seriously compromised. Likewise, the place of circumcision, the covenant with the patriarchs, and the Torah, all these relate to the correlative concern: is faith in Jesus to be located within Israel? Once that concern has been stated, confirmed as an interest in the sources, and traced in its specifics, the question of James' standing in Jesus' movement obviously becomes crucial. If he indeed stands for the Church within Israel, and is effectively the leader of the movement, then Israel must have been the fundamental category of Christian social doctrine, at least until James' death in 62 C.E. (and probably after that).[6]

The hopelessness of the same list is that it presents these questions as if they were purely historical. Both in conceptual terms and in

---

[5]   For a typical presentation, see the table of contents of Bernheim's book.

[6]   Just this insight is central to the perspective of the principal donor to the consultation, Frank T. Crohn; see *James: His Brother's Keeper* (Skidmore College: Master of Arts, 1997).

pragmatic terms, a merely historical approach offers no prospect of success.

In conceptual terms, to understand a figure of Christianity in relation to Judaism requires more than the tools of biography. Biographical treatment assumes an understanding of the context in which a person developed. A recent biography of Robert Kennedy,[7] for example, engages with the social history of the United States and the consequences of immigrant families amassing wealth and adopting the perspectives and political agenda of liberal, aristocratic families in turn of the century America. The interface between social context and an individual's evolution is so evident and so intense, current biographical work does not even need to make out the case for exploring that connection. But in the case of James, or any figure of primitive Christianity (Jesus included), the issue of context is at least as problematic as the evidence concerning the particular person involved.

In pragmatic terms, the purely historical approach is even more obviously bankrupt in the case of James. The few mentions of James in Paul, the Gospels, Josephus, Acts, the *Gospel according to the Hebrews*, the Clementine literature, and Eusebius, even were they to be taken at face value, do not provide a coherent, a structured, or even a broad account of Jesus' brother. Each of those sources argues as it unfolds for a particular view of the relationship between Judaism and Christianity, and each was produced within the terms of reference of that relationship as it existed at the time the source was produced. By the time these documents were written, James was more the pawn than the pawnbroker he might once have been.

The conceptual and pragmatic poverty of a purely historical approach has already been illustrated by the course of recent discussion of Jesus. The *Journal of Biblical Literature* recently presented a lively exchange concerning the sustained attempt by John Dominic Crossan to style Jesus as Cynic philosopher.[8] The consensus appears to be that the fit Crossan proposes is not sustained by the evidence, but little attention has been paid to the question of why Crossan would have so completely identified Jesus with *any* urban

---

7   See Michael Knox Beran, *The Last Patrician: Bobby Kennedy and the End of American Aristocracy* (New York: St. Martin's, 1998).

8   See Paul Rhodes Eddy, "Jesus as Diogenes? Reflections on the Cynic Jesus Thesis," *JBL* 115 (1996) 449-69, and the response by F. G. Downing, "Deeper Reflections on the Jewish Cynic Jesus," *JBL* 117 (1998) 97-104.

Hellenistic movement in the first place. He himself provides the answer, in his most complete treatment of Jesus. Rather than contend with the many varieties of Judaism attested within the first century, Crossan makes the categorical assertion, "There was, in the world and time of Jesus, only one sort of Judaism, and that was Hellenistic Judaism."[9] Once Jesus' environment has been homogenized by that generalization, the way is open to put him in a context quite different from the setting in provincial Galilee which recent archaeology has elucidated.[10] Judaism has been denatured by a stroke of the pen, to be identifiable with Hellenistic philosophy, and little ingenuity is then required to proceed to clothe Jesus in the garb of popular philosophy.

So this allegedly historical Jesus truncates any consideration of the religious identity of Jesus' movement, by constructing a consistent picture of him within a thoroughly implausible setting. The conceptual creativity of Jesus and his movement is collapsed into the contention that all such teachers were philosophers of one sort or another, and the pragmatics of exegesis are conflated into the contention that, as a Cynic, Jesus was an example of "hippies in a world of Augustan yuppies."[11] Few sentences in modern scholarship are as apt, and at the same time as self-revealing. The particular failings of this Cynic-hippie portrait of Jesus are a matter of ongoing discussion,[12] but it is evident that a surmised social setting is here used to truncate both the conceptual and the pragmatic dimensions of analysis. What I have styled an historicist fallacy has perennially impoverished an assessment of Jesus,[13] because history has been used

---

[9]   J. D. Crossan, *The Historical Jesus: The Life of a Mediterranean Jewish Peasant* (San Francisco: HarperCollins; Edinburgh: T. & T. Clark, 1991) 418. In the preface of his book, Crossan admits to bewilderment at the variety of Judaisms during the first century (see p. xxvii).

[10]   See the sustained criticism of Crossan's picture in Richard A. Horsley, *Archaeology, History, and Society in Galilee: The Social Context of Jesus and the Rabbis* (Valley Forge, Pennsylvania: Trinity Press International, 1996). For criticism in regard to literary evidence, see Chilton, "Jesus within Judaism," in J. Neusner (ed.), *Judaism in Late Antiquity. Part Two: Historical Syntheses* (Handbuch der Orientalistik 17; Leiden: Brill, 1995) 262-84.

[11]   Crossan, *The Historical Jesus*, 421.

[12]   See B. Chilton, *Pure Kingdom: Jesus' Vision of God* (Studying the Historical Jesus 1; Grand Rapids: Eerdmans; London: SPCK, 1996).

[13]   See B. Chilton, *The Temple of Jesus: His Sacrificial Program Within a Cultural History of Sacrifice* (University Park: The Pennsylvania State University

to reduce Jesus' theology and Jesus' public acts to the supposition that he merely instantiates one cultural norm or another. Why someone who merely typified a cultural form should have been remembered as being thoroughly untypical is not explained. Further, since the context of Jesus is as mysterious as the figure of Jesus, no advance is made by trying to identify him with a totalizing model drawn from a mere supposition concerning his cultural environment.

The historicist impoverishment is even more debilitating in the study of James, whether on the conceptual or the pragmatic side. Conceptually, James can only be located within, and vigorously stands for, a emphatic concentration on the Temple in Jerusalem which distinguishes him from every other Christian teacher. The evaluation of James therefore demands an assessment—consequently, a construction—of that sort of practice, before Christian claims of the complete transcendence of sacrificial worship became dominant with the publication of the Epistle to the Hebrews. Absent such an assessment, one simply finds reassertions of the claim of the Tübingen school during the nineteenth century, that James stood in a diametrical opposition to Paul, holding the place of law in the confrontation of law and grace. That, of course, is a Pauline antinomy, and results in the persistent claim that James insisted upon the circumcision of all male believers, when both Acts and the Clementine *Recognitions* assert just the contrary. Protestant intellectuals since the Enlightenment sought to read their doctrines into history, and James has been a perennial victim of that program. That kind of historicism forecloses any conceptual appreciation of James from the outset.

In pragmatic terms, the sources which portray James are much more disparate than those which portray Jesus, and the references to James are, comparatively speaking, fragmentary. What makes matters even more difficult, none of the major sources which refer to James does so from the point of view of James' own followers. This is the principal reason for which the immediate recovery of something like the historical James is simply impossible.

The Gospels, when they refer to James at all, do so with no great sympathy. He is listed at the head of Jesus' brothers in the Synoptic Gospels, but in a statement of a crowd in Nazareth which is skeptical that one whose family they know can be responsible for wonders

---

Press, 1992).

(Mark 6:1-6; Matt 13:53-58). In John, he is presumably included among the unnamed brothers who argued with Jesus about his refusal to go to Jerusalem for a feast (John 7:2-10), and James is also referred to anonymously in the Synoptics as among the brothers whom, even with his mother, Jesus refused to interrupt his teaching in order to greet (Mark 3:31-35; Matt 12:46-50; Luke 8:19-21). A possible inference would be that Jesus and James were at odds during this period, but that is scarcely provable. More immediately, one can say that James and his brothers are marginalized by such references, so that there can be no question of their controlling Jesus during his life. The distance which the Gospels posit between Jesus and James may or not accurately reflect their relationship, but it does suggest a desire to qualify the assessment of James' influence within the communities which produced the Gospels.

Despite the Gospels' qualification of James' influence, Acts attributes to James (and to James alone) the power to decide whether non-Jewish male converts in Antioch needed to be circumcised. He determines that they do not, but proceeds to command them to observe certain requirements of purity (so Acts 15:1-35). That may help to explain why emissaries from James make their appearance as villains in Paul's description of a major controversy at Antioch. They insisted on a separate meal-fellowship of Jews and non-Jews, while Paul with more than equal insistence (but apparently little or no success) argued for the unity of Jewish and non-Jewish fellowship within the Church (Gal 1:18-2:21). How James came to such a position of prominence is not explained in Acts, although Paul does refer to James as a witness of Jesus' resurrection (1 Cor 15:7), and the *Gospel according to the Hebrews* (approvingly cited by Jerome, *Liber de Viris Illustribus* 2) presents a full account of his fasting prior to his vision.

Acts also associates James with the Temple in Jerusalem, as the head of the community of Jesus' followers there, and particularly portrays him as concerned with the fulfillment of Nazirite vows, a practice in which he involves Paul (Acts 21:17-35). That fits with Josephus' account of James' martyrdom at the Temple (*Ant.* 20.9.1 §197-203), an account which is considerably filled out by Hegesippus, who stresses James' asceticism, and the privilege he enjoyed within the Temple as a result (as cited by Eusebius in his *Hist. Eccl.* 2.23.1-18). Hegesippus' account of James prominence is confirmed by Clement, who portrays James as the first elected bishop in Jerusalem (also cited by Eusebius, *Eccl. Hist.* 2.1.1-6), and by the pseudo-Clementine *Recognitions*, which makes James into an almost papal figure, providing the correct paradigm of preaching to Gentiles. (Paul is so much the butt of this presentation, the *Recognitions* [1.43-71] even relate that, prior to his conversion to Christianity, Saul assaulted physically James in the Temple. Martin Hengel refers to this presentation as an apostolic novel [*Apostelroman*], deeply influenced by the perspective of the Ebionites, and probably to be dated within the third and fourth centuries.)[14]

It is telling that, in his attempt to draw together the material relating to James, Jerome cites the *Gospel according to the Hebrews* alongside the New Testament, Hegesippus, and Josephus. The conflation attests the fragmentary nature of the references, as well as the appearance they give of having been spun out of one another, or out of cognate traditions. For all that use of these sources is unavoidable, as the necessary point of departure for any discussion of James, they all make James into an image which comports with their own programs. The Gospels' James is kept at bay so as not to deflect attention from Jesus *until the resurrection*, when James implicitly or explicitly (in the case of Paul and the *Gospel according to the Hebrews*) becomes an important witness; the James of Acts reconciles the Church within a stance which leads on to the position of Paul; Paul's James divides the Church; Josephus relates James' death to illustrate the bloody mindedness of Ananus, the high priest; Hegesippus does so to illustrate the righteousness of James and his community; Clement makes James the transitional figure of the apostolic tradition, and the *Recognitions* use and enhance that standing in order to attack the figure of Paul.

Right the way through, James is deployed in these sources to assert

---

14   See M. Hengel, "Jakobus der Herrenbruder—der erste 'Papst'?" in E. Grässer and O. Merk (eds.), *Glaube und Eschatologie: Festschrift für Werner Georg Kümmel zum 80. Geburtstag* (Tübingen: Mohr [Siebeck], 1985) 71-104, here 81. The ordering of Peter under James is clearly a part of that perspective, as Hengel shows, and much earlier Joseph Lightfoot found that the alleged correspondence between Clement and James was a later addition to the Pseudo-Clementine corpus (see J. B. Lightfoot, *The Apostolic Fathers* 1 [London: Macmillan, 1890] 414-20). But even if the Pseudo-Clementines are taken at face value, they undermine Eisenman's view (or the view of the "Tübingen school," as Hengel [p. 92] points out is the source of such contentions): they portray James as the standard for how Hellenistic Christians are to teach (see *Recognitions* 11.35.3).

what is held to be an authoritative construction of Jesus' movement. Accordingly, he is marginalized (in the Gospels), appealed to as an authoritative witness (in Acts and Paul), criticized (in Paul), portrayed as a victim (by Josephus) or a hero (by Hegesippus), hailed as both a source of unity (by Clement, in the tradition of Acts) and the trump card to use against Paul (in the *Recognitions*). Everything which makes the figure of "the historical Jesus" in an historicist understanding problematic makes "the historical James" in that sense out of the question.

But an appropriate posing of the question of Jesus has in any case proven to be feasible in critical terms, once the myth of an historical Jesus immediately recoverable from the sources is dispensed with. For all that a Jesus of history is not "in" our sources, there is no doubt but that there is a Jesus of literary history. That is, the Gospels, as well as other documents refer back to Jesus as their point of generation, and we may infer what practices Jesus engaged in, what beliefs he adhered to, so as to produce the accounts concerning him in the communities of followers which produced the documents. The framing world of those practices and beliefs in the formative period of the New Testament (whether in the case of Jesus or his followers) was Judaism. For this reason, the much maligned word "primitive" is suitably appended to refer to the Christianity of this period. Practices and beliefs are attested in the documents manifestly, whether or not their attribution to Jesus is accepted, and that is a suitable point of departure for the genuinely critical question of Jesus. That question can not be formulated as, What did Jesus really say and really do? The critical issue is rather, What role did Jesus play in the evolution of practices and beliefs in his name?[15]

That generative question may be broadened, of course, to apply not only to Jesus and the Gospels, but to primitive Christianity and the New Testament.[16] In the present case, however, the challenge is to apply a generative approach to James, and that involves specifying the practices and beliefs which attach to James within the sources, and seeking to understand his place within them. Not every practice, not every belief may be assumed to be correctly attributed to James, but the various streams of tradition the documents represent do come

---

[15]   For my development of this perspective, see Chilton, *The Temple of Jesus*, and idem, *Pure Kingdom*.

[16]   See B. Chilton and J. Neusner, *Judaism in the New Testament: Practices and Beliefs* (London and New York: Routledge, 1995).

together in what may be called nodes, to constitute stable associations
of practices and beliefs with James. The nodal issues of practices and
beliefs, not "facts," represent our point of departure. Just those nodal
issues are addressed in our papers for "The Consultation on James."

Unless we make a generative concern with practices and beliefs
our priority, our portraits of figures in the New Testament other
than Jesus will become even more distorted than our constructions of
Jesus himself. The findings of the Jesus Seminar in regard to John
the Baptist are illustrative. The Fellows deployed their much-
discussed skepticism to doubt that Jesus ever referred to John as a
prophet, but then cast their beads to decide that John was such a
prophet.[17] That, without an analysis of John's practices and without
addressing the embarrassing fact that Josephus (who is not exactly
parsimonious in his use of prophetic language) does not call John a
prophet. If this finding is skeptical, it is with the skepticism of the
nineteenth century, which expected to find facts covered up, but to
find them nonetheless.

Within the terms of reference of early Judaism and primitive
Christianity, no single issue can compare in importance to that of the
Temple. The Nazirite practice attributed to James and those in
contact with him provides a highly focused degree of devotion to the
Temple. Professor Neusner's paper, "Vow-Taking, the Nazirites, and
the Law: Does James' Advice to Paul Accord with Halakhah?,"
therefore opens our consultation with the most pertinent question in
relation to James' definition as a son of Israel. The definition of
Israel, of course, is fundamental to Paul's perspective, particularly in
his letter to the Galatians, where he insists that those who believe in
Jesus are "sons of Abraham" (Gal 3:1-7), identifiable as "the Israel
of God" (Gal 6:16). There is no accident that, precisely as Paul is
working out that radical definition, he provides us with the only
references there are to James from someone who actually knew him.
Although Paul is scarcely James' disciple, he brings us closer to that
figure than any of the sources we will consider, so that Professor
Farmer's lucid and evocative paper, "James the Lord's Brother,
according to Paul," is a pivotal contribution. The setting of the confrontation between Paul and those whom he describes as emissaries

---

17   R. W. Funk and R. W. Hoover (eds.), *The Five Gospels: The Search for
the Authentic Words of Jesus* (Sonoma: Polebridge Press; New York: Macmillan,
1993) 132, 178-79.

from James, with Peter and Barnabas caught in between, is Antioch, a center which has attracted considerable interest in recent years. Dr Bockmuehl's paper, "Antioch and James the Just," brings that discussion to bear, but also opens out an exciting possibility in regard to the geographical evaluation of Antioch in a positive relationship to Israel within the sources of early Judaism and Rabbinic Judaism. These initial essays are all socially historical in the proper sense: they assess the practices and beliefs of James and his circle as compared to well attested practices and beliefs in contemporary Judaism and Christianity.

As usually practiced, of course, the social history of primitive Christianity and early Christianity as been Hellenistic in orientation. That is predictable and defensible, given the actual provenience and language of the New Testament and the bulk of the corpus of Christianity in late antiquity. Still, social histories such as those of Wayne Meeks,[18] Abraham Malherbe,[19] and Dennis Smith and Hal Taussig[20] have tended not to engage the sources of Judaism, and especially the Judaism of Aramaic and Hebrew sources, with the same vigor that has been applied to the Hellenistic dimension of analysis. That is perfectly understandable, given the particular documents they have dealt with, and the specific questions which they applied to those documents. But a figure such as James will simply remain a cipher, and in all probability a cipher for some form of Paulinism or another, as long as he is not located within the milieu which not only produced him, but which was taken as a consciously chosen locus of devotion and activity. Many teachers associated with the movement of Jesus managed at least partially to avoid the Temple altogether; James is virtually found only there after the resurrection.

The specificity of that location raises the issue of James' relation to other forms of Christianity, to other forms of Judaism, and especially to those responsible for the operation of the Temple. Here the analysis of James in socially historical terms comes closest to classic history, in its specificity. But these are specifics which are clearly related to the nodal issue of the Temple. In "James and Jesus," Professor Evans takes up the issue of the relative continuity and

---

18   See *The First Urban Christians: The social world of the Apostle Paul* (New Haven: Yale University Press, 1983).

19   See *Social Aspects of Early Christianity* (Philadelphia: Fortress, 1983).

20   See *Many Tables: The Eucharist in the New Testament and Liturgy Today* (Philadelphia: Trinity Press International; London: SCM Press, 1990).

discontinuity manifest in the positions of Jesus and James, especially in regard to the Temple and interpretive traditions focused on Psalm 118. The Temple is also a central concern in the definition of the Essenes, and Professor Davies approaches the Essene affinity of James by means of a consideration of the work of Robert Eisenman in "James in the Qumran Scrolls." Finally, within this section of more specifically focused, socially historical essays, Professor Bauckham approaches the intriguing question of the motivation and occasion for James' execution by the priestly authorities in Jerusalem.

Whether in the key of an emphasis on the "social" (as in the first three essays) or the "historical" (as in the next three) within socially historical analysis, what emerges from our consideration is a distinctive, cultic focus upon the validation of the covenant with Israel on the authority of Jesus, understood in his resurrection to be identifiable with the "one like a son of man" of Daniel 7. Once that distinctive focus has been isolated, it is natural to ask: how great was its impact upon the corpus of primitive Christian and early Christian literature? It has been argued, for example, that passages within the Synoptic Gospels might well bear the stamp of James' perspective. Within the narrative of Jesus' passion in the Synoptics, only one passage makes the last supper correspond to Passover (Matt 21:1-11; Mark 11:1-10; Luke 19:28-40), and that presentation conflicts with the Johannine and Pauline presentations. That would limit participation in the meal and in its commemoration to those circumcised, in the case of males (see Exod 12:48), a move which would accord with James' Israelite construction of the church.[21] Similarly, the teaching attributed to Jesus in regard to vowing property as *qorbana*, a gift to the Temple, manifests an interest in and a familiarity with cultic institutions, as well as a style of exegesis associated with the *pesharim* of Qumran, which better accords with James than with Jesus (Matt 15:1-20; Mark 7:1-23).[22] Lastly, the story of the demons and the swine of Gerasa, with its emphasis on the impurity of non-Jews (Romans especially; Matt 8:28-34; Mark 5:1-20; Luke 8:26-39) has been linked with a Jacobean cycle of tradition, and the secret knowledge of the demons that Jesus was *Nazarenos*, a Nazirite, is

---

21   See B. Chilton, *A Feast of Meanings: Eucharistic Theologies from Jesus through Johannine Circles* (NovTSup 72; Leiden: Brill, 1994) 93-108.

22   See Chilton, "A Generative Exegesis of Mark 7:1-23," *The Journal of Higher Criticism* 3.1 (1996) 18-37.

plausible linked to the same cycle.[23]

The transition from evaluating the James of the literary and social history of the New Testament to the attribution of material to James and his circle is evidently a second order of inference, developed from the initial, literarily historical inference of James' theological influence. That transition is most directly confronted in the question of the authorship of the letter attributed to James in the New Testament. That issue is taken up by Peter Davids in "Palestinian Traditions in the Epistle of James," a paper which enables us to look into the entire range of such attributions, not only within the New Testament, but also in Gnostic literature, beginning from the statement in the *Gospel according to Thomas*, where James is presented as the one for whom the heavens and the earth were created (*logion* §12). The consideration of attributions, in turn, must be embedded in a more comprehensive vision of James' place within the development of primitive Christianity and early Christianity, and Professor McKnight has provided us with an occasion to seize such a vision in "A Parting within the Way: Jesus and James on Israel and Purity."

Just as it is possible to move from the inference of James in literary history and social history to the secondary inference of attributions to James, so a third order of inference is possible. The historicist questions we began with are by no means the beginning and end of analysis, but it would be a strange king of history (literary or social) which simply ignored them. Responses to them are implicit in much of our work, and—by way of hypothesis—I take this opportunity to respond to them explicitly. Richard Bauckham has given new currency to what he calls the Epiphanian view of Jesus' relationship to James:[24] Joseph was the father in each case, but Miriam was Jesus' mother, not James', since Joseph had a wife prior to his marriage to Miriam. Joseph's relatively advanced age might account for his early departure from the narrative scene

---

23 See J. Neusner and B. D. Chilton, *The Body of Faith. Israel and the Church* (Christianity and Judaism – The Formative Categories 2; Valley Forge: Trinity Press International, 1996) 98-101, and Chilton, "Getting it Right: Jesus, James, and Judaism," given at a conference at Bard College in 1997 entitled "The Missing Jesus: Rabbinic Judaism and the New Testament," to be published in a volume under the same title by Hendrickson.

24 See "The Brothers and Sisters of Jesus: An Epiphanian Response to John P. Meier," *CBQ* 56 (1994) 686-700.

of the Gospels, while James' emphasis on the Davidic identity of the Church (see Acts 15:16) is easily accommodated on this view. His seniority relative to Jesus might just be reflected in the parable of the prodigal (Luke 15:11-32). The story of those with Jesus seizing him in the midst of exorcism (Mark 3:21) may well reflect the kind of almost parental concern an older brother might feel for a younger brother, and the proximity of that story to the account of Jesus refusing to see his own family (Mark 3:31-35) might be eloquent.[25]

James' devotion to the Temple and to his brother as the Danielic Son of Man after the resurrection made him the most prominent Christian leader in Jerusalem. The practice of the Nazirite vow was his distinguishing feature, and his belief in his brother as the gate of heaven, the heavenly portal above the Temple, made him a figure to be revered and reviled in Judaism, depending upon one's evaluation of Jesus. Among Christians, he promulgated his understanding of the establishment of the house of David by means of an interpretation reminiscent of the Essenes, although he insisted that baptized, uncircumcised non-Jews had an ancillary role. As the overseer (*mebaqqer*) of his community, he exercised a function which entered the Greek language as *episkopos*, and the influence of his circle is attested in the New Testament and Gnostic literature.

But such hypothetical statements can only be taken by way of example. Whatever may or may not be said of James, such statements can not plausibly be made of him as he is under the texts or behind the texts. The only James we can know is within the sources, properly contexted in the practices and beliefs of Judaism and Christianity, just as those two religions were emerging with the systematic structures we recognize them by. Our literary and social inferences, the second-order inference of attribution, and the third-order inference of historical hypothesis, each to be corrected and refined, these are the substance of our knowing, not any alleged figure abstracted from the sources.

---

[25]   See "Getting it Right."

JAMES IN THE QUMRAN SCROLLS

Philip R. Davies

JAMES IN THE QUMRAN SCROLLS?

As far as I know, the theory that James the brother of Jesus is alluded to in the Qumran texts is exclusively associated with the name of Robert Eisenman, who first advocated it in two slim volumes published in 1983 and 1986.[1] Eisenman identifies James with the "Teacher of Righteousness," Paul with the "Liar" (alias "Man of Lies" and "Spouter of Lies"), and the High Priest Ananus with the "Wicked Priest"—the three main protagonists of a text, the *pesher* on Habakkuk, still thought by many to carry the secrets of Qumran origins. But as the title of Eisenman's first volume suggests, these identifications have been achieved in the context of a wider thesis about the existence of a Jewish movement that bore many names throughout its history and combined fervent nationalism with rigid adherence to the law of Moses in a cult of "righteousness" (Heb: צֶדֶק). By recognizing this movement under the guise of "Maccabees," "Zadokites," and "Nazoreans," as well as attributing to them the authorship of the Qumran scrolls, Eisenman presents an alternative to the increasingly accepted view both that the Judaism of the late Second Temple Period was characterized by a number of different versions of "Judaism"—even, indeed, a number of "Judaisms." On the contrary, he simplifies the picture of Palestinian Judean religion considerably by effectively proposing a duality between the "righteous," nationalistic, and popular Judaism of his "Zadokites" and the religiously corrupt Judaism of the political and religious authorities who were also politically compliant with the occupying power, Rome: Sadducees, Herodians, Pharisees, and high priests.

---

[1] *Maccabees, Zadokites, Christians and Qumran: A New Hypothesis of Qumran Origins* (SPB 34; Leiden: Brill, 1983); *James the Just in the Habakkuk Pesher* (SPB 35; Leiden: Brill, 1986). These have now been republished in a single volume, together with later studies, in *The Dead Sea Scrolls and the First Christians* (Shaftesbury, Dorset: Element Books, 1996).

The most controversial aspects of Eisenman's theory propose that the production of the Qumran scrolls and the origins of Christianity both lie within this popular Judaism of "righteousness" and that some of the Qumran scrolls actually emanate from the earliest Christian community, the earliest followers of Jesus led by James the Just (הַצַּדִּיק). Debate about the relationship between the Qumran scrolls and Christianity (or the New Testament) has a long and fascinating history, of course, ranging from the view of both Dupont-Sommer and Allegro in the 1950s that Christianity was essentially anticipated by Essenism (and the more extreme expression of this by Wilson)[2] to the now more commonly accepted opinion that while there are several points of resemblance between the Scrolls and the New Testament, there is no organic or systematic connection between the two. There is a further dimension to this relationship, namely that many of the Scrolls originate from a messianic sect and thus offer an interesting social parallel to the messianic sect of Jesus's early followers. From this perspective, several parallels (community of goods, council of twelve, belief in imminent vindication) but also differences (attitude to purity laws, especially) can be accommodated. Unfortunately, the public is eager for rather more positive evaluations of the connection and is being to some extent pandered to by a good deal of print and television journalism.

At any rate, the relationship between the "Jewish" and "Christian" contexts of the Scrolls has been pondered again recently, as the course of Qumran scholarship has undergone a strong shift in recent years away from a Christian near-monopoly towards a strong Jewish participation. This has been in part the reason for an increased recognition of the importance of legal issues in the Scrolls.[3] Eisenman's intervention in the debate about the "Jewishness" of the

---

[2]   John Allegro, *The Dead Sea Scrolls: a Reappraisal* (Harmondsworth: Penguin Books, 1956 [²1964]); E. Wilson, *The Scrolls from the Dead Sea* (New York: Oxford University Press, 1955); A. Dupont-Sommer, *Les écrits esséniens découverts près de la Mer Morte* (Bibliothèque historique; Paris: Payot, 1959); ET: *The Essene Writings from Qumran* (Oxford: Blackwell, 1961); cf. T. Gaster, *The Dead Sea Scriptures* (Garden City: Doubleday, 1956).

[3]   I say "in part" because the contents of the Temple Scroll, the Halakhic Letter, and the Cave 4 manuscripts of the Damascus Document would, under any publication regime, have drawn attention to the importance of halakhic matters to the writers of the Scrolls. That all of these were published exclusively or largely by Jewish scholars does not obscure this fact.

Scrolls has, in this context, certainly been taken as provocative. Lawrence Schiffman, whose major work on the Scrolls is entitled *Reclaiming the Dead Sea Scrolls*,[4] has claimed that Eisenman is "taking away the heritage of the Jewish people" by making, or appearing to make, the authors of the Scrolls Christians. A contrary interpretation of Eisenman's position could, however, be argued: that he is really trying to take away the heritage of Pauline Christians by claiming that Paul was an enemy of the first and closest followers of Jesus, and that these followers espoused a devotion to the Mosaic law and political opposition to the ruling class and the Romans that Paul certainly did not share. While I do not think that the kind of link that Eisenman ties between early Christians and Qumran is effective, I have no difficulty in the proposition, of which Eisenman makes a good deal, that for many first-century Palestinian Jews devotion to the law and militaristic fervour easily combined. But that opinion is in any case one that most students of late Second Temple Judaism would be happy to share. The once-mooted division between "legalistic" and "apocalyptic" species of Judaism (which led respectively to rabbinic Judaism and to "Christian theology") has certainly been definitively buried, if that were needed, by the evidence of the Qumran scrolls. That rabbinic Judaism did in fact develop broadly and eventually in the one direction and Christianity in the other should not obscure the fact that the two attitudes sit very comfortably together at the time just before either religious system came into existence.[5]

The problem I personally face with Eisenman's work is that while I find his argumentation both hard to follow and often based on a chain of associations, and some of his assumptions inadequate, I nevertheless regard some of his ideas about the nature of the earliest community of Jesus' followers intriguing and even plausible. The treatment of James the brother of Jesus in the synoptic Gospels[6] strikes me, as it does Eisenman, as suspicious in the way these writings either dissociate him from the followers of Jesus (see Mark

---

[4]   *Reclaiming the Dead Sea Scrolls* (Philadelphia: Jewish Publication Society, 1994).

[5]   The two are closely intertwined in the book of Ezekiel, which was highly influential among the Qumran documents. Nor should it be forgotten that a tradition of keeping the divine law remained in Christianity, and an interest in apocalyptic among the rabbis.

[6]   The Fourth Gospel makes no reference to any James at all.

6:3 parr.) or distinguish his mother Mary from the mother of Jesus (Mark 15:40, 16:1 parr). But these suspicions are not my business in this paper. Rather, my primary question is: does Eisenman actually make a reasonable case for James as the "Teacher of Righteousness" of the Habakkuk *pesher* (and some other *pesharim* also)? If I were to concentrate purely on this question, I could offer a very succinct paper. For while it is not technically beyond the bounds of scientific possibility that *some* of the Qumran texts that mention the "Teacher of Righteousness" might have been composed sufficiently late to permit James to have been the intended bearer of that title, it is virtually impossible that all such texts do. For such Qumran manuscripts include also the fragments of the *Damascus Document* from Cave 4,[7] which are very hard to assign all to such a period.

Indeed, if Eisenman insists, as he does, that "one must make one's determinations on the basis of internal data—internal allusions and perspective of the document itself,"[8] then he will have to acknowledge that the internal evidence of the Scrolls as a whole is against him. All the *known* historical allusions in the Scrolls (as has been recently demonstrated by Wise, Abegg, and Cook[9]) can be assigned to the first century B.C.E. There is simply no ground from which to argue that certain others *must* nevertheless refer to the first century C.E. and that James could therefore be mentioned in the Qumran Scrolls.

But if James was not the "Teacher of Righteousness" of the Scrolls (assuming that this figure is identifiable with a single historical person), then may he nevertheless have been the leader of the same movement that included among its many manifestations the "Qumran sect"? Eisenman, with many earlier Qumran scholars, assumes the Scrolls to be the products of a single community, for which the term "Qumran sect" was an appropriate designation. But much of current scholarship doubts that the Scrolls all originated at Qumran, while how much of the archive is "sectarian" (and how many sects may be represented) is now disputed, as is the nature of the Qumran site

---

[7]   Now published in full by Joseph M. Baumgarten, *Qumran Cave 4: The Damascus Document (4Q266–273)* (DJD 18; Oxford: Clarendon Press, 1996).

[8]   *James the Brother of Jesus: Recovering the True History of Early Christianity* (London: Faber & Faber, 1997) 82.

[9]   M. O. Wise, M. G. Abegg Jr., and E. Cook, *The Dead Sea Scrolls: A New Translation* (San Francisco: HarperSanFrancisco, 1996) 26-32.

itself.[10] However, Eisenman's theory would gain some strength from the view that the Qumran texts represent a wider spectrum of Jewish religious ideas, emanating perhaps from a wider "movement" or even interconnected groups. If this is the case, has Eisenman, regardless of his precise claims about the presence of James in the Scrolls, any useful contribution to make to understanding either the Scrolls or the movement that James led?

Eisenman has certainly had considerable success in convincing writers of popular books of his thesis. In their *Dead Sea Scrolls Deception*,[11] Baigent and Leigh accepted Eisenman's claim that the Scrolls contained accounts of the true origins of Christianity in suggesting that the Vatican had initiated a conspiracy to suppress their publication. More recently still, Neil Asher Silberman also endorsed Eisenman's account of the background of the Scrolls.[12] None of these writers is a Scrolls specialist, nor indeed a student of early Christianity or Second Temple Judaism. Baigent and Leigh, of course, had in addition very good reason to accept Eisenman's thesis, since without it there is little basis for a conspiracy theory. Only Eisenman currently provides any basis for such an accusation.[13] Silberman was perhaps attracted by the ideological issue of Christian versus Jewish interpretation of the Scrolls. And perhaps some of the allure of Eisenman's portrait of first-century C.E. Palestinian Judaism is that it offers a dualism of popular and elite, pure and corrupt, official and unofficial, patriotic and unpatriotic, reflecting the dualism of the many of the Scrolls themselves, and imposing a modern version of that on ancient Judaism.

In contrast with the writers just mentioned, the circle of Scrolls specialists has almost unanimously dismissed Eisenman's views. This reaction is not entirely because of the reasons given earlier that render his conclusions at best very improbable. There are in addition

---

[10] For a convenient summary of the recent debate, see Philip R. Davies, "Was There Really a Qumran Community?" *Currents in Research: Biblical Studies* 3 (1995) 9-35.

[11] Michael Baigent and Richard Leigh, *The Dead Sea Scrolls Deception* (London: Jonathan Cape, 1991).

[12] Neil Asher Silberman, *The Hidden Scrolls: Christianity, Judaism and the War for the Dead Sea Scrolls* (New York: Putnam, 1994).

[13] The views of Barbara Thiering are not amenable to any scholarly discussion and will not be considered here. By her own logic, she also writes in a form of code, and I do not claim to be able to understand her *pesher*.

two other factors: his manner of argumentation and his unwillingness to negotiate or debate his views. (The latter is a trait he shares with Norman Golb: both seem to represent themselves as modern "teachers of righteousness" standing against the wicked priesthood of establishment scholarship.) Eisenman himself does not easily engage in discussion or compromise. He is quite convinced of his correctness, and therefore knows that those who disagree with him are wrong. But the lack of real dialogue also stems from a manner of argumentation that is rather difficult to apprehend, let alone evaluate. Here is perhaps the place to attempt a description.

At the core, as he constructs it, of Eisenman's thesis lies the term "sons of Zadok," which occurs in the Damascus Document and the Rule of the Community and is taken by him, as well as many other scholars (wrongly, I think, but that is another matter) as a self-designation of the "Qumran sect." He then notes that the name Zadok "definitely has a component in 'Righteousness,'"(sic) and asserts that this "in other language might be characterized as 'zeal for the Law'—phraseology current at Qumran,"[14] Thus the root ts-d-q by associative logic, is linked with the root q-n-'. Further: since צַדִּיק is also used of the "Servant" in Isaiah, Jesus can be linked to this terminology; and, moreover, since the Servant brings "knowledge" (דַּעַת), we can add this term too to the network of allusive and specialized vocabulary that will, in Eisenman's process of argument, always point to the same movement. Proceeding further still, since Jesus was a צַדִּיק, as were the Hasmoneans and sons of Zadok, "to his heirs belongs the High Priesthood," for, after all, the name Melchizedek also contains the key root.[15] James also bore the title "The Just" (צַדִּיק) and thus (whether because of the connecting chain of associations or because of the Zadokite dynasty is not clear; it could be both) functioned as a high priest. The priestly aspect of the root can then be linked again with "zeal" through the story of the priest Phinehas, the archetypal zealous Jew of Numbers 25, to whom Mattathias, patriarch of the Hasmonean dynasty, refers in his speech in 1 Macc 2:26.

These interlinking words and allusions, claims Eisenman, are "not all separate reckonings, but rather esoteric or poetic variations around the same theme, 'Righteousness' and/or 'zeal.'" To such a

---

[14]   *The Dead Sea Scrolls*, 17; cf. *Maccabees, Zadokites*, 4.
[15]   *The Dead Sea Scrolls*, 19; cf. *Maccabees, Zadokites*, 5.

cluster of alternative terms he then adds אֶבְיוֹן, חָסִיד, קְדֹשׁ, and תָּמִים by the same associative process. These all function as "interchange-able metaphors"[16] in such a way that the presence of one such term in a Qumran text, or a letter of Paul, links that text to other texts where it occurs and confirms that it participates in a tissue of sectarian vocabulary. (There is something reminiscent in this of the rabbinic *middah* of *gezerah shawa*). In particular, the phrase "Doers of the Law," a phrase "used at Qumran" points clearly to the connec-tion with the Letter of James, where "doing the law" represents an allusion to the same movement.[17]

The tissue that Eisenman offers as his argument is a material called "allusion," a word which Eisenman uses quite frequently, but which most of his readers feel needs to be more rigorously applied. The use of a common term in Jewish and Christian texts that are historically or ideologically connected (or even those that are not) does not automatically count as proof that the texts participate in the same esoteric or technical discourse. The obvious example is "righteous-ness," which occurs over two hundred times in the Hebrew Bible (in nearly every book) and nearly a hundred times in the New Testament (again, in nearly every book). It is certainly possible for the most common terms to acquire esoteric meanings within *fairly closed* groups, as part of a mechanism of self-identification and ideological solidarity. But it needs to be demonstrated that such terms function in this way, not merely from their frequent occurrence, but from distinct understandings that do not apply outside the group.

Again, where a term is in fairly common use, it cannot auto-matically be asserted that every usage in one text is an allusion to another usage in another text. Allusion built upon allusion in the Eisenman manner is capable of rendering the entire corpus of Qumran scrolls univocal, and expressing a Judaism attached not only to works of law and to righteousness, to true priesthood and messianism but to every recurrent item of terminology that the scrolls employ. One need only ponder what the same method could make of the book of Psalms, for instance, to see the danger of an uncontrolled application. Here again, then, there seems to be a lack

---

[16] *The Dead Sea Scrolls*, 21-22; cf. *Maccabees, Zadokites*, 6.

[17] See e.g. R. Eisenman and M. Wise, *The Dead Sea Scrolls Uncovered* (Shaftesbury, Dorset: Element Books, 1992) 196, where 4QMMT is connected with the Letter of James.

of methodological precision and rigour.

We now move to the next stage of Eisenman's argument. The terms (selectively) associated by the chains of allusion are interpreted as representing a set of values, notably hatred of the ruling priestly class. Now this attitude is admittedly quite evident from many of the Qumran scrolls. But in his view the antagonism is directed towards a particular target. The particular criticisms made of the priests—amassing wealth illegally, marrying within forbidden orders, collusion with foreigners—are regarded by Eisenman not typical accusations of any hierarchy but as distinctively characteristic of the Herodian establishment. This conclusion, in Eisenman's view, puts the Scrolls close enough to the time of James. It should be conceded that Eisenman's documentation of the activities of the Herodians and their appointed high priests does match very well the accusations in the Scrolls. But two cautions need to be expressed. One is that these criticisms could to a very large extent have been applied by any dissident group to a number of ruling establishments in late Second Temple Judah. Another is that the "Herodian" period is being made to stretch rather far. Herod himself deceased in 4 B.C.E. Here again, as with the issue of vocabulary, the chronology in Eisenman's method of arguing seems rather more flexible than it should, since while he sometimes argues very strongly for a particular date for one piece of evidence (CD or 1QpHab, for example), he can also assert that the ideology itself persists over a long period of time, so that what really matters is to demonstrate the *pattern* of ideas. But it is surely necessary to distinguish carefully items that point to a particular date from those that are offered as typical of the movement throughout its history. What is characteristic of one generation need not be characteristic of another. This concern is especially well-founded when Eisenman wishes to identify with his one movement the groups known as Maccabeans, Zadokites, Zealots, and Nazoreans.

It is thus hard to disagree with Schiffman's reaction to Eisenman's associative method, published in a volume of conference papers as part of the discussion following Eisenman's paper.[18]

---

[18]   The paper is R. Eisenman, "Theory of Judeo-Christian Origins: The Last Column of the Damascus Document," in M. Wise, N. Golb, J. J. Collins, and D. Pardee (eds.), *Methods of Investigation of the Dead Sea Scrolls and the Khirbet Qumran Site* (New York: New York Academy of Sciences, 1994) 355-67; the

The problem with your associative technique is that most of the things we're talking about exist in Judaism from day one. Militancy, for example, versus more accommodationist approaches, existed at day one, as they exist today in American Jewish and Israeli politics, because they're part of the different views within Judaism . . . You can't take different views within Judaism and then pick them out and simply say that they must be matched up with somebody who happens to fit into one or another trend, whether it be Paul, whether it be James, whether it be Jesus, John the Baptist, or anyone else.

At the same session, M. Klinghardt also addressed Eisenman's chronological imprecision, referring to "non-specific parallels," and asked Eisenman which specific Qumran texts reflected the early history of Christianity. To which Eisenman replied,

I didn't say that we had the history of early Christianity here, I said there were parallels. You don't see what we're doing here. The parallels are strong. The thing is that the ideas are fixed, the categories are fixed, the ethos is fixed . . .

This response illustrates clearly what Eisenman believes he is illustrating: fixed ideas and categories that manifest themselves in different historical configurations. Such phenomena he calls "parallels."

Klinghardt pursues the question:

So it's your point that the early Jewish Christian theology is similar to what we find in the scrolls?

and, while insisting that he is speaking of *first century* Jewish Christianity, "the Jerusalem Church of James the Just, Palestinian Christianity," Eisenman agrees.

KLINGHARDT: I'm absolutely pleased.

The continuing discussion, however, shows that Eisenman does not think in terms of a distinctive, novel "Jewish Christianity"—a sectarian movement that is not yet a religion separated from other forms of Judaism—but a stage in the evolution of the (one single) messianic movement in Palestine, for which he would prefer the term "Zadokites, "though "Messianic Sadducees" he also finds attractive. The earliest Christianity, then, is marked not by any new departure but by an ongoing affirmation of long-held and purely Jewish values. It is, as observed earlier, Christianity that Eisenman wishes to deprive of its heritage, not Judaism! James the Just is a

discussion occupies pp. 367-70; quotations are from pp. 367-68.

Jewish, not a Christian hero.

I hope that I have now sufficiently (and fairly) indicated both Eisenman's vision and the methods he uses to support it. The vision is one of a broad, united Jewish messianic movement that uses of itself (or has used of it) many different names, and which employs in a technical manner a range of terminology that in its texts enables it to be identified as the author. But the texts themselves may come from any time between the second century B.C.E. and first century C.E., because this movement began with the Maccabees and ended with the destruction of the Temple, more or less.

In his recent work on James, Eisenman has in fact moved the emphasis away from the Scrolls and onto classical and patristic sources, particular the Pseudo-Clementine *Recognitions*. I do not feel myself competent to pass judgment on his use of these, though I see some similar difficulties with his over-interpretation of evidence and too-easy identifications. But there is no doubt that a large amount of research has been done on this material, and that Eisenman is capable of seeing in texts things that many others have failed to see. While I suspect that most of these are simply not there, there remains, I think, a likelihood that some of the questions Eisenman has raised concerning the role of James and traditions about him could be fruitfully revisited.

At the conclusion of this section of my paper, I return, then, to the issue of late Second Temple Judaism, where the Scrolls belong. In effect, Eisenman is doing exactly what Schiffman does: making the Qumran scrolls into an expression of "mainstream Judaism." But while Schiffman characterizes this Judaism as centred on the interpretation of the law of Moses, Eisenman makes it centre on "righteousness," zeal for the law, true priesthood, and militant nationalism.

We might ask: regardless of the respective manner of argumentation with respect to the Scrolls, which of these two views gives us the truer picture of late Second Temple Judaism? Both, in fact, follow in a clear scholarly heritage. Schiffman on the one hand champions the view that there was a "mainstream" in Judaism that is faithfully reflected in rabbinic Judaism, though he is careful to pay heed to the elements of variety. On the other hand, Eisenman's view reflects the tradition that popular Judaism in the time of Jesus was anti-Roman and that the majority of Jews heartily longed for a Davidic messiah. This view remains, for example, that of Geza Vermes, although he does not appear to think (as did Brandon, for example) that Jesus in any way behaved politically in an anti-Roman fashion. In favour of Eisenman's view remains the fact (if facts exist at all in this domain) that Jesus was executed by Romans for a political crime and that three decades later the majority of Jews participated in a revolt against Rome. The crucial difference would seem to be that while for Eisenman, rabbinic Judaism was an abandonment of the essence of Judaism, for Schiffman it was its culmination. These differing attitudes probably mirror their authors' respective attitudes towards modern forms of Judaism.

In favour of Eisenman's view of James is that this "messiah" was apparently succeeded by his brother, in the manner of the Maccabees and the founders of other Jewish revolutionary movements at the time. It may also be that Eisenman is correct in claiming, as Wise, Abegg and Cook now also argue,[19] that the Qumran texts are not necessarily anti-Hasmonean, as was once taken for granted, but that some may even be pro-Hasmonean, such as the text 4Q448.[20] And Eisenman's claim that the writers of the scrolls were non-orthodox Sadducees is embraced even by Schiffman himself (whom Eisenman has accused of stealing it without acknowledgement).

It may be unfortunate in the eyes of many that the place of Jesus' brother within Judaism and within Christianity has been championed by Robert Eisenman, and then on the basis of a claimed appearance in the Dead Sea Scrolls—and unhelpful that the portrait of late Second Temple Judaism has been unduly simplified in the process. But if Eisenman's manner of argumentation is elusive and cannot really deliver the conclusions, there are features of his thesis that constitute a useful challenge to some orthodoxies about the nature of Palestinian Judaism(s) and the curious process by which a universal religion sprang from the teachings of Jesus. That James is a key figure in the Scrolls must be firmly denied: but that he might, like the Scrolls, hold a key to understanding the nature of first century

---

[19] *The Dead Sea Scrolls*, 26-27.
[20] See E. Eshel, H. Eshel, and A. Yardeni, "A Qumran Composition Containing Part of Ps. 154 and a Prayer for the Welfare of King Jonathan and his Kingdom," *IEJ* 42 (1992) 199-229. While Eisenman and Wise (*The Dead Sea Scrolls Uncovered*, 273-81) regard the hymn contained here as addressed to the Hasmonean Alexander Jannaeus, Geza Vermes ("The So-called King Jonathan Fragment (4Q448)," *JJS* 44 [1993] 294-300) prefers the brother of Judas and Simon, Jonathan.

Palestinian Judean religion seems worth careful reflection. Eisenman may well turn out to have been partly right, even if largely for the wrong reasons. It happens often enough in scholarship.

QUMRAN AND THE JESUS MOVEMENT

In this rather brief second section I want to do no more than suggest one line of possible connection between the Scrolls and early Christianity, and may (it can be expressed no more strongly) have a bearing on the role of James. That connection runs through the Gospel of Matthew. The features of Matthew that attract my attention are the themes of "righteousness" and "law" and the impression that the Gospel is written for a community struggling to retain a place within Judaism on the basis of its commitments to righteousness and law.

The word δικαιοσύνη ("righteousness," "justice") occurs 92 times in the New Testament, only ten times in the Gospels, and seven of these in Matthew.[21] (It is used 34 times in Romans and three times in the letter of James.[22]) The word νόμος ("law") occurs eight times in Matthew, but nine in Luke and 13 in John (Romans includes 74 references and James ten.) The raw statistics are perhaps not as revealing as the cumulation of scholarship that has recognized "righteousness" and "law" to be a dominant theme of the letter to the Romans and, to a less prominent extent, also of the Gospel of Matthew and the letter of James, though the last two are usually held to represent contrasting opinions on the important of faith as against works in fulfilling the righteousness required by the law.

It is more useful, I think, to consider the function of "righteousness" and "law" in the communities that generated the Scrolls and the Gospel of Matthew. Since in the case of the Scrolls there may be more than one community, I shall focus on that of the Damascus Document. That community appears to have living under the laws revealed to it (though in fact derived by exegesis of the scriptural law) during the "period of wickedness" until the arrival of "one who will teach righteousness at the end of days" (CD 6:11). I have argued

---

[21]   The references are 3:15; 5:6, 10, 20; 6:1, 33; 21:32.

[22]   δίκαιος ("righteous," "just") occurs 79 times in the New Testament, 30 in the Gospels, and nine of these in Matthew, seven times in Romans, and twice in James.

elsewhere[23] that this figure is messianic, since in CD 12:23 the figure
that ends the "period of wickedness" is called the "messiah of Aaron
and Israel." I thus identify a somewhat overlooked messianic profile:
that of teacher, among the Qumran documents. It would seem, from
the reference to this figure in the past (CD 1 and the *pesharim*) that
this person was believed by his followers to have come (and gone:
see CD 19:35–20:1). But the importance of this figure for the history
of communities in the Qumran texts is another matter. I want simply
to suggest that for the Damascus community righteousness, achiev-
able only through perfect obedience to the law, was to be finally
revealed by an eschatological messianic teacher. One can also go a
little further and show that the words of this "teacher" were placed
alongside the law as of equal authority to the community among
whom this person was received. In 20:27-28, where we find a
reference to those who "hold fast to these rules (*mishpatim*) by going
in and out according to the Law, and listen to the voice of the
Teacher." The phrasing very clearly adds to the authority of the law
that also of the teacher. The implication in CD 6:11 that this person's
arrival would have an effect on the "law for the period of
wickedness" seems confirmed; the Teacher was, the phrase implies,
regarded as having an authority alongside the law. The legal
authority of the Teacher is reiterated in 20:32, where indeed the
Teacher's voice now represents what are called חקי הצדק—and no
reference to other laws or commandments are mentioned!

This understanding of the messiah-teacher may be compared with
what Graham Stanton says about the Gospel of Matthew:[24]

> Matthew's gospel provided the 'new people' with a new set of authoritative
> traditions to be set alongside the law and the prophets . . . Matthew's Jesus
> does not repudiate the law: its continuing importance is affirmed very
> strongly . . . In some respects, however, the sayings of Jesus (and
> Matthew's gospel as a whole) must *in practice* (though not in theory) have
> taken priority over the law and the prophets in the community life of the
> 'new people'.

In an earlier section of the same book (i.e. "Matthew's Gospel and
the Damascus Document in Sociological Perspective"), Stanton

---

[23]   Forthcoming in T. H. Lim and L. Kreitzer (eds.), *The Dead Sea Scrolls in
Their Historical Context* (Edinburgh: T. & T. Clark, 1999).
[24]   Graham N. Stanton, *A Gospel for a New People: Studies in Matthew*
(Edinburgh: T. & T. Clark, 1992) 382-83.

compares and contrast the two communities reflected in the texts, mainly in terms of boundaries, social conflict and legitimation.[25] He does not, however, explore the ways in which both communities exploit the issue of right understanding of the law in negotiating their sectarian identity, nor the function of their beliefs in an imminent end to the age. Such an exploration would perhaps reveal closer similarity between the two messianic Jewish sects. It is even more disappointing that in his treatment of Matthew's apocalyptic eschatology, in which he briefly includes comparisons with Qumran, Sim does not deal explicitly with the figure of the eschatological teacher of the law.[26] Equally neglectful is Overman's treatment of Matthew and Judaism, in which the Damascus Document occupies no more than a few lines.[27]

The relevance to the figure of James of a comparison of the Damascus Document and Matthew's Gospel (which has yet to be properly undertaken, and which I have merely tried to outline) is expressed in Stanton's observation[28] that Matthew has either modified an earlier tradition or has used his own words in expressing the distance between his own ἐκκλεσία and the συναγωγή that stands for the Judaism that his community has now quit. With many other commentators, Stanton concludes that Matthew's community had only recently, and painfully, made this separation. By comparison, "there is no comparable use of different terms for community self-identification in the Damascus Document." It is true that the term יחד may function partly in this way among those who followed the Teacher (and who, in my opinion, also redacted the Damascus Document so that it reflected the arrival of the eschatological Teacher),[29] but the framers of the Damascus Document expressed their difference from historical Israel through their adherence to a *new* covenant. For them, it was their continuity with the *true* historic

25   Stanton, *A Gospel for a New People*, 85-110.
26   David C. Sim, *Apocalyptic Eschatology in the Gospel of Matthew* (SNTSMS 88; Cambridge: Cambridge University Press, 1996).
27   J. Andrew Overman, *Matthew's Gospel and Formative Judaism: The Social World of the Matthean Community* (Minneapolis: Fortress Press, 1990). See pp. 9-10, 21, 31.
28   Stanton, *A Gospel for a New People*, 97.
29   For a full argument of this view of the Damascus Document, see Philip R. Davies, *The Damascus Covenant: An Interpretation of the Damascus Document* (JSOTSup 25; Sheffield: JSOT Press, 1983).

Israel that mattered, and they equally stressed the continuity of their contemporaries with the *faithless* historic Israel that had suffered exile and spiritually still did.

But Matthew's community, like the members of the Damascus Covenant, had once thought of itself as a part of Israel in the fullest sense, as possessors of the full meaning of the law, as able to fulfil true righteousness through the teaching of their messiah. Both communities point us to a the phenomenon of a sectarian group in the process of breaking with what it saw as the erring Judaism of outsiders, and taking issue precisely over the key shared issues of law and the righteousness that comes from true observance to that law. For both, one who "teaches righteousness at the end of days" is the key to membership of the true Israel.

Whether these two sectarian documents enable us to understand better the profile of a dimly-perceived community led by James the *Dikaios*, the *Tsaddiq*, those loyal to the law and aiming to "fulfil righteousness," requires to be tested. If, as I believe, there is room for a responsible investigation on these lines, then in some way, however small, the contribution of Robert Eisenman should be acknowledged.

PALESTINIAN TRADITIONS IN THE EPISTLE OF JAMES

Peter H. Davids

The issue addressed in this chapter is the presence of Palestinian Jewish-Christian[1] traditions as markers of provenance in the Epistle of James, as opposed to, for example, Graeco-Roman traditions (unmediated through their influence upon Palestinian Judaism) or, to the degree that they can be distinguished from Palestinian Judaism/ Jewish-Christianity, Diaspora Jewish/Jewish-Christian traditions (e.g. Philonic influence). We will not attempt a definitive answer as to the personal source of those traditions, although we will suggest a possible answer. That is, despite this chapter's being part of a work on James the brother of Jesus, we will not attempt to argue that James *must* be the source of any of the material contained in the epistle that bears his name, although we will suggest that he *may* be the it source of much of the material. There are two reasons for this limitation. First and foremost, outside of Acts (which presents its own historical difficulties, particularly in terms of the content of speeches), we have only two first century samples of Jacobean material. These are Paul's cryptic references in Galatians 2[2] (in

---

[1]   I will use the term "Jewish-Christian" because it is the traditional term for Jewish adherents of the first-century Jesus movement. However, neither they nor Paul (even with respect to gentile followers of Jesus) saw themselves as members of a new religion, but rather as a variety of Judaism. In their eyes its was eschatologically restored Judaism, much as the people of the Dead Sea Scrolls saw themselves as "the faithful in the land" in the midst of other Judaisms. Thus the term Christian Judaism would be equally applicable, although it obscures the fact that the leaders of the gentile Christian movement who left records also saw themselves as a version of Judaism.

[2]   No words of James are preserved in either of the two references in Galatians 2. The first merely includes him among the "pillar" apostles who approved the Pauline gospel, but did not want Paul's independence to include a failure to care for the Jerusalem poor. The second refers to some people "from James" who caused the defection of Peter and Barnabas in Antioch. That they were "from James" explains their influence and thus the effect they had on Peter and Barnabas. However, Paul does not explain whether James was the source of their teaching or whether they came for other reasons altogether but were listened to when they

which we never hear the actual voice of James) and the Epistle of James itself.[3] With no other relatively contemporary Jacobean literature with which to compare it (as opposed to the case of the Pauline corpus), one cannot conclusively evaluate the attribution of authorship in the letter. Second, the letter itself appears to be a collection of traditions, so even when one agrees that James is the major source (and in that sense, author), this would not make him the author of all of the material included in the letter.[4] In our view, the most one can demonstrate with a high level of probability is that the material in James appears to come from the environment in which James lived and functioned and thus *could well* stem from James.[5] This environmental location is what we will attempt to

---

reacted to Paul's law-free gospel because of their status as "from James." In other words, we learn nothing certain about James from Paul other than that he was the most significant leader in Jerusalem.

3   To this we could add the reference in Josephus (*Ant.* 20.9.1 §197-203). There is of course second century or later (at least in the form we have it) material concerning James, such as the citations of the *Gospel of the Hebrews* in Jerome (*Liber de Viris Illustribus* 2), the tradition of Hegessipus in Eusebius (*Eccl. Hist.* 2.1.4-5; 2.23.3-25), *Gospel of Thomas* (log. §12), the *First Apocalypse of James*, the *Second Apocalypse of James*, and the *Apocryphon of James* (the latter three all from Nag Hammadi). In Josephus' account James does not speak, and while he speaks in some of the other literature, whatever is genuine is difficult of separate from the encrustation of tradition and later ideologies. Richard Baucham's article in this work addresses this issue in part.

4   Indeed, it is very unlikely that he is. For example, some sayings in James, e.g. Jas 1:12, 18; 3:18; 4:5-6, 17; and 5:20, have been muted by some scholars to be agrapha (e.g. James Adamson, *The Epistle of James* [NICNT; Grand Rapids: Eerdmans, 1976] 181, 301-303). While such a thesis, based solely on the criteria of coherence, cannot be proved, we do know that 5:12 depends on a form of the Jesus tradition (cf. Matt 5:33-37 and Justin, *Apology* 1.16.1, the latter being one of several early Christian writers witnessing to a non-Matthean form of the saying). Given that this known teaching of Jesus is cited without attribution, it is naturally possible that more than one such saying occurs in James. However, while one could argue on the basis of the criterion of coherence that a saying *could not* have come from Jesus, one cannot prove that one *must* come from Jesus, since by definition an agraphon does not occur in a work attributing it to Jesus. However, simply raising the issue points out that by the same token we cannnot be sure that all of the sayings in James come from the same author.

5   Naturally, there is the attribution of authorship in Jas 1:1. And it is true that in its simplicity it also fits a first century *Sitz im Leben*. That is, we find none of the exalted titles attributed to him in later literature (e.g. see Hegessipus, cited above),

demonstrate.

In pursuing our argument, we lack the strongest type of evidence, both internal and external. Since the Epistle of James is not cited by name before Origen (d. 253), we lack the most solid external evidence linking the work to a specific date and place. And since there is no other work thought to be by the same author, we cannot apply the tools of stylistic analysis to demonstrate common authorship, as we can in the case of Paul.[6] Furthermore, there are no references to datable contemporary individuals, events or cultural features (especially people, events or items that passed in obscurity after a given date), partly because we are not dealing with narrative.[7] Thus we are left with the relatively indirect evidence, which points more to a socio-cultural milieu than to a specific date and place. We divide this evidence into four general areas: genre evidence (Is the genre of James similar to that of other works originating in Palestinian Judaism?), linguistic evidence (Does the language of James show evidence of originating in a Palestinian milieu?), incidental references (Are there idioms or cultural allusions in James that point to a Palestinian milieu?), and tradition-critical evidence (Do the traditions in James appear to stem from a Palestinian environment or elsewhere?). In each of these areas the use of the Septuagint in Diaspora Jewish communities as well as in Christian gatherings complicates the matter, for it introduced Palestinian

---

nor even a reference to him as the brother of Jesus. That much is agreed to, for example, by W. G. Kümmel (*Intruduction to the New Testament* [NTL; Nashville: Abingdon, 1966] 290) and H. Windisch (*Die Katholischen Briefe* [HNT 15; Tübingen: Mohr [Siebeck], 1951] 3), neither of whom is otherwise inclined to accept Jacobean authorship. However, to use Jas 1:1 as direct evidence would be circular. That is, we would be using as evidence the very data we would be trying to investigate, i.e. the attribution of authorship. Thus for our purposes we are bracketing it.

6   Accurate stylistic analysis depends, not upon vocabulary, which may vary with the topic discussed, but with unconscious features of literary style. Thus it requires a sufficiently large piece of literature, which is the reason why not all Pauline works qualify for such analysis.

7   For example, since the five-porched pool of Bethsaida was covered during the destruction of Jerusalem in 70 C.E., there is evidence that the story in John 5 comes from someone who knew Jerusalem in the pre-destruction period. Of course, even if we had such evidence in James, as in the Gospels it would only prove that a particular tradition originated before a certain date or is linked to a certain date, not the whole work originated before that date.

images and Hebraic expressions into a non-Palestinian, Greek-speaking population. Naturally we will try to control for this influence by not weighting as strongly evidence that might come from the Septuagint. Furthermore, some of these types of evidence are stronger than others. For instance, tradition-critical evidence is the most difficult to tie down, since traditions can be transmitted by groups that do not understand them, while the incidental evidence is more weighty is that it tends to be unconscious and thus less liable to falsification. Finally, we realize that in any effort of this type no one piece of evidence is strong enough to bear the full weight of the argument. There is always the possibility that someone outside Palestine might have written using any given expression or idea that we discuss. Thus by nature the argument is cumulative. The more data one finds that are associated with the Palestinian environment, the less likely that someone outside that environment could have written this epistle. However, first we need to look at other attempts to locate James.

THE CASE FOR OTHER SOCIAL LOCATIONS

There certainly have been significant scholarly arguments for other social locations for this epistle. While the dating of the *Tübingen-Schule* (i.e. a late second century date) has been by and large abandoned, among other reasons because James lacks any evidence of the Christological controversies of that period or any reflection of Gnostic thought or episcopal church structure, there certainly has been a significant attempt to locate James in Rome in the late first century (or early second).[8] Since the earliest indirect external evidence for the use of James comes from Rome (e.g. *The Shepherd of Hermas*, particularly in his uses of δίψυχος, and often *1 Clement* as well are frequently viewed as being dependent upon James), one might well think of Rome as a logical place of origin.

---

8   The principle proponents of this location have been Bo Reicke, first in his *Diakonie, Festfreude und Zelos* (UUÅ; Uppsala: University of Uppsala Press, 1951), and then in *The Epistles of James, Peter and Jude* (AB 37; Garden City: Doubleday, 1964), which abstracts the more detailed argument of his monograph, and S. S. Laws, first as S. S. C. Marshall, *The Character, Setting and Purpose of the Epistle of James* (dissertation, University of Oxford, 1968), and then in *A Commentary on the Epistle of James* (BNTC; London: A. & C. Black, 1980), as well as in numerous articles.

Further evidence adduced for Rome include: (1) the quality of the Greek and especially the use of the Septuagint in the quotations of the Hebrew scriptures, (2) the apparent knowledge of Paul's writings (in Jas 2:14-26), (3) some references to social customs (the clothing of Jas 2:2, which Prof. Reicke argued indicated a campaigning Roman of Equestrian rank), and (4) indications of a superficial knowledge of Judaism on the part of the author. While several of these topics will be discussed below, a brief response is in order at this point. In our view the linguistic parallels between James and *Hermas* are the strongest part of this evidence. When one finds a rare term like δίψυχος used repeatedly in a context of prayer as it is in James, along with other parallels between the two works, for example, the attitude displayed towards wealth, one has every right to suspect that the later work is dependent on the former. While the case is not conclusive (we lack the sustained parallel linguistic structures needed to prove *literary* dependence), it is indeed strong.[9] As for the other evidence, (1) there is, as we will argue below, no reason why a first century Palestinian Jewish community writing to Diaspora Jews would not use good Greek and cite the Septuagint; (2) a comparison of Jas 2:14-26 to Romans in particular makes it unlikely that the author of James had ever seen the work (see below), which would make a composition in late first century Rome unlikely; (3) Jas 2:2-4 is a hyperbolic "what if" type of structure, not a reference to a specific incident (and the "shining" clothes of James do not necessarily mean a white candidate's toga),[10] and (4) in our view, James is more Jewish than Laws in particular admits, although James is

---

[9]   P. H. Davids (*Themes in the Epistle of James that are Judaistic in Character* [dissertation, University of Manchester, 1974] 63-66, 472-73) examines these two themes in James and *Hermas* and finds a different use of the synoptic tradition (i.e. without attirbution in James and with attribution in *Hermas*) and a more vivid, immediate eschatology in James, as well as a trend in *Hermas* towards toning down the piety-poverty equation. Thus he comes to the conclusion that while *Hermas* knew James, James is the earlier work. G. Kittel ("Der Jakobusbrief und die apostolischen Väter," *ZNW* 43 [1950] 54-112; cf. idem, "Der geschichtliche Ort der Jakobusbriefes," *ZNW* 41 [1942] 71-105) comes to a similar conclusion on faith and works in James.

[10]   While Reicke's "local colour" is questionable, Laws's main effort is directed at arguing that what appears to be Palestinian cultural and geographic references are nothing of the sort, rather than demonstrating that there are similar actual unconscious references to Roman culture and geography.

relaxed in his Judaism in that it is not under attack in his community.[11] Equally important, there appears to be no reason why someone writing in Rome would attribute a work to James, who was not (to our knowledge) particularly revered in Rome. Such an attribution would seem to deliberately set the work up for what did in fact happen, i.e. the disappearance of references to James or evidence of its use in the West for 200 plus years. We suspect that one reason for this was the increasing popularity of Paul's letters in Rome and the regions it influenced and a concomitant unease with James.

One could, of course, try to link James to an Egyptian point of origin. In is in this area that we find James first accepted as scripture, with the evidence indicating this acceptance spreading north and west in the fourth century. Also, the fact that there are three Jacobean works in the Nag Hammadi codices indicates that there was a continuing interest in James in that area. This has not been a popular option,[12] however, for there is no evidence of Philonic thought in James (e.g. there is no significant similarity in their use of λόγος) nor any cultural references that begin to look Egyptian. Here the external evidence is virtually the only evidence. What it may explain is the preservation of the work due of contact between Egyptian Christians and those in Palestine (e.g. Jerome, Origen, both of whom cite James) and/or the migration of Jewish Christians to Egypt, probably around the time of the Second Jewish Revolt (i.e. ca. 135 C.E.).[13] Whereas James' perceived conflict with

---

[11]   We recognise that we are, for the sake of brevity, conflating Laws and Reicke and thus are in some ways unfair to either and in others strengthening both. Laws, for instance, argues that James circulated in a non-Pauline church circle in Rome, which allows her to overcome to a degree the problem that James does not seem to know the Pauline letters, although the evidence for such a circle is only that it is needed to support her position. Reicke did not, like Laws, argue that the author of James was only tangentially in contact with Judaism.

[12]   In fact, most typically James is located on the fringes of Palestine, e.g. Caesarea or Syria. J. H. Ropes, *A Critical and Exegetical Commentary on the Epistle of St. James* (ICC; Edinburgh: T. & T. Clark, 1916) 49, is typical in this regard. J. Moffatt, *The General Epistles* (MNTC; London: Hodder and Stoughton, 1928) is a rare example of someone who suggested that James comes from Egypt, largely due to the wisdom theme of the book.

[13]   As Jewish-Christians became increasingly marginalized in the church, especially after Jerusalem became the gentile city Aelia Capitolina after 135 C.E., James could have become a lost book, perhaps known only from fragments, along

Paul could explain its disappearance from the areas where Paul was active (Syria around through Rome), Paul was not the local hero in Egypt, and there was every reason to preserve a work that one could refer to as "one of their own" and perhaps even use to defend one group's antiquity against those who had other Jacobean traditions.[14]

Thus we need to turn to examine the strength of the evidence linking James to a Palestinian milieu. It is to this task and its implications that the rest of this chapter is devoted.

GENRE EVIDENCE

The genre of James has been variously evaluated. Martin Dibelius labeled it paraenesis, by which he meant that it was a gathering of ethical traditions loosely connected together. James was, so to speak, an ethical string of pearls, much as the gospels were viewed in the same period as collections of Jesus traditions.[15] In that case one might compare James with Proverbs and the wisdom tradition or with parts of Epictetus.[16] While few today would deny wisdom materials in James,[17] Dibelius' position, which prevents him from seeing any purpose or theme in James as a whole, has long been abandoned. Most writers on James since the 1960's have argued for its being a unitary work, although they have not agreed on the nature

with the *Gospel of the Hebrews* and other works belonging to that segment of the church. That it did not may well have to do with Egyptian Christianity and its interest in Palestine in general and James in particular.

14   Its eventual church-wide acceptance may well have been due to the church as a whole becoming more interested in a more legal approach to the faith (i.e. rules) and the influence of leaders from the Egyptian area (e.g. Athanasius), who could presumably allay fears that James might not be consistent with Paul. Interestingly enough, even in the early period, *Hermas*, whom James appears to influence, was more interested in drawing strong boundaries on the basis of works than other roughly contemporary Roman works.

15   Martin Dibelius, *James* (Hermeneia; Philadelphia: Fortress, 1976) = *Der Brief des Jakobus* (rev. H. Greeven; MeyerK; Göttingen: Vandenhoek & Ruprecht, 11th ed., 1964). Greeven's revisions do not affect Dibelius' basic position on this matter.

16   Although today scholars are inclined to argue for structure and purpose in Proverbs, as a survey of commentaries over the past decade or so would show.

17   William R. Baker (*Personal Speech-Ethics in the Epistle of James* [Tübingen: Mohr (Siebeck), 1995]), for instance, has demonstrated the presence of Ancient Near Eastern and in particular Jewish speech-ethics in James, speech-ethics being a significant part of the wisdom tradition.

of this unity.[18]

Another line of genre studies came from Rudolf Bultmann in his description of the diatribe.[19] This description of a longer literary structure found in Epictetus and other Cynic–Stoic philosophers, initially applied to Paul, soon generalized to James and especially to James 2; yet it did not solve the problem of genre. First, this literary form applies only to parts of James (indeed, Dibelius would come after Bultmann and point to diatribes in James, but view them as some of the "pearls" strung together). Second, the diatribe is itself simply vivid oral discourse. It cannot be distinguished formally from vivid oral discourse coming from other cultural settings.[20]

One reason for the disagreement is the fact that up until the work of F. O. Francis writers were not taking the epistolary form of James seriously. Of course scholars recognized that James begins with an epistolary salutation, but they viewed it as something tacked onto another type of work, such as a tract of some type. It was F. O. Francis who pointed out that the letter form extended to far more than the first verse of James, and included much of chapter one plus the ending of chapter five (5:7-20). The evidence for this was the parallels between James and other published letters in the Jewish and

---

[18]   Franz Mussner (*Der Jakobusbrief* [HTKNT 13.1; Freiburg: Herder, 2nd ed., 1967]), was one of the first in the German-speaking world. C. Leslie Mitton (*The Epistle of James* [London: Marshall, Morgan and Scott, 1966]) started the trend in the English-speaking world, followed by James Adamson, *The Epistle of James* (NICNT; Grand Rapids: Eerdmans, 1976). Adamson, of course, had already argued for a similar position in his Cambridge dissertation. One of the most promising recent approaches to the structure of the epistle combines literary data with discourse analysis: Kenneth D. Tollefson, "The Epistle of James and Dialectical Discourse," *BTB* 21 (1997) 62-69. This in turn builds on work such as that of Ralph B. Terry, "Some Aspects of the Discourse Structure of the Book of James," *Journal of Translation and Textlinguistics* 5 (1992) 106-25.

[19]   Rudolph Bultmann, *Der Stil der paulinischen Predigt und die kynisch-stoische Diatribe* (Göttingen: Vandenhoeck & Ruprecht, 1910).

[20]   Peter H. Davids, *A Commentary on the Epistle of James* (NIGTC; Grand Rapids: Eerdmans, 1982) 12, 23. Specifically, all of the characteristics of the diatribe (e.g. dialogue [rhetorical questions, questions and answers, imaginary opponent], direct address of the auditor, variety in subject matter, alliteration and harsh speech) can be found in the synagogue homily as described by W. W. Wessel; cf. Duane F. Watson, "James 2 in the Light of Graeco-Roman Schemes of Argumentation," *NTS* 39 (1993) 118-20.

Hellenistic literary corpus.[21]

Recently this analysis has been extended. Karl-Wilhelm Niebuhr has suggested that James is very similar to early Jewish letters to the Diaspora.[22] In saying this, Niebuhr does not necessarily imply that the letter is anything other than a literary composition, a published rather than an actual letter. That is, he compares James with such works as the letters at the beginning of 2 Maccabees, the Letter of Jeremiah, and the letter at the end of the *Syrian Apocalypse of Baruch*. All of these were composed in Greek as letters from leaders in Palestine to groups of Jews in Diaspora synagogues. All demonstrate a thematic similarity to James. What is significant is not the genuineness of the letters in these works, but that all of this literature likely originated in the general area of Palestine and drew upon known literary conventions. This letter-to-the-Diaspora form, even when purely literary, was modeled on the actual letters of the period, particularly those from leading Jewish authorities in Palestine to Diaspora communities.[23] Thus, while this evidence can not determine whether James is only the implied author or the actual author of our letter, it does place the Epistle of James into a particular literary world. In other words, the genre of James fits the Palestinian milieu. Furthermore, it fits the need of the early Christian movement centered in Jerusalem to extend its instruction to Diaspora Christian communities.

If the themes and overall structure of James are that of a Diaspora-letter, how can one account for the disjointedness that Dibelius pointed to? The best response to this is the observation that James is probably an edited work. That is, it is true that one can view James as a series of sayings and sermons (diatribes, if one will). One does

---

21   F. O. Francis, "The Form and Function of the Opening and Closing Paragraphs of James and I John," *ZNW* 61 (1970) 110-26. It makes no difference whether or not the letters he cites are genuine letters—most are probably the literary creations of the author of the book containing them (although Francis does cite some papyri letters that are certainly authentic letters)—for they nevertheless show the form in which those authors felt a proper letter should be written.

22   Karl-Wilhelm Niebuhr, "Der Jakobusbrief im Licht frühjüdischer Diaspora-briefe," *NTS* 44 (1998) 420-43.

23   Richard Bauckham ("James and the Jerusalem Church," in R. Bauckham [ed.], *The Book of Acts in its Palestinian Setting* (*The Books of Acts in Its First Century Setting*, vol. 4 [Grand Rapids: Eerdmans, 1995] 423-25) marshals evidence for this practice.

sense that many of the "pieces" could stand on their own. Other units are linked by link-words rather than by smooth transitions. In some cases proverbial sayings, which could easily have been originally independent, are used as transitions. Furthermore, there are some inconsistencies in the vocabulary of the work. For example, the first chapter stresses ὑπομονή as the term for patient endurance, while in chapter five μακροθυμέω suddenly appears. Πίστις changes its meaning from one unit to another ("the faith" in 2:1; "faith" in the sense of orthodox belief in 2:19 and apparently in 2:14-26 as a whole; "commitment" in 1:3, 6, and probably 2:5). Such inconsistencies are marks of the bringing together of originally independent sayings and sermons. While problematic in a composition one believes a single author wrote over a short period, this evidence is not inconsistent with the idea of James as a Diaspora-letter, for is it not likely that Jewish-Christians would be interested in collecting and sending out to Diaspora congregations within their sphere of influence teaching attributed to their greatest leader? And might not his death —thus the silencing of his live voice—have served as a trigger for such a collection?

LINGUISTIC EVIDENCE

A major factor in placing the origin of James outside of Palestine has been the quality of its Greek, which, while not up to the quality of Luke-Acts, Hebrews, or parts of 1 Peter, is certainly very good.[24] While people in Palestine, especially those living in mixed Jewish and gentile areas such as Galilee, often knew some Greek, the argument goes, would a Palestinian peasant like James have known such fluent Greek? Would he not have spoken a heavily aramaized Greek, given that Aramaic was the language of Palestinian Jews? This argument must now be rejected for two reasons.

First, there is significant evidence for the extensive use of Greek within first century Jerusalem, let alone the rest of Palestine.[25] One

---

[24]   We have already noted Laws, *James* (1980), who places the origin of James in Rome, partially on the basis of his Greek that she considers too good for a Palestinian Jew.

[25]   This was demonstrated as far back as J. N. Sevenster, *Do You Know Greek?* (NovTSup 19; Leiden: Brill, 1968) 190-91; and E. R. Goodenough, *Jewish Symbols in the Graeco-Roman Period*, vol. 5 (Bollingen Series 37; New York: Pantheon Books, 1953-65) 13, 51, 56, 184-98.

even finds evidence for the knowledge and use of Greek philosophical ideas, including Cynic and Stoic ideas within Palestinian literature.[26] Thus there is no *prima facie* reason why a Galilean Jew would not have grown up bilingual and have spoken decent Greek, although such a person might rely upon an amanuensis for literary style.[27] There is even less reason to suppose that a Jewish-Christian group in such an environment would not use good quality Greek to write to Diaspora adherents of the movement.[28]

---

[26]   Marjorie O'Rourke Boyle ("The Stoic Paradox of James 2.10," *NTS* 31 [1985] 611-17) does indeed argue that Jas 2:10 reflects the Stoic idea of the unity of virtues and vices, as found in Seneca, *De beneficiis* 4.27.1; 5.15.1 (which use in Seneca indicates that the idea was circulating in James' time). However, she also notes that 4 Macc 5:19 already has the idea, "minor sins are just as weighty as great sins, for in each case the Law is despised." However, while Boyle, Dibelius, *James* 146, and R. B. Townshend (in R. H. Charles, *APOT* 2.672) all argue that 4 Macc 5:19-20 is evidence of a conflation of Jewish and Stoic tradition by the first century C.E., H. Anderson (in J. H. Charlesworth *OTP*, 2.550 n. f) denies this, arguing that Jewish antecedents were fully sufficient to explain this passage (and by extension, Gal 3:10 and Jas 2:10). Thus, while it would not be surprising to find Greek thought in a Jewish setting, this is one case where parallelomania is more likely than true dependence. More careful work was done by F. Gerald Downing ("Cynics and Christians," *NTS* 30 [1984] 584-93), who feels that Christian material was shaped to be understandable to persons influenced by Cynics (including persons in the Eastern Mediterranean), but does not claim dependence. He sees this shaping especially in "Q" material, special Matthean material, and aspects of Mark and James (perhaps because James is so close to Matthew's form of "Q").

[27]   If, as Paul assumes in 1 Cor 15:7, James became part of the Christian movement shortly after Easter, and if he was a significant leader by the late 40's C.E. at the latest, as Galatians 2 appears to assume, then James himself had by then up to twenty years experience in a bilingual movement as he rose to prominence and then a number of years as leader of a movement that perforce functioned in both Aramaic and Greek. By his death around 61 C.E. he had had at last 15 and perhaps 30 years of leadership. His peasant origins (which themselves required dealing with customers from various linguistic backgrounds) were a long way behind him; his literary style would have improved with his frequent need to teach and preach before a variety of groups. And of course other leaders in the Jerusalem-based movement may well have been more fluent and more educated than he.

[28]   Since it was rare for a person, especially an important person, to write his or her own letters, some sort of amanuensis was certainly used, and a trusted amanuensis would likely improve the style of a letter. Obviously, without knowing more about James from some other source than this letter, we cannot know if this would be necessary or not in his case. However, if we are correct, as argued above, that the Epistle of James is a composite work edited together from sermons

Second, the Greek of James does contain a significant amount of Semitic influence. It is precisely such influence that one would expect if the Greek were being written in an environment where Aramaic was the other prominent language.

Examples of Semitic influence in James abound. Some terms such as ποιητὴς νόμου (4:11), ποιήσαντι ἔλεος (2:13), and ἐν ταῖς πορείαις αὐτοῦ (1:11) are indeed Semitic, but may be derived from the Septuagint.[29] Other phenomena are more difficult to explain on this basis: e.g. parallelism (1:9, 11, 13; 4:8-9; 5:4), the frequent placement of the possessive pronoun immediately after the noun (57 times in James, starting with Jas 1:2, versus 29 times in 1 Peter and 28 times in Colossians, works of similar length), repetition of pronouns (2:6), the frequency of the use of the imperative participle (e.g. 1:1, 6, 21), the frequent use of ἰδού, the pleonastic use of ἄνθρωπος and ἀνήρ (e.g. 1:7, 12, 19), the frequency of the use of the genitive of an abstract noun instead of an adjective (e.g. 1:25; 2:1; 3:13; 5:15), subordination without the use of conjunctions or the use of paratactic constructions where the logic is hypotactic (e.g. 2:18; 4:7-10; 1:25; 2:2-3; 3:5; 4:17), the use of paraphrastic conjugations with εἶναι (e.g. 1:17; 3:15), the use of the dative similar to the Hebrew infinitive absolute (e.g. 5:17), and certain individual terms and expressions (e.g. γέεννα, 3:6 [on which see below]; σώζειν ψυχήν, 1:21; 5:20; passive used to avoid God's name, 1:5; 5:15). Certainly these vary in their value. Some are not un-Greek; it is only their frequency of use that makes them important. Others might come from church or Diaspora Jewish linguistic conventions. Still, one gets the impression that the author of this epistle, although fluent in

---

and sayings of James, then there certainly was an "amanuensis" cum editor responsible for the work. Furthermore, while Watson ("James 2," 94-121) applies the categories of deliberative rhetoric to James 2 and thus implies a Hellenistic origin for the rhetoric, we do not know (1) whether this structure stems from the original author of the material or a later editor or (2) whether James or some other Jewish-Christian leader writing to the Diaspora would have consciously chosen these categories of thought or whether they stem from an amanuensis. Furthermore, James 2 is the most structured part of James, although Watson has tried to apply this analysis to other, more classically structured parts of James. See Duane F. Watson, "The Rhetoric of James 3:1-12 and a Classical Pattern of Argumentation," *NovT* 35 (1993) 48-64.

[29] Mussner (*Der Jakobusbrief*, 31) lists some 20 examples of such "Bible" language.

Greek, lives in a bilingual environment from which Semitic expressions seep into his speech and writing.

One particularly interesting example of this phenomenon is ποιηταὶ λόγου in Jas 1:22. According to standard Greek usage, this phrase should mean a writer, poet or orator (e.g. 2 Macc 2:30, where ποιεῖσθαι λόγων means in context "historian"). That, however, is not James' meaning. Rather, building on the Hebrew expression of a "doer of the law" (Deut 28:58; 29:28; etc.), translated in the Septuagint as ποιητὴς νόμου in one passage (1 Macc 2:16; the related ποιήσις νόμου in Sir 19:20; 51:19 refers to doing the law rather than a doer of the law) our author creates a parallel expression without example in (and, given that there is only one analogous usage, possibly without influence from) the Septuagint.[30]

INCIDENTAL REFERENCES

One of the primary ways that foreign infiltrators are detected within a culture is by their use of idioms and metaphors that have their origin in their home culture but are foreign to the host culture.[31] We notice a number of these within James. Naturally, in each case we need to ask whether these stem from the Septuagint, i.e. whether a "Bible-reader" is using "Bible-language." In several of the cases this is unlikely.

---

30 One must remember that 2 Maccabees was also part of the Septuagint. It is difficult to tell whether or not the author of James knew the Septuagint. All of his biblical citations come from places where the Septuagint translates the Hebrew text fairly literally, so an independent translation could be identical to the Septuagint. Furthermore, some citations which might be viewed as exceptions (e.g. the citation of Prov 3:34 in Jas 4:6) are used multiple times in early Christian literature, indicating that they were in common circulation within the church and could be picked up without knowing the Septuagint itself. However, there is no reason why a Christian leader in Jerusalem would not use the Septuagint when dealing with Greek-speaking house churches or visitors to the city. After all, copies of these books were found at Qumran, which no one suspects of being a Hellenising community. Use of the Septuagint indicates nothing about where the author lived and worked, only that he could read Greek.

31 E.g. when I taught in Germany in the mid-70's one of my students commented to my wife, "We like Mr. Davids because he puts things so . . . so differently." What he meant was that my idioms and metaphors were frequently translated from American (or perhaps English) usage and thus sounded fresh, as well as marked me out as not being a German (although my accent would have done the latter far more quickly).

James 2:1-4 presents a picture of some type of church meeting. R. B. Ward has argued that it is a church court,[32] while many others assume that it is a church service (i.e. a Jewish-Christian synagogue gathering). Ward's reasoning comes from the unlikelihood that multiple postures would be encouraged at the same time in a church service combined with the observation that rabbinic sources refer to different postures (sitting vs. standing) and different clothing (rich vs. poor) as *prima facie* evidence that a court is showing discrimination, which is the accusation leveled in 2:4. Another line of reasoning, one not necessarily incompatible with Ward's, is even more interesting. In an excursus to an article on the synagogues of Jerusalem, Rainer Riesner notes that in Jas 2:2-3,

> There is a fixed seating order. Apparently the leader of the service stands or sits on a raised place. This cannot be merely a stool, but presupposes ascending benches or a raised platform. Next to the leader's position are sitting places. One part of the room is free for standing.

His point is that this fits known synagogue architecture of the period and that James' reference to a person εἰσέλθη εἰς συναγωγήν is a reference to the place of gathering, a Jewish-Christian synagogue, not to the gathering itself (James refers to the community as ἐκκλησία in 5:14). This fits with first century Palestinian terminology for a synagogue, but not with Diaspora terminology, which referred to synagogues as a προσευχή.[33] If this argument is accepted, then we have first of all evidence for a Jewish setting for James, and in the terminology evidence for a specifically Palestinian setting.

In Jas 3:6 there is a reference to the tongue being "set on fire by Gehenna" (φλογιζομένη ὑπὸ τῆς γεέννης). Richard Bauckham has recently argued that the correct meaning of this phrase is that the sinful tongue will be tortured in the fire of Gehenna.[34] His agument roots the image in various strands of first century Judaism. These do

---

[32] R. B. Ward, "Partiality in the Assembly: James 2:2-4," *HTR* 62 (1969) 87-97.

[33] Rainer Riesner, "Synagogues in Jerusalem," in Bauckham (ed.), *The Book of Acts in its Palestinian Setting*, 179-211. The excursus on Jas 2:2-3 is on pp. 207-8.

[34] Richard Bauckham, "The Tongue Set on Fire by Hell (James 3:6)," read in the Apocalyptic in the New Testament Seminar of the Studiorum Novi Testamenti Societas meeting in Copenhagen 6 August 1998.

not include the Septuagint, for in fact the term γέεννα does not occur there. In the New Testament the word appears in Mark 9:43, 45, 47, Luke 12:5, seven times in Matthew,[35] and here. It was not a favorite Christian expression, since it does not occur in any Christian tradition from a non-Palestinian milieu, but rather appears in traditions originating in Palestine. This is consistent with Bauckham's evidence for the use of the term in non-Diaspora Jewish sources.[36]

Yet another example of such cultural references is that to the "early and latter [rain]" in Jas 5:7. This phrase does occur five times in the Septuagint (Deut 11:14; Jer 5:24; Hos 6:3; Joel 2:23; Zech 10:1), although there the term ὑετός (usually in the accusative) occurs, rather than "rain" being the understood referent as in James.[37] Not only is there this linguistic difference, but also none of the Septuagintal passages refer to farmers, to waiting for rain, or to waiting at all. Instead they refer to the rains as God's provision and especially to a return to YHWH resulting in his response of restoring the rains. Thus out of the Septuagintal passages only the two adjectives remain, not the explicit references to rain nor the theology of the passages using the phrase. Furthermore, the expression does not occur in non-Palestinian Jewish or Greek (including Christian) literature. It is therefore far more likely that James is using a proverbial expression rooted in the same geographical area as the Hebrew *Vorlage* of the Septuagint. The phenomena of the early and latter rains is characteristic of the eastern end of the Mediterranean, and in particular of the southern half of that region.[38] That is, this is an unconscious indication of the geographical area in which the

---

[35]   That is, it occurs in one Marcan passage (and its parallels), one "Q" passage, and two special Matthean passages.

[36]   The phrase τὸν τροχὸν τῆς γενέσεως also appears in Jas 3:6. However, the lack of understanding of the original meaning of this Orphic expression shows that James has picked up a phrase that was used by Jews, as its occurrence in Jewish literature demonstrates, rather than that he has any independent knowledge of Greek philosophy.

[37]   F. Spitta, *Der Brief des Jakobus untersucht* (Göttingen: Vandenhoeck & Ruprecht, 1896) believed that καρποί should be supplied as in *Geoponica* 1, 12, 32. However, while the *Geoponica* does include much older material, the work itself is tenth century C.E. That is hardly a solid basis for arguing for first century usage.

[38]   Denis Baly, *The Geography of the Bible* (London: Lutterworth, 1957) 47-52.

author has lived or was living.[39]

One should couple this phrase with the description of "the rich" in
5:1-6, since the waiting is a response to the situation created by "the
rich." All of the occupational images used in this prophetic
denunciation are agricultural, which of course fits the situation of
first century Palestine and its absentee landlords. One might become
wealthy through trade (although Palestine was not a trading
country), but one established status by purchasing farmland, even if
one normally resided in a city (especially Jerusalem). Furthermore,
"the rich" have fields that are "mowed" or "reaped" by hired
"workers," since they deserve wages. Neither of these is
characteristic of the Septuagint. That is, the Septuagintal contexts
referring to reaping fields (Lev 25:11; Deut 24:19; Isa 17:5; 37:30;
Mic 6:15) usually pair sowing and reaping and never speak of
injustice; nor does the Septuagint use the term ἐργατής (except in 1
Macc 3:6 for "workers of lawlessness"). The form of the prophetic
woe speech in James is traditional, but the content is not coming
from the Septuagint. Instead it reflects the situation in first century
Palestine, where absentee landlords (and also those who were not
absentee) used hired workers to work their farms rather than slaves
(as was common elsewhere in the Roman Empire and in the period
when the Hebrew scriptures were being written).[40] Thus we have
another unconscious indication that the Palestinian agricultural
situation is in view, not that elsewhere in the Roman Empire. This
information reinforces the impressions that we received from the

---

[39] If, for example, the author had grown up using such an expression, even a
move to another geographical area would not preclude a slip in which he use a well-
worn phrase from his past, even though it was inappropriate to where he now
lived. Thus the phrase could indicate either the author's origin or his location at the
time of writing.

[40] The reason for this phenomena was that slaves had to be released in the
sabbatical year (gentile slaves could become proselytes and enjoy this same
privilege), while hired labourers did not involve an investment that could be lost.
Also, there was a plentiful supply of such labour in Palestine in the first century
through the displacement of tenant farmers, the loss of farms due to indebtedness,
and the need of younger sons to find work independent of the family farm.
Naturally, with the uncertainties of the Palestinian climate there was a further
advantage in that slaves had to be fed in times of drought, but hired labourers were
not the responsibility of the landowner who used them. See F. M. Heichelheim,
"Roman Syria," in T. Frank (ed.), *An Economic Survey of Ancient Rome*, vol. 4
(Baltimore: Johns Hopkins Press, 1938) esp. 146-50, 164-65.

reference to the "early and latter" rains.

Therefore there are indications in the unconscious usages of our author that he is located in (or comes from) Palestine. As noted above, there is nothing comprable in the work that would indicate another cultural location, and a number of pieces of evidence pointing to a Palestinian location.

TRADITION-CRITICAL EVIDENCE

It is clear that James contains pre-existing traditions. These come in two forms. The first form is his use of preformed sayings and/or sermons found in his pool of tradition. One clear example is the Jesus logion in Jas 5:12 (cf. Matt 5:34-37). In this case James has the shorter form of the Jesus saying, while Matthew has a longer, more Semitic version. While this is the one clear citation of a saying of Jesus, as noted above, there may well be other logia that are agrapha, which means that only the criterion of coherence might help us discover them and even then it would only prove that they *could* be sayings of Jesus. More significantly, one can discover up to 35 allusions to the Jesus tradition in James.[41] Most of these are to the "Q" material behind the Sermon on the Mount/Plain, which is what one would expect from the paraenetic nature of James. However, while his closeness to the Jesus-tradition does differentiate James from Paul (perhaps because for the most part Paul did not address topics that the Jesus tradition also discusses), the existence of the four gospels suggests that the Jesus tradition was valued in various parts of the early church, gentile (e.g. Mark) as well as Jewish (e.g. Matthew).[42] The fact that James is not dependent upon any written form of the gospel tradition only helps one to avoid the mistake of

---

[41]   For a chart listing these, see Davids, *James*, 47-48; cf. Gerhard Dautzen-berg, "Ist das Schwurverbot Mt 5,33-37; Jak 5,12 ein Beispiel für die Torakritik Jesu?" *BZ* 25 (1981) 47-66, for a discussion of the single clearest passage.

[42]   It is interesting that in terms of content James is closer to Matthew than to any other gospel, although in the sharpness of his denunciation of the rich and in his exaltation of the poor he is closer to Luke (and *1 Enoch*). Patrick J. Hartin ("James and the Q Sermon on the Mount/Plain," in David J. Lull [ed.], *Society of Biblical Literature 1989 Seminar Papers* [SBLSP 28; Atlanta: Scholars Press, 1989] 440-57) in a detailed examination argues that James knows the Q Sermon and how it developed in the Matthean community, but not the final Matthean redaction. His affinities with the Lukan form of the sermon only reveal knowledge of the Lukan material in Q, not how the material developed in Lukan tradition.

dating James too late.[43]

There is clearly a relationship to Jewish traditions in James.[44] The piety-poverty material in James echoes themes in Qumran and *1 Enoch*, although it appears to be mediated to James through the Jesus tradition. Only some of the material on speech-ethics appears to come through the Jesus tradition (e.g. the sayings about anger in 1:19 and those on judging), while the rest stems directly from the massive amount of material on wisdom, the tongue, and speech found in such places as Proverbs and Sirach.[45] It is, however, in James' use of the *yēṣer* tradition that one sees his most interesting dependence upon Jewish materials. His rejection of "doubleness" (Jas 1:7; 4:8), his insistence that sin comes from desire within (Jas 1:14), his reference to the internal struggle among desires (Jas 4:1), his connection of desire to death (Jas 1:15), his reformulation of the testing tradition in terms of Job (Jas 1:13; cf. his description of God's character in 1:17-18), and his proposal of wisdom as the solution to the issues raised by testing and desire (Jas 3:13-17) all recall the *yēṣer* tradition. This is not the developed rabbinic form of the tradition (the two *yēṣerîm*, the Torah as the solution—although James is not without his references to the Law—and the debates about the origin of *yēṣer*) nor the less developed form found in the later Jewish wisdom literature such as Sirach and Wisdom, but somewhere in between.[46]

---

43   James does have in common with Matthew his use of the term παρουσία, which could be seen as pointing to a later date for James, if we view Matthew as introducing the term into the little apocalypse. However, there is no specific reference to Matthew in James, and the term itself is used for the return of Jesus in more than one tradition (1 John 2:28; 2 Pet 3:12; 2 Thess 2:1) and especially in 1 Cor 15:23, where Paul is probably drawing on traditions that he has received. Thus the use of the term appears to have been widespread in the church and certainly known by Paul several years before the martyrdom of James.

44   So much so that Phillip Sigal ("The halakhah of James," in D. Y. Hadidian [ed.], *Intergerini Parietis Septum (Eph 2:14): essays presented to Markus Barth on his sixty-fifth birthday* [Pittsburgh Theological Monograph Series 33; Pittsburgh: Pickwick Press, 1981] 337-53) does speak of James' teaching as halachic.

45   Interestingly enough, the virtue and vice catalogue in Jas 3:13-18 is closer to that found in 1QS 4 (although James uses wisdom language rather than spirit language) than to any other Jewish or Christian virtue-vice catalogue. On wisdom in James. See Ernst Baasland, "Der Jakobusbrief als Neutestamentliche Weisheits-schrift," *ST* 36 (1982) 119-39.

46   Lewis J. Procter ("James 4.4-6: Midrash on Noah," *NTS* 335 [1989] 625-27) notes the *yēṣer* references; however, his argument that they stem from a midrash

James' use of Jewish haggadic traditions also appears to place him in this same temporal and spatial area. His Abraham and Rahab are dependent upon the traditions of later Judaism.[47] His Elijah is moving towards the Elijah of the rabbis, for he is a man of prayer (a characteristic found as early as 4 Ezra 7:109), and his Job reflects the traditions later embodied in the *Testament of Job*, especially ὑπομονή.[48] Again we find that James fits best in the context of Judaism, a Judaism that was most developed in Palestine.

James has traditionally been seen as having some relationship to the Pauline tradition, for there is a linguistic overlap between some of the material in 2:14-26 and Pauline concerns, phraseology, and examples. In particular, James overlaps some of Paul's language in Rom 3:27–4:12. This relationship has been variously evaluated. As recently as 1987 Martin Hengel could argue that James' passage (and to a large extent the whole letter) was vehement polemic against Paul.[49] On the other hand, other scholars have observed that James does not depend on any known Pauline letter and thus might not be

---

on Noah (Gen 6:5; 8:21) is unconvincing. Cf. Joel Marcus, "The Evil Inclination in the Epistle of James," *CBQ* 44 (1982) 606-21.

[47]   See R. B. Ward, "The Works of Abraham: James 2:14-26," *HTR* 61 (1968) 283-90, as an example of one of the first to point this out.

[48]   For more detailed evidence see Peter H. Davids, "Tradition and Citation in the Epistle of James," in W. W. Gasque and W. S. LaSor (eds.), *Scripture, Tradition, and Interpretation* (Everett F. Harrison Festschrift; Grand Rapids: Eerdmans, 1978) 113-26.

[49]   Martin Hengel, "Der Jakobusbrief als antipaulinische Polemik," in G. F. Hawthorne and O. Betz (eds.), *Tradition and Interpretation in the New Testament. Essays in Honor of E. Earle Ellis* (Tübingen: Mohr [Siebeck]; Grand Rapids: Eerdmans, 1987) 248-78. Prof. Hengel, of course, is not alone. For example, Jack T. Sanders (*Ethics in the New Testament* [Philadelphia: Fortress Press, 1975]) uses this conflict as a key to New Testament ethics, in this case opting for James against Paul. And of course Martin Dibelius (*James*) takes a similar position. An important part of this argument is the interpretation of Gal 2:12 as indicating that James sent messengers not just to correct some Pauline practices in Antioch, but to oppose fundamental parts of his theology. If that is the correct interpretation of this verse, however, then the harmony with James concerning the gospel that Paul goes to great lengths to discuss in Gal 1:19 and 2:1-10 was short lived and the portrayal of James in Acts 15 and 21 is inaccurate. Those discussions, however, are outside the scope of this essay other than to note that Paul could have been clearer had he wished to indicate that his real conflict was with James rather than simply with Peter and that one can defend the essential accuracy of the portrayals of James in Acts (see Bauckham, "James and the Jerusalem Church," 441-50, 452-80).

opposing Paul himself. This difference of opinions calls for a look at the data.

The terminological overlap consists in the use of Abraham as an example, the citation of Gen 15:6, and the terms "faith" (πίστις), "works" (ἔργων), and δικαιόω (we are deliberately leaving this term untranslated).[50] What one realizes upon analysis is that if James is opposing Pauline thought, then he clearly does not understand Paul. Paul always speaks of "the works of the law," meaning the markers of Judaism, especially circumcision and dietary laws, never of works *per se*.[51] James speaks of works, and the one work of Abraham he cites is not the circumcision of Isaac from Genesis 17, but the binding of Isaac from Genesis 22.[52] The former fits the Pauline argument, while the latter fits the Jacobean context of testing (πειρασμός). Paul speaks of faith in Jesus Christ in the sense of commitment to him (cf. Rom 10:9-10 for something of a definition), while James speaks of faith in the sense of commitment to the *Shema*ᶜ, i.e. God is one. Paul speaks of the justification (δικαιοσύνη) of the unrighteous. James, on the other hand, speaks of Abraham (as an example) being declared righteous (δικαιόω) on the evidence of his deeds (Gen 22:12, 15-18 are surely the divine statements James has in mind). Thus James must at least be misunderstanding Paul, as Joachim Jeremias pointed out years ago.[53] If he had had direct contact with Pauline thought as expressed in Romans, we would indeed have to say, "Frère Jacques, dormez-vous?"[54] It makes more sense of the data to assume that James had never seen a Pauline letter and instead at most had had contact with an antinomian distortion of Paul's teaching.[55]

---

50   Significantly, James does not himself use the nominal form, διακαιοσύνη; this noun only occurs in his quotation of Gen 15:6, not in his own composition.

51   There are exceptions in which Paul says only "works," but in those cases the full phrase has been mentioned earlier in the same passage.

52   Perhaps drawing with it a reference to the charity of Abraham, as argued by Ward, "Works of Abraham," 283-90.

53   Joachim Jeremias, "Paul and James," *ExpTim* 66 (1954-55) 368-71; cf. John G. Lodge, "James and Paul at cross-purposes: Jas 2:22," *Bib* 62 (1981) 195-213, for another approach to reconciling James and Paul.

54   Klaus Haacker ("Justification, salut et foi," *ETR* 73 [1998] 183) first applied this nursery song to the issue.

55   See further Peter H. Davids, "James and Paul," in G. F. Hawthorne, R. P. Martin, and D. G. Reid (eds.), *Dictionary of Paul and His Letters* (Downers Grove: InterVarsity, 1993) 457-61.

More recently Klaus Haacker has examined the most relevant passages (Jas 2:14-26; Rom 3:27-4:12) from a linguistic standpoint, distinguishing between theme (θέμα) and language (ῥῆμα, *parole*).[56] Beginning with the thesis statements of each passage (Jas 2:14; Rom 1:16) he demonstrates the totally different issues that each passage is discussing (θέμα). While there is overlapping vocabulary (ῥῆμα), there are more critical terms in each passage that find no parallels in the other than those that do. Finally he examines the language of faith in James (faith saves/ does not save/ have faith) and notes that such language appears in Paul only in 1 Cor 13:2, a non-soteriological context that finds its origin in the Jesus tradition (Matt 17:20; 21:21; Mark 11:23).[57] It is precisely in this tradition where one also finds the language of faith saving (e.g. Mark 5:34 = Matt 9:22; Luke 8:48; cf. Acts 14:9). That is, James is dialoguing with ideas coming from the healing narratives about Jesus, a tradition with which he is clearly in touch (Jas 5:14-16).[58] James' issue appears to be with the distinction between the faith that always saves (= heals) in Jas 5:15 and the faith that is not sufficient to save (= eschatological salvation) unless it shows through actions that the heart is truly submitted to God. In this context both the teaching and the Abraham example are fully in line with Jewish usage.[59] This also explains why James uses δικαιόω in the sense it normally has in Jewish sources rather than in the Pauline sense. In other words, a careful linguistic examination of James and Paul demonstrates that the relationship is only superficial and apparent. Everything that James says has ample precedent and basis in the Jesus tradition and Jewish teaching about Abraham. Nothing requires contact with Pauline thought for an explanation. Again the book seems more at home in the Palestinian communities where Jewish tradition mixed with the pre-written Gospel tradition (since James shows no contact

---

56   Haacker, "Justification, salut et foi," 177-88.

57   Paul does not say that faith saves. That would be quite unpauline. He would attribute salvation (which in itself is not the preferred pauline term) to the death of Jesus or the action of God, not to faith.

58   Not only does James connect the "prayer of faith" to saving (using σῴζω), but he also refers to anointing with oil, which is paralleled elsewhere only in the disciples' practice in Mark 6:13.

59   Cf. Ferdinand Hahn, "Genesis 15,6 im Neuen Testament," in H. W. Wolff (ed.), *Probleme biblischer Theologie: Gerhard von Rad zum 70 Geburtstag* (Munich: Kaiser Verlag, 1971) 90-107.

with the written gospels) than anywhere else.

CONCLUSIONS

The arguments presented above vary in their value. For example, some evidences gains significance because it coheres with the more weighty evidence. The point we have argued throughout, however, is that whether one looks at the genre of James, its linguistic data, its incidental references (precisely because they were probably unconscious), or the traditions it uses, one gains the impression that this work is culturally and linguistically at home in Palestine. True, it is possible that a person whose native environment was Palestine wrote James while living somewhere else, but in that case that author has done an excellent job of not leaving any clues about their new environment.[60] In all probability, then, James should be viewed as a letter to the Diaspora (meaning the scattered renewed Israel, including the gentile converts who were "in their midst") coming from Jerusalem (for what other Christian group in Palestine would have felt they had the authority to write such a letter).

Can we go beyond this conclusion? We stated at the start of this essay that the most one could demonstrate was that James fits into a particular socio-cultural context (which includes a particular linguistic context). That is what we have argued for. But given the context, the logical source within this context was Jerusalem, for up through 70 C.E. (and in their own eyes, perhaps even long after 70 C.E.) it was *the* centre for the church, not only in Palestine, but even for the whole eastern Mediterranean and beyond.[61] Furthermore, where else would a letter to the Diaspora originate from? Thus the probabilities are that this is a letter stemming from the (Jewish-Christian) church in Jerusalem.

If that point is accepted, however, then even without looking at the

---

60   J. Daryl Charles (*Virtue amidst Vice* [JSNTSup 150; Sheffield: Sheffield Academic Press, 1997]) makes the major point of his book that the basically Palestinian material in Jude shows the effects of reworking it in a gentile context in 2 Peter. There are no such non-Palestinian contextual indicators in James.

61   Even Paul assumes the importance of the Jerusalem "pillars" in Galatians 2, or else he could not have implied that their disapproval of his message would have meant that he had "run in vain" (Gal 2:2). Certainly Jerusalem has influence in Antioch according to Gal 2:11-14 as well as Acts 11:22; 15:1-2. See further Bauckham, "James and the Jerusalem Church."

salutation it would be likely that James was at least in part the author, if the letter were written before 61 C.E., and that he had at least shaped the perspective if it were written after.[62] That is, no major scholar dates James before the persecution of the church by Herod Agrippa I (i.e. the 41–44 C.E. period). And between that persecution and his martyrdom James was clearly the pre-eminent voice in the Jerusalem church. That is the testimony of Paul (who lists James first in Gal 2:9) as well as Acts, the *Gospel of Thomas* (*logion* §12) and Hegesippus.[63] That being the case, then the salutation may well be authentic. At the least it is free of the more elaborate titles that we find attributed to James in later works. Instead it uses a title that at least one contemporary, Paul, did use of himself (although Paul often added "apostle" as did 2 Peter; Jude is closer to James and probably comes from the same milieu). Given that James does not use other titles that Paul uses, it was not modelled on the Pauline letters themselves, nor shows any need to compete with them (e.g. James could have added without controversy "brother of our Lord" or "apostle," since Gal 1:19 appears to indicate that Paul himself would have granted him such titles). Thus given the context from which we believe the letter comes, the salutation is not improbable at all. In our view it is likely that the Epistle of James is either a product of James himself or, more likely, a Diaspora letter preserving his sayings for the church at large shortly after his martyrdom. If one accepts this, then in this letter one is hearing the voice of James or at least the perspective of the church in Jerusalem that he led.

How, then, can we describe this perspective? Or, to put it another way, what voice does James contribute to the overall voice of the

---

62   The disruption of the Jerusalem church during the Jewish War of 66–70 and its weakened state after 70 make it unlikely that James was written after the Jewish War. Furthermore, with the decline of the church in Jerusalem no strong alternative centres developed within Palestine; instead the influential church centres afterwards were north (Antioch, Asia Minor, Rome) or south (Alexandria) of Palestine. (While a gentile church did develop in Jerusalem after 135 C.E., it did not have the influence of the other major centres and certainly not of the Jewish-Christian church that preceded it.)

63   Eusebius, *Eccl. Hist.* 2.23.4-9. While Hegesippus is reporting legend that is certainly exaggerated and in places quite improbable, the core of the account is that James was the main leader of the Jerusalem church, although he likely led as the first among equals in a group of elders. See further Bauckham, "James and Jerusalem," 448-49.

Christian canon?

1. It is a perspective in which the one God is central. When James wants to cite the creed, it is the *Shema*ʾ, precisely what one would expect of a Jew. While the "Judge" at the door in chapter five may be Jesus, the "one Lawgiver and Judge" of chapter four is not. In fact, the theocentric nature of James was what led Spitta to argue that it was a Jewish work lightly retouched by the addition of two verses (1:1; 2:1).[64] In one sense Spitta is correct: the author saw himself as a Jew, worshipping the Jewish God according to a Jewish creed. What Spitta missed, however, was that the whole Jewish-Christian movement saw themselves this same way.

2. In James the law is assumed, not argued for. As in Matthew, with which, as we have seen, James has affinities, there is a Torah-piety underlying James. The law is the "perfect law of freedom" or the "royal law." One can argue from the law (as in 2:1-14), but one does not need to argue for the law. This relaxed attitude towards the law, not that the law was not follow strictly, but that the observance of the law is something that one does not need to argue for, is precisely what one would expect within a Jewish community.

Unlike the James portrayed in Hegesippus or Acts 21, or the early Christian community in Acts 2, Temple piety does not play a significant role in the Epistle of James. There are certainly cultic images (perhaps with meanings going beyond the cultic) that could come from either Temple piety or the Hebrew scriptures (e.g. 4:7-8), but there is no clear reference to Temple rites or cultic purification. However, this does not mean that the author and his community did not practice Temple piety. If we are correct that the Epistle of James is a Diaspora letter, then Temple piety was not a possibility for the majority of its intended audience. Even for those that made the pilgrimage, it could at best be only a rare experience. James is interested in purity, but the purity he mentions is due to repentance, separation from "the world", and the like—all possible in a Diaspora context.

3. James is Christian. Jesus is the "glorious Lord" of the church in whose name they were baptised, who is likely the coming Judge and whose teaching is authoritative (much as that of the Teacher of Righteousness was in Qumran). That is, the many allusions to the

---

    64   F. Spitta, *Der Brief des Jakobus untersucht* (Göttingen: Vandenhoeck & Ruprecht, 1896).

teaching of Jesus show that for James' community Jesus was the source of the correct interpretation of the Hebrew scriptures. This is consistent with a view of Jesus as the exalted leader of the messianic community, the purified Jewish nation. It is likely that he is "the Lord" who heals in 5:14-15. He certainly is the one in whose name they pray.

4. One might add that while James reflects a Jewish-Christian community, the epistle itself does not inform us of the relationship of Jewish believers to gentile believers within the context of the renewed Israel. James addresses the communities he writes as Israel ("Twelve Tribes in the Diaspora"). Does that mean that gentile believers are now part of the renewed Israel or do they relate to it as would a pious gentile who came to the synagogue or are they simply not in the picture? The letter itself does not tell us. Since that information would clarify the relationship of the letter to Pauline teaching, this is from a scholarly viewpoint unfortunate.

5. The burden of the letter is dealing with such pressures as might make one compromise ethically. The two major themes are speech-ethics, consistent both with Proverbs and the Jesus tradition, and economic ethics, more the concern of the Jesus tradition. James' community is "the poor" over against the outsiders, among whom are "the rich" (functioning very much as "the wicked" function in the prophetic sections of the Hebrew scriptures). In this James reflects terminology that would be at home in Qumran, and especially in apocalyptic groups such as that behind *1 Enoch*. In the light of pressure, both in terms of shaming and of economic persecution from "the rich," James argues for community solidarity in terms of charity and unity.

Thus while authorship cannot be proved, our evidence points us back towards a specific cultural location, Palestinian Jewish-Christianity, after which one's judgment about the authenticity of the salutation and the historical probabilities of the period will be what lead one to attributing or not attributing this work to James the Just. In our judgement, however, either we are hearing (largely) his voice, or we are at least hearing the collective voice of the community that he led.[65]

---

[65] So also Pierre-Antoine Bernheim, *James, Brother of Jesus* (London: SCM Press, 1997) 244.

VOW-TAKING, THE NAZIRITES, AND THE LAW: DOES JAMES' ADVICE TO PAUL ACCORD WITH HALAKHAH?

Jacob Neusner

After this Paul stayed many days longer . . . at Cenchreae he cut his hair, for he had a vow.

Acts 18:18

They said to him, "You see, brother, how many thousands there are among the Jews of those who have believed; they are all zealous for the law . . . What then is to be done? They will certainly hear that you have come. Do therefore what we tell you. We have four men who are under a vow. Take these men and purify yourself along with them and pay their expenses so that they may shave their heads. Thus all will know that there is nothing in what they have been told about you, but that you yourself live in observance of the law."

Acts 21:23-24

Pretty much everyone concurs that Paul's haircut had to do with a Nazirite vow, in line with the provisions of Numbers 6, and, further, James' party counseled Paul to show himself observant of the law by supplying the Nazirites with the offerings that they required to complete their Nazirite vows in the Temple rites specified at Numbers 6.[1] The happenstance that Paul himself had taken such an oath, had completed the span of time subject to the Nazirite rule, and was expected to present the necessary offerings need not detain us. Within the halakhah of the Mishnah, one had the possibility of taking a vow to supply Nazirites with their offerings; a father might so commit himself to his son, or the son to the father, for instance. So the picture is clear: James deemed vow-taking in general, and the Nazirite vow in particular, to signify loyalty to law-observance in the framework of the Torah, and Paul concurred, having himself taken such an oath. Now, everyone knows, one significant figure in the same framework will have found such counsel puzzling, and that

---

[1]   For recent and representative assessments of the pertinent passages, see R. Pesch, *Die Apostelgeschichte* (2 vols., EKKNT 5.1-2; Zurich: Benziger Verlag, 1986) 2.154-56, 218-21; J. A. Fitzmyer, *The Acts of the Apostles* (AB 31; New York: Doubleday, 1998) 633-34.

is Jesus himself, to whom the Sermon on the Mount attributes the explicit statement (Matt 5:33-36), "You have heard that it was said to the men of old, 'You shall not swear falsely, but shall perform to the Lord what you have sword.' But I say to you, Do not swear at all, either by heaven . . . or by earth . . . or by Jerusalem . . . And do not swear by your heard, for you cannot make one hair white or black.'"[2]

The statement on its own presents a puzzle. For the context of the statement carries us to swearing in two categories that are kept separate in the halakhah, "swearing" referring to an oath by God's name in court, and "vows," e.g. the Nazirite vow, such as would be represented by "swearing by your head," or "by the hairs of your head." But in treating the two matters together, the statement leaves no doubt of the intent. Hence James's advice to Paul certainly presents a puzzle. I propose to show that the rabbis, represented later on by the Mishnah and the other halakhic and aggadic documents also, will have identified more eloquent media for the expression of piety than vowing and keeping vows in general, and the Nazirite vow in particular; and it is to make that point that I wish to spell out in an exposition of the halakhic sources on both issues. With the halakhah in hand, the truly jarring effects of James's advice will make their impact.

I. THE HALAKHAH OF NEDARIM

A survey of the halakhah of vowing, in tractate Nedarim of the Mishnah, Tosefta, Yerushalmi, and Bavli, and the halakhah of the Nazirite vow in particular will show us how the sages, start to finish both expounded the topic and evaluated it. When, thereafter, we take up the religious statement that the halakhah makes and identify the corresponding position of the aggadic writings, we shall see a uniform judgment of the matter, start to finish. The halakhah set forth in the Mishnah, Tosefta, and two Talmuds deems language the

---

2   For a critical assessment of this "antithesis," see W. D. Davies, *The Setting of the Sermon on the Mount* (Cambridge: Cambridge University Press, 1964; repr. BJS 186; Atlanta: Scholars Press, 1989) 239-42; D. C. Allison Jr., and W. D. Davies, *A Critical and Exegetical Commentary on the Gospel according to Saint Matthew*. Volume I: *Introduction and Commentary on Matthew I–VII* (ICC; Edinburgh: T. & T. Clark, 1988) 533-37; H. D. Betz, *The Sermon on the Mount* (Hermeneia; Philadelphia: Fortress, 1995) 243-59, with bibliography on 240-43.

mirror of the soul; the words we use expose man's heart, articulate and give effect to his intentionality. The key to the entire system comes to expression in the language of the halakhah, "An act of consecration done in error is not binding or consecrated." And from the viewpoint of the Torah's halakhah, what we intend makes all the difference: God responds to what we want, more than to what we do, as the distinction between murder and manslaughter shows in an obvious way. For the critical dialectics of the Torah embodies the conflict between God's and man's will. That focus upon the definitive, taxonomic power of intentionality explains, also, why if a man says to a woman, "Lo, you are consecrated . . .," and the woman acquiesces, the intentionalities matching, the woman is thereby sanctified to that man and forbidden to all others; the act of intention formulated in words bears the power of classification upon which the entire system builds. But—self-evidently—not all intentionality finds Heaven's approval, and that is so even though Heaven confirms and acquiesces therein. And that brings us to the vow, which realizes in words the intentionality of the person who takes the vow and imposes upon himself restrictions of various kinds. And, inseparable from the vow, in sequence comes the special vow of the Nazirite.

Stated simply, the sages' position, in the halakhah and the corresponding aggadah, rejects vow-taking as disreputable, for reasons I shall explain. Not only so, but the Nazirite vow in particular is singled out as an act of personal arrogance, not of piety at all. The dismissive judgment of the halakhah upon the vow is fully exposed in the rule, "He who says, 'As the vows of the suitable folk' has said nothing whatsoever. Such a statement does not constitute a euphemism for a vow. Why not? Because suitable folk (keshérim) do not take vows. And the rest follows. But most people do take vows, and in the exemplary language of the halakhah they are particularly common in the life of the household, meaning, in relationships between husband and wife. For the vow is the weapon of the weak, the way by which the lesser party to a transaction exercises power over the greater. If the wife says to the husband, "By a vow, I shall not derive benefit from you," or "What food you feed me is qorban," she removes from herself her husband's control, so too, the guest to the host. But the vow also stands for the release of discipline, it is an expletive and an outcry, an act of temper, and no wonder sages do not respect those that take vows. Now let us see matters in more general, theoretical terms.

The power of the word to change the status of persons and things defines and sustains the household above all, which rests in the last analysis upon the foundations of commitment, responsibility, and trust—all to begin with embodied in language. The sanctity of one's word forms a corollary of the proposition that the language we use bears the power of classification, and, in the present context, of therefore effecting sanctification. If, after all, by declaring a woman consecrated to a man, or an animal to the altar or a portion of the crop to the priesthood, one brings about the sanctification of the woman or the beast or the grain, then what limits to the power of language to affect the everyday world are to be set? In that same framework, after all, God communicates and is communicated with: in the present age, with the Temple in ruins, worship is through prayer, which takes the form of words whether spoken or not.

But why focus the discussion of vowing as a component of the law that pertains within the household (in the received organization of the Mishnah, within the division devoted to the family), when vows can take place in the larger framework of the Israelite social order? Scripture imposes its judgment on the point, within the social order, at which vows become pertinent when it presents the matter as a dimension of the life of wives with their husbands or daughters with their fathers. That fact emerges from the pertinent verses of Scripture at Num 30:1-16:

> Moses said to the heads of the tribes of the people of Israel, "This is what the Lord has commanded. When a man vows a vow to the Lord or swears an oath to bind himself by a pledge, he shall not break his word; he shall do according to all that proceeds out of his mouth.
>
> "Or when a woman vows a vow to the Lord and binds herself by a pledge, while within her father's house in her youth, and her father hears of her vow and of her pledge by which she has bound herself and says nothing to her, then all her vows shall stand, and every pledge by which she has bound herself shall stand. But if her father expresses disapproval to her on the day that he hears of it, no vow of hers, no pledge by which she has bound herself, shall stand; and the Lord will forgive her, because her father opposed her. And if she is married to a husband while under her vows or any thoughtless utterance of her lips by which she has bound herself, and her husband hears of it, and says nothing to her on the day that he hears, then her vows shall stand, and her pledges by which she has bound herself shall stand. But if, on the day that her husband comes to hear of it, he expresses disapproval, then he shall make void her vow which was on her and the thoughtless utterance of her lips, by which she bound herself; and

the Lord will forgive her. But any vow of a widow or of a divorced woman, anything by which she has bound herself, shall stand against her.

"And if she vowed in her husband's house or bound herself by a pledge with an oath, and her husband heard of it, and said nothing to her and did not oppose her, then all her vows shall stand, and every pledge by which she bound herself shall stand. But if her husband makes them null and void on the day that he hears them, then whatsoever proceeds out of her lips concerning her vows or concerning her pledge of herself shall not stand; her husband has made them void. But if her husband says nothing to her from day to day, then he establishes all her vows or all her pledges that are upon her; he has established them, because he said nothing to her on the day that he heard of them. But if he makes them null and void after he has heard of them, then he shall bear her iniquity."

These are the statues that the Lord commanded Moses, as between a man and his wife, and between a father and his daughter, while in her youth, within her father's house.

The generalization, that a person is not to break his word but keep "all that proceeds out of his mouth," meaning, his vows, immediately finds its amplification in the framework of the household.

The halakhah of vows (drawing in its wake the halakhah of the special vow of the Nazirite) concerns matters of personal status: what may a person do or not do by reason of a self-imposed vow? The halakhah so reveals what it finds especially interesting in marriage, which is, relationships: shifts and changes in the relationship of the wife to the husband. That is consistent with the points pertinent to the status of a woman in relationship to a man at which the halakhah begins and ends: the creation of the marriage through Heavenly action (the halakhah of Yebamot) or human intervention (Qiddushin, Ketubot); the cessation of a marriage through Heavenly action (death) or through the writ of divorce (Gittin). Now we raise the question about the interplay between responsibilities to Heaven, on the one side, and to the husband, on the other, that the woman takes upon herself—the gray area in which the woman owes fealty to Heaven and to husband alike. Here we find ourselves in dialogue with the three pertinent chapters of the Written Torah that all together address the matter, Numbers Chapter Five for the woman investigated for faithfulness; Numbers Chapter Six for the Nazirite vow; and Numbers Chapter Thirty for the ordinary vow.

The most general statement of matters then invokes the matter of relationships with Heaven that affect relationships on earth, that is, the woman's vow to Heaven that affects her relationships with her husband and family. That is what is at stake in the halakhah of Qiddushin and Gittin as well—only now in the reverse. Acts of consecration involve declarations made on earth and confirmed in Heaven, e.g. consecration of a woman to a particular man. Here we address the effects of declarations made to Heaven that shape a woman's status and relationships on earth, and that means, in the nature of things, with her father before marriage and with her husband in marriage.

The presentation of the halakhah starts with the definition of a vow and proceed to consider the affects of a vow upon what a person may or may not do, mainly, eat. We conclude with close attention to how one may gain absolution from a vow, releasing its binding character by reason of diverse grounds or pretexts. That is the whole story, beginning, middle, and end, a structure that is simple and logical. That vows principally locate themselves within the household—the premise of the Scripture's statements and the halakhah's presentation throughout—guides the articulation of the details of the law. But the halakhah as the Written Torah defines it and the formulation of the halakhah by the Oral Torah do not coincide in one fundamental way. Scripture treats the matter as principally one involving women— wives and daughters—while the halakhah of the Oral Torah presents it as a sex-neutral one, involving vows by man or woman alike. What is nearly the whole story of the topic in Numbers is handled in Nedarim as subordinate and secondary. Rather, the halakhah of the Oral part of the Torah wants to know about the language that makes the vow effective, the results of vows, the release of vows—topics implicit, but not explored, within the Scripture's account of the matter.

The halakhah spreads a broad net over the language people use, treating every sort of euphemism as effective in imposing the vow. The halakhah of definition yields no problematics I can discern, only a principle richly instantiated that any sort of language that resembles the language of a vow takes effect. The essay on language that the halakhah embodies proceeds to language that is null, or language used without adequate reflection, e.g. vows of incitement, on the one side, vows of exaggeration, on the other. In both cases the vow does not follow much thought. Or, more to the point, the intention behind the language is inappropriate. Vows of incitement —to purchase an object at a given price—embody inappropriate intentionality; they are meant to influence the other only. Vows made in error, like acts of consecration made in error, do not stand for the intentionality of the speaker, and so are null. Finally, vows broken under constraint are null. Along these same lines, one may intentionally take a false vow to save life or limb or to deceive the thief and the tax-collector (regarded as one and the same).

The second important problematics that provokes legal inquiry provides a systematic exercise in differentiating the genus from the species, embodied in the distinction between a vow against deriving benefit from the genus, which encompasses all the species of that genus (the genus, house, the species, upper chamber), and a vow against deriving benefit from a particular species, which leaves available the other species of the same genus (upper chamber, house). That exercise is worked out in vast detail, repeating the same point throughout. The difference between genus and species (wool, shearings) and between two distinct genera (clothing, sacking) accounts for a broad range of the issues dealt with here, and the matter of speciation covers much of the rest. Thus we differentiate cooking from roasting or seething. So too, language that is general is interpreted in minimal ways, "pickling" applying only to vegetables. In all, the exercise of speciation and its effects accounts for many of the concrete halakhic problems that are set forth, and a few generalizations, even given in abstract terms, would encompass much of the halakhah in its details.

If speciation explains a broad range of rules, the matter of causation accounts for another. Specifically, the third type of problem addressed by the halakhah concerns the effects of vows, e.g. the result of general statements about deriving benefit for specific types of benefit. A vow against deriving benefit from his friend leaves the friend free to perform certain general actions, e.g. paying the man's half-sheqel tax to the Temple and restoring what he has lost. The distinction between forbidden and permitted benefit is subtle, and so far as I can see rests upon the difference between efficient cause and proximate cause, benefit deriving from actions in the category of efficient causes being forbidden, the other kind permitted.

That that distinction governs is shown, among other cases, by the rule that allows the fellow, forbidden by the man's vow to give him any benefit, to hire a storekeeper to give what the man cannot directly give himself. The rule is worth reviewing: The fellow goes to a storekeeper and says, "Mr. So-and-so is forbidden by vow from

deriving benefit from me, and I don't know what I can do about it."
And the storekeeper gives food to him who took the vow and then
goes and collects from this one against whom the vow was taken. [If]
he against whom the vow was taken had to build the house of the one
prohibited by vow from deriving benefit, or to set up his fence, or to
cut the grain in his field, the fellow goes to the workers and says to
them, "Mr. So-and-so is forbidden by vow from deriving benefit
from me, and I don't know what I can do about it." Then the
workers do the work with him who took the vow and come and
collect their salary from this one against whom the vow was taken.
Clearly, the difference between direct and indirect action governs.
But if we differentiate indirect from direct cause, we also focus upon
direct cause in its own terms, e.g. fruit, what is exchanged for the
fruit, what grows from the fruit. So from an exercise on the
difference between genus and species we here proceed to one on the
difference between direct and indirect causation.

Vows are remitted or lose effect when the conditions specified in
them have been realized or proved null. They also are remitted when
the purpose of the vow is shown spurious, e.g. "Did you not speak
only to do me honor? But this [not taking your wheat and wine for
my children] is what I deem to be honorable!" Further, vows cannot
in the end take effect so as to bring about the violation of existing
obligations or contracts. A vow against what is written in the Torah
is null; one that violates the marriage-contract is ineffective; one that
requires dishonoring parents is null. Vows that contradict the facts
explicitly invoked in making them are null. The point is then
obvious: language takes effect only when the facts embodied in the
language to begin with are valid.

The power of the husband or the father, as the case may be, to
annul the vows of the wife or the daughter presents no surprises. We
deal with the familiar range of cases, e.g. the interstitial status of the
betrothed girl, over which both father and husband enjoy power.
Once the woman is on her own, it goes without saying, no man may
nullify her vows. The husband may annul the vows of the wife once
she comes into his domain. The action must take place on the spot,
through the day in question; it cannot be done in advance. The
halakhah clearly makes provision for the autonomous woman, not
subject to father or husband, and treats as valid whatever vows she
makes on her own account.

II. THE HALAKHAH OF NAZIR

The special vow of the Nazirite, like the vow in general, draws in its wake consequences for the life of the family of which that individual that takes the vow is (by definition) a key member: the householder, his wife, children, and slaves. Not drinking wine, not shaving the head, not contracting corpse-uncleanness are matters that are personal and impinge upon the household; they do not pertain in any weighty way to public life, on the one side, or to relations between the people, Israel, and God, on the other. The Nazirite cannot attend to the deceased, cannot drink wine with the family, and subjects himself to his own rule when it comes to his appearance. As is the priest to the family of Israel, so is the Nazirite to the household of Israel, a particular classification of persons, distinguished in consequential and practical ways as to nourishment and comportment.

Nor should we miss the negative case. The vow does not encumber all Israel in relationship to God. It is not an obligatory act of service, as an offering is, but a votive one. And while other votive acts of service, e.g. the thank-offering or the peace-offerings, engage the priesthood in the Temple, the vow does not, and the Nazirite vow brings about offerings given to the priest at the door of the tent of meeting, in the manner of the offerings of the person afflicted with the skin ailment described in Leviticus Chapters 13 and 14; and there he stays.

Hence the special vow of the Nazirite forms an event at the door of the Temple courtyard but in the heart of the household. That is not all that explains why the tractate is situated, in the Mishnah, where it is, in the division on the family ("Women"), even though it bears upon men as much as upon women. The Nazirite vow forms a subdivision of the category, vows, and is treated as continuous with the exposition of that topic. That is because the right of the husband to annul his wife's vows extends to the Nazirite vow that she may take. That is surely the formal reason that justifies situating the tractate where it is. Scripture deals with two topics, the restrictions self-imposed by the vow, and the offerings required in connection therewith. The relevant verses of Scripture are at Num 6:10-21. The exposition of the law set forth by Scripture, which preoccupies the halakhah of the Oral Torah in the present case, explicitly concerns husband-wife relationships at M. 4:4-7, the husband's annulling the vows of the wife, the affect upon the wife of the husband's sudden death without an act of nullification, and the like. Not only so, but the tractate commences with a formulation modeled upon that of Mishnah-tractate Nedarim. But the true continuities, which make the two tractates into a single, continuous statement, will impress us only when we have reviewed the halakhah of the Nazirite vow.

The Written Torah finds two points of interest in the present topic, the prohibitions upon the Nazirite, the offerings that come as the climax of the vow. The Nazirite then is comparable to a *kohen* or priest: subject to certain prohibitions and is assigned a particular position in the conduct of the Temple cult. The priest cannot serve if he is drunk or contaminated by a corpse or bald (a bald-headed man is invalid to serve as a priest, so *m. Bekh.* 7:2A). A single paradigm pertains, a single analogy governs. From the perspective of Scripture, once the Nazirite vow takes effect, prohibitions are invoked against wine, hair-cutting, and corpse-uncleanness; the other point of interest is the offerings that are required if the Nazirite is made unclean with corpse-uncleanness and when the Nazirite completes the vow in a state of cleanness. All this the halakhah both takes for granted and in the main simply ignores. What Scripture holds does not require detailed analysis, by contrast, is the process by which the woman or man becomes a Nazirite, that is to say, the vow itself. To that problem fully half of the halakhah as defined by the Mishnah with the Tosefta is devoted.[3] So while the triple taboo is merely restated by the halakhah of the Oral Torah, it is the exposition of the vow that defines the tough problems, generates interesting conundrums, and entails the rich exposition that the Tosefta and two Talmuds would ultimately provide.

But in the Oral Torah, the halakhah, for its part, characteristically ignores what is securely classified and instead takes up interstitial problems, generated by intersecting rules or classes of data. In the present case, the halakhah focuses upon not the black-and-white language that invokes the vow, but on euphemisms that may or may not pertain, just as we saw with Nedarim. Language that is similar in

---

[3]   As usual, the contribution of the Talmuds to the formulation of halakhah proves negligible. Their interest is in analysis, not legislation. The Yerushalmi's formulations show little augmentation of the law, much amplification; I give no indication of the speculative problems explored therein, which are as usual imaginative and rich, but add nothing to the halakhah in its classical formulation except refinements.

sound or in sense takes effect. What about stipulations that might affect the vow, conditions under which the vow is or is not invoked, the taking of sequences of Nazirite-vows at a single moment? That is the next problem. The duration of the vow, undefined in Scripture, occupies attention. Then comes the intervention of the husband into the applicability of the vow his wife has taken. We turn, further, to designating the diverse animals that are to serve as the Nazirite's offerings at the end of the vow, with special attention to situations in which the animals are not used in accord with the original language of sanctification.

It is no surprise that the problematics of the halakhah, then, finds acute interest in the working of euphemisms. But that is not only because of the unclear status of euphemistic language—does it mean what it seems or not? Language, the halakhah recognizes, conveys sense and meaning in many ways. Language stands for what is intensely personal and private. But language also conveys meanings of general intelligibility. It is by definition a public act. With what result for the halakhah? What is private (mumbled, unintelligible, gibberish) bears no consequence, what is intelligible by a common-sense standard takes effect. That is how the halakhah sorts matters out. Thus, when it comes to euphemisms, all of them take effect; for what matters about language is not adherence to the governing formula, though it matters. What makes all the difference is the perceived and publicly comprehensible intent. If the intent conveyed by the language is clear and unmistakable, then the language has done its task of embodying intentionality. And then the language is affective. If the intentionality is not vividly conveyed, however indirectly, then the language is null. The power of language lies in its capacity to convey, to embody, inchoate intentionality, to realize in the shared world of public transactions the individual and private attitude or intentionality that motivates action. To that matter we shall return when we ask about the religious meaning of the halakhah.

And that accounts for the halakhah's recognition of the special status of a Samson-Nazirite: the language that is used signals the intentionality to accept the model of Samson, and hence fully exposes the will of the one who takes the special vow. Whether or not the Oral Torah has invented the category of the Samson-Nazirite to build upon the implications of its theory of the relationship of language to intentionality—the necessary connection between language and intention, public metaphor and private attitude and will—we cannot surmise. It is the simple fact that once the important questions pertinent to the topic at hand center upon the power of language to embody and realize, confirm and convey the attitude, the (mere) details of language will precipitate the formation of specificities of the halakhah. The main problem addressed by the halakhah pertaining to the language of the vow to be a Nazirite is how to standardize matters, so that private meanings and personal stipulations do not corrupt discourse. Then the prevailing solution is to identify what is general and intelligible and dismiss the rest. One example serves. That is why if someone specifies a detail as incumbent, then all the details of a Nazirite vow pertain to him. Nothing remains private, personal, idiosyncratic, once language serves. Even what affects the household in particular is framed for effect for all Israel.

The Tosefta's contribution to all this is, predictably, expansive: Just as euphemisms for Nazirite-vows are equivalent to Nazirite-vows, so euphemisms for Samson-vows are equivalent to Samson-vows. The vow applies in the Land and abroad, to hirsute and bald alike, and—it goes without saying—whether or not the Temple is standing. The intention is the key, not the limitations of circumstance. And that same governing principle accounts for the interpretation of the language, "I will be a Nazir like the hairs of my head" or "like the dust of the earth." That is taken to mean, for an unlimited period of time. The net effect of the halakhah is to generalize upon specific and idiosyncratic usages. Individual conditions are null, e.g. If one said, "Lo, I am a Nazir on condition that I shall drink wine and become unclean with corpse uncleanness," lo, this one is a Nazir. But he is prohibited to do all of these things that he has specified as conditional upon his vow. If he said, "I recognize that there is such a thing as Naziriteship, but I do not recognize that a Nazir is prohibited from drinking wine," lo, this one is bound by the Nazirite oath. But legitimate stipulations bear consequences, e.g. conditions that do not violate the law of the Torah: ". . . if my wife bears a son" or "a daughter."

Because the husband has the power to nullify the vows of the wife (or the father of the daughter), the halakhah attends to the case of nullification. But I see nothing of special interest in the laws, except that while the husband may nullify the wife's vow, he may not nullify his own. If his vow is contingent upon her vow, by contrast, neither is subject to the Nazirite rule. Limits are set upon intentionality; if one intended to violate the vow but in fact was not subject to the vow, there is no penalty: If her husband annulled the vow for her, but she did not know that her husband had annulled it for her and nonetheless continued to go around drinking wine and contracting corpse uncleanness, she does not receive forty stripes. So too, someone who violated the vow but had a sage annul it is not penalized; the vow never took effect. Here intention to violate the vow is insufficient to precipitate sanctions; the actualities intervene. Or, to put it otherwise, improper intention not confirmed by improper deed is null. Mere intention on its own is null—language and action decide everything, and, when it comes to the vow, the language constitutes the act.

When it comes to the offerings of the Nazirite, the halakhah—as at Pesahim and elsewhere—takes special interest in the interstitial case of the beast that has been consecrated but cannot be offered in fulfillment of the intent of the sacrifier: what to do with a beast designated for a given purpose that no longer is needed for that purpose? That involves the general rules that pertain. If a beast is designated as a burnt offering, it is presented in that designation; so too, a peace offering, differentiated from the Nazirite's peace-offering as to accompanying gifts. When it comes to the disposition of the coins that are designated for the purchase of an animal to be consecrated for the stated purpose, the rules follow the same lines. The upshot is, the language that is used to designate the animal or the coins takes effect, even though the purpose for which the animal or coins is required is nullified by circumstance. What is the stopping point? It is the tossing of the blood. At that point, the vow has been fully carried out and can no longer be annulled.

When it comes to the restrictions upon the Nazirite, which the Written Torah has defined, the Oral Torah devotes its halakhah to the familiar problem of differentiating among a sequence of actions of a single type, that is, the general theme of the many and the one, the one and the many, that preoccupies the halakhah in one topic after another. This routine problem comes to expression in the language, A Nazir who was drinking wine all day long is liable only on one count. If they said to him, "Don't drink it! Don't drink it!" and he continues drinking, he is liable on each and every count [of drinking. The problem is particular, the resolution and consequent rule not. So too the conundrum about the high priest and the Nazirite, both of them subject to the same restriction against corpse-uncleanness, who share the obligation to bury a neglected corpse requires us to hierarchize the sanctity of each in relationship to that of the other. This too represents a particular form of a general problem of the halakhah in its work of hierarchical classification, here of competing sanctities: who is holier than whom, and so what? For the same reason, we need not be detained by the halakhah covering cases of doubt. They merely illustrate prevailing principles on how cases of doubt are to be resolved; another tractate provides the systematic statement of governing principles of the matter, the present one, merely concrete problems for solution.

III. RELIGIOUS PRINCIPLES OF NEDARIM-NAZIR

The halakhah of Nedarim-Nazir takes up the theme, the power of language to impose changes in status. That is a common theme of the halakhah, paramount in the halakhah of Israel's relationships with God as much as that of Israel within the household walls. In words a magic dwells. In relationship to God what is at issue is the designation of what belongs to God or God's surrogates. Here at stake is personal status. The former then concerns how language affects the tangible world of wine and grain and oil, the latter, the intangible but very real world of a person's standing in the sight of Heaven and Israel alike. By using certain language, a man or woman effects an alteration in his or her condition, e.g. in relationships with other people, or in food that may or may not be eaten, or situations that may or may not be entered into. In both realms of being words affect the world of tangible substances and real relationships. Here, as we noted earlier, by words a man declares himself analogous to a priest—and his actions confirm his intention, realized in language.

What the vow does is to call down Heaven's sanctity upon the benefit, material or otherwise, that the donor wishes to give over for the sake of Heaven. No wonder then, that in analyzing vows, we call upon the conceptions of the gift to Heaven that form the center of Holy Things. The intention of the farmer to consecrate the beast, expressed in the proper language, is confirmed: the beast enters the status of sanctification even before it is set on the altar and slaughtered, its blood tossed at the corners of the altar. "Qorban," "Nazir," and other effective language—these form a single classification, words that transform by reason of the intent with which they are spoken, which they realize because they are spoken.

To state matters in more general terms: at stake in the vow and in the special vow of the Nazirite is the realization of intention brought about through the use of language. But language used for vows, so sages portray matters, does not sanctify, it contaminates, that language ought to express reflected-upon intentionality—like the designation of an animal to expiate an inadvertent, newly-realized sin —but it conveys the outcome of temper and frustration. Designating a beast as consecrated realizes a noble, godly intention; designating benefit one receives from one's spouse as "qorban" uses language to embody a lowly and disreputable intention, one to humiliate and reject and disgrace the other. Sages' message registers that language is dangerous because it realizes intentionality, which had best, therefore, be expressed with probity and restraint. And these virtues form the opposite of the traits of mind and character of the vow-taking Israelite, wife or husband, host or guest, salesman or customer, as the exemplary cases of Nedarim have shown us.

All the consequences of the use of special language—the illustrative materials of both bodies of halakhah, Nedarim and Nazir —concern relations of husbands and wives, or parents and children, or the localized transactions of the household and the service-economy round-about (the shop-keeper for example), thus the household and the conduct of life therein. Only rarely does the language, e.g. of the vow or of the special vow of the Nazirite, spill over into the public affairs of Israel in general. Being private, the vow and the Nazirite vow have no consequences for the relationship of Israel to God in general; breaking the vow or failing to observe what is pledged concerns the individual and God, the community being a bystander to the transaction and bearing no stake therein. The category-formations involved in vows and Nazirite vows do not encompass transactions within the social order, never alluding to a Nazirite's cow that gored the cow of a woman, or a man subject to a vow who struck another and injured him; the compensation is unaffected by the status of the Nazirite or the person who has taken a vow, in the way in which compensation is shaped by the status, e.g. of the slave, the minor, or the idiot:

m. Baba Qamma 8:4
A. A deaf-mute, idiot, and minor—meeting up with them is a bad thing.
B. He who injures them is liable.
C. But they who injure other people are exempt.
D. A slave and a woman—meeting up with them is a bad thing.

E. He who injures them is liable.

F And they who injure other people are exempt.

No such provision in public law ever takes account of the status of the Nazirite or the person subject to a vow; these do not define classifications of persons for which the social order publicly makes provision. The exemplary cases in Nedarim-Nazir reenforce the essentially private circumstance of matters, their restriction to the household or the village formed by households. The matter of accepting gifts or hospitality hardly registers as a social event. In two of the three dimensions of Israel's world order, its public relationship with God and the conduct of its social order, vows and special vows make no material difference.

But language on its own is a public event, not subject to private manipulation. Language matters because of what it represents and conveys, which is, the solemn intentionality of the one who uses the language, and that is the key to all else. Language makes public and attracts public attention to the intentionality of the private person, forms the point of intersection ("the interface") between the individual and the community. So the classification of the law at hand within the framework of the Israelite household, while appropriate, somewhat misleads. For when it comes to the theme and problem at hand—the interplay of intentionality and language—the halakhah uniformly explores the matter in its impact upon Israel's relationship with God, Israel's social order, and Israel's life within the household, all three. But sages' category-formation, setting Nedarim-Nazir in the framework of home and family, and mine, placing the halakhah within the walls of the household, find ample justification.

That is because, as one may see, also, with reference to Hullin, Qiddushin, Ketubot, and Nedarim, the halakhah of Nazir carries us deep into the recesses of Israel in its tents, within the walls (whether tangible or otherwise) of its households—there alone. Intentionality matters in many category-formations of the halakhah, but in connection with vows and the Nazirite vow in particular do sages localize their statement on the matter. Here they say, people bear direct, personal responsibility for what they say, and while statements made in error are null, those made in jest bear real consequences. That is why, as we have seen in the consideration of both bodies of halakhah, euphemisms form so central a concern. There is no fooling around with God, no language exempt from God's hearing. Accordingly, the halakhah of vows and the Nazirite vow finds an appropriate situation here because it is coherent in its generative problematics with the halakhah of the household in general. For what makes the Nazirite vow effective is language that an individual has used, and it is the power of language to bring about profound change in the status of a person that forms the one of the two centers of interest of the halakhah of life within the walls of the Israelite household—the focus of sanctification. That formal fact explains the topical pertinence.

The halakhah of Nedarim-Nazir investigates is the power of a person through invoking the name of Heaven to affect the classification in which he or she is situated and so his or her concrete and material relationships with other people. This is done by stating, "May what I eat of your food be prohibited to me as is a sacrifice prohibited to me," all conveyed in the word "Qorban." Having said that, the person may not eat the food of the other. The reason is that the other person's food has been declared by the individual who took the vow to be in the status of a sacrifice. We know that what makes an ordinary beast into a holy beast, subject to the laws of sacrilege and set aside for the alter, is a verbal designation as a sacrifice. Here too what makes ordinary food into food in the status of Holy Things, so far as the given individual is concerned, is the verbal designation of that ordinary food as Holy Things. The difference is that designating an animal as a beast for sacrifice is a public act, affecting society at large. No one then can make use of said animal. Declaring that a dish of oatmeal is in the status of a qorban by contrast, has no affect upon the cereal, except for the person who made that declaration.

That language confirms and conveys the intentionality to effect sanctification hardly presents a surprise at this point in our study; it is, after all, the governing principle of Qiddushin for the spoken word and Ketubot for the written word, the legal document. But what sages wish to say in the halakhah before us differs from their message concerning Qiddushin and Ketubot, even though all four tractates take up the power of language to bring about changes in status. Sages revere the language that brings about sanctification of a woman to a man, and they treat with great punctiliousness the language of the marriage-contract, which, indeed, they subject to the closest exegetical processes of reading and interpretation. If they wished to say, language bears its own power (for the reason stated earlier, its capacity to embody intentionality), they could have no superior choice of topic than the halakhah of Qiddushin and Ketubot (and Gittin).

IV. SAGES' EVALUATION OF VOW-TAKING
AND OF THE NAZIRITE VOW

But what if they wanted to say, language bears power even for purposes of which we (and Heaven) disapprove? And what if their intent was to warn, watch what you say, hold your tongue and keep your temper, because in expressing intentionality, your words give effect to your will, and you will be unable to retract? In other words, if sages wanted to make the point that people had best use in a wise and astute manner the power of language, how would they best say so? Within the framework of the halakhah, vows, inclusive of the special vow of the Nazirite, present the particular and appropriate medium for such a message. That is not only because sages want to tell people to watch their words and not pretend to joke when it comes to matters where intentionality makes a difference as to personal status. That is also because sages to begin with take a negative view of vowing. While of oaths taken in court with full deliberation, invoking the name of God, they approve, vows they despise. They are explicit on that matter: people who take vows show their weakness, not their strength. Vows represent the power of the weak and put-upon, the easy way to defend oneself against the importunities of the overbearing host, the grasping salesman, the tormenting husband or wife. But sages do not honor those who take the easy way, asking God to intervene in matters to which on our own we ought to be able to attend.

Sages do not treat respectfully the person who takes vows. Vow-takers yield to the undisciplined will, to emotion unguided by rational considerations. But intentionality must (ideally) take form out of both emotion and reflection. Vows explode, the fuel of emotion ignited by the heat of the occasion. "Qonam be any benefit I get from you" hardly forms a rational judgment of a stable relationship; it bespeaks a loss of temper, a response to provocation with provocation. Right at the outset the halakhah gives a powerful signal of its opinion of the whole: suitable folk to begin with do not take vows, only wicked people do. That explains in so many words why, if one says, something is subject to "the vows of suitable folk," he has said nothing. Suitable people—*keshérim*—make no vows at all, ever. A distaste for vowing and disdain for people who make vows then characterize the law. People who take vows are deemed irresponsible; they are adults who have classified themselves as children. They possess the power of intentionality but not the responsibility for its wise use. That is why they are given openings toward the unbinding of their vows; they are forced at the same time to take seriously what they have said. Vows are treated as a testing of Heaven, a trial of Heavenly patience and grace. Sanctification can affect a person or a mess of porridge, and there is a difference. Expletives, with which we deal here, make that difference; these are not admired.

But because the halakhah begins and ends with the conviction that language is power, the halakhah also takes account of the sanctifying effect of even language stupidly used. That is the message of the halakhah, and it is only through the halakhah at hand that sages could set forth the message they had in mind concerning the exploitation and abuse of the power of language. It is a disreputable use of the holy. And language is holy because language gives form and effect to intentionality—the very issue of the halakhah at hand! That is why we do admit intentionality—not foresight but intentionality as to honor—into the repertoire of reasons for nullifying vows, as we note in the halakhah of Nedarim:

> M. 9:1 In a matter which is between him and his mother or father, they unloose his vow by [reference to] the honor of his father or mother.

> M. 9:9 They unloose a vow for a man by reference to his own honor and by reference to the honor of his children. They say to him, "Had you known that the next day they would say about you, 'That's the way of So-and-so, going around divorcing his wives,' "and that about your daughters they'd be saying, 'They're daughters of a divorcée! What did their mother do to get herself divorced' [would you have taken a vow]?" And [if] he then said, "Had I known that things would be that way, I should never have taken such a vow," lo, this [vow] is not binding.

The normative law rejects unforeseen events as a routine excuse for nullifying a vow; foresight on its own ("had you known . . . would you have vowed?") plays a dubious role. But when it comes to the intentionality involving honor of parents or children, that forms a consideration of such overriding power as to nullify the vow.

So sages' statement through the halakhah of Nedarim-Nazir is clear. Vows are a means used on earth by weak or subordinated person to coerce the more powerful person by invoking the power of Heaven. They are taken under emotional duress and express impatience and frustration. They are not to be predicted. They do not follow a period of sober reflection. They take on importance principally in two relationships, [1] between friends (e.g. host and guest), [2] between husband and wife. They come into play at crucial, dangerous points, because they disrupt the crucial relationships that define life, particularly within the household: marriage, on the one side, friendly hospitality, on the other. They jar and explode. By admitting into human relationships the power of intentionality, they render the predictable—what is governed by regularities—into a source of uncertainty, for who in the end will penetrate what lies deep in the heart, as Jeremiah reflected, which is beyond fathoming? But language brings to the surface, in a statement of will best left unsaid, what lurks in the depths, and the result, Heaven's immediate engagement, is not to be gainsaid. That is why vows form a source of danger. What should be stable if life is to go on is made capricious. So far as marriage is concerned, vows rip open the fabric of sacred relationships.

Language represents power, then, and it is a power not to be exercised lightly. In the cases examined in Ketubot as those laid out here, the weaker side to the party is represented as taking a vow—whether the milquetoast husband, whether the abused wife. It is the wife against the husband, the harried guest against the insistent host, the seller against the buyer, the boastful story-teller against the dubious listener, the passive against the active party, that the vow is taken. The strong incites, the weak reacts, and the language of reaction, the vow, contains such power as is not to be lightly unleashed even against the one who gives and therefore dominates, whether in sex or food or entertainment. Vows then are the response: the mode of aggression exercised by the less powerful party to the relationship. The weak invoke Heaven, the strong do not have to. A vow will be spit out by a guest who has been importuned to take a fourth portion in a meal he does not want to eat. A wife will exclaim that she will derive no benefit whatsoever from her husband. A whole series of cases emerges from a vow taken by a person not to derive benefit from his friend, with the consequence that the friend, who wants to provide some sort of support for the dependent person, does so through a third party. The dependence then is less obtrusive. So, once more: who gives, dominates, and the vow is the instrument to escape earthly domination in the name of Heaven.

V. THE AGGADIC READING OF THE HALAKHIC CIRCUMSTANCE

As usual, what the halakhah states in its way, the aggadah expresses in its manner too. Here is the Bavli's topical composite on losing one's temper, which is deemed the basis for taking vows:

B. Ned. 3:1A-D I.14/22A Said R. Samuel bar Nahman said R. Yohanan, "Whoever loses his temper—all the torments of Hell rule over him: 'Therefore remove anger from your heart, thus will you put away evil from your flesh' (Qoh 11:10), and the meaning of 'evil' is only Hell: 'The Lord has made all things for himself, yes, even the wicked for the day of evil' (Prov 16:4). Moreover, he will get a belly ache: 'But the Lord shall give you there a trembling heart and failing of eyes and sorrow of mind' (Deut 28:65). And what causes weak eyes and depression? Stomach aches."

B. 3:1A-D I.16/22b Said Rabbah bar R. Huna, "Whoever loses his temper —even the Presence of God is not important to him: 'The wicked, through the pride of his countenance, will not seek God; God is not in all his thoughts' (Ps 10:4)."

B. 3:1A-D I.17/22b A. R. Jeremiah of Difti said, "[Whoever loses his temper]—he forgets what he has learned and increases foolishness: 'For anger rests in the heart of fools' (Qoh 7:9), and 'But the fool lays open his folly' (Prov 13:16)."

B. R. Nahman bar Isaac said, "One may be sure that his sins outnumber his merits: 'And a furious man abounds in transgressions' (Prov 29:22)."

B. 3:1A-D I.18/22b Said R. Ada b. R. Hanina, "If the Israelites had not sinned, to them would have been given only the Five Books of the Torah and the book of Joshua alone, which involves the division of the Land of Israel. *How come?* 'For much wisdom proceeds from much anger' (Qoh 1:18)." [Freedman, *Nedarim, ad loc.*: The anger of God caused him to send prophets with their wise teachings.]

Sages leave no doubt as to their view of matters, which they express with the usual explicit clarity.

The same negative view pertains to the Nazirite vow. It is a mark of arrogance. The special vow of the Nazirite arrogates to the person who takes it the special status of a holy man or woman, even though Heaven has not endowed him or her with that status by nature, by birth. The priest by birth cannot function drunk or subject to corpse-uncleanness. The Nazirite takes on himself the same prescriptions and beautifies himself with abundant hair, held by sages a mark of pride.

T. *Nazir* 4:7 A. Said Simeon the Righteous, "In my entire life I ate a guilt-offering of a Nazir only one time.

B. M'SH B: "A man came to me from the south, and I saw that he had beautiful eyes, a handsome face, and curly locks. I said to him, 'My son, on what account did you destroy this lovely hair?'

C. "He said to me, 'I was a shepherd in my village, and I came to draw water from the river, and I looked at my reflection, and my bad impulse took hold of me and sought to drive me from the world.'

D. "I said to him, 'Evil one! You should not have taken pride in something which does not belong to you, in something which is going to turn into dust, worms, and corruption. Lo, I take upon myself to shave you off for the sake of Heaven.'

E. "I patted his head and kissed him and said to him, 'My son, may people like you become many, people who do the will of the Omnipresent in Israel. Through you is fulfilled this Scripture, as it is said, "A man or a woman, when he will express a vow to be a Nazir, to abstain for the sake of the Lord'" (Num 6:2).

But the Nazirite is one who lets his hair grow long, cutting it only at the end of the process, when the vow has been fulfilled. So the Nazirite has undertaken important restrictions incumbent on the priesthood and beautified himself with long hair. Only at the end does the Nazirite make himself praiseworthy, in line with Simeon's judgment, by cutting off all the hair. In line with this statement of matters, sages treat the Nazirite vow as they treat vows in general, as a mark of inferior character or conscience, here, of pride. Here is where James's advice registers: go, help Nazirites pay for their vows (and do your own), and so show your adherence to the Torah. But that does not change the fact that Simeon does not approve of the vow except in the most unusual case.

What is at stake, then, in the halakhah of Nedarim-Nazir? It is sages' interest in defining the source of the power of language. This they find in Heaven's confirmation of man's or woman's affirmation. By using formulary language man or woman invoke the response of Heaven more really by throwing up words toward Heaven and so provoking a response in Heaven. That is how patterns of behavior and relationship, such as are defined by the vow, the Nazirite-vow, the act of sanctification of a woman to a particular man or a marriage contract, are subjected to Heaven's concerned response. Relationships and deeds are subjected to Heaven's engagement by the statement of the right words. So the halakhah explores the effects of words, and it is in the halakhah of the Oral Torah—and not that of the Written Torah, with its powerful bias toward priestly concerns

—that that exploration takes place.

VI. DOES JAMES' ADVICE TO PAUL ACCORD WITH THE HALAKHAH?

The halakhah of the Oral Torah answers the question, what can a man or a woman say so as to become obliged to do or not do a specified range of deeds? And the answers to that question respond to yet another, still more profound question. It is, how is Heaven mindful of man and woman on earth? The ornate essays into the trivialities of language and the use of language that we find in the halakhah of Qiddushin, Ketubot, Nedarim, Nazir, and Gittin respond to that question. The halakhah speaks large and simple truths in conveying a remarkable vision of humanity in God's image. Man and woman are so like God as to be able through what they say to provoke, and even encumber, God's caring and concern. That is because man and woman know how to say the ordinary words that make an extraordinary difference on earth and in Heaven. The message of the halakhah of the Oral Torah is, we are responsible for what we say—there is no such thing as "mere words"—because what we say brings to full articulation what we want, words bearing the burden of intentionality. After all, the first act of creation is contained in the statement, "And God said . . . ."

When it comes to the Nazirite vow in particular, sages recognize the Nazirite and respect his obedience to the provisions of the law. But they take note that the Nazirite puts on airs, grows his hair long and imposes upon himself restrictions indicative (otherwise) of priestly status. So they take the view, "If you take the vow, carry it out," but they do not counsel the pious to show their piety by taking the vow. If James were to have advised Paul to take the vow and keep it for the requisite thirty days, he would have given poor advice. Telling Paul to complete the vow and help out others in the same position—that represents a mediating position. Advising Paul not to keep the vow at all would have marked the other extreme.

But so far as James had in mind for Paul to make a public affirmation of his adherence to the law of the Torah, the case at hand proves ambiguous, the advice bearing a measure of irony: if that's what you have done, then do it up and do it right. It accordingly is self-evident that James's advice on how to show oneself obedient to the law will not have scandalized the sages, but it also will not have found agreement among the rabbis of the Mishnah represented by the halakhah of the Mishnah, Tosefta, Yerushalmi, and Bavli. Whether or not their view of matters circulated—if not under their auspices, let alone in formulations later on cast by them into halakhic language —is not subject to doubt. Jesus said exactly the same thing in the Sermon on the Mount. But that carries us to the very crux of the issue that separated James from Paul.

A PARTING WITHIN THE WAY:
JESUS AND JAMES ON ISRAEL AND PURITY

Scot McKnight

One of the most intriguing questions historians ask of the extant evidence for first century Christian development revolves around the relationship of first century Judaisms and first century Christianities: how did a restoration vision of Israel as enunciated and enacted by Jesus of Nazareth part from its original vision as a form of Judaism to become a separate faith as opposed to the varieties of Judaism by the time of the second Jewish revolt (132–135 C.E.)? Or, how did a form of Judaism, or various forms of Judaism that were similar, eventually establish themselves as a separate religion, even if inherently diverse? Surely one of the more significant studies in this regard is the monograph of J. D. G. Dunn who, with a sensitivity to details of the texts and history as well as to the broader sweep of Christianity and Judaism, examines four pillars of Judaism to see how these four pillars were eventually challenged, in varying degrees of intensity and directness, by the emerging new faith associated with Jesus. Theses four pillars are: (1) God is one, (2) election: a covenant people, a promised land, (3) covenant focussed in Torah, and (4) the Land focussed in Temple. His conclusion, now well known, is that the "partings of the ways" took place over time, in different ways and with different results—but, still, by the middle of the second century C.E. there were two faiths: Christianity and the foundations of formative, or rabbinic, Judaism.[1] I suggest that it is the scholarly discovery of the diversity of both Judaism and Christianity as well as the renewed interest in Jesus, and his vision for Israel, that invigorates recent investigation into James, the brother of Jesus. Why? Because it is James who may well represent the movement that did not, in social shape, part from Judaism or, put

---

[1]   J. D. G. Dunn, *The Partings of the Ways: Between Christianity and Judaism and their Significance for the Character of Christianity* (Philadelphia: Trinity Press International, 1991). The main lines were set fourteen years earlier in his *Unity and Diversity in the New Testament: An Inquiry into the Character of Earliest Christianity* (Philadelphia: Trinity Press Internatinal, 1977; rev. ed., 1990).

differently, with James we might find a parting within the way of
Judaism and thus find another form of Judaism, a "Christian Judaism." James, I believe, was a Jew, a faithful Jew, who both embraced
the vision of his brother, Jesus, as well as the faith of his ancestors,
what we now call Judaism.[2] While it would be desirous to set out all
the the shapes and nuances of James, and the Jerusalem-based
Christian Judaism movement he directed,[3] it shall be my goal merely
to try to set out this direction of Jacobite Christian Judaism by
looking at the intersection of two concerns: (1) the national direction
of Jesus' vision and the place purity plays within that vision, and (2)
how the various pieces of evidence about James fit into that vision of
Jesus about purity. I shall in what follows provide a preliminary
view of purity that sets the stage for Jesus' vision for Israel and then
show how James fits into that picture. I shall develop the picture of
Jesus a little more completely than one might expect in a study of
James but I do so in order to highlight the historical developments of
James and to put in proper nuance the vision of James for Israel.
Furthermore, since there is virtually no bibliography on James and
purity I shall attempt a survey of the issue, hoping that I might put
some elements pertaining to James in perspective. There is for
James, so far as I know, no traditional or innovative position to
overturn but, as I shall argue, there is enough to be said that the
discussion ought to begin.

I. ISRAEL AND PURITY

Without setting out an exhaustive analysis of purity in ancient
Israel, a study of purity shows at least four separate traditions that
feed into what an Israelite of the first century might have understood
purity to be.[4] The *foundation and details of purity* in ancient Israel

---

[2]   Recently B. D. Chilton has proposed that a connection between Jesus and
James can be explored along the lines of a Nazirite vow. See his "The Brother of
Jesus and the Interpretation of Scripture," forthcoming. In addition, see M. O.
Wise, "Nazarene," in J. B. Green, S. McKnight, I. H. Marshall (eds.), *Dictionary
of Jesus and the Gospels* (Downers Grove: InterVarsity Press, 1992) 571-74, who
proposes a linguistic solution for the ambiguities over the name "Nazarene."

[3]   An excellent analysis, if at times a bit laden with too many difficult-to-prove
hypotheses, is J. Painter, *Just James: The Brother of Jesus in History and Tradition*
(Studies on Personalities of the New Testament; Columbia: University of South
Carolina Press, 1997).

[4]   See the survey of J. Milgrom, *Leviticus 1–16* (AB 3; New York: Double-

have been expressed most completely in the Priestly and Holiness traditions of Leviticus where a comprehensive set of laws is set out for Israel if it wishes to live in the Land with the glory of God attending its sacrifices. Place is paramount in the levitical codes: Land is broken into generic and particular, with the particular holy place broken into degrees of holiness and purity which map the Land's purity. Holy place is to be understood as the symbolization of purity, with God's particular sanctuary the focal point for purity and sacrificial restitution. But the tradition bequeathed to Israel not only rules and regulations for a place but set out a myriad of practices for turning everyday life into a quest for purity as well as a life that could be governed by purity. It was especially the food laws, corpse impurities, and the various laws concening body fluids that impacted so much of the everyday life of ordinary Jews in both their own meals, which brought into expression their view of the nation and purity, as well as in their social relations with the Gentiles (cf. Leviticus 11–16). All of these laws, however, are not without basis and Bruce Chilton has expressed this emphasis both on place as well as on the function of purity within Israel clearly: "The land, in Leviticus, is not for Israel; Israel is for service of God in his land."[5] That is, *the laws of purity were designed to keep Israel in a worthy condition for "housing" YHWH, for keeping him there, and for worshipping/ serving him in his holiness. That is, fundamentally, purity is about order, social conditionedness and national security.*[6] Nuance and

---

day, 1991) 3-13.

    5   B. Chilton, "Purity and Impurity," in R. P. Martin and P. H. Davids (eds.), *Dictionary of the Later New Testament and Its Developments* (Downers Grove: InterVarsity Press, 1997) 989.

    6   On the vast topic of purity in ancient Israel, see J. Neusner, *The Idea of Purity in Ancient Judaism* (SJLA 1; Leiden: Brill, 1973); M. Douglas, *Purity and Danger: An Analysis of the Concepts of Pollution and Taboo* (London: Routledge & Kegan Paul, 1966); E. P. Sanders, *Judaism: Practice and Belief 63 BCE – 66 CE* (London: SCM Press; Philadelphia: Trinity Press International, 1992) 214-30; idem, *Jewish Law from Jesus to the Mishnah. Five Studies* (Philadelphia: Trinity Press Internatinal, 1990) 29-42, 131-254; of the more recent social-scientific approach to purity, see J. H. Neyrey, "Unclean, Common, Polluted, and Taboo: A Short Reading Guide," *Forum* 4 (1988) 72-82; B. J. Malina, *The New Testament World: Insights from Cultural Anthropology* (rev. ed., Louisville: Westminster/ John Knox Press, 1993); for direct examination of the implication of recent study for the relationship of Judaism and the early Christian movement, see J. J. Pilch, "Sickness and Healing in Luke-Acts," in J. H. Neyrey (ed.), *The Social World of*

variation apart, the deuteronomic traditions maintain a similar fundamental national orientation even if less attention is given to the priestly focus.

An illustration of this priestly focus of a levitical orientation can be found in the charming parable of Hag 2:10-14:

> 10 On the twenty-fourth day of the ninth month, in the second year of Darius, the word of the LORD came by the prophet Haggai, saying: 11 Thus says the LORD of hosts: Ask the priests for a ruling:
>
>   A. 12 If one carries consecrated meat in the fold of one's garment, and with the fold touches bread, or stew, or wine, or oil, or any kind of food, does it become holy? The priests answered, "No."
>
>   B. 13 Then Haggai said, "If one who is unclean by contact with a dead body touches any of these, does it become unclean?" The priests answered, "Yes, it becomes unclean."
>
> 14 Haggai then said, So is it with this people, and with this nation before me, says the LORD; and so with every work of their hands; and what they offer there is unclean.

Evidently preaching in the Temple courts, Haggai simply asks for a ruling (*torah*) from the priests: the animal used for a sin offering was "most sacred" (Lev 6:25) and, inasmuch as priests did have to wave such holy offerings in their sacrificial presentations (cf. Num 6:20), it is likely that such offerings were carried about in the priests garments. But, as the ruling is clear, such a garment did not become a source of contagion for purity (A). On the other hand, items that were impure were a contagion for impurity (B; cf. Lev 11:28; 22:4-7). Israel, because of its contaminating contacts with impurities, is spreading impurity as a contagion on the run; consequently, their sacrifices which are intended to render impure things pure again are also impure. Purity, then, is not a contagion.

Second, Ezekiel (Ezekiel 40–48) expands the so-called priestly

---

Luke-Acts: Models for Interpretation (Peabody: Hendrickson, 1991) 181-209; in the same volume, see J. H. Elliott, "Temple versus Household in Luke-Acts: A Contrast in Social Institutions," 211-40; J. H. Neyrey, "Ceremonies in Luke-Acts: The Case of Meals and Table-Fellowship," 361-87. Neyrey's reading guide, however, fails to note the significance "group" played in the early study of purity by J. Neusner where he drew attention to the sectarian debates over purity. A recent, and ground-breaking, dissertation has been penned by Jonathan Klawans, *Impurity and Sin in Ancient Judaism* (Ph.D., Columbia University, 1997; UMI, 1997), in which the connection between sin/moral impurity (as opposed to ritual impurity) and purity laws is explored. The effect of this research is to challenge the view that "moral defilement" is merely metaphorical.

traditions and offers a vision of restoration to the Land and renewal of an immaculately-ordered Temple in which YHWH would dwell gloriously (43:1-5) and the priests would conduct worship, providing Israel with another *place of purity and holiness: the New Temple of YHWH in a reordered Israel.* Zooming in from the east and entering through the eastern gate, which therefore is never to be opened again, YHWH enters the Temple and dwells in glory (43:1-5; 44:1-3; cf. 46:1-8). What was once abandoned by Israel's God now houses God himself. Now that YHWH fills the new Temple with his glory, the Zadokite[7] priests are ordered to live according to the Law both as covenant members and mediators/teachers of God's purity (43:18-19; 44:15-16, 23-24) so that the Temple will be holy and no longer profane God's name (43:7-9, 12). A new prince administers the Land (45:7-8). Nothing expresses this vision better than 43:12:

> This is the law of the temple: the whole territory on the top of the mountain all around shall be most holy. This is the law of the temple.

Finally, if the people of Israel desires to participate in this glorious Temple and restoration, then that people must repent and put away its idolatry (cf. 43:6-12). Any who so choose, including the *gerim*, may dwell in the Land (cf. 44:7-8 and 47:22-23).

Third, another vision of purity which influences the purity program of some early Christians can be found in Zechariah.[8] Transporting himself into an ideal age, after the Day of YHWH, Zechariah envisions those that survive that Day will all worship YHWH of hosts annually in Jerusalem at the Feast of Sukkoth and if survivors choose not to attend the feast they shall experience the classical covenant curses (14:16-19). Three features of this vision of Zechariah may well have set the tone for Jesus' vision of purity: first, there is here a purging fountain that gushes forth from Jerusalem in order to offer endlessly to the nation both forgiveness and cleansing from impurities (13:1; 14:8); second, there is within Zechariah's vision an inclusiveness, greater than Ezekiel's, as the YHWH of hosts reigns over the whole earth and survivors from all nations worship him in Jerusalem (cf. 14:9 and 14:16-19); third,

---

[7]   In Ezekiel's vision the Levites are assigned a lesser role of priest attendants due to sinfulness (cf. 44:10-14).

[8]   See here B. D. Chilton, *The Temple of Jesus: His Sacrificial Program within a Cultural History of Sacrifice* (University Park: Penn State University Press, 1992) 135-36.

Zechariah's castigations are particularly directed at the leaders, especially the prophets, at the shepherds of the nation (13:2-9). As Bruce Chilton has observed, this purity of program, like Jesus', is not based on sacrifice but by a unilateral action of YHWH.[9] It is not surprising then that the final scene of Zechariah revolves around the utter purity of everything—the bells on the horses, pots in the house of YHWH, as well as the bowls before the altar (14:20-21). He concludes with words that governed the final action of Jesus in public: "and there shall no longer be traders in the house of the LORD of hosts on that day" (14:21).

Fourth, there is evidence in the Hebrew Bible for *moral impurity*, that sin can cause defilement.[10] The biblical sources call certain sins impurities, including sexual sins (Lev 18:24-29), idolatry (20:1-13), and bloodshed (Num 35:33-34). These very sins, according to the biblical authors, defile the sinner (Lev 18:24), the Land (18:25; Ezek 36:17), and the sanctuary (Lev 20:3; Ezek 5:11) and so the people are cut off from the Land (Lev 18:28; Ezek 36:19). However, moral and ritual impurity are to be distinguished and carefully defined: (1) as to *source*, whereas ritual impurity results from bodily flows, corpses, and the like, moral impurity has its source in sins; (2) as to *effect*, ritual impurity leads to a temporary, but contagious condition whereas moral impurity effects the desecration of sinners, the Land, and the sanctuary; and (3) as to *resolution*, ritual impurity requires bathing and waiting whereas moral impurity requires atonement, punishment and even exile from the Land. The burden of Klawans's research is that labeling "moral impurity" as "metaphor," in the sense that no real defilement has taken place, misses the force of the biblical tradition for in his view the sinner, the Land, and the sanctuary are degraded in status.

To summarize: these visions of purity are rooted in the levitical legislations of ancient Israel but express that purity concern in various degrees of congruence with those original concerns of people, practices, space, time, things, and behavior. The fundamental idea of purity, whether mundane or eschatological, seems to be *orderliness*, both in *approach to God* and in a moral, and apparently real, sense *in relations to others*, not to mention the order that pertains to anomalies of nature as expressed in the impurities found in

---

9   Chilton, *Temple of Jesus*, 135.
10 See Klawans, *Impurity and Sin*, upon whom I rely here.

foods and body fluids. One is pure then when one is fit to approach God, to live in the Land, to participate in the sanctuary, and to relate to others. No less important for understanding purity is that *it pertains to a people*, namely, to Israel as the holy people of God and scholars are nearly united in seeing such a dimension of purity as a contrast to other peoples in the ambient culture. Since God is holy, *his meeting place* with Israel must be pure, and so there develops the rituals connected with worshipping YHWH in the Tabernacle and Temple. In addition, purity has dimensions in the *body*, in *things*, and in *time. Fundamentally, then, when one looks at purity one is looking at a nation who must be fit to come into the presence of YHWH in order to worship him and to live out his Torah for that nation—and when that happens (enter the prophets and eschatology), everything is in order and nothing is out of place—for Israel is pure.* On the other hand, synthesis of this sort cannot be done without careful attention to the details of the specific systemic context from which they emerge. It will not do simply to synthesize the "ancient Jewish traditions" about purity and then think we have purity now in hand. It is highly likely, in fact, that just as any one ancient view of purity was embedded in a systemic context, so when we approach Jesus and James we will need to understand their views of purity within their systemic reflections. To anticipate, I will argue that while Jesus used "moral purity" for his larger systemic point of entry into the world of purity, James was much more traditional in using ritual purity as fundamental in his systemic ordering of purity concerns.

A point of method: if purity is substantively Israel's, or an Israelite's, condition of being fit to worship and relate to YHWH in the right order, then purity encompasses nearly everything about each New Testament writer as well, though those authors rarely express themselves in the categories of purity. As a consequence, I shall focus in what follows on Israel, the body politic, and specific injunctions that pertain more directly to the specific purity concerns of ancient Israel. If Peter, according to the author of Acts, sees Gentile conversions as being heart purification by faith (15:9), Paul might say the same thing under the category of justification and Peter under new birth—but rarely does scholarship of earliest Christianity think of justification or new birth as terms associated with Israel's purity legislation. Accordingly, some narrowing of focus is required.

II. JESUS, ISRAEL, AND PURITY

Jesus operated with a system of purity but because his vision for Israel altered the landscape found in the traditions of Israel his vision of purity was different because it enacted that new vision. Put differently, Jesus in some senses redefined who the pure people of YHWH was and provided two rituals that enacted that definition: his regular table fellowship as well as the more symbolic last supper with his followers. I shall sketch Jesus' vision of purity to set the table for our understanding of James.

Israel and Purity

How then does one become pure for Jesus? It must be recalled from our discussion above that purity was connected in ancient Israel to place, to priests, to moral and ritual practices and to the people—and, in general, each element is to be understood in context of being fit for approaching God or for being in relation to God's people. And, as noted above, purity did not revolve around "individual salvation" but instead centered upon Israel as the people of God and its condition of being fit to approach God. So, when we look to Jesus, we need to look not to statements about how individuals might purify themselves in order to find salvation but instead to how Jesus envisioned the nation: how is Israel to be pure?

First, *Jesus saw Israel becoming pure when it joined the movement set in motion by John to repent in order for the nation to be restored.* For John and Jesus repentance can be seen in two dimensions: internal and external. The latter, which I shall not examine here, refers to the "things" the Israelite is called to give up in order to become part of the restoration of Israel. On the other hand, internal repentance, by which I refer to the individual Israelite's attitude toward himself/herself in the context of the nation's bondage to Rome and in the context of a personal relationship to the Covenant God made with Israel, clarifies what purity means for Jesus. This is obvious from the Jewish context, a context that must be recalled every time we attempt to articulate what Jesus means by repentance: in the history of Israel the call of God through the prophets was a call for the nation to turn from its idolatries, its sinfulness, its injustices, its religious harlotries, and its unfaithful alliances with other nations for protection—to turn from these sins back to the God of the Covenant who brought them out of Egypt, who protected them, and who recalled them to their ways by continual acts of discipline, and who will forgive their sins and restore them to a twelve-tribe nation with YHWH's glory flooding the Temple (e.g. Isa 44:21-22; 45:22; 55:7; Amos 3–6).[11] This context forms the contours for the call of Jesus to his nation but this call is fundamentally a call to Israel to form a new Israel, an Israel that is pure because it has turned to this eschatological cry of Jesus. With this as the substructure for Jesus it becomes clear that Jesus operates with a view of purity that is quite similar to the view outlined above as moral purity: if repentance effects purity, then the impurity is caused by sin. In fact, the whole picture of Jesus is one dealing with Exile and Exile, as noted above, is the result of moral impurities.

Beginning with John the Baptist and continuing through the ministry of Jesus, the call to repentance is a dyadic[12] decision and this dyadic dimension shows that repentance is about purity, about making Israel fit to approach YHWH and by returning from Exile. The first century Israelite shapes his or her identity in the context of how the nation fares and how one fits into that nation because only if that nation was fit to worship could the individual stand before God in righteousness. Thus, repentance in that context calls a person to undertake an individual action for the good of the nation, for the sake of Israel's purification, and for the sake of God's return to the nation. This obtains as much for Jesus' own baptism as for the followers of Jesus: as Jesus' baptism signified his agreement with John's call to the nation, so Jesus' call to repentance invokes a similar corporate response on the part of those who wish to see the visions of John and Jesus actualized for the nation.[13] Put differently, the

---

[11]   A brief survey of the evidence in Judaism can be found in E. P. Sanders, *Jesus and Judaism* (London: SCM Press; Philadelphia: Fortress, 1985) 106-108; N. T. Wright, *Jesus and the Victory of God* (Minneapolis: Fortress, 1996) 246-52.

[12]   See B. J. Malina, *The New Testament World: Insights from Cultural Anthropology* (rev. ed., Louisville: Westminster/John Knox Press, 1993) 63-89; J. J. Pilch and B. J. Malina, *Biblical Social Values and Their Meaning. A Handbook* (Peabody: Hendrickson, 1993) 70-73 ("Family-Centeredness," by M. McVann); B. J. Malina and R. L. Rohrbaugh, *Social-Science Commentary on the Synoptic Gospels* (Minneapolis: Fortress, 1992) 99-101 (on surrogate family).

[13]   The term repentance deals with "not just a change of mind about something but also a change of attitude, of intention, of will, if not a total transformation of one's conduct and orientation"; so W. Schrage, *The Ethics of the New Testament* (Philadelphia: Fortress, 1988) 41-42. This statement also typically illustrates the individualism characteristic of scholarship on the ethics of Jesus.

individual acts for the nation in repentance rather than just for his or her own personal salvation. This national focus of repentance explains more accurately the call Jesus issues to the whole *nation* rather than just to the *wicked sinners* who are clearly in need of moral reform and personal religious conversion (cf. Matt 11:21-24 par; 12:38-42 par; Luke 13:1-5). To be sure, Jesus' call included the Zacchaeuses and the Matthews, but it also included those like Simeon (Luke 2:25-35) as well, and it may have been the latter who were most attracted to Jesus' vision for Israel. We have no reason to believe that either Peter's or Zebedee's family were especially in need of moral reform; we do have good reason to believe, however, that many Israelites of the period were looking for the final day of redemption and would therefore eagerly join a call to national repentance.

Repentance then becomes a national analysis that leads to self-condemnation of one's own standing before God within his covenant with Israel. It recognizes one's unworthiness before an all-holy God but, instead of running away from this God, willingly goes to God in the hope of purification, mercy, forgiveness and restoration. Those who so respond to Jesus believe that he is the end-time prophet who can restore Israel from exile and lead the nation one more time in the fulness of righteousness, purity, peace and holiness. The repentance of those who follow Jesus, in other words, has a national component: turning to the vision of Jesus is a return to the covenant of YHWH with Israel in such a manner that God looks kindly upon the nation and restores its fortunes. Repentance then is purification, it is preparation for approach to God. One scholar who sees this eschatological and national component to repentance is A. N. Wilder, who concludes:[14]

> For repentance had come to be especially assigned to the days of the end, and the very fact of a general call to repentance on the part of John and Jesus could be interpreted as an indication of the approach of the end of the age . . . . That is, now is the time of the promised, divinely aided restoration of Israel to its proper disposition and obedience as preliminary to the great things of salvation and renewal that had been promised.

Those wicked Israelites (and any who wish to enlist in his movement) no doubt find in John's and Jesus' call to righteousness a powerful

---

[14]   A. N. Wilder, *Eschatology and Ethics in the Teaching of Jesus* (rev. ed., New York: Harper & Bros., 1950) 76, 78.

conviction of their own sinfulness and a need for moral reformation, even though they were surely aware of the national significance of this term. But both emphases are present, with the national standing first in line. The nation needs to change but it does so only when individuals strike out in repentance from their nation's past and walk in the faith that Jesus envisions for the people of God. I shall now mention three other features of purity for Jesus.

Second, *for Jesus purity is more a matter of the heart than a matter of external rite.*[15] Though the contexts in both the Markan and Matthean text are redactional (Mark 7:1-4; Matt 15:1), we have good reason to think they reflect an authentic setting for the life of Jesus. The issue is that Jesus is challenged over what amounts to purity with respect to handwashing, a dominating concern of the Pharisees.[16] By appealing to Isaiah's distinction between lip-service and heart-service (Mark 7:6), Jesus accuses them by continuing the citation of Isaiah with its blanket condemnation of the people's pretext of obedience under the guise of human ordinances (7:7). And it is this distinction of the prophet that forms the basis for Jesus' counter-approach to purity itself. If heart is more important than lip (and here we must not pretend to hear some new Christian innovation for it is to Isaiah that Jesus appeals), and if human commandment is connected to lip, then lip can be repealed in order to foster heart. Insight into Qorban is merely illustration. The logical point of Jesus is found in Mark 7:14-23 and it is here that Jesus offers a hermeneutical insight into purity that is ultimately derived

---

[15]   In summarizing what is stated in Mark 7:15 here, I have used the recent theory that grammatically Jesus may be saying that he is "more" concerned with moral purity than ritual purity while not disavowing the importance or ritual impurity. I hold this to be the effect of the grammar. However, I am more convinced that Jesus, at the rhetorical level, is overstating his case to make his point clear and even inflammatory. In other words, I doubt Jesus eliminated all purity concerns and I doubt also that for him purity was *only* a matter of the heart. By way of extension, when James continues the ritual purity concerns of Israel I doubt also that he is moving away from Jesus. On the authenticity of Matt 15:11 and Mark 7:15, see J. D. G. Dunn, "Jesus and Ritual Purity: A Study of the Tradition-History of Mark 7:15," in *Jesus, Paul, and the Law: Studies in Mark and Galatians* (Louisville: Wesminster/John Knox Press, 1990) 37-60. On p. 51 Dunn concludes for the "more important than" view.

[16]   See esp. J. Neusner, *The Pharisees: Rabbinic Perspectives* (SAJ; Hoboken: Ktav, 1984), a handy summary of his three volume set, *Rabbinic Traditions about the Pharisees before 70* (3 vols., Leiden: Brill, 1973).

from Leviticus itself: *purity is a matter of the heart*. The things that enter into a person do not make a person impure (the Greek expression is κοινῶσαι αὐτόν; 7:15a); instead, the things that come from within are τὰ κοινοῦντα τὸν ἄνθρωπον (7:15b). Food, Jesus says, enters and exits (7:19a).[17] Sins, however, are what defile and sins begin in the heart (7:20-23). In particular, as Klawans has observed, the specific sins mentioned here by Jesus correspond conceptually to what ancient Jews saw as morally defiling and, as such, they show that Jesus is fully within the orbit of Judaism is so defining purity and defilement.[18]

Other Jesus traditions show the emphasis he gave to heart as the source of purity (Q: Matt 6:19-21 par; 6:22-23 par; 7:16-20 par; 12:33-37 par; 23:25-26 par) while the mission of the Twelve/Seventy implies that all food is to be eaten rather than observed with regard to its status (cf. Mark 6:10 with Matt 10:11-13; Luke 10:5-9).[19] Thus, for Jesus either all of Israel is pure (and impurity is found when Israelites/Israel sin/sins) or the eschatological Israel he is forming is pure (and impurity is found when eschatological Israelites/Israel sin/sins). "Fundamentally, Jesus' concern appears similarly to have been with cleanness as a matter of production rather than of consumption."[20] Related to this observation about heart is the corollary that for Jesus *purity concerns access to YHWH rather than restrictions from YHWH or strictures within Israel and society*.[21] When Jesus says that the Sabbath is for persons rather than persons for the Sabbath (Mark 2:27), he is expressing a general orientation toward purity, albeit purity as time. Accordingly, purity is here subsumed under larger categories. Subordination of purity concerns for the sake of relations and compassion is memorialized famously by Jesus in the Parable of the Good Samaritan (Luke 10:30-37). As

---

17   The Markan comment in 7:19b, not shared by Matthew in either passing it on or agreement in mind, is redactional.

18   See *Impurity and Sin*, 308-10.

19   I would argue that the Pauline mission and Gentile Christian orthodoxy based its attitude to the Law on this kind of teaching, as well as Jesus' practice of indiscriminate table fellowship. James, however, would not have understood Jesus as obliterating all senses of levitical purity. On the mission instructions, see B. D. Chilton, "Purity and Impurity," 991-92.

20   Chilton, "Purity and Impurity," 990.

21   See the summary comments of Neusner, *Idea of Purity*, 118: "All rites of purification aimed at one goal: to permit participation in the cult."

B. J. Malina has said:

> Hence any interpretation of the purity rules should be in the direction of the
> welfare of Israel . . . . What results is the embedding of the purity rules of
> the Torah within the Torah as a whole instead of fitting the Torah as a whole
> into the purity rules . . . .[22]

I think it fundamental for understanding Jesus that he was neither
against Israel nor the Torah; rather, he used a different hermeneutic
derived from the Torah in order to put in perspective some
prominent features of the Torah as expressed in his culture. That
hermeneutic, as Klawans has recently demonstrated, owes its origins
to passages like Leviticus 18 where moral sins defile and where
purity is seen in moral, as opposed to ritual, terms.[23]

Third, for convenience we can amalgamate the traditions about
lepers, menstruants and unclean spirits to summarize another dimension of Jesus and purity: *purity is a contagion for Jesus*. In contrast
to the clear teachings of the levitical codes, and appealed to as they
are by Haggai (2:10-14), where only impurity is a contagion, Jesus
seemingly thinks that Israel, embodied now in holy, pure Israelites
like himself, acts a contagion of purity itself, in a manner not unlike
the Eschaton set out in Zechariah's vision of water gushing from
Jerusalem (cf. 13:1; 14:8). Jesus, by touching people, turns them
from impure Israelites into pure Israelites. This is a staggering
innovation on the part of Jesus, and may well lay behind such a belief
as is found in Paul's understanding of children and spouses who have
believing parents (cf. 1 Cor 7:12-14). Thus, when in Mark 1:40-44
parr. Jesus is touched by the leper, he is not contaminated because his
purity is both powerful enough to resist the contagion but also active
enough to purify the leper himself. That Jesus saw himself as more
than just the one who declared purity can be seen from Mark 1:42:
the man's leprosy was removed because Jesus was a contagion of
purity. Though Jesus assumes the role of the priest in declaring the
man "clean" (7:41), he still operates within the strictures of Temple
service by sending the pure Israelite back to a levitically-based priest
in order to be declared ceremonially pure (7:44). As for menstruants
(Mark 5:24-34) and demons, who are sometimes described as
"unclean spirits" (Mark 1:23, 26, 27; 3:11, 30; 5:2, 8, 13; 6:7; 7:25;
9:25), the same kind of observation needs to be made: stopping the

---

22   B. J. Malina, *New Testament World*, 173, 174-75.
23   See his study of Jesus in *Impurity and Sin*, 298-312.

flow of blood or exorcisms, though surely to be connected with the Kingdom itself, are in part *purifications of unclean Israelites* and *Jesus is the pure Israelite who, because he is contagious with purity, can purify these unclean Israelites.*[24]

Purity then is what happens to the nation when it repents and returns to God; purity happens when people come into contact with Jesus who is a contagion of purity. Purity, fourth, must also be seen as fundamentally *moral* for Jesus in the sense that *it describes Israel as now conformed to God's will as Jesus teaches it.* This point needs some clarification. Above we observed that for Jesus purity is more a matter of the heart than a matter of consumption or avoidance. And at that location we observed the Markan text which explains that which comes from the heart as moral factors (Mark 7:20-23) though this emphasis on morality would probably for Jesus not have meant no ceremony and no rite—after all, he is known in the rite he established (Mark 14:12-25 pars). But there is something fresh and group-defining for Jesus when it comes to his emphasis in matters of morality. For Jesus, morality is no longer *just Torah but now it is Torah as defined by love.* [25] This is the consensus of nearly every kind of scholar on Jesus: Jesus taught that the Law was climaxed in the *Shema* as combined with Lev 19:18—in love of God and love of others (Mark 12:28-34 pars; Matt 5:43-48; 7:12). It needs to be noted here that in contrast to the Johannine traditions where love is seen as a "new" commandment (John 13:34-35), for Jesus in the Synoptic tradition it is not so much new as it is a revitalized and reactualized ancient Israelite tradition, a fresh combination of Leviticus and Deuteronomy that permits the Law to be fulfilled and easily perceived (Mark 12:28-34 pars). Thus, in the words of E. P. Sanders:

> Just as Jesus' citation of the Shema[c] ('love God', Deut. 6.4f.) as the greatest commandment would have caused no surprise, neither would this quotation of Lev. 19.18 as the second greatest commandment (Mark 12.28-34). Both these passages are presented in the Bible itself as summarizing the

---

[24]   In his otherwise fine study of Jesus, G. H. Twelftree (*Jesus the Exorcist: A Contribution to the Study of the Historical Jesus* [Peabody: Hendrickson, 1993]) omits any exploration of the significance of "unclean" with respect to the demons and Jesus' mission, and therefore misses the import of purity for exorcism. But cf. Neusner, *Idea of Purity*, 60-63.

[25]   Schrage, *Ethics*, 68-85; R. Schnackenburg, *Die sittliche Botschaft des Neuen Testaments* (HTKNT, Supplementband 1.1; Freiburg: Herder, 1986) 88-97.

two aspects of the law: the commandments that govern relations with God
and those govern relations with others.[26]

Once again, however, this commandment of Jesus, or comment on
the commandments of Moses, is not simply an individualistic morality or salvation. It is fundamentally a vision for the pure eschatological Israel which is now being reconstituted around the Twelve.

Thus, Jesus envisions Israel becoming pure in a manner contrasting with the ancient ritual traditions that were expressed in Leviticus,
Ezekiel and Deuteronomy: that is, one does not become pure by
observing certain rituals connected with the people, Land, or Temple
or by living according to levitical legislations, even if these features
of Israel's life might be involved in the new Israel. Instead, Jesus'
vision of purity is compatible with portions of Leviticus and that
view of Ezekiel and Zechariah when they describe a vision for a
restored Israel which is fully committed to the will of God—though
an actual Temple plays no role for Jesus. That is, *Jesus' vision of
purity is more devoted to morality, people and time than it is to
place and things.* And, because it is focussed on people and not place,
the Temple is shoved to the side and eventually scorned by Jesus so
that he can enact his own vision of purity and Israel.[27] Instead of a
repentance so that Israel might have a pure Temple (Leviticus, Ezekiel), Jesus has a repentance that leads to a pure people who, instead
of worshipping in the Temple, are sitting equally around a table.[28]

It was this commitment which led Jesus to enact his purity
program in table fellowship with Israelites (and, I suppose, anyone
else who cared to join in the Zecharian vision) as he dined in the
evenings in Galilean villages. It is not the place here to develop
either Jesus' regular practice of table fellowship nor his last
enactment of that fellowship in his counter-proposal for purity in
eating with his followers near Jerusalem in his last week. I suspect
that, as sacrifices purified the sanctuary in ancient Israel,[29] so Jesus

---

[26]   Sanders, *Judaism: Practice and Belief*, 231. Only an insensitive hermeneutic
can attribute to Jesus a novelty with respect to the fundamental relations of persons
to God and others when he expresses this double love-commandment.

[27]   It is not impossible that Jesus' rhetoric against the Temple and priestly
establishment are derived from John, who almost certainly had priestly roots. On
this, see C. H. Kraeling, *John the Baptist* (New York: Scribner's, 1951).

[28]   See J. H. Elliott, "Temple versus Household," who charts the differences in
cultural evocation.

[29]   J. Milgrom, *Leviticus 1–16* (AB 3; New York: Doubleday, 1991) 253-61.

saw his own last meal and death as means of purifying the Temple/
city/Land and nation.

III. JAMES, ISRAEL, AND PURITY

How then does James, the brother of Jesus, fit into all this? In
broad sweep it was James, the brother of Jesus, who carried on the
vision of Jesus in its most consistent form and it is from the Jacobite
tradition, as compared with the Pauline tradition, that we gain
glimpses of the Jesus tradition in retrospect. However, the obstacle
we must hurdle in order to gain these conclusions is that the
Christian tradition nearly blocked out the Jacobite tradition. Thus, a
critical examination of the texts of the New Testament does, at times,
yield insights into James, surely a "towering figure," and the form of
Christianity he represented.[30]

For instance, though Christian interpreters have nearly always
contended that James, the brother of Jesus, was not a follower of
Jesus during the lifetime of Jesus and that, in fact, he became a
believer only when convinced by the unassailable evidence of his
resurrection from the dead, it is not altogether clear that such a
tradition is as secure as once believed. John Painter, in his thorough
attempt to resurrect James from under the rubble of Christian
suppression, contends that John 7:5 could be presenting the brothers
of Jesus in a manner similar to others who followed Jesus but, as he
concludes:

> By Johannine standards of 'authentic' or ideal belief neither the disciples
> nor the brothers qualified until after the resurrection of Jesus and the coming
> of the Paraclete.[31]

He appeals to a similar position with respect to the mother of Jesus

---

30   See Painter, *Just James*, 1; for a sketch of "Jewish Christianity." see Dunn,
Unity and Diversity, 235-66; see also M. Hengel, "Jakobus der Herrenbruder—der
erste 'Papst'?," in E. Gräßer and O. Merk (eds.), *Glaube und Eschatologie: Festschrift für Werner Georg Kümmel zum 80. Geburtstag* (Tübingen: Mohr [Siebeck],
1985) 71-104. On p. 72 Hengel writes: "Ganz gewiß ist dieses Zurücktreten des
Bruders Jesu, das sich in den Apostolischen Vätern und bei den Apologeten
fortsetzt, ein Zeichen für die einseitige, tendenziöse Auswahl der uns überlieferten
historischen Nachrichten im Kanon und der frühen Literatur des 2. Jh.s, die
deutlich macht, daß man in der heidenchristlich geprägten Großkirche nach 70 von
Jakobus und den anderen Brüdern Jesu bald nicht mehr wissen wollte."
31   Painter, *Just James*, 16; cf. pp. 16-18 for the full defense of his view. See
Eusebius, *Comm. Pss.* 68:8-9; Hengel, "Jakobus," 84-85.

(John 2:1-11) and the parallel gains in its support when we observe that in both contexts is a word about Jesus' hour not being yet (cf. 2:4 and 7:8). Painter goes on to show how this very text has had a massive impact on other ancient traditions about the brothers of Jesus and James, most notably, the Jesus traditions found now in Mark 3:20-21 and 3:31-35, neither of which unambiguously confirms that Jesus' family members were outside his circle of followers. In conclusion, Painter argues that the Christian interpretation of James has been colored by unsupportable historical interpretations which have been both generated and carried on by a view of Christianity that had more intention to exalt Paul and suppress Jewish Christianity than by historical realities.[32]

Though I cannot subscribe to every detail of Painter's thesis, a more careful examination of the data shows that James was indeed a significant figure, a (perhaps *the*) dominant leader of the Jerusalem church and the spokesman for the earliest form of Jerusalem-based Christian Judaism.[33] For instance, from Acts 1:14 and 12:17 we can infer that the brothers of Jesus were both at the chronological basis of the Jerusalem churches as well as the core leaders of that movement.[34] If this is the case, it seems highly unlikely that the brothers of Jesus did not believe until after the resurrection unless, at the same time, one accords the Jerusalem believers a capacity to grant them both immediate forgiveness and authority! When Paul visited Jerusalem after his conversion for the first time, though he first mentions his obtaining of information from Peter,[35] he quickly mentions that he also met with James and he calls him both an

---

[32]   See the older study of E. Stauffer, "Zum Kalifat des Jacobus," *ZRGG* 4 (1952) 193-214; now translated in "The Caliphate of James," *Journal of Higher Criticism* 4 (1997) 120-43.

[33]   R. Bauckham speaks eloquently for the traditional view that the Twelve governed the Jerusalem-based Jewish Christians until the persecutions of Agrippa I gave to James greater prominence. See his "James and the Jerusalem Church," in *The Book of Acts in Its Palestinian Setting* (The Book of Acts in its First Century Setting 4; ed. R. Bauckham; Grand Rapids: Eerdmans, 1995) 415-80, here pp. 427-41. Hengel ("Jakobus," 98-99) then is in the majority in seeing the order of Gal 1:18-19 as compared to 2:1-10 as a change in leadership.

[34]   Especially if the three of Mark 9:1 in addition to the four brothers of Jesus (Mark 6:3) are the so-called "seven" pillars of the Church; see Bauckham, "James and the Jerusalem Church," 447-48.

[35]   See Dunn, *Jesus, Paul, and the Law*, 110-13, 126-28.

"apostle" and the "Lord's brother" (Gal 1:18-19).[36] In the same
letter, now describing an event more than a decade later, Paul refers
to James as a "pillar" (cf. 2:2, 6, 9) and, more significantly, he lists
James first when he is clearly delineating the leadership at Jerusalem,
ahead of both Peter and John (cf. 2:9). This leadership of James best
explains why it is that both Peter and Barnabas, two stalwarts of the
emerging Christian movement, backtracked from their vulnerable,
but quite Pauline, practice of eating with Gentiles in unobstructed
fellowship (2:11-14). It was only when some ἀπὸ᾽Ιακώβου arrived
that they withdrew from mixed fellowship and, to make matters
worse, the influence of these men from James led Peter to compel
Gentile Christians to go the whole way from Gentile status to proselyte status: he compelled them to Judaize (πῶς τὰ ἔθνη ἀναγκάζεις
ἰουδαΐζειν;).[37] This status of James, so imposing to force even
notable Christian leaders to bow to its pressure, was not a passing
phase in Jerusalem, for at least two decades after the resurrection
James still wields enough force to be appealed to by Paul in Corinth.
Paul asks, when defending his rights to accept payment or support
for his ministry, if he doesn't have even the rights to be accompanied
by a wife—ὡς καὶ οἱ λοιποὶ ἀπόστολοι καὶ οἱ ἀδελφοὶ τοῦ κυρίου
καὶ Κῆφας (1 Cor 9:4). Accordingly, in his list of those to whom

36   Because Paul seems to take note of James on this visit makes me think
James was already a significant leader, and this well before the persecutions under
Agrippa I. This evidence, I suggest, works against the theory of Bauckham,
"James and the Jerusalem Church," 440-41. Bauckham may see this only in connection with the rise of James over Peter. Thus, it is not the persecutions of
Agrippa I that explain the rise of James and, in addition, this leaves open the reason
why James was not persecuted while the others were. Such a view makes tenable
the older theory that James survived because of his closer adherence to the Torah
and greater respect among non-Christian Jews in Jerusalem (so e.g. Hengel,
"Jakobus," 99-102). Further, when Paul comes to Jerusalem later (Gal 2:1-10) he
is concerned to present his ideas to the "pillars" and the first one mentioned is
James. I infer from this that James, Peter and John are in positions of authority in
Jerusalem. If so, it appears that at least two of the apostles returned, perhaps after
the death of Agrippa I in 44 C.E., and resumed their positions. It is unclear,
however, when Peter and John returned and I leave as an open question whether
they returned before or after 44 C.E.

37   I am inclined to think that the use of ἀνακάζεις is with reason: Peter was
actually using force to Judaize the Gentile Christians. Cf. Gal 2:3; 6:12; see also
Acts 9 and 26:11. Such use of force would not be without parallel in the annals of
Jewish practice; cf. S. McKnight, *A Light Among the Gentiles: Jewish Missionary
Practice in the Second Temple Period* (Minneapolis: Fortress, 1991) 68, 79-82.

Jesus appeared, Paul mentions Peter, the Twelve, five hundred brothers, James, then to all the apostles, and finally to himself (15:5-7).[38] Finally, when at the very end of Paul's missionary work as recorded in Acts he returns to Jerusalem to deliver his collection, which was for him a consuming passion that expressed the unity of the Jewish and Gentile churches, he does so by first finding and meeting with James (Acts 21:17-26).[39]

James, then, according to a careful examination of the surviving evidence, embedded as it is so often in disputes, was a powerful, towering figure who led the Jerusalem church and whose leadership and influence extended well out into the Diaspora.[40] In the words of Richard Bauckham:

> James in the period of his supremacy in Jerusalem was no merely local leader, but the personal embodiment of the Jerusalem church's constitutional and eschatological centrality in relation to the whole developing Christian movement, Jewish and Gentile.[41]

Such a historical position should remind us again of the theological and social conditioning in the canonization of Christian Scriptures where surely the Christian Judaic viewpoint was not given an equal voice—owing no doubt to the growing influence of the Gentile Christian movement, a movement spearheaded and determined by the apostle Paul, the archrival of James and the Jerusalem churches (Acts 21:17-26). Canon, then, is a viewpoint on books that emerges from a viewpoint on the kerygma, a kerygma that seems to have had little room for the immediate successors of Jesus.[42] Thus, in the words of Martin Hengel:

> One of the tragic developments in the history of Christianity is that the 'church of the Jews', which showed great powers of perseverance even after AD 70, was not tolerated and supported in the further history of the

---

38   I offer as a suggestion that the so-called "Christ" party of 1 Cor 1:12 may be code language for James and the other brothers of Jesus who represent Jesus, or at least a party representing the Jerusalem-based Jewish Christianity.

39   See S. McKnight, "Collection for the Saints," in G. F. Hawthorne, R. P. Martin, and D. G. Reid (eds.), *Dictionary of Paul and His Letters* (Downers Grove: InterVarsity Press, 1993) 143-47, with bibliography.

40   See Hengel, "Jakobus," 81-85, 102, who traces the early Christian traditions regarding the authority of Peter.

41   Bauckham, "James and the Jerusalem Church," 450.

42   See the further developments about James as described by R. Bauckham in the chapter in this volume.

Church of the Gentiles, despite the warning given by Paul in Rom. 11.17ff.[43]

In turning now to James I shall examine two features of James' teaching: his perception of Israel and his view of purity and ethics. For each, I will begin with the evidence from Acts and the Pauline letters before turning to the letter attributed to him. In using the letter, however, I will suspend judgment about authorship until the conclusions where I shall make comparisons with the evidence from Acts and the Pauline letters. In what follows Israel has been separated from purity even though Israel for both the James of Acts and of the letter the former category is a fundamental dimension of the latter. Separating them, however, keeps the discussion from being too unwieldy.

James and Israel: Acts and the Pauline Evidence

Jesus redefines Israel, a primary locus of purity, as those who have been purified by baptism under John and who have also decisively repented in such a manner that they turn to the restoration mission of both John and Jesus. How does James see Israel?

First, recent analysis of Acts 15:13-21 has argued that at least the interpretation of Amos 9:11-12 attributed to James can be reasonably assigned to James, the brother of Jesus, or at least to the leadership of the Jerusalem-based Christian Judaism when James was the leader.[44] After a moving presentation by way of the *experience* at the

---

[43]   See M. Hengel, *Acts and the History of Earliest Christianity* (London: SCM Press, 1979) 121, 125-26; also his "Jakobus," 91.

[44]   R. Bauckham, "James and the Gentiles (Acts 15.13-21)," in B. Withering-ton III (ed.), *History, Literature, and Society in the Book of Acts* (Cambridge: Cambridge University Press, 1996) 154-84, here pp. 178-84. See also Bauckham, "James and the Jerusalem Church," 452: "The most important question is not whether the speech of James in Acts 15 reports what James actually said at the council, which is not likely, but whether it accurately reflects both the considered view of the Jerusalem church leadership, in which James was pre-eminent, as to the relation of Gentile Christians to the Torah, and also the exegetical arguments on which this view was based and with which it was recommended." I was made aware of J. Wehnert's study, *Die Reinheit des 'christlichen Gottesvolkes' aus Juden und Heiden: Studien zum historischen und theologischen Hintergrund des sogenannten Apostel-dekrets* (FRLANT 173; Göttingen: Vandenhoeck & Ruprecht, 1997), but was unable to acquire a copy for use in this essay. In light of a forthcoming review of this book by Bockmuehl (for *JTS*), however, what needs to be said that Wehnert also connects the prohibitions with the resident aliens of Leviticus 17–18 showing

hands of Peter, Barnabas and Paul, James clinches the argument by an *exegesis* of Amos 9:11-12. We can immediately infer from Acts 15:16-18a that James sees in Jesus' ministry the beginning of the reversal of fortunes for Israel and that Israel, *as a nation*, is now being restored. That is, James sees the Judaism he leads to be *primarily, if not totally, an expression of a restored Israel and not a separate religion—and this at least fifteen years after the ministry of Jesus.* To be sure, James' purpose in appealing to Amos, who predicts not only the rebuilding of the Temple but also the permanence residence of the nation in the Land, is to locate a text that includes Gentiles (see below), but by appealing to Amos 9:11-12 James shows clearly that for him Gentile conversion is *inclusion in Israel*. In the words of Bruce Chilton:

> In the argument of James as represented here, what the belief of gentiles achieves is not the redefinition of Israel (as in Paul's thought), but the *restoration* of the house of David.[45]

The same is probably also to be seen in Acts 15:14 where λαός is used, not ἔθνη, for the Gentile converts: thus, Gentiles become part of the people of God, namely, Israel.[46] What James grew up seeing in the names of his brothers, and I believe at the knees of his family, was that God would someday restore the fortunes of Israel; he now believed that his brother, Jesus, was the one through whom God chose to start the process—and he is continuing that restoration of the nation through the Jerusalem-based Christian Judaism community.[47]

---

that a consensus is beginning to emerge for seeing the prohibitions as emerging from exegesis of the Torah with respect to resident aliens and, thus, that James and the Jerusalem church may well have seen the Gentile converts in such a category.

45 B. D. Chilton and J. Neusner, *Judaism in the New Testament: Practice and Beliefs* (London: Routledge, 1995) 106; in greater depth, see Bauckham, "James and the Jerusalem Church," 457-62.

46 J. Painter argues, on the basis of Gal 2:1-10, that there were two missions and two goals for people like James. See his *Just James*, 61-67. If this could be established, it could be confirmed in Acts 15:14 by suggesting that λαβεῖν ἐξ ἐθνῶν λαὸν τῷ ὀνόματι αὐτοῦ describes, not "inclusion into Israel", but an actual separate "people." Since I am not convinced that the genitives of Gal 2:7-8 (e.g. τὸ εὐαγγέλιον τῆς ἀκροβυστίας, or εἰς ἀποστολὴν τῆς περιτομῆς, κ.τ.λ.) can carry a weight that much different from the accusatives of Gal 2:9 (ἡμεῖς εἰς τὰ ἔθνη, αὐτοὶ δὲ εἰς τὴν περιτομήν), I am even less convinced that Acts 15:14 could suggest a "Gentile Church" as distinct from a "Jewish Church."

47 See the discussion of Bauckham ("James and the Jerusalem Church," 423,

Second, *James himself was observant of the Torah.* [48] After
growing up in Galilee, James apparently came to settle in Jerusalem
after the crucifixion and resurrection of Jesus where observance was
in the majority. When the followers of Jesus tried to put together
what had happened, just after the "ascension" of Acts 1:9-10, they
returned to the city of Jerusalem, gathered together, and spent
regular time in prayer (1:14: οὗτοι πάντες ἦσαν προσκαρτεροῦντες
ὁμοθυμαδὸν τῇ προσευχῇ). James, being a brother of Jesus, is
included in the company of what we might call the "core group" of
believers in Jesus' vision for the restoration of Israel (cf. 1:6!).
While we might imagine they were having a typical "Prayer
Meeting," it is far more likely that what Luke is here describing is
Jewish piety with respect to holy days. Whether James returned to
Galilee or not is not known, but we do know that Acts records James
back in Jerusalem, this time clearly as a point leader, when Peter
escapes from prison (Acts 12:1-17). Notable here is that a Jewish
holy day is involved (Unleavened Bread; 12:3), that danger would
have been apparent to any of the leaders connected with Jesus, and
that James is the first one the "fugitive Peter" chooses to inform of
his status (12:17). In short, James *is depicted here as a Torah-
observant Jew who is leading the Christian Judaism of Jerusalem.*
For good reason James was called "James the Just/Righteous." Well
has Martin Hengel said:

> ... ursprünglich wird der Bruder Jesu diesen Ehrennamen aufgrund seines
> vorbildlichen Toragehorsams und seiner vom Gebot Jesu geprägten
> Lebensführung erhalten haben, die wohl nicht nur die Judenchristen
> beeindruckten, wobei wir annehmen können, daß Jakobus Vertreter einer
> spezifisch judenchristlich-jesuanischen Halacha war. [49]

Third, the evidence of Acts indicates that *for James the Torah was
still a defining boundary for determining the extent of the people of
God.* Even though the τινὲς ἐξ ἡμῶν [ἐξελθόντες] of Acts 15:24
may be alluding to 15:1, the τινας ἀπὸ Ἰακώβου of Gal 2:12 leads

---

442-50) on the eschatological Temple (i.e. the Jerusalem church) and the role of the
pillars in establishing that Temple. Chilton ("The Brother of Jesus and the
Interpretation of Scripture") confirms an emphasis on the Temple in the Acts
portrait of James.

[48] For a good analysis of James and the Law, see Chilton, "The Brother of
Jesus and the Interpretation of Scripture"; see also C. A. Evans, "Jesus and James:
Martyrs in the Temple."

[49] Hengel, "Jakobus," 80.

me to think that the referents of Acts 15:24 were other than those of Acts 15:1. That is, we find the persuasion of James in Acts 15:1 and then only later (15:19-21) did he offer a conciliatory proposal and, judging from later evidence about Jewish practice (21:17-26), maybe only a temporary conciliation. The evidence of Gal 2:11-14 clearly shows that James' authority was used for a law-based expression of the gospel about Jesus Christ. And even if Acts 15:1 refers to a group other than James, the "compromise" proposal of Acts 15:13-35 still maintains some Jewish distinctives as at least "minimal requirements." Exceeding those minimal expectations would have been more than acceptable to James. In fact, Bruce Chilton has argued that even these minimal expectations are a fundamental confession on the part of the Gentiles:

> In Acts, James himself, while accepting that gentiles cannot be required to keep the whole law, insists that they should *acknowledge* its entirety—ethical and cultic—as Moses' constitution for Israel, by observing basic requirements concerning fornication and blood.[50]

This law-based boundary definition for Israel is further confirmed by Acts 21:20, 21, 24. As Peter "reported" to James in 12:17, so also Paul did the same when he returned to Jerusalem (21:18) and, when he reported what God had been doing among the Gentiles, they praised God (21:20). At this point we find that the Christian Judaists within James' circle are both numerous (πόσαι μυριάδες) and πάντες ζηλωταὶ τοῦ νόμου ὑπάρχουσιν.[51] Those who were so "zealous," and surely we are not to think of them as anything but observant Christian Judaists, had heard things about Paul that disturbed them: that (1) he was teaching Jewish believers in Jesus of the Diaspora to abandon Moses (21:21: ἀποστασίαν διδάσκεις ἀπὸ Μωϋσέως), (2) that he was teaching them not to circumcise their children (cf. Gal 2:7) and (3) that he was teaching them not to live according to our customs. A simple mirror-reading of this text leads us to infer that James taught each of these, and he may have learned these very things from his older brother, Jesus: Moses, circumcision, as well as the customs of Jewish observance. For the Christians associated with James, then, the Torah and observance of the Torah,

---

50   Chilton and Neusner, *Judaism in the New Testament*, 108.

51   There is no better study of "zeal for the Law" than the Ph.D. dissertation of M. Hengel, *The Zealots: Investigations into the Jewish Freedom Movement in the Period from Herod I until 70 A.D.* (Edinburgh: T. & T. Clark, 1989) 146-228.

even the customs that characterized Jewish life in the Diaspora, defined the true people of God. The solution was to get Paul to pay for himself and others in performing a ritual vow (Num 6:1-21) so he could demonstrate to the Christian Judaists of Jerusalem that αὐτὸς φυλάσσων τὸν νόμον (21:24).[52]

Fourth, at the recommendation of James *it was decided that Gentile converts to faith in Jesus should refrain from certain practices without suggesting for a moment that Jews would bend from their own customs* (Acts 15:13-35).[53] After Barnabas (who has suffered the same treatment as James and whose influence may have been widespread) and Paul explained to the council what God was doing among the Gentiles in the Diaspora who were hearing the gospel, James spoke up,[54] alluding first to what God had done through Συμεών,[55] Peter's Jewish instead of Christian name, and then appealing for support for Barnabas and Paul by use of Amos 9:11-12. Though his design is to justify the inclusion of Gentiles in the final restoration of Israel, James concludes with two points: (1) that Christian Judaism ought not to make it difficult for Gentiles to convert ἐπὶ τὸν θεόν (15:19), an expression that clearly indicates the direction of James' faith—it is faith in the God of Israel who is restoring Israel at these last times,[56] and (2) that the Gentiles who convert to God should abstain from certain practices (15:20). James feels legitimated in this appeal to Jewish customs for Gentiles because

---

[52]   For fuller details, see J. Neusner's chapter in this volume.

[53]   On letter regulations, see Bauckham, "James and the Jerusalem Church," 423-25.

[54]   That Luke describes James' decision in forensic terms (15:19: διὸ ἐγὼ κρίνω) clearly implies the stature of James in the Jerusalem community as well as his position as an arbiter of interpretation; see C. K. Barrett, *The Acts of the Apostles* (2 vols., ICC; Edinburgh: T. & T. Clark, 1998) 2.729.

[55]   R. Riesner has recently mounted a case for seeing here the Simeon of Luke 2:29-32 rather than Simon Peter. See "James's Speech (Acts 15:13-21), Simeon's Hymn (Luke 2:29-32), and Luke's Sources," in J. B. Green and M. Turner (eds.), *Jesus of Nazareth: Lord and Christ. Essays on the Historical Jesus and New Testament Christology* (Grand Rapids: Eerdmans, 1994) 263-78. This suggestion, while certainly clever, seems highly unlikely.

[56]   Conversion to "God" as distinguished from Christ is consistent both with the orientation of conversion for Jesus and the vision James has of God's restoring of the house of David. Further, the language may be that of proselytes to Judaism (cf. Barrett, *Acts*, 2.729).

of the ubiquity of Moses' teachings (15:21).[57]

Jewish mercy emerges in the decision μὴ παρενοχλεῖν (15:19) the converts, that is, the decision not to require circumcision, while Gentile commitment to the roots of Israel's faith comes to the fore in the expectations of the decree (15:20: ἀλλὰ ἐπιστεῖλαι αὐτοῖς τοῦ ἀπέχεσθαι [1] τῶν ἀλισγημάτων τῶν εἰδώλων καὶ [2] τῆς πορνείας καὶ [3] τοῦ πνικτοῦ καὶ [4] τοῦ αἵματος; cf. also at 15:29; 21:25).[58] But what is the purpose of this list of prohibitions? First, it has customarily been argued that James here simply rehearses the so-called *Noahide laws* as an expectation for Gentile converts in their social and physical contacts with Jews, including here observant Christian Judaists (cf. Gen 9:4-6; Lev 17:10; Deut 12:16, 23-25).[59] Second, B. Witherington, III, has recently argued both that this explanation would not adequately cover the number and complexity of issues that would arise in a "mixed community" and, further, that these regulations can be more simply explained as *prohibitions of participation in a pagan temple feast or ritual.*[60] If Witherington is accurate here, James' "conciliation" is simply a demand on Gentile converts to God that they no longer participate in religious pagan festivals rather than specific guidelines, however minimal, for social interaction between Jews and Gentiles. He argues that it is only the temple feasts that can adequately unify both the various features prohibited here and the later practices of Paul (cf. esp. 1 Thess 1:9; 1 Corinthians 8–10) whereas if James were expecting Gentiles to refrain from eating meat improperly drained he would be adding a considerable burden to their life. This proposal results in a James more completely compatible with Paul. If Witherington has given a

---

57   On the role of James as mediator of the Jesus tradition in early Christian tradition, cf. Hengel, "Jakobus," 85-88.

58   For details, see Barrett, *Acts*, 2.731-36.

59   See K. Lake, "The Apostolic Decree of Jerusalem," in K. Lake and H. J. Cadbury (eds.), *The Beginnings of Christianity. Part 1. The Acts of the Apostles. Volume 5. Additional Notes to the Commentary* (repr. Grand Rapids: Baker, 1979) 195-212. A variant on this view can be seen in Chilton and Neusner, *Judaism in the New Testament*, 108, where the Noahide laws are combined with a view that sees (rooted in the purity laws of Leviticus and the love command of Jas 2:8, which is found in Lev 19:18) a call to exclusive worship. This view begins to touch on the view of Witherington III noted above. Barrett concludes: "The parallel is not close, and there is nothing in the text of Acts to call Noah to mind" (*Acts*, 2.734).

60   B. Witherington III, *The Acts of the Apostles: A Socio-Rhetorical Commentary* (Grand Rapids: Eerdmans, 1998) 460-67.

more evidentially-based interpretation of the four clauses of this "compromise" over against the traditional view, he has at the same failed to see the significance of James in the burgeoning Jewish Christian churches of Jerusalem, the weight James gives to the Torah (in both Acts and the letter of James), his power to keep even "moderate" Jewish Christians like Peter and Barnabas from falling under a stand for purity food laws (Gal 2:11-14), as well as the argument against Paul in Jas 2:14-26 (if a part of the historical James). In addition, one is struck by the redundant, if not otiose, nature of this proposal: Gentile "converts" are required not to participate in pagan temple feasts, which one would think is what is involved in the term "converts."

Thus, third, a recent study of R. Bauckham proposes that James, or the leadership of the Jerusalem-based churches, by exegeting Amos 9:11-12 through several other prophecies lands back in Leviticus 17–18 and this provides the most reasonable basis for these four specific commands: each is for the "resident alien" who dwells in the Land.[61] The citation from Amos 9:11-12 is framed by Hos 3:5; Jer 12:15; and Isa 45:21 so that

> we can see that all variations of the text of Acts 15.16-18 from that of Amos 9.11-12 LXX belong to a consistent interpretation of the text with the help of related texts which refer to the building of the eschatological Temple (Hos. 3.4-5; Jer. 12.15-16) and the conversion of the nations (Jer. 12.15-16; Zech. 8.22; Isa. 45.20-23) in the messianic age.[62]

It is Acts 15:14b, in the expression λαβεῖν ἐξ ἐθνῶν λαὸν τῷ ὀνόματι αὐτοῦ, that forms the exegetical basis for James's exegesis. In addition, it is in Lev 17:10, 12, 13; and 18:26 that we find (1) the expression "in your midst", (2) the four prohibitions of Acts 15:29 and (3) this "in your midst" is also present in Jer 12:15-16 (cf. also Zech 2:11). Thus, by framing Amos 9:11-12 with Jer 12:15-16 James provides a connection back to Leviticus and the four prohibitions of the Apostolic decree.[63] Though some might be put

---

61   Bauckham, "James and Gentiles." Bauckham summarizes this article in "James and the Jerusalem Church," 452-67. After noting this view, Barrett (*Acts* 2.734) suggests that the prohibitions emerge from those matters for which a Jew was to give his life. He, however, notes that such a view provides no basis for the πνικτόν prohibition.

62   Bauckham, "James and Gentiles," 165.

63   Chilton ("The Brother of Jesus and the Interpretation of Scripture") offers support for the view of Bauckham by arguing that such restrictions are connected to

off by the cleverness of such a proposal, no one familiar with Jewish exegesis would be surprised to find such allusory observations and careful exegesis. In fact, we can readily assume that the Jerusalem-based Christian Judaists, so committed to the Torah, would have made such connections had they been given the challenge of what requirements might be expected for the eschatological Israel when Gentiles come to join in their worship at Zion. Thus, they conclude, "while these Gentiles are not obliged to become Jews and to observe the Law as a whole, the Law itself envisages them and legislates for them."[64] In my estimation, this proposal has resolved an old problem. Consequently, what we have here is an innovative Jewish exegesis of the Torah revealing that for James (and the Jerusalem-based Christian Judaism he represents) the Torah contains the answers to life's complex problems, including specific problems about which laws Gentile resident aliens will have to obey in the eschatological renewal. All this is based, of course, on a spiritualized or eschatological understanding of "in your midst."[65]

Fifth, *James still does not express any mission to the Gentiles because his understanding is that God is restoring Israel.* This can be seen in three interlocking observations. To begin with, scholarship is fairly united now in arguing that Judaism at the time of Jesus and the earliest Jewish churches was not a missionary religion in any sense like the activity of Paul and early Gentile Christianity. Since this is a supporting presupposition and since I have argued this at length elsewhere I will not offer here any further support.[66] A second observation is that Jesus himself prohibited his followers from invading Gentile cities and from evangelizing among the Samaritans because his mission was directed solely to Israel (Matt 10:5-6;

---

the law of love (Lev 19:28), which is found in Jas 2:8.

64 Bauckham, "James and Gentiles," 179.

65 By way of confirmation for James connecting Temple and Torah, along with Israel, one needs to note that CD 7:15-20 (cf. also 4Q174 3:10-14) applies the "fallen hut of David" to the Torah, an exegetical move not out of keeping with Amos 2:4.

66 See McKnight, *A Light Among the Gentiles* ; M. Goodman, *Mission and Conversion: Proselytizing in the Religious History of the Roman Empire* (Oxford: Clarendon, 1994); see for a contrary minority view, L. H. Feldman, *Jew and Gentile in the Ancient World: Attitudes and Interactions from Alexander to Justinian* (Princeton: Princeton University Press, 1993). For a recent statement, see Bauckham, "James and the Jerusalem Church," 425-26.

15:24).[67] Thirdly, we note that though the Lukan presentation has James *including* Gentiles (15:17-18), his real concern is that the Christian Judaists should not make it difficult for the Gentiles to convert to God (15:19). This stance of James is one of *passive acceptance of converts* rather than *active evangelism of Gentiles* and such a stance is precisely consistent with ancient Judaism as well as the ministry of Jesus, for whom Gentile converts were exceptions rather than the "objects" of his mission. It thus needs to be concluded that, while James does envision at the present moment an eschatological restoration of Israel, the presence of Gentiles in that restoration is one of acceptance and toleration rather than active involvement in evangelizing the Gentile world. Such a stance with regard to the mission of the Gentiles might be inferred from Acts 21:17-26 when James, after hearing of the manifold work of God among the Gentiles, praises God but then gets right down to (his kind of) business, saying in effect, "Good, Paul. Now will you show the Jerusalem-based Christians that you are not against the Law." In other words, it appears James bifurcated the restored Israel into those who observed the whole Torah and those who, on the periphery, kept only some of it. Bruce Chilton may have it right when he says:

> Where Paul divided the Scripture against itself in order to maintain the integrity of a single fellowship of Jews and gentiles, James insisted upon the integrity of Scripture, even at the cost of separating Christians from one another."[68]

How then does James see Israel? And, for our purposes, is he consistent with Jesus in this regard? James sees Israel as an eschatological community that is living out the vision of Jesus but which is fully and totally committed to the Torah as the revelation of God for his people, even the Gentiles "in their midst" (read:

---

[67]   Both of these logia come from the "M" traditions of Matthew. Interestingly, reviving the older theories of B. H. Streeter, Painter (*Just James*, 85-95) argues that the M traditions derive from the circle of James.

[68]   Chilton and J. Neusner, *Judaism in the New Testament*, 108. In this connection of framing two churches, it needs to be observed that Paul needed James' approval as the first of the pillars (Gal 2:1-10). Not only did Paul need James' approval, he got it because James thought the inclusion of the Gentiles was part of the plan of God for the eschatological Israel. However, I am not convinced that James had the unity of the Church in mind as does Hengel, "Jakobus," 92-93, 97-98.

"resident aliens"). This Torah was practiced by James, was the defining boundary between the Jewish world, including those Jews who were part of the restoration of Israel, and the Gentile world, and was the foundation for what was expected of the Gentiles who did convert to the God of Israel. In my judgment, there is a certain lack of concern on the part of James for the Gentile world and even for Gentile converts; the latter only interested him to the degree that they confused the status of Christian Judaism in Jerusalem. Israel was for James a pure body, the eschatological community of Jesus, but when James so construes Israel he does not at the same time contend, so far as I can see, that those Jews who did not believe in Jesus were to be classed with pagan Gentiles. For James "salvation" was of the Jews and through the covenant God made with Abraham and was now renewing through Jesus' vision of the Kingdom.

James and Israel: The Letter of James

The opening salvo of this letter, if interpreted appropriately, establishes a fundamental position for James with respect to the question of Israel.[69] The letter is sent ταῖς δώδεκα φυλαῖς ταῖς ἐν τῇ διασπορᾷ. The options are at least three-fold: (1) a biblical metaphor for the Christian Church in general, using an image so expressive of the eschatological fulfillment of covenant restoration; (2) a metaphor for Christian Judaism, in which the term is both literal (for ethnic Jews) and metaphorical (for ethnic Jews who believe in Jesus; "twelve" being used not for a real physical description but for the fulfillment of the restoration of the Twelve Tribes in the Jews who found redemption in Jesus as Messiah); (3) a description of ethnic Jews who are now residing outside the Land of Israel. The evidence (e.g. Matt 19:28; Rev 21:12), I would argue, best fits a combination of options two and three, since I think the options have been reified in Christian scholarship: rather than seeing here "Jewish Christianity" one is probably more justified in seeing "Christian Judaism" and this letter seeks to regulate the Christian Judaism of the Diaspora.[70] *Thus, James' concern is with Israel, the eschatological Israel.*[71]

---

69   Authorship by the brother of Jesus is not hereby implied; instead, I use the term "James" here for convenience. The inquiry presently being conducted may well shed light on the question of authorship.

70   See R. P. Martin, *James* (WBC 48; Waco: Word, 1988) 8-11.

71   In contrast to the "eschatological Temple" that James focusses on in Acts

Even if James alludes to the ἐκκλησία (5:14), this term need not be interpreted in the Pauline sense of the term, and the use of συναγωγή (2:2) neatly balances the evidence to reveal either a form of Judaism that is Christian or a form of Christianity that is still dominantly Judaism. To be sure, the presence of Jesus traditions throughout James (e.g. 5:13-14),[72] as well as the use of Ἰησοῦ Χριστοῦ (1:1; 2:1),[73] indicate that the "Twelve Tribes" find in Jesus the time of restoration for Israel but the exemplary nature of Jewish "heroes" rather than Christian figures, especially the absence of the appeal to Jesus as is done in 1 Peter (cf. 2:18-25), reveals that *this movement is securely within Judaism.* Thus, we find appeal to Ἀβραὰμ ὁ πατὴρ ἡμῶν (2:21), to Rahab (2:25-26), to Job (5:7-11), and to Elijah (5:17-18).

Furthermore, the debate within James is more probably explained by seeing a distinction between "poor" and "rich" Jews, with the former characterizing the Twelve Tribes and the latter those who have not found in Jesus the restoration of the nation, rather than between "Jews" and "Christians." Exegesis of 1:9-11 reveals this very distinction.[74] The crux for our angle is that while ὁ ταπεινός is clarified by ὁ ἀδελφός (1:9), the coordinate ὁ πλούσιος (1:10) does not have a similar clarification and the careful reader then asks why. Examination of 1:9-11 leads to finding the same themes at 2:1-12 and 5:1-6, especially in their use of ὁ πλούσιος for the oppressing Jewish rich (cf. 2:7; 5:1), and such results indicate that 1:9-11 contrasts the "poor brother" with the "rich" who are only "brothers" in an ethnic sense but who because of their behavior cannot be given such an honorific and intimate title. It is justifiable to see here a distinction between "insiders" and "outsiders" but the reticence of James reveals the precise condition of its community: *they are Jewish and they believe in Jesus but their belief in Jesus does not lead them away from Judaism.*

That this Twelve-Tribe Israel, located in the Diaspora, is under-

---

15:13-21, the letter of James shows no interest in the Twelve-Tribe Israel as the eschatological Temple.

[72]   A complete analysis can be found in J. B. Adamson, *James: The Man and His Message* (Grand Rapids: Eerdmans, 1989) 169-94; see also the shorter summary in Painter, *Just James*, 260-65.

[73]   Κύριος at times clearly refers to Jesus as well (cf. 2:1; 5:7, 8; but cf. also 1:7; 3:9; 4:10; 5:10-11).

[74]   See Martin, *James*, 22-28.

stood within the categories of *restoration* is not only clear from the choice of the category of Twelve Tribes, and surely the Twelve Apostles are the "phylarchs,"[75] but from the subdued though nonetheless presence of eschatological imminency: 5:7-8 and perhaps 4:8.[76] The language of 5:7-8 is unquestionably Christian, certainly transcending and even transforming the language of Jesus (cf. ἤγγικεν ἡ βασιλεία τοῦ Θεοῦ in Mark 1:15 with Jas 5:8, where Kingdom has been supplanted by ἡ παρουσία τοῦ κυρίου), but nonetheless expressing the imminent expectation of earliest Christian Judaism. James sees the appearing of the Lord to be not only "near" but he also states that ἰδοὺ ὁ κριτὴς πρὸ τῶν θυρῶν ἕστηκεν (5:9). A note of eschatological restoration may be found in 4:8: ἐγγίσατε τῷ θεῷ καὶ ἐγγιεῖ ὑμῖν. Traditionally, scholars have understood this axiom of James in cultic and moral terms,[77] but not only does P. H. Davids point to eschatological contexts and connotations in the notion of "God coming/returning to his people" (cf. 2 Chr 15:2-4; Lam 3:57; Zech 1:3; 2:3; Mal 3:7) but the work of N. T. Wright on Jewish hope as it impacts Jesus has shown the fundamental nature of Jewish expectation for God one more time to return to Zion, to draw near to his people.[78] I suggest then that is possible James is building on this expectation here and urges a call to the Twelve Tribes to cooperate in God's final coming to Zion by humbly drawing near to him and so discard Satan and sin (4:7-10). *In conclusion, James sees Israel as did Jesus: the new community around Jesus is the eschatological, restored Israel.*

James and Purity : Acts and the Pauline Evidence

Because I am skipping across the terrain of the evidence about James and am trying to present an overall survey of his understanding of purity, which begins fundamentally with his view of

---

75   See W. Horbury, "The Twelve and the Phylarchs," *NTS* 32 (1986) 503-27.

76   On the eschatological expectation associated with Judaism, Christian Judaism, and James, see J. Jeremias, *Jesus' Promise to the Nations* (SBT 24; London: SCM Press, 1958); Bauckham, "James and the Jerusalem Church," 425-26.

77   Martin, *James*, 153.

78   P. H. Davids, *The Epistle of James: A Commentary on the Greek Text* (NIGTC; Grand Rapids: Eerdmans, 1982) 166 (though he prefers a cultic interpretation). See N. T. Wright, *The New Testament and the People of God* (Minneapolis: Fortress, 1992) 280-338; also his *Jesus and the Victory of God, passim*.

Israel, I will provide a sketch of the main features of purity.[79] In particular, we need to see how that picture of purity compares to the vision of purity outlined above with respect to Jesus for whom purity was (1) obtained through repentance in order to become part of the restoration of Israel, (2) found more in the heart than in the hand, (3) spread like a contagion by contact with Jesus, and (4) fundamentally realized in the morality of the Torah as interpreted by Jesus through the commandments to love God and others. How does James fit into this picture?

First, it needs to be noted at the outset that, like Jesus, *James connects purity and the eschatological Israel as defined by the Torah.* The logic of Acts 15:19-21 carries fundamental import for James: since Moses is read everywhere (15:21), which means "since everyone is familiar with the Torah of Moses", we can expect the Gentile converts to God who now dwell "in their midst" to live within a minimal adherence to levitical codes (15:19-20). Purity, then, is rooted in Torah and is a minimal expectation for Gentiles and a maximal expectation for those in Christian Judaism as Acts 21:20-21, 24, make abundantly clear. When the Christian Judaists of Jerusalem are called ζηλωταὶ τοῦ νόμου (21:20) and are grievously concerned about the rumour that Paul encourages even the Jewish converts to Jesus μὴ περιτέμνειν τὰ τέκνα μηδὲ τοῖς ἔθεσιν περιπατεῖν (21:21) and to demonstrate so by performing a Nazirite vow in order to show that he is στοιχεῖς καὶ αὐτὸς φυλάσσων τὸν νόμον (21:24),[80] we see in sharp profile the importance of Torah for defining Israel as well as the significance of purity for the restored Israel and as the impracticability of the Pauline ethic for Christian Judaism.[81] If

---

[79]   For a recent analysis of Acts and the theme of purity, see R. Wall, "Purity and Power according to the Acts of the Apostles," *Wesleyan Theological Journal* 34 (1999) forthcoming. I am grateful to the author for the opportunity to read his study and for the comments he offered on my paper. Wall sees the narrative of Acts 15:13–28:28 to be an unfolding of the results of the Jerusalem council and, in particular, of the midrash on Amos 9:11-12 in Acts 15:19-21. A key thematic is how the pure Jew could intermingle with the unclean Gentile. Even further, Wall contends that Paul's Gentile mission contaminated his status (18:20; 21:26).

[80]   The volatile connotations of teaching Jews not to circumcise their children or to break with traditional custom cannot be overestimated. The Maccabean traditions show the immensity of such actions; cf. 1–2 Maccabees. One of the finest studies remains E. Bickermann, *Der Gott der Makkabäer: Untersuchungen über Sinn und Ursprung der makkabäischen Erhebung* (Berlin: Schocken, 1937).

[81]   Paul's cooperation here is precisely that: cooperation rather than commit-

Gentile converts to God were expected to observe some levitical purity codes, eschatological Israelites were fully committed to the whole of the Torah.

Within this commitment to Torah purity, though there is a so-called "minimal" expectation for Gentile converts (see below), *for the Jew the whole Torah, including full observance of purity laws, is expected*. It is not just that the Christian Judaists are all zealous for the Torah (21:20) but that they are afraid Paul is teaching them to stop circumcising the boys and to abstain from walking in Jewish customs (21:21). If we pause to ask which commandments James might have had in mind we miss the point: all of the Torah is in mind when one is zealous for the Torah. The so-called compromise of the purity laws in Acts 21:25 had no influence on Christian Judaism: they did not back away from some laws in order to meet halfway with the Gentile converts. Instead, they carried on in their normal observance of Torah and Torah observance means all of it (cf. Jas 2:10-11), including purity laws. (Paul surely is on target then when he contends that those who are circumcised are committing themselves to the whole Torah [Gal 5:3]. Further, Paul probably was also right in coming to a completely different position, seeing the Law as *adiaphora* [5:6; 6:15], because he perceived that "partial" observance was an unworkable proposal.) We see this commitment to the purity laws in (1) the vow of Paul (21:22-26), where Paul assumes the pay for four Jewish Christians who have undertaken a Nazirite vow and, to complete his return from contacts with Gentiles, Paul is purified himself (cf. Num 6:1-21; *m. Nazir* 6:5-6; *m. Ohol.* 2:3; 17:5; 18:6; Josephus, *Ant.* 19.6.1 §294) and (2) the concentration on Temple purity in James' statements, where a reminder of Gentile impurity is witnessed in structure (cf. Acts 15:16; 21:26). One needs to recall in this connection *GThom.* §12 as well as the church traditions about James attributed to Hegesippus (Eusebius, *Hist. Eccl.* 2.23.1-9).

Second, since Torah defines the restored Israel, *purity restrictions*

---

ment to the Torah as a defining boundary. Paul operated on the basis of another agenda (Gal 5:6; 6:15; 1 Cor 9:19-21) and it is highly likely that, though at the external level, Paul was now "off the hook," others knew Paul well enough to realize his commitments were located elsewhere and the Christian Judaism represented by these "zealots for the Torah" would still be unsatisfied. On Paul's attitude to the decree, see Bauckham, "James and the Jerusalem Church," 470-75; Hengel, *Acts*, 116-19; idem, "Jakobus," 94-95.

are expected for Gentile converts. The ambiguity of Acts 15:14 in its reference to either a separate people altogether (two churches with two missions) or a separate people within the restored Israel (one church, two dimensions) is only partly clarified by James's recommendation that the Gentile converts to God cooperate with the purity traditions of Israel by acknowledging the more elementary ones (15:20, 29; 21:25). This, of course, is a step back from the Pharisaic Christian demands of 15:1 and 15:5, but, if the Gentile converts do not acknowledge at least these basic purity regulations, they are either not part of Israel or part of another church altogether—recall that the issue of Acts 15:1 is not just social relations but salvation and the demand of the Pharisaic Christians is that the Gentiles observe the Torah of Moses.[82] Though James is in danger of both forcing Gentiles to convert completely to Judaism, becoming "Gentile proselytes to Christian Judaism," or of splitting the growing movement into two irreconcilable churches, he still maintains that the Gentiles will have to be "somewhat pure" if they are to be part of the restoring of the house of David and remain separate from the ambient Gentile world.[83]

A third, though less secure, dimension is derivative: *if James is agreeing with Peter, James sees purity to be in the heart and that it results from the Holy Spirit and faith* (Acts 15:8-9 and 15:13-14). In light of Paul's attention given to the Holy Spirit, who is the replacement of the Torah (cf. Gal 5:1, 5, 16, 18), and the inevitable conflict between James and Paul, it is not surprising that James has little emphasis on the Holy Spirit. Thus, when James agrees with Simeon in the debate in Jerusalem it is more than a little problematic but, nonetheless, it is possible that James does see purity as obtained through the Spirit when one exercises faith in Jesus (15:8-9). Another feature, found also in the letter of James (4:8) and clearly important to Jesus, is the issue of the location of purity: for Simeon

---

82   *Contra* Witherington III, *Acts*, 460-67, it would be odd for James merely to require them to affirm their fundamental conversion (which his view implies) by abstaining from pagan religious feasts when the issue is post-conversion expectations or, in the terms of the Pharisees, full conversion vs. partial conversion.

83   The recent work of Bockmuehl on the extent of the "Land of Israel" within Jewish perceptions of various texts would support the view here presented. That is, it is just possible that James' concern with the Antiochene community of Christian Judaism needs to shore up its obedience to the Law *because it is within the Land itself*. See his chapter in this volume.

it is found in the heart (15:9). Perhaps James is also agreeing to this perception of purity. Since the overall impact of this encounter masks the deep-seated differences between James, Peter, and Paul, one suspects that the Lukan presentation may well have influenced the presentation of James here but it remains, in my opinion, a possiblity that James and Simeon agree in some basic matters pertaining to purity—after all, it was the arrival of the party of James that led Peter to move back to table purity (Gal 2:11-14).

James and Purity : The Letter of James

Assuming the previous discussions about Israel which, as a people, forms the locus of purity for James, we need now to look at what James says directly about purity for this Twelve-Tribe, restored Israel (1:1).[84] First, as with Jesus and the picture of James in Acts, for the letter *purity is found in adherence to the Torah of Moses.* Proper standing before God, as a simple definition of purity, is found in obedience to the Torah, now understood to be perfect, liberating, and royal, and expressed centrally in the command to love one's neighbor (Jas 1:25; 2:8, 12). No text of James expresses this more cleanly than 1:26-27:

> Εἴ τις δοκεῖ θρησκὸς εἶναι μὴ χαλιναγωγῶν γλῶσσαν αὐτοῦ ἀλλὰ
> ἀπατῶν καρδίαν αὐτοῦ, τούτου μάταιος ἡ θρησκεία.
> θρησκεία καθαρὰ καὶ ἀμίαντος παρὰ τῷ θεῷ καὶ πατρὶ αὕτη ἐστίν,
> (1) ἐπισκέπτεσθαι   (a) ὀρφανοὺς καὶ
>   (b) χήρας ἐν τῇ θλίψει αὐτῶν,
> (2) ἄσπιλον ἑαυτὸν τηρεῖν ἀπὸ τοῦ κόσμου.

---

84   The work of J. H. Elliott needs to be mentioned here. See his "The Epistle of James in Rhetorical and Social Scientific Perspective: Holiness-Wholeness and Patterns of Replication," *BTB* 23 (1993) 71-81. His study is a macro-level explanation of James in terms of purity (as defined in the school of interpreters following Mary Douglas and B. J. Malina), abstracting from the binary oppositions of James a pattern of wholeness (= purity) and division (= impurity/pollution). Four problems lead our study away from his: (1) he opts for questionable exegeses of too many major sections in the letter (e.g. in 2:14-26 or 5:12), (2) his study assumes a singular community when it is not at all clear that a single community is in mind at 1:1, (3) his work lacks a sense of historical context for both purity and the issues of Jewish Christianity, and (4) he gives too much weight heuristically to 1:2-4 and its vocabulary. Unlike Elliott, I do not see "purity" as a cental theme of the letter. Though we might be able to extract features of his view of purity and do so in a seemingly coherent manner, we should not at the same time think that purity was the central category of James.

James here uses the language of purity to highlight the centrality of a life that is acceptable to God and these items are to be seen as the "life of Torah": καθαρά (Gen 7:3; 8:20; Lev 4:12; 7:19; 11:32; 15:13) καὶ ἀμίαντος (Lev 5:3; 11:24; 18:24; Deut 21:23). Thus, inasmuch as the royal law is to love one's neighbor, "looking after" orphans and widows (Exod 22:22; esp. in the deuteronomic tradition: Deut 10:18)[85] is θρησκεία[86] καθαρὰ καὶ ἀμίαντος παρὰ τῷ θεῷ καὶ πατρὶ because it embodies the royal law of love as also is caring for the destitute (2:14-17; cf. Matt 25:31-46) and therefore gains approval from God.

A second feature of θρησκεία καθαρὰ καὶ ἀμίαντός is ἄσπιλον ἑαυτὸν τηρεῖν ἀπὸ τοῦ κόσμου.[87] To maintain a "spotless" (cf. 1 Pet 1:19; 1 Tim 6:14) life vis-à-vis the world is to follow the Torah in such a manner that one's relation to the world does not prevent observance of Torah. The world is in opposition to God (cf. 2:5; 3:6; 4:4). The theme of avoiding sin, as an act of purity in relation to Torah observance, is found elsewhere in the letter: 1:12-14, 21; 3:2. But for James this purity by avoiding sin finds a special manifestation in control of the tongue:

> καὶ ἡ γλῶσσα πῦρ·
> ὁ κόσμος τῆς ἀδικίας ἡ γλῶσσα καθίσταται ἐν τοῖς μέλεσιν ἡμῶν,
> ἡ σπιλοῦσα ὅλον τὸ σῶμα καὶ φλογίζουσα τὸν τροχὸν τῆς γενέσεως καὶ φλογιζομένη ὑπὸ τῆς γεέννης (3:6).

Our concern is with the third statement here for the language of purity is used: the tongue is capable of "defiling" (cf. the α-privitive in 1:27; σπιλόω) the whole body since it can erupt as a fire or set loose a world of unrighteousness. The tongue defiles the whole body in the way a false teacher defiles Israel.

We need to delve more deeply into James' view of Torah purity since *the pure Israel of the last days is an Israel defined by the Torah.* If one suspects some Christian vocabulary in the use of λόγος in 1:22 (cf. 1:18, 21), that suspicion is quickly clarified when in 1:25 James refers to the same object with ὁ δὲ παρακύψας εἰς νόμον

---

[85]   This action may be seen as a sign of the eschatological fulfillment of Israel since oppression of orphans and widows characterizes the "tribulation"; cf. Isa 1:10-17; 58:6-7; Zech 7:10).

[86]   This term refers to the external, observable features of the Twelve-Tribe Israel; cf. R. Wall, *Community of the Wise: The Letter of James* (New Testament in Context; Valley Forge: Trinity Press International, 1997) 100.

[87]   On world in James, see Elliott, "Epistle of James," 75-78.

τέλειον τὸν τῆς ἐλευθερίας καὶ παραμείνας. Evidently, the *logos* and the *nomos* are one and the same for James. By way of confirmation, the ποιηταὶ λόγου (1:22) are also ποιητὴς νόμου (4:11). The same interaction of what appears to be Christian vocabulary is interwoven once again with Torah vocabulary in 4:11-12: James prohibits judging one another since the action of condemning and judging[88] one's brother is the same as condemning and judging the Torah (4:11b) and, he infers, the one who judges the Torah is no longer subservient to the Torah (οὐκ εἶ ποιητὴς νόμου) but has become its κριτής (4:11c). But this is arrogant nonsense since, for James, there εἷς ἐστιν ὁ νομοθέτης καὶ κριτής and he is ὁ δυνάμενοις σῶσαι καὶ ἀπολέσαι, terms previously used for what the λόγος (cf. 1:18, 21) or what πίστις (2:14b) can accomplish.[89] Whatever one might think of the logical steps James here takes, he clearly identifies the Twelve Tribes as those who are subject to the Torah.[90] It is perhaps an innovation on James' part to think, in addition, that one must do the whole Torah if one wants to be considered righteous (2:10-11) but, regardless of its rather unique sharpness, the point remains the same: identity is framed by Torah purity.

The *polemical* [91]*nature* of some of the phrases in James is almost certainly intended to counter Paul or his (mis)representives, and in a style quite authoritarian: of the 104 verses, there are more than 54 imperatives.[92] Because 2:14-26 has drawn so much attention in this regard, I shall concentrate on but one term: δικαιοσύνη. Paul's use of δικαιοσύνη is well-known but what needs to be seen here is that James' usage is nearly identical to that of Matthew and to the classical use in Judaism both of which see in this term a description of the

---

88   James makes a close connection between "condemning"/"slandering" and "judging."

89   For parallels, see L. T. Johnson, *The Letter of James* (AB 37A; New York: Doubleday, 1995) 294.

90   I follow here the exegesis of Davids, *James*, 168-70.

91   That Torah, and by derivation purity, were part of sectarian debates has been shown by Neusner, *Idea of Purity*.

92   On this see esp. M. Hengel, "Der Jakobusbrief als antipaulinische Polemik," in G. F. Hawthorne and O. Betz (eds.), *Tradition and Interpretation in the New Testament* (E. E. Ellis Festschrift; Grand Rapids: Eerdmans, 1987) 248-78. Hengel finds anti-Pauline rhetoric throughout the letter (1:2-4; 1:13-17; 2:14-26; 3:1-12; 4:13-16; 5:7-20). Perhaps the most interesting is the suggestion that the "rich traveller" of 4:13-16 is Paul.

faithful Jews' adherence to the Torah through behavior,[93] as opposed
to Paul's use of the term for the "non-behavioral" standing before
God.[94] The axiom of 1:20, ὀργὴ γὰρ ἀνδρὸς δικαιοσύνην θεοῦ οὐκ
ἐργάζεται, is best translated: "man's anger cannot accomplish God's
Torah" where "God's Torah" denotes "the behavior God expects of
his people."[95] A similar usage of the term for human behavior that
conforms to God's Torah can be seen in 3:18: καρπὸς δὲ δικαιο-
σύνης ἐν εἰρήνῃ σπείρεται τοῖς ποιοῦσιν εἰρήνην. When James
castigates the weathly Jewish landlords, he ultimately condemns them
for killling τὸν δίκαιον, a term that can only mean "the representative person, or even martyr, who consistently practices the Torah"
(cf. Matt 1:19).[96] Finally, James contends that the δέησις δικαίου is
greatly effective (5:16c) and he then appeals to the example of the
great Jewish prophet, Elijah (5:17-18). Though it is possible that
James has in mind the example of James the brother of Jesus, if that
is the intended reference in 5:6,[97] it is more likely that James is using
the term δίκαιος here in its typical Jewish meaning: the person who
lives according to Torah. This emphasis on behavior that conforms
to the Torah is further confirmed by the use of ποιέω in James,
especially when it has been turned into the noun that describes the
person who is "doer of the Law/Logos" (1:22, 23, 25; 2:8, 12, 13;
3:18; 4:11). Unlike Paul, James commends "doing" the Torah.

It is in this context that 2:20-26 needs to be understood. James can

---

[93]   It is acceptable to say "adherence to God's will" but God's will is found in
"Torah."

[94]   An excellent study here is that of B. Przybylski, *Righteousness in Matthew
and His World of Thought* (SNTSMS 41; Cambridge: Cambridge University Press,
1980) 13-76; a recent careful examination of the term in recent Pauline thought can
be seen in K. L. Onesti and M. T. Brauch, "Righteousness, Righteousness of
God," in Hawthorne and Martin (eds.), *Dictionary of Paul and His Letters*, 827-37.
It ought to be noted here that the use in James conforms to what scholars have
frequently assigned to the "M" traditions of Matthew; that is, the position of Painter
(*Just James*, 85-95) ought once again to be noted that "M" and James are to be
connected.

[95]   See Davids, *James*, 93; also M. Dibelius, rev. H. Greeven, *A Commentary
on the Epistle of James* (Hermeneia; Philadelphia: Fortress, 1976) 111.

[96]   In the history of scholarship some have seen here a veiled reference either to
Jesus Christ or to James himself (cf. Davids, *James*, 179-80; Martin, *James*, 181-
82).

[97]   See Martin, *James*, 211 (maybe James); Davids, *James*, 196 (a Christian in
good/obedient standing within the community); Johnson, *James*, 335.

offer some perfectly Pauline expressions, as can be found in 2:21, 23, 25, but in each case *James has redefined the concept of justification over against the Pauline expressions*. For James, to be sure, one's standing before God can be called "justification" but one is justified, οὐκ ἐκ πίστεως μόνον but ἐξ ἔργων (2:21, 25). In fact, James turns the classical Pauline text, Gen 15:6, on its head by seeing the action of Abraham that best expresses that evaluation in the offering of Isaac (Jas 2:21)—a position so self-evident to James that he appeals to this event in a rhetorical question. Christian theologians have battled endlessly over whether James is opposing Paul or a (mis)representative of Paul but this misses the target dramatically for, as anyone can see, whether James is responding to Paul or some overzealous Pauline disciple, James sees the logic of justification differently than does Paul: for James one is justified by observing Torah, by obedience and by doing rather than by believing alone. Since these terms speak of final acceptance by God, we must conclude that for James purity is by way of Torah obedience.

But James' view of the Torah purity has an important dimension that cannot be neglected for it opens up a new wall into the meaning of a "restored Israel": *James sees the Law as fulfilled in the commandment to love neighbor*. The critical expression in the scholarly discussion of this point in James scholarship is found in 1:25: εἰς νόμον τέλειον τὸν τῆς ἐλευθερίας. Three terms are noteworthy: (1) Law, (2) perfect, and (3) freedom. There is no discussion of the meaning of "Law" here; it refers to the Torah of Moses. However, the descriptives attached there to show that it is not simply Torah; it is a perception of the Torah. In using the term τέλειον as an attribute of the Torah, James is describing its completeness, its perfection, as well as its moral excellence (cf. 1:4, 17; 2:22; 3:2), and surely we are to think of the majestic words of Pss 19:7-10 and 119.[98] The term ἐλευθερία, however, has generated considerable debate since it leads quite naturally into Pauline theology or into what might be understood as an anti-legalistic perception of the Law —but such findings are theological eisegesis rather than historically-sensitive exegesis. It would not have been surprising to a Jew to be told that the Law "brings" freedom (cf. *m. 'Abot* 3:5; 6:2; *m. B. Qam.* 8:6; *b. B. Qam.* 85b; joy is attached to Law observance in Pss

---

[98]   Again, only Matthew appeals to this concept of τέλειος; cf. Matt 5:48; 19:21.

1:2; 19:8, 10; 40:8; Sir 6:28; 51:15, 29; Bar 4:4). If Paul can describe the Torah as bringing slavery and advocating the Spirit who brings freedom (cf. Gal 5:1-6), James can anchor the same freedom in the Torah itself![99]

But these two descriptions of Law do not yield the clarity for understanding James' context that can be found when one examines 2:1-13. In a context of describing a practice of partiality shown to poorer Jews and who are therefore assigned humbler, less accepting seats in the synagogue (2:1-4), James launches into a direct assault against the rich Jews who oppress the poorer Jews (2:5-7). In this context, James urges the brothers to observe the νόμον βασιλικόν (2:8). To the two adjectives of "perfect" and "freedom" we now have "royal." Walter Bauer contended long ago that βασιλικός here denoted "royal" because "it is given by the king (of the kingdom of God)"[100] and, since James as just mentioned the kingdom (2:5) and proceeds to appeal next to a distinguishable logion Jesu, even if he is quoting Lev 19:18 (cf. Mark 12:31 parr.), his position is most likely correct.[101] The "royal," "free," and "perfect" Law of James then is to love one's neighbor as oneself.[102] That is, James' perception of the Law derives from Jesus: God's commandments are best expressed in the commandment to love one's neighbor.

Examples of loving one's neighbor abound in James though the issue of "who is my neighbor?" seems not to have been an issue for the Twelve-Tribe Israel. Since poverty emerges as a focussed social axis in which everything comes together, it is probably accurate to see poverty behind the exhortation to consider each opportunity of suffering to be an opportunity for character development (1:2-4 connects to 1:9-11). Poverty is certainly the context in which James exhorts the restored Israel to show mercy toward orphans and widows (1:27) as well as mercy to the oppressed ones who are shoved into the synagogue corners (2:1-13). The straw man illustra-

---

[99]   See Wall, *Community*, 83-98. Wall sees a connection here with Jubilee theology (Leviticus 25; Deut 15:1-11; Isa 61:1-2) and its specific manifestation in liberation of the poor (Jas 2:1-13).

[100]   BAGD, 136.

[101]   See also Davids, *James*, 114; Johnson, *James*, 230; Wall, *Community*, 96-97, 122-24, who again sees a connection to Jubilee theology.

[102]   That James intends the "perfect" and "freedom" Law of 1:25 to be connected with the "royal" Law of 2:8 is nearly proven by his use of "freedom" again in the context of 2:8 at 2:12, where he also attaches "mercy."

tion of 2:15-16 may, as it turns out, not be a straw man at all: some of the Twelve Tribes were destitute as a result of oppression (cf. 1:2-4, 9-11; 5:1-6). When James strikes out against the wealthy, arrogant business man who ventures off in utter confidence, he has in mind at the same time the oppression against the poorer members of the community (4:13–5:6). In each of these cases, then, James is explicating what he means by the "royal law of loving one's neighbor." James then defines Israel as an eschatologically-restored Twelve-Tribe nation that is defined by the Law as articulated by Jesus, by the Law of love, but it is still the Law that defines this Twelve-Tribe nation.

A final point of clarification in James' perception of the Law is that this Law is the λόγος ἀληθείας (1:18) which recreates Israel (not just individuals) to be a kind of (τινα) first fruits of creation[103] and is also ὁ ἔμφυτος λόγος which has the ability σῶσαι τὰς ψυχὰς ὑμῶν (1:21). No clearer perception of an eschatologically-recreated Israel (cf. Deut 32:18; Jer 2:3; Hos 11:1-4; Rom 8:23; 11:16; 16:5; 1 Cor 15:20, 23; 16:15; Col 1:10; Eph 2:15; 4:21-24; 5:26; 1 Pet 1:23) that lives the life of the Torah can be offered than this. As God created originally by his spoken word (Genesis 1) so now he recreates through his word (Jas 1:18). But this word, as was anticipated by Jer 31:31, is implanted (as opposed to "innate")[104] in the Twelve Tribes and it will save them, i.e. deliver them, so that they will now live the life prescribed by the Torah (as understood by Jesus). *The Torah purity that defines this Twelve-Tribe Israel is (1) the Torah of Moses, (2) that has been interpreted by Jesus according to Lev 19:18, the Torah of love, and (3) this Torah has been implanted in them so they might be the pure Israel that does the Torah of love.*

Second, the Twelve-Tribe Israel that is marked by wise purity (3:17-18) becomes a *contagion of purity for Israel*. Two texts of James suggest that James may well have seen the Twelve Tribes as embodying purity and, therefore, as a contagion capable of spreading purity. I would suggest that we can see this in the exhortation to anoint with oil in 5:13-16. Besides its obvious connections with ritual sacrifices (e.g. Exod 29:40; Lev 2:1), olive oil was used for healing

---

[103] It is possible, but highly unlikely, that James has in mind a Gentile mission here. See Martin, *James*, 40-41.

[104] See Johnson, *James*, 202.

(Isa 1:6; Mark 6:13; Luke 10:34). This is especially seen in the context of lepers (Lev 14:15-20): after sprinkling oil seven times before YHWH, the priest is to place some oil on the leper's right ear, on the right thumb, on the right big toe, and on the guilt offering; then the priest is to put what remains in his left hand on the leper's head and make atonement for the leper. When Jesus sent out the Twelve they anointed sick persons (including lepers) with oil as a form of purification in which action the Twelve function in a priestly manner (Mark 6:13). This provides the most likely context for the action of the elders in James. If one remembers that Jesus healed lepers as a contagion of purity, I think it is not too far from reality to think that James saw the elders as conveying the embodied purity of the community of the Twelve Tribes. In that context (Jas 5:13-16), one finds the presence of sin, confession, anointing, and healing. It is possible that a continuance of the view that Jesus was a contagion is involved. A second text like this is the restoration of a brother to the community (5:19-20). In the word "turning back" (ἐπιστρέφω) we might have an allusion to the community that considers itself a *sanctorum communio*, and even further a *contagion* of salvation. That is, it is the community to which the wanderer returns and that community is the Twelve Tribes, the restored Israel. Certainly our discussion of Israel above leads one to think that the Twelve Tribes of Israel is pure.

Third, there are other features of James that may express a concern with *particular features of purity*. James occasionally brings the demonic world into view and, if a part of traditional Jewish thought, one would have to think of "unclean" spirits and purification (2:19; 3:6, 15; 4:7). Oddly enough, in the verses just prior to the two features of purity as a contagion James exhorts his readers *to avoid using oaths*, verbal actions connected with the Temple.[105] If this is a purity issue, then it is possible to explain the last three features of James 5 to be "purity concerns."[106] On the other hand, P. H. Davids sees James prohibiting the use of oaths in the course of normal conversation.[107] In Jas 4:8, cultic language emerges in exhortations pertaining to purity:

---

[105] See the discussion of Davids, *James*, 189-91.

[106] Scholars have been vexed in their attempt to explain both the logic of this section on oaths and why the letter tails off the way it does.

[107] Davids, *James*, 190-91.

ἐγγίσατε τῷ θεῷ καὶ ἐγγιεῖ ὑμῖν.
καθαρίσατε χεῖρας, ἁμαρτωλοί, καὶ ἁγνίσατε καρδίας, δίψυχοι.

While I am inclined to see the first line to be associated with the Jewish expectation of the restoration of Israel and the return of God to Zion, the second line appears to be metaphorical language for moral exhortation for many scholars. The neat parallelism of the two commands proves this: καθαρίσατε is connected with ἁγνίσατε; χεῖρας is connected with καρδίας; ἁμαρτωλοί is connected with δίψυχοι. If this is so, the purification commands are directed at the opprobrious categories of James' community (cf. 5:20; 1:8; 4:4); the term "hands" corresponds to "heart" so that a spiritual, as opposed to a physical, dimension is in mind; and the two commands are to be synthesized as: purify yourselves.[108] On the other hand, R. P. Martin contends that James has both in mind: a physical and a spiritual condition is used to connote whole body dedication.[109] If this latter interpretation is followed, James has a concern with "handwashing" (cf. Mark 7:1-23). Finally, as with Jesus and perhaps with the James of Acts 15 who agrees with Peter (15:8-9), James does see purity *connected to the heart* though no emphasis is given to this locus of purity (Jas 4:8b).

Finally, as with Jesus and with the James of Acts, *the James of the letter has no concern with the Gentiles.* To be sure, this is an argument from silence but it is a louder silence than is sometimes the case: since neither Jesus nor the James of Acts shows any real concern with the Gentiles becoming pure, we can see the absence of Gentiles in a letter supposedly written to the Twelve Tribes who are now living among Gentiles (1:1) may well speak to the lack of concern with Gentiles and the absence of the Apostolic decree witnesses to this. After all, the James of Acts 15 only addresses the Gentile question about how much Torah was required for salvation because of issues that emerged in the Diaspora (15:1). I would suggest that had the Twelve Tribes been much concerned with Gentiles then James would have had to bring it up because for James the identity of the group is connected to the Torah and the Torah certainly would have raised issues about purity and the Gentiles. We cannot even assume that James implies that the Gentile converts will need to acknowledge even minimal expectations.

---

108 See the exegesis of Davids, *James*, 166-67.
109 Martin, *James*, 153-54.

CONCLUSIONS

Jesus

Grasping the visions of the prophets, especially that of Zechariah, Jesus set out a vision for Israel, a pure Israel, in which God's new people would be restored to the Twelve-Tribe expectation. He calls Israel to national repentance, first along with John in a baptism of purification, and then independent of John and extended through his chosen followers, the Twelve. For Jesus, if Israel is to be pure, all Israel must repent (and not just the wicked) and those who do so repent at his call to the Kingdom become part of the eschatological Israel. For Jesus the purity associated with the Kingdom is manifested most especially morally, in the Torah of loving God and loving neighbor (regardless of the condition of the neighbor). Though Jesus may push the boundaries of what a pure Israel is, as can be seen in his table fellowship with sinners and other unlikely persons of Jewish culture, for Jesus Israel was still an ethnic category and hence he had no Gentile mission. As a corollary to this, Jesus did not value the Temple but his valuing of table fellowship, and even the establishment of an alternative sacrifice in his last meal, but neither the devaluation of Temple nor the elevation of table fellowship as an alternative form of grace gave him impetus to stretch the ethnic nature of Israel. Other categories, however, became the backbone for the later Gentile mission of the Church for stretching the meaning of Israel: in particular, one thinks of his emphasis of purity being a matter of the heart. Finally, it appears that Jesus envisions himself as a contagion of purity in that he demonstrated his mission of the Kingdom through his contact with the impure and this contact purified those so affected.

James of Acts and Paul

Building on the vision of Jesus, James defines Israel similarly: though a restoration movement of the Eschaton, this Israel remains an ethnic body as it fulfills the destiny of the House of David. It is likely that the James of Acts and Paul saw purification take place through baptism inasmuch as the early Christian movement was a baptismal movement and James shows no aversion to such practices in his encounters with the expanding churches. Where James apparently differs from Jesus in the matter of the pure Israel is in his emphasis on Israel as the eschatological Temple wherein there may have been assigned pillars and his lack of emphasis on repentance as a requirement for entry (though this is but an inference from silence).

If Jesus softened the Torah as central to defining a pure Israel, James hardened the Torah, for he seems unrelenting when it comes to matters of the Torah. Not only was his reputation as "the Just" established through his own practice, but he fought against Paul on the centrality of Torah and established, through no lack of exegetical effort, that Gentile converts to God who join in the worship of the eschatological Israel were to do just what Torah had commanded for "resident aliens" who are living "in their midst." Such ruling, therefore, is hardly to be seen as a "compromise" on the part of James: one does not compromise when one requires just what Torah says. Furthermore, as we can see from the dialogues of Acts 21, it is highly likely that James expected ethnic Jews of the pure Israel to adhere to the whole Torah and to be "zealous" for its completion. This emphasis on Torah probably leads James also to value the Temple more than his older brother: for James, the Temple was not only a place for prayer but also the express image of what Christian Judaism is, the eschatological Temple. It is possible that James held on to the tradition of Jesus in offering table fellowship indiscriminately, but there is no evidence for such a practice on James' part. In fact, it is more likely that James' view of table fellowship was less expansive and more like the later rabbinic practices. Purity then is defined by Torah for James.

Accordingly, like Jesus, James has no Gentile mission though he is keen on regulating the moral life of the Gentile converts both for reasons of purity and politics. Gentile converts are to follow the minimal expectations of Torah for "resident aliens." Again like Jesus, if we can think that James' agreement with Peter in the speech of Acts 15 reflects also James' position, we can infer that James also saw the heart as the primary locus of purity because it had been purged by faith through the Holy Spirit. However, since our evidence for James is limited to two, highly-charged encounters, we simply cannot be sure that James would have seen the heart as purified by the Spirit through faith. There is no evidence that James sees Jesus or the eschatological Israel as a contagion of purity; the evidence suggests that, though the eschatological Israel is pure, one must be pure through Torah obedience in order to remain within this Israel. I hold it as a remote possiblity, however, that James would have agreed with Peter's, Paul's, and Barnabas' extension of Israel into the Gentile world in which action one might detect a perception of Israel as a contagion of purity.

James of The Letter of James

James here heightens both the ethnic and eschatological dimensions of a pure Israel when he defines the eschatological Israel as the Twelve Tribes (1:1). He thus continues both the vision of Jesus for a national restoration around the Twelve apostles and the vision of James in Acts wherein a rebuilding of the house of David is envisioned. In contrast to Jesus, James of James does not mention repentance, baptism, or the Twelve apostles (though each could be inferred from an assumption of Christian standing). In contrast to the James of Acts, James of James does not use any Davidic imagery. But, in general, there is continuity in the concept of who is Israel: Israel is ethnic and Israel is restored around the concept of twelve.

Purity for James of James, like James of Acts and Paul, is defined by Torah though the James of James associated Torah now with Logos, probably a Christian innovation. Significant continuity with respect to the Torah between Jesus and James of James is found when Torah is defined by the Torah of loving others (though James here does not mention the Shemaᶜ aspect of loving God, perhaps because his context for raising love pertains to others, not God). This dimension of Torah love is extended through the adjectives "perfect," "liberating," and "royal." Such a stance is unlike the James of Acts and Paul. On the other hand, I see more emphasis on Torah purity in James of James than in Jesus; like James of Acts, the James of James has a more hardened view of Torah. The James of James, perhaps due to his context, has no regulations for Gentiles who are "in the midst" of the Twelve-Tribe Israelites of the diaspora and he also has no vision for a Gentile mission. Such a stance continues the practice of Jesus and is similar to the view of James in Acts. The James of James, furthermore, polemicizes about the Torah: if in Acts the polemic is not as clear as it is in the letter, one suspects that the polemic revolves around the same problem (Gentile behavior and expectations for inclusion in the pure Israel). The James of James, unlike the James of Acts, has no emphasis on the Temple as a place of purity or purification, though it is possible that James of James has a hope of God's return to Zion in Jas 4:8. But neither does the James of James have any interest in table fellowship, let alone with sinners—this contrasts with Jesus and shows dramatic similarities to the James of Acts. A unique feature of James of James is his view that the Torah as both "implanted" and the same as the Logos; nothing like this can be found in either Jesus or in the James of Acts, though we might suspect that this perception of James (in James) is a part of the gradual perception in earliest Christianity of the Holy Spirit's role in the life of the Christian.

On the other hand, James of James does show continuity with Jesus and perhaps the James of Acts in purity being a matter of the heart (Jas 4:8b) but, perhaps like the James of Acts or Paul, he also may see a place for hand purity (Jas 4:8a) and this would be unlike Jesus. Unlike the James of Acts, the James of James may well see the Twelve-Tribe Israel as a contagion for purity (as did Jesus) though the evidence is hardly unambiguous.

Ambiguities apart, we can conclude that the vision of Jesus was substantially carried on in both the James of Acts and the James of James, but not without modifications and supplementations. For each, God was at work in restoring Israel and the Torah had a significant part in that restoration, even if it was Torah as defined by love of God and neighbor. For each, the community connected to Jesus was the restored, Twelve-Tribe Israel. If the substantive continuity of each with Jesus can be established, we must also add that there is enough difference between the James of Acts and the James of James to make one wait until further evidence is garnered before one can conclude with any degree of confidence in the matter of the authorship of the letter connected with James.[110] But, the two presentations of James are a witness to the kind of Christian Judaism that continued the vision of Jesus into the next generation as this form of faith in Jesus led to a parting yet within the way of Judaism.

---

[110] See the chapter by P. H. Davids in this volume.

PART TWO

JAMES AND JEWISH CHRISTIANITY

JAMES THE LORD'S BROTHER, ACCORDING TO PAUL

William R. Farmer

INTRODUCTION

What can be inferred about "James the Lord's brother" by gleaning information from the four brief but explicit references to James in the letters of Paul? James is mentioned three times in Paul's letter to the Galatians, and once in 1 Corinthians. We shall begin our essay by some initial reflection on the three references in Galatians and treat the one reference in 1 Corinthians in relation to what we can glean from Galatians.

In Gal 1:19 Paul refers in passing to "James the Lord's brother." In 2:9 he refers to "James and Cephas and John" as persons reputed to be "pillars" in the Jerusalem church. In 2:12 he refers to "certain men who came from James," whose coming to Antioch led Peter out of fear of their coming to withdraw from table fellowship with Gentiles.

The first question to settle is whether Paul is referring to the same person in all three cases. There is nothing to indicate that the James identified as "the Lord's brother" in Gal 1:19 is not the same person as is mentioned by the name of "James" in 2:9 and/or 2:12. The decisive consideration in arriving at this conclusion is the literary convention that requires an author of a closely argued narrative to stipulate that a different person is being referred to (should that be the case) when the same name recurs in the same account. Otherwise intended readers could be misled or at least confused, and the narrative account judged a literary failure.

There are exceptions to every rule and we should remain open to any consideration that may lead us to conclude that Paul has a person other than "James the Lord's brother" in mind when he refers to "James" in 2:9 and/or 2:12. However, at the outset of this essay I wish to acknowledge that I think that Paul is referring to the same person in all three cases.

Assuming this to be the case, it follows that Paul, in giving an account of his relationship with Peter and the pillars of the Jerusalem church, refers to no other associate of Peter as often as to James. In no case does Paul refer to James alone or in his own right. Furthermore, he always refers to James in connection with some pivotal moment in the life of the church.

Peter functions as Paul's alter ego in this autobiographical account. James appears to be a secondary character. As such he functions as an alter ego to Peter. Or to put the matter in another way, while Peter, Paul and James are the three chief characters in this dramatic account, James only comes into the picture when Paul is narrating events in which Peter is playing a primary role, or in which he is the dominant character. So far as we can tell from Paul's account, he could have omitted reference to James completely in the first two cases, and the narrative, on the surface, would have been quite intelligible.

That James, under these circumstances, appears in Paul's narrative suggests that he had an unexpressed importance that constrained Paul to mention him by name. Paul clearly expects his readers to know who James is. And these three references to him in this tight-knit narrative serve to impress upon even Paul's unintended readers that Paul has at least on some occasions in the past moved in the same circles as James, while not always necessarily having been in full agreement with him.

Let us proceed to an in-depth analysis of the relevant portions of the text of Galatians 1–2, taking up these three references to James in the order in which they appear in Paul's account.

I

On the principle of moving from the known to the unknown, let us begin by reviewing what we know about why Paul was in Jerusalem when he had the meeting with James referred to in Gal 1:19.

A. Paul's fifteen-day visit with Peter in Jerusalem

In Gal 1:15-20, Paul tells his readers that when it pleased the one who separated him from his mother's womb to reveal His Son to (or in) him he did not go up to Jerusalem to see those who were apostles before him, but rather he went into Arabia. From there he returned to Damascus, implying that it had been from Damascus he had entered Arabia. Then after three years, according to Paul, he went up to Jerusalem to visit Peter. On this visit Peter also met James, the Lord's brother, as we have noted. But before focusing on Paul's fifteen-day visit we should ask what it was that Paul was doing during those three years between the time he returned from Arabia and Damascus and the time he went up to Jerusalem to visit Peter. In Gal 1:21-24, Paul relates that after his fifteen-day visit in Jerusalem he went into the regions of Syria and Cilicia. But *at that time,* according to Paul's account, he remained unknown by face to the Churches of Christ in Judea. Those churches only knew him by reputation , and what they heard was to the effect that the Paul (Saul) who formerly persecuted the Church "was now proclaiming that faith that formerly he had ravished (Gal 1:23).

We suggest that during the three years in question, Paul had been preaching the gospel outside Judea, possibly in the area of his former persecuting activity, and that during this period of evangelization he laid the groundwork for beginning a westward mission to the Gentiles. His going to Jerusalem must of necessity have proceeded from the reality of these three years of preaching and from his decision to embark on this far-reaching mission.

In Gal 1:18 Paul states that he went up to Jerusalem to visit Peter. The verb translated "to visit" is ἰστορῆσαι. But this verb can also have other meanings. In this context we can best understand this verb if we begin with the cognate noun form ἵστωρ. The ἵστωρ in ancient Greece functioned as examiner and arbiter in legal matters. He was learned in the law and skilled in examining witnesses. He knew how to ask the right questions of people who were being examined in order to ascertain the truth in matters of dispute. The truth he was after was not philosophical truth in some abstract metaphysical sense, but rather the kind of truth that can issue in practical wisdom. In the final analysis the ἵστωρ was a judge.

The verb ἰστορῆσαι can mean to inquire into or about a thing, or to inquire about a person. Or it can also mean to "examine" or "observe." Such a questioner or observer would then become "one who is informed" about something, or "one who knows."

In this context we should not shy away from accepting the plain meaning of what Paul writes in reference to going to Jerusalem: He went to question Peter.[1] Paul is not making himself subservient to

---

[1]   For the full argumentation for this conclusion, see William R. Farmer, "Peter and Paul and the Tradition concerning the 'Lord's Supper' in 1 Corinthians 11:23-26," in B. F. Meyer (ed.), *One Loaf, One Cup: Ecumenical Studies of I Cor. 11 and other Eucharistic Texts* (Leuven: Peeters and Leuven University Press; Macon:

anyone in his decision to ask questions. This apostolic concern to "get it right" is foundational for Christian life and faith. Paul is not forensically diminishing his authority by "making inquiry" of Peter. On the contrary his use of ἱστορῆσαι in this context conceptually places Peter in the witness box. Paul is the ἵστωρ. Peter is the one being cross-examined. What is at issue is the truth in a whole range of practical matters which Paul wants to discuss with Peter—none, we conclude, extending to the heart of his gospel. That much Paul appears to rule out decisively in what he says about how he received his gospel in Gal 1:1-17.

Paul in going to Jerusalem to question Peter, is moving up the stream of church tradition to its very source, that is, to those eyewitnesses who first carefully formulated it.

Paul's use of ἱστορῆσαι at this point serves very well his purpose of establishing both his apostolic independence and his apostolic authority. He is not just an independent apostle who has seen the risen Jesus. He is an independent apostle who stands in a close relationship to Peter. By implication, everything that Paul did or said in the church after that meeting carried with it the implicit authority of both Paul and Peter. That was the risk Peter took in agreeing to the meeting. The risk that James took in meeting Paul was different but no less real. We have no way of knowing from any statements made by Peter or James on the subject of how they viewed Paul's coming to Jerusalem. But the practice of risk-taking out of love, even love of a potential enemy, has been endemic to Christian faith from its origin in the heart of Jesus.

B. Galatians 1:19 ". . . others of the apostles I did not see . . ."

Before we begin our reflection on this text, we need to look at the fourth reference to James by Paul. In 1 Cor 15:7 Paul, in giving an account of the resurrection appearances, mentions that Christ appeared to James and then "to all the apostles." This does not require us to think that Paul regarded James as an apostle, but it could be read in this sense: he appeared to James , and then "to all the (rest of) the apostles." In Gal 1:19, however, Paul writes, "Others of the apostles I did not see, except James the brother of our Lord." From this reference it is clear that Paul was prepared to regard James as an apostle.

Mercer University Press, 1993) 38-43.

Paul went to Jerusalem to see Peter. While Paul did not see any of the other apostles, he did see James. So, for the sake of those who regarded James as an apostle (and Paul appears to have been such a person), in order to set the record straight, Paul makes clear that there was an exception to his statement: "other of the apostles I did not see." He did see James.

In fact Paul may have seen James more than once during his fifteen day visit. But if he did it is likely it would have been when Peter was also present. While there is nothing explicit in Paul's account to suggest that Paul went to Jerusalem with the purpose of seeing James, we can not rule out the possibility that to see James may have been one of his purposes.

In any case, the relationship between Paul and Peter was such as to prepare the way for the two to adjust their respective schedules for this time together. Granting the importance of James as one of those apostles reputed to be pillars of the Jerusalem church, it is not unreasonable that Paul went to Jerusalem open to the possibility that his visit with Peter would or might lead to his seeing James.

If the question of whether Paul would or would not require circumcision of his Gentile converts came up during his fifteen day visit, it seems likely that Peter would have seen the merit of bringing James the brother of Jesus into the discussions, or at least bringing the two, Paul and James, face to face under appropriate circumstances. Certainly, if those two men had never met before—and this is a distinct possibility—Peter, as one of the apostles open to Paul's ministry, would have been interested in taking advantage of any opportunity to expedite the gospel through arranging for Paul and James to meet. After all, the three were united by the bond of having a shared experience of decisive apostolic importance: the resurrected Christ had appeared to each of them. This fact alone, in the case Paul had never met James before, could have justified Peter in arranging for Paul to see James.

This is a good point at which to pause and reflect on a matter of some importance. For Peter to have Paul as an ally opened up a whole new world of missionary potential. As a Pharisee of some influence—for example we know that Paul was skilled in arguing for his position from the scriptures—Paul as an ally of Peter would have greatly enhanced public respect in certain circles for the Galilean fisherman—namely, in circles that understood and appreciated the tradition that the Pharisees sat in Moses' seat. For Paul, a Pharisee, to risk everything on the basis of Jesus' appearance to him, and for him to present Peter to his hearers as the first to whom Jesus had appeared, elevated Peter wherever Paul spoke to those who heard him favorably. Paul was in effect a "front man" for Peter in all circles where his pharisaic credentials enabled him to speak with authority on the law. We have to think of the Roman Emperor joining the church in the fourth century if we wish to gage the magnitude of the ecclesial change that flowed from the social impact of Paul becoming Peter's partner in the Lord. At the time the two joined forces, Peter in partnership with Paul more than matched the stature of James. This partnership was not forged all at once. It began at the personal level during their fifteen-day visit, was openly confirmed at the Jerusalem conference fourteen years later, and refined by fire in Antioch.

For Paul to meet James at some time during his visit with Peter, assuming he had not met James before, would have been an apostolic consideration of overriding importance. It is almost certain that the explicit bond of each having seen the risen Lord, a bond shared by Peter, would have played a decisive role in constraining both to give a high priority for at least a short visit while Paul was in Jerusalem, should James have been in the city even for a few days of the two-week visit.[2]

In any case, it so happens that we have every reason to expect that at some point during the fifteen days, if not very early in the visit, the question of the Law and the circumstances of its binding force for Gentile converts would have come up.

The point is that it would be wrong to conclude in advance that because Paul only mentions James in passing in Galatians, there was very little contact between the two during that fifteen-day visit. We just do not know. At this point, we must, in the nature of the case, suspend judgment on this important question. It is an important

---

[2]   We should not underestimate the importance of being listed among those to whom the Risen Christ had appeared during the earliest formative period of the infant church. It is unlikely that Paul's name was included on all such lists. Each such list no doubt had its own history. To have one's name added to any authoritative list would require assent from those responsible for authorizing the particular list. For the list Paul later passed on to his churches, this would probably have involved the authorization of both Peter and James. This would have called for face-to-face discussions about the respective resurrection experiences these men shared.

question because once we consider the possibility that Paul's contact with James during this Jerusalem visit was more than a merely casual matter, it opens the door to serious conjecture on a wide range of important topics.

A fifteen-day visit with Peter, unbroken by meetings with any other apostle—with one exception—not only focuses attention on the apostle whom Paul chiefly wanted to visit (i.e. Peter), it perforce also focuses attention on that apostle who was the singular exception to the statement: "others of the apostles *I did not see*" (i.e. James).

In Gal 1:17, Paul had been at pains to say: "when it pleased God to reveal his Son to (or in) me, I neither conferred with flesh and blood nor did I go up to Jerusalem to those who were apostles before me."

Presumably those apostles with whom he could have conferred in Jerusalem immediately following his revelatory-conversion-resurrection experience, included some of the same apostles Paul had in mind when he assured his readers that he saw "none of the other apostles except James."

Considerations such as these lead us to conclude that James the Lord's brother mentioned by Paul only in passing in Gal 1:19 and 2:9, and as a person active behind the scenes in Gal 2:12, was by inference someone who played an important role in the life of the Jerusalem church, a role through which he exerted influence not only in places as far away as Antioch, but also in churches as distant from Jerusalem as those in the important Roman province of Galatia.

II

A. Galatians 2:9: "James, Cephas, and John"

James, Cephas and John had the reputation of being staunch leaders of that ecclesial body which had the authority to convene apostolic conferences. These "pillar" apostles bore the responsibility of offering leadership not only for the "circumcised," but for the "uncircumcised" as well (Gal 2:9-11). That these three apostles would be named together by Paul, and in the particular order: James, Cephas, and John, is probably not accidental.

Just as Peter held the dignity of place, consequent to being mentioned first in the received arrangement of the resurrection appearances, so in the case of Paul's listing the names of those who by reputation were leaders at the Jerusalem conference in Gal 2:1-10, it is James who enjoys the dignity of being named first. However, in this case it cannot be because the resurrected Christ appeared to James before he appeared to Peter, he did not. It must have been some other consideration that accounts for this notable fact. Most likely it has to do with James being the brother of Jesus combined with the tradition that he was numbered among those to whom the Lord appeared after his death, burial and resurrection.

This points to a particular importance of Paul's relationship to Peter. Peter appears to have functioned as Paul's contact with the Jerusalem leadership of the church Paul once persecuted, but whose faith, after his conversion, he began to preach (Gal 1:23).

This means that Paul's seeing James while he was visiting Peter in Jerusalem was at the very least a serious courtesy call on the brother of Jesus. It is most unlikely to have been simply a casual matter.

B. The Importance of James

Much of what is inferred about James under this heading is in the nature of the case speculative. Nonetheless, when data is limited, as it is in this case, the historian has little alternative but to speculate. We will begin, however, with some sound inferences that can be drawn from something Paul relates in 1 Cor 9:1-6. In this passage Paul is responding to some of his critics. What is at issue is not clear, but for our purposes this is not important. For our purposes what is important is *what* Paul discloses in passing in his argumentation. Paul, in referring to Barnabas and himself, asks, "Have we not the power to lead about a sister, a wife, as well as the other apostles, and (as) the brethren of the Lord, and Cephas?" Something important about the social history of primitive Christianity is inadvertently disclosed in this rhetorical question, namely that there were groups in primitive Christianity whose members were extended special rights, and one such group was "the brothers of the Lord." So, to begin with, James *as a brother of the Lord* was a member of a privileged group. That he was also a member of another privileged group, i.e. the apostles, marked James out as especially important. Thus for those apostles like Paul, who recognized James as an apostle, James enjoyed a twofold basis for being privileged, i.e. as an apostle and as one of the Lord's brothers. This two-fold basis for privilege would have given James exceptional power. His standing among the brothers of the Lord was enhanced by his being an apostle, and vice versa. This helps explain why James is listed ahead of Cephas and John as a pillar of the church.

One further point is to be made in connection with this informa-tion about the brothers of the Lord being granted the privileged right to "lead about a sister, a wife." It is important to emphasize that what is at issue is not the right to have a wife, but rather whether *having* a wife (or a sister), one had the right *to be accompanied by this wife* or sister. This right or privilege would have entailed an extra financial burden upon the church, and could not have been granted without good reason. And the reason for granting this special privilege to the "brothers of the Lord," we may presume, was similar if not the same as the reason it was granted to Cephas, Paul, Barnabas and the other apostles including James. These were all baptized members of the body of Christ, engaged in expediting the Gospel of Jesus Christ in some meaningful way. In no case should this be regarded as a blanket privilege extended to any and all relatives of Jesus without reference to whether or not they embraced the faith of the church.

As the brother of Jesus to whom the risen Christ had appeared, James would have been a singularly well qualified relative to represent the family of Jesus in the apostolic leadership of the church. He would, for example, have represented Mary, who, as a woman—even though she was the mother of the Lord, and possibly the most influential voice in the very earliest church —because of the patriarchal realities of the time most likely would have exercised her influence in ecclesial conferences through that male member of her family to whom her crucified son had appeared in his risen glory. In his unique role in the primitive church, when James spoke, the other apostles listened! (or so we can imagine).

James could have represented the family of Jesus in the apostolic monitoring of the translation of Jesus' teaching into languages in which Jesus himself had not taught. On the other hand, the known history of missionary translation work suggests that there would always have been the need to do this work carefully with as much expertise and conscientiousness as would have been possible under ever-changing circumstances. In any case, it is altogether likely that any such monitoring would have been quite informal as long as transmission of Jesus' teaching remained primarily in an *oral* state. But the need to authorize *written* translations of his teaching would have called for more formal monitoring. Of course specialists in the respective languages concerned would be needed and they would have an important role to play in this process. But disciples of Jesus who had been closely associated with him during his ministry, and his family, could also have played important consulting roles in the overall translation process. Jesus' disciples would have been the ones best equipped to speak with authority on what Jesus had actually taught. Jesus' family would have been needed primarily in cases where the proper nuancing of his idiomatic expressions required a first-hand acquaintance with the linguistic culture in which his speech was formed.

The way in which Jesus learned to speak at his mother's knees and while playing with James and other children in his home and neighborhood environment and while growing up and assisting in the family place of business, was the final court of appeal in resolving any question about the meaning of the words and idiomatic expressions Jesus used in formulating teaching for his disciples. We are not suggesting that James would himself have had the responsibility of doing all this work. Certainly it was not a chief responsibility. But since such translation work, for the most part, would have been centered in Jerusalem where linguistic talent was concentrated, there is no way James, while playing a leadership role in Jerusalem, could have avoided responsibility in this area, especially when the matter of Jesus' idiomatic usage was involved. This would have required reliable acquaintance with Jesus' mother tongue. For this reason alone, as minor a consideration as it might appear to us to have been, James would have been highly respected by the other apostles, including those who had been Jesus' disciples, like Peter. On matters like this Peter would have deferred to James. Their apostolic partnership or concurrence on such a matter would have been important.

C. Paul, Peter, and James

In 1 Cor 15:5 Paul passes on a tradition he had received which mentions the appearance of Christ to Peter at the very beginning of his list of appearances. Next he mentions the twelve. This tradition gives Peter pride of place among the twelve and among all who accepted this tradition, including Paul.

But this is not the only tradition on this matter. According to a text preserved in the Gospel of Matthew, Jesus appeared to women closely associated with him in his ministry before he appeared to Peter and any of the other twelve disciples. And in the Gospel of John we have a tradition that gave John pride of place vis-à-vis Peter in entering the tomb before Peter.

In the end, as we know, the family of Jesus lost influence in the Church of the Apostles (i.e. the Church for which the two chief apostles were Peter and Paul). How did this happen? In answering this question we note first that the tradition Paul received and passed on to the Corinthians, and presumably to other if not all of his churches, was a tradition he received from the church he persecuted (1 Cor 15:1-7). We say this because Paul, after telling the Galatians about his fifteen-day visit with Peter, wrote: "Then I went into the regions of Syria and Cilicia—and I was [at the time] unknown by face to the churches of Christ in Judea. They only knew me by reports they heard: 'The one who formerly persecuted us now preaches the faith he formerly ravaged'" (Gal 1:23). This means that the faith Paul preached after his conversion was a pre-Pauline faith—namely the faith of the church he had been persecuting. If Paul received the post-conversion faith he preached from the church he had been persecuting, we conclude, in the absence of any evidence to the contrary, that he also received the tradition he passed on to his churches from the same church.

In passing on to the Corinthians the tradition preserved in 1 Cor 15:1-7, without reference to any conflicting or rival tradition like that preserved in Matthew or John, Paul is casting the weight of his apostolic authority in favor of giving to Peter pride of place not only among the twelve, but among all the apostles, including James. This is a reversal of the order of the preeminence between Peter and James given in Gal 2:9.

As Gal 2:9 indicates, Peter was not preeminent among the leaders of the Jerusalem church, James was. Peter provided Paul entree into the circle of apostolic leadership in Jerusalem. The best explanation for James to have been the only other apostle Paul met in Jerusalem while he was visiting Peter could be the simple fact that, granting James' preeminent role among the pillars, for word to pass among the other apostles that Paul had met with James would have satisfied the essential requirements of apostolic protocol. On the other hand, the simplest explanation for Paul's preference for Peter as the apostle he wanted to visit in Jerusalem is that Peter had been the chief apostle in the mission that brought into being the church that Paul (Saul) had persecuted. It was this church that had been engaging in practices which excited Paul's pre-Christian "zeal for the law" and had led to his persecuting activity (for the connection between "zeal for the law" and Paul's persecuting the church, see Phil 3:6).

This leads us to infer that Peter was from a very early date—and this means before the conversion of Paul—an advocate and defender of an apostolic mission that was open to and in favor of admission of Gentiles into the intimacy of table fellowship with apostles of Jesus Christ—certainly including the Apostle Peter.

What I am suggesting is this: there was a very close connection between Peter eating with Gentiles in the church persecuted by Paul, and (1) Peter being willing to receive a visit from a Pharisee who had formerly persecuted this church for such legal offenses, but who was now preaching the faith he formerly ravaged; (2) Peter's opening the doors in Jerusalem for a meeting of the pillars of the Jerusalem church with Paul and Barnabas upon Paul's return to Jerusalem after fourteen years of missionary activity; and finally (3) his eating with Gentiles in Antioch (Gal 2:11).

(1) James meeting with Paul during his fifteen-day visit with Peter; (2) his presence at the Jerusalem conference fourteen years later; and (3) his sending a delegation of the circumcision party to Antioch, must all three be seen against the backdrop of Peter's deep involvement with a mission that at least in part was open to Gentile converts. The fact that James agreed to meet Paul in Jerusalem when he came up to see Peter, and especially that fourteen years later he participated in extending to Paul and Barnabas the right hand of fellowship in order that Paul and Barnabas might go to the Gentiles and they to the circumcised, makes it clear that James and possibly other members of the family of Jesus were in principle open to an understanding of the Gospel which called for opening the doors of the church to Gentiles. How we understand James' involvement at all three stages in this ecclesial development must make sense as a whole, and always in close relation to the roles of both Peter and Paul in these pivotal moments in church history.

On the basis of this proposed reconstruction it can be seen that Peter was the apostle primarily responsible for the conversion of Paul. Not that Peter had any direct contact with Paul before the fifteen-day visit, though that possibility cannot be ruled out, but that the church Paul had been persecuting and from which he received the faith he preached among the Gentiles, can only have been a church which received this faith from those who were apostles before him—and this appears to have included Peter. In any case it was pro-Petrine. This much is clear from 1 Cor 15:5.

That Paul would have wanted to have an extended visit with Peter before embarking on his mission to the regions of Syria and Cilicia is altogether appropriate under the circumstances. And that Peter would have been open to this visit and viewed it appropriate for Paul to see James, under the circumstances, would mark out Peter as a mediating figure in the Jerusalem apostolate.

The far-reaching consequences of this fifteen-day visit could hardly have been foreseen at the time.[3] The emergence of Peter (with Paul) as one of the two Apostles into whose hands the pillars of the church, including James, fourteen years later, would entrust the twin missions to the circumcised and to the Gentiles, would be a conciliar decision of the greatest importance. This act of formalizing the apostolic partnership between Peter and Paul would have vastly increased the potential power of Peter vis-à-vis that of James, and, at least in part, would have paved the way for the eventual freezing out of James as a major player in the development of an apostolic church which became more and more Gentile in its membership and culture.[4] Antioch foreshadows the handwriting on the wall. We turn now to this pivotal event in church history.

III

A. Galatians 2:12 ". . . fearing those of the circumcision party"

James himself did not accompany those who came to Antioch because of their concern over the "circumcision" question. Nonetheless, this group is identified by Paul as being under the influence—if not direct leadership—of James. This is implied in Paul's saying that these men came "from James." This is blunt language. James is represented by Paul as the apostolic sponsor of this delegation. It is to be noted that "when Peter came to Antioch" (Gal 2:11), he was followed very soon thereafter by this party from James (2:12). If there was to have been some kind of scheduled meeting in Antioch—at which among other things how the matter of the law was to be handled for the Gentile converts was to have been discussed—the plan appears to have called for a preparatory visit by

---

3   See "And I remained with him fifteen days," in Farmer, "Peter and Paul, and the Tradition concerning 'The Lord's Supper'," 44-46.

4   This does not preclude other factors contributing to the diminishing of James' influence in the church. We think of the destruction of Jerusalem, and in close association with this destruction, the emergence of Rome as the place where the two chief apostles, Peter and Paul, were martyred.

Peter. In any case we now turn to the crucial question.

B. What Happened in Antioch?

On the basis of the agreement reached at the Jerusalem conference we should not anachronistically jump to the conclusion that this "delegation" was sent to Antioch to check up on what Peter was doing there. There is nothing in the text that requires this interpretation.

First of all, Paul makes no derogatory references to these representatives of those concerned with the question of circumcision, such as the charge against the "false brethren" who "were brought in to spy out the freedom of Christ" at the Jerusalem conference (see Gal 2:4).

It is clear that after Peter had arrived in Antioch, but before the arrival of the men "from James," he had been eating with Gentile Christians. It is altogether probable that what Peter was doing was in principle in accord with his and Paul's understanding of the agreement reached at the apostolic conference in Jerusalem (Gal 2:1-10). There is no suggestion that eating with Gentiles was anything exceptional for Peter. There must, however, have been something out of the ordinary that set the stage for the disaster which followed. I see no point in trying to guess what the "out of the ordinary" circumstance might have been.

It is better to begin with what we do know and work our way out from that point of knowledge. We do know that Peter and Paul were both in Antioch at the same time. This we know from Paul's statement that he confronted Peter to his face—something that would have been difficult to accomplish if either was somewhere else at the time. So much is common knowledge. What is not generally realized, however, is that this being together was no accident. First of all, there was an audience to see and hear what was said and done. When Paul wrote that he confronted Peter to his face in the presence of all, this presumably included an assembly made up of persons who had gathered for the purpose of receiving some report on what had happened or for a discussion of this report or both. It follows that Peter would have agreed to be present, but not that he had agreed to be present only to be confronted by Paul over his troublesome behavior in response to the coming of the men from James. No, Peter's agreement to be present in Antioch at all at a time when Paul and others were to be there must have been an agreement reached well in advance of the actual assembly. That would have been true both for his presence in Jerusalem for the Jerusalem conference and for his presence there for the visit from Paul fourteen years earlier. There is no reason to think that his presence at Antioch at this particular time was not also agreed to well in advance.

So what would have been the governing purpose of Peter's presence in Antioch at this time? We have to assume that it had something to do with the presence of the others involved in Paul's report. This means it had to do with Gentiles, who in Pauline terms had become members of the Body of Christ, it also had to do with whatever led James to send a delegation whose members were concerned over what to do about the Law's requirement of circum-cision, and above all it had to do with Paul and Paul's responsibility for the mission to the Gentiles. The main and possibly the only reason for Peter to be present was to represent the interests of the apostolic mission entrusted to him at the Jerusalem conference. It follows that this would have been a conference involving the partici-pation of the two chief apostles responsible for the twin missions to the circumcised and the uncircumcised.

It is possible that this conference was solely or primarily convened to settle local problems that had arisen in Antioch. However, it must be recognized that Antioch was also well situated to serve as a "Jerusalem-oriented" forwarding base for missionary work, not only for the regions of Syria and Cilicia, but for all provinces west of the Cicilian gates. In other words, the possibility cannot be ruled out that Paul's readers in Galatia understood without needing to be told what was at stake at Antioch during this particular conference. Paul's whole mission to the Gentiles was at stake.

Nor are we to think that the group "from James" was the only delegation that arrived from outside the area of Antioch to attend this high-level meeting. There is nothing in the text that requires us to think that other interest groups were not also present. In fact, that Paul can assume that his readers in Galatia know about James and the meeting in Antioch is best explained if the churches in Galatia had direct information about some of the things that had transpired in Antioch (possibly but not necessarily through reports from their own representatives).

Paul's purpose was not to tell his readers *that* there was a conference at Antioch, but rather what really *happened* at Antioch, and what lay behind the no-doubt controversial action Paul had taken vis-à-vis Peter. The whole Antioch mission was at stake. That is what Paul is at pains to make clear.

This all makes more sense once we realize the nature of Paul's narrative account. Only those who do not realize what the name "Antioch" conjured up in the minds and hearts of his readers can dismiss Paul's account as exaggerated or egocentric. Those of us living in the United States would have to think in terms of place names like "Selma" or "Gettysburg" to understand the magnitude of what "Antioch" meant to Paul's readers. This was a nation-making/nation-breaking event, and Paul's account would have been as riveting for its intended readers as our reading Lincoln's second inaugural, or any account King ever gave of what happened that day on that bridge between yesterday and tomorrow for the American people.

The problems at issue in Antioch, whatever they were, were effectively in the hands of Peter *and* Paul. Informed apostolic discussions concerning the status of Gentile Christians were of the most delicate nature. Peter's eating with them was a clear sign of their future full acceptance in the church. That much had been settled in Peter's mind from a very early period in the history of the church. It was presupposed in the discussions that took place during the fifteen-day visit. And it was underscored by Paul at the Jerusalem conference by his bringing Titus, who was a Gentile, with him into the Jerusalem meeting.

Paul must have known and agreed in principle to the arrangement that some kind of a delegation from James would come to Antioch to take part in what I propose we consider to have been intended to function as the first trial conference over which Paul was to preside with his fellow apostle Peter at his side. Or perhaps it was to have been the other way around. We simply do not know. What was important, however, was for these two apostles (representing the two separate missions) to symbolize their unity in the faith as they moved together to expedite the Gospel among both "circumcised" and "uncircumcised."

A meeting of the kind I conjecture was intended to take place would have functioned as a model of how at points of potential conflict over the vital and potentially conflicting interests of the two missions, problems of mutual concern were to have been worked out. There would have been no need for James himself to be present, physically present, that is. But there would have been a place for responsible representation of what could have been termed the "circumcision party." The responsibility of this group would have been to be sure that the voices of those committed to the Jerusalem accords, but sharing deep anxieties over potential dangers inherent in any unnecessary neglect of the law, would be heard. We assume that James had a decisive voice in selecting the names of those included in that delegation.

Such an arrangement, in my opinion, would have been acceptable to Paul. What neither he nor Peter, nor James for that matter, foresaw, was the inadvertent and unanticipated behavior of Peter. Paul says that this behavior was caused by fear on Peter's part over how the men from James (not necessarily, be it noted, how James himself) might have reacted to his eating with the uncircumcised. It is important that Paul makes no claim that the uncircumcised Titus actually *ate* with the circumcised in Jerusalem.

Perhaps Peter went farther in this matter than he had ever intended to go. We do not know the details. We only know the outcome. Peter unexpectedly and disastrously withdrew, and subsequently Paul confronted him face to face in the presence of all, for "not walking in a straightforward manner with reference to the truth of the Gospel" (Gal 2:14). I repeat, when Paul writes that he did this in the presence of all, in my opinion this would have included the presence of Gentile representatives as well as representatives of the circumcision party, most likely including at least some of the members of the "delegation" from Jerusalem sent by James.

James would have received a report on what happened. How he would have responded to such fraught-with-danger developments is a topic worthy of some discussion.

CONCLUDING REMARKS

One purpose of this essay has been to set the stage for a critical assessment of the supplementary but later tradition concerning James and his relationship to the church in Antioch, preserved in the Acts of the Apostles.

However highly we may regard Acts as a source of reliable historical information, any inclination to accept this later and secondary tradition at face value needs to be checked by a careful evaluation of what can be learned from Paul's letters. Paul knew James, and he prepared his account for readers who had some understanding of James' importance. Paul knew that his words would be measured against the testimony of others. Some of this testimony probably went back to "eyewitness" accounts which had reached the Galatians. Paul's credibility in the eyes of those to whom he was writing was at risk. This was not a time for him to misstate the facts, nor to omit anything that was essential for his readers to know in order to make a sound judgment. At the same time, Paul's account must be seen as highly selective, and therefore, correspondingly tendentious. It is like a legal brief that concentrates on a single point of decisive importance.

Another purpose of this essay has been to set the stage for a critical assessment of the significance of the witness of Ignatius of Antioch to the effect that for the Church of Antioch and the churches of Asia Minor Peter and Paul were the two chief apostles. James is clearly not in the picture for Ignatius, and the twin martyrdoms of Peter and Paul are already fused into a single and normative witness for the whole church.

Historians offer no explanation for the evidence of some profound "togetherness" of Peter's and Paul's martyrdoms.[5] Our reflections serve to open up for discussion the possibility that there was a profound apostolic reconciliation that followed the Antioch incident, and I would like to ask: What role could James himself (or his martyrdom) have played in that reconciliation?

In any case there are, in my opinion, good reasons for us to give considered weight to what we have gleaned from Paul's brief but important references to that wrongly maligned historical figure whose righteous life and death have brought us together in this colloquy.

Epilogue

At one point in the colloquy an objection was made to my reconstruction in part III. This objection was defended on the grounds that I had not taken sufficient account of the fact that while the Acts account is tendentious, Paul's account in Galatians is also tendentious. The implication was made that I had given more weight to Paul's account in Galatians 1 and 2 than to the parallel accounts in Acts on the assumption that Paul's account was less tendentious than the accounts in Acts. After reflecting upon this objection to my analysis I

---

5   See W. R. Farmer and R. Kereszty, *Peter and Paul in the Church of Rome: The Ecumenical Potential of a Forgotten Perspective* (New York: Paulist Press, 1990).

JAMES THE LORD'S BROTHER, ACCORDING TO PAUL   151

would like to make a statement for the purpose of clarification.

What is at issue in my analysis is not whether one author's account is more or less tendentious than the other. What is at issue is the distinction between testimony from an eyewitness compared to testimony that is not from an eyewitness in a disputed matter.

Paul knew James and Peter on the basis of face-to-face meetings. He was present and participated in a meeting with Peter and James in Jerusalem. Fourteen years later he returned to Jerusalem and was present and participated in a meeting that included these same two apostles along with John and others. Later he was present in Antioch, where he spoke with Peter face-to-face over the issue of his withdrawing from table fellowship. That cannot be said about the author of the Acts account, whoever it might have been. There is no evidence that he participated in the events in Antioch, which he describes.

The historian is well advised to follow the rules of evidence that obtain in courts of law. In fact his role is analogous to that of a presiding judge in questions of this kind. That is what it means to call a historian a critic. Any judge who fails to observe the rule that greater weight should be given to eyewitness reports than to reports based upon hearsay is laying the grounds for judicial appeal of his ruling.

On the basis of this distinction between "primary" and "secondary" sources I have decided to make an analysis beginning with what Paul has to say about James, leaving open the question of how this analysis is to be used by those who want to go on to take into account the extremely valuable information that can be judiciously gleaned from the "hearsay" evidence that comes to us from the author of Acts. Any historian who refuses to be guided by this procedure and insists on treating the account in Galatians 1 and 2 as having no more evidential value than the largely hearsay testimony preserved in Acts 1:1–16:10 will be producing reconstructions that are methodologically problematic from the start.

On a completely different matter, I was very interested in learning from the colloquy discussions that the food laws in the Torah applicable to resident aliens may have guided the primitive church in settling the problem of how the food laws were to be binding upon Gentile converts in the earliest days of the church. This knowledge provides an insight into the situation in the early church of some importance. For example, it is now possible to say that in the situation in which Paul found himself when he first began to preach the faith that formerly he had ravished, he probably accepted the practice of the church he had been persecuting in these matters in the initial phases of his own evangelistic activity. However, at some point Paul apparently found himself in situations where Christian accommodation to the food laws governing resident aliens would have become increasingly problematic. We know that his letters reflecting his handling of such matters outside of Palestine—certainly in the provinces of Galatia, Asia and points east—indicate that he was relatively if not completely free of any tendency to make use of the distinction between the way in which the food laws were binding upon Jews and the way in which they were binding upon resident aliens, and for this he had good reason, because outside of Palestine, this distinction would no longer have been of much or any use.

The importance of the distinction between Christian practices in areas where there are "resident aliens" and in areas where there are few or no "resident aliens" helps us to understand the complexity of the kinds of problems that had to be adjudicated between Peter and Paul as they respectively sought to give leadership to their closely related but administratively separate missions to the Gentiles and the circumcised. Antioch on the Orontes would have been an especially interesting place, geographically and culturally, in the light of this distinction. In those parts of the city where Jewish legal authority was strong, the use of the legal provision for "resident aliens" presumably would have made more sense than in parts of the city where Jewish legal authority was weaker. Against the background of this kind of cultural complexity, the potential for the kind of misunderstanding and/or sharp disagreement reflected in Paul's account of what happened in Antioch is certainly increased.

Finally, I can add to my paper the point that since I am convinced that Paul's trip to Jerusalem to visit Peter was pre-arranged and must have had the approval of James, it would follow that at that time Paul could hardly have been thumbing his nose at James over the question of how he (Paul) had been handling the question of food laws for gentiles during the prior three-year period he had been preaching the faith that formerly he had ravished. This suggests that there may have been some development in Paul's thinking about the matter of gentiles' observance of the food laws, and that it was primarily during the fourteen-year period that he spent establishing churches in Asia Minor and Greece, where the food laws for resident aliens would have had little practical meaning for Paul's converts, that Paul's position on the law reflected in his letters coming from this later period in his ministry would have become decisive for his mode of expediting the Gospel.

ANTIOCH AND JAMES THE JUST

Markus Bockmuehl[1]

It was in Antioch, Luke tells us (Acts 11:26), that the disciples were first called "Christians" (Χριστιανοί), quite plausibly an offici-al Roman designation for the adherents of a man called Χριστός.[2] But this is only the beginning of many puzzling questions. Were the followers of Jesus not previously identified with him as Messiah? Is it perhaps true after all that "Christianity," as a movement publicly recognisable by its messianic belief in Jesus, was the invention of certain Hellenised Jews in Antioch?

And what was the role played by the Jerusalem leadership in all this? Protestant Pauline scholarship has long found in Galatians 2 proof positive of a deep and irreconcilable division between a law-free Gentile mission based at Antioch and the Jerusalem reactionaries under James the Just, who were very much the villains of the piece. They were irritated by Paul's cavalier approach to the Torah; and it was they who therefore invented the so-called Apostolic Decree *ex post facto*, as an attempt to extract from the Gentile mission at least a measure of Jewish respectability and decorum: "we cannot ask for the whole Law but we must have some of it."[3] All of Paul's troubles with Judaizing opponents from Galatia via Corinth to Rome can be understood as caused by Jerusalem's attempt to impose on his Gentile churches the Apostolic Decree (or something rather like it), and by

---

[1]   This paper was first read on 3 November 1998 to the New Testament Seminar at the University of Cambridge, and on 20 November 1998 to the Consultation on James hosted in Orlando, Florida by the Bard College Institute for Advanced Theology. I am grateful to those present on both occasions, and to Prof. William Horbury, for helpful suggestions.

[2]   See recently J. Taylor 1994; Hengel and Schwemer 1997: 230. Note further Hengel and Schwemer 1998: 350-51 on an inscription identifying the supporters of Cn. Calpurnius Piso, Roman governor of Syria in Antioch from 5 BC to AD 19, as *Pisoniani* and those of his adversary Germanicus as *Caesariani*.

[3]   So e.g. Barrett 1997: 335; note the quotation from F. C. Baur and the reference to M. D. Goulder. At the same time, Barrett considers the Decree to be the invention of Hellenistic Christians, which Paul then did not accept: e.g. 1998: 712.

his own stalwart resistance, for the sake of the "law-free" gospel, to both the letter and spirit of that document.

Was it *really* quite like that? We may or may not endorse this assessment, which with minor variations remains common to a majority of German and a good deal of British and American scholarship. But whatever our view of this matter, there can be no doubt that the real human and doctrinal dynamics of the apostolic church will remain a closed book to us until we can understand the beliefs and motivations of Simon Peter and James the Just. Their role and influence in the fledgling church is arguably every bit as significant as that of Paul.

The so-called Antioch incident has been a central question for New Testament scholars for most of the past two centuries, and one that has given rise to an unmanageable deluge of secondary literature.[4] Recent times, moreover, have also seen a lively renewal of interest in the person of James himself.[5] This continuing flood of new scholarship has been largely published in the absence of new textual or archaeological data to add to our very limited basis of factual knowledge. As a result, the study of James the Just and his relationship with Antioch, Paul and the Gentile mission has lent itself to an unchecked proliferation of hypotheses. In New Testament scholarship, Antioch still seems to be a matter of *quot homines, tot sententiae*.

The issue at present is still mired on the one hand in methodological problems pertaining to the two rather tricky sources we have in Acts and Galatians. On the other hand, one glance at recent treatments such as those of C. K. Barrett, M. D. Goulder or M. Hengel shows the extent to which the problem also continues to be bound up in a peculiarly intractable history of scholarly and confessional dispute. The developmentalist Hegelian view of early Christian history, as determined by conflicts over opposing fundamentals and deeply intractable antagonisms, is still alive and well among the present-day heirs of F. C. Baur. (What is less well understood is the

---

4   A recent full history of (mainly German) research is offered in Wechsler 1991: 30-295; see earlier Kieffer 1982.

5   Recent studies and surveys of the literature include Pratscher 1987; Adamson 1989; Wechsler 1991; Goulder 1994; Bauckham 1995, 1996; Painter 1997; Eisenman 1997; Bernheim 1997; Wehnert 1997. For a survey of recent research on the Epistle of James see also Hahn and Müller 1998.

extent to which this point of view also perpetuates an ancient tradition of Christian supersessionism, such as that expressed by Jerome in his grumpy old man's rebuke of Augustine on the subject of the Antioch incident, *Ep.* 112.4-18.)

Given such a state of scholarship, this short study cannot hope to "solve" any of the major problems, nor to achieve anything by propounding yet another comprehensive hypothesis. My aim is merely to shed a little light on the view that James the Just is likely to have taken of the city and the fledgling church at Antioch. My first step will be to examine how the city and the Jewish community of Antioch might have been viewed by an inhabitant of Jerusalem in the mid-first century. The second part of this chapter will then go on to propose for discussion a number of relatively lightly argued theses on the likely rationale for James' view of Antioch. Whether the latter arguments are eventually judged right or wrong, it is my hope that they may focus our consideration on certain key points of controversial significance, points that will in my view need to be resolved if future attempts at a fuller treatment are to become less arbitrary and subjective.

FIRST-CENTURY ANTIOCH

As Frank Kolb recently reminded us in the *Festschrift* for Martin Hengel, the nature of our sources makes it virtually impossible to gain any sort of lifelike impression of the city of Antioch in the first century. Our primary epigraphic sources extend to barely 200 inscriptions over the entire period of the city's ancient history, an extraordinarily poor basis on which to assess a metropolis of Antioch's size. (One might compare the small city of Philippi, with only 10,000 inhabitants, which has thus far produced nearly 1,400 inscriptions.) With one mysterious exception,[6] none of the inscriptions relate directly to the Jewish community in the early imperial period. There are indeed a large number of coins, but these offer limited information on anything other than the political setting and

---

6   The word ΓΟΛΒ is inscribed on a stele with menorah. See Downey 1952: 15-51 and No. 24. Might this have marked a Jewish spelt store (Aram. גולבא, e.g. *b. Pesaḥ.* 35a; *b. Menaḥ.* 70b; cf. כסמין in Mishnaic Hebrew)? The significance of spelt, both as a basic staple and for halakhic reasons, is well documented in rabbinic sources: e.g. *m. Peʾa* 8:5; *m. Kil.* 1:1, 9; *m. Ḥal.* 1:1; 4:2; *m. Pesaḥ.* 2:5; *m. B. Meṣ.* 3:7; *m. Šebu.* 3:2; 4:5; 5:3; *m. Menaḥ.* 10:7; *m. Ṭ. Yom* 1:5.

the city's pagan cults; Jewish coins from Palestine are attested only in small numbers.[7] Other written sources for the first century include scattered comments of Josephus and the sometimes fanciful sixth-century chronicle of Malalas.

The excavations carried out in the 1930s admittedly had to contend with a vast ancient city repeatedly destroyed by earthquakes and now buried 6-10 metres under a flood plain.[8] Nevertheless, it now seems very disappointing that the work was executed on such a relatively small scale, consisting only of a few long sections and individual probes along the city's main North-South axis.[9] Nothing of substance emerged, for example, in relation to the entire Jewish quarter. The modern city of Antakya was re-created on a deserted site around 1800; one hundred years later, it still occupied only a very small footprint on the vast area of ancient Antioch.[10] At the end of the twentieth century, however, it has grown to a population of 130,000, complete with high-rise tenements, office blocks and increasing suburban sprawl; and the remaining scope for excavation of ancient Antioch is shrinking week by week.

It is a telling fact of the *status quaestionis* in Antioch scholarship that very little has moved since Downey's masterful work of 40 years ago.[11] Kolb concludes, not unreasonably, that on the basis of the archaeological material we can say almost nothing about those cultural, ethnic and other aspects of Antioch's first and second-century setting that would be of particular interest for an under-standing of early Christianity in that city.[12] Despite the confidence displayed in a number of scholarly treatments, there seems little

---

[7]   On the Jewish coins see Waage 1952: 87. Both Hasmonean and later Herodian (only Archelaus and Agrippa I) periods are represented, as well as the Roman procurators of the period from Augustus to Nero; perhaps the most interesting and revealing find is a "Year 2" (i.e. AD 67–68) coin of the war against Rome.

[8]   Cf. Kolb 1996: 97; Lassus 1984: 361; on the problem of flooding, with the concomitant need for canalisation, see also Feissel 1985; Grainger 1990: 74-75; Wallace and Williams 1998: 168; Millar 1993: 86-89.

[9]   Kolb 1996: 105; cf. Lassus 1977: 56-60, and see the excavation reports.

[10]   See Grainger 1990: 73-74 and cf. Lassus 1977: 59, who reproduces H. Paris's mid-century map of modern Antioch superimposed on the ancient site.

[11]   Downey 1961; cf. Hengel and Schwemer 1997: 430 n. 949: "The standard work is still Downey"; similarly Brown and Meier 1983: 22 n. 51.

[12]   Kolb 1996: 99.

point in talking about the Jewish and Christian communities of Antioch without a clear acknowledgement that we still know very little.

The Jewish Community

In the Christian story, Antioch first features in the person of Nicolas of Antioch, a Gentile proselyte to Judaism who had emigrated to Jerusalem and there joined the Christian community, eventually becoming one of the seven first Deacons (Acts 6:5). By this time, the Jewish community of Antioch already had a long and sometimes tortuous history.

Antioch itself was, like Alexandria, a relatively brash upstart in the ancient Mediterranean world when compared to cities like Jerusalem, Damascus, Athens or Ephesus. It was only founded by Seleucus I Nicanor in 300 BC on the crossroads of important trade routes to Persia and the Far East, to Asia Minor in the North and to Egypt in the South. Although the city itself was landlocked, the nearby harbour city of Seleucia Pieria connected Antioch with destinations around the Mediterranean Sea. Despite its susceptibility to earthquakes and its desirability as the prize of successive warlords, Antioch continued to grow into a major metropolis of the ancient world, being ranked before long with Alexandria and Rome.[13] Antioch had grown in stature throughout the first centuries BC and AD, becoming the natural capital of the Roman province of Syria. Seleucia Pieria had been turned into a major naval base, and Julius Caesar had built new temples, baths, an aqueduct, a theatre and an amphitheatre. Not to be too far outdone, Herod the Great likewise furnished the city with a magnificently paved main street—even if Josephus' report of a marble colonnade over a length of 3.5 km may be somewhat exaggerated.[14]

Josephus claims that Jews had been granted citizenship rights at Antioch by the founder himself (*Ant.* 12.3.1 §119). Aside from this statement, the earliest evidence of Jewish settlement in Antioch is in the 170s BC, when the famous High Priest Onias III took refuge

---

[13] Josephus (*J.W.* 3.2.4 §29) ranks it as "indisputably third" (τρίτον ἀδηρί-τως ... ἔχουσα τόπον) after Rome and Alexandria.

[14] Josephus, *Ant.* 16.5.3 §148; *J.W.* 1.21.11 §425. Kolb 1996: 111 points out that the archaeological record points more plausibly to a colonnade dating from the time of Tiberius (as is claimed by Malalas).

from his Palestinian rival Menelaos in Antioch's "Beverly Hills," the pleasurable suburb of Daphne (2 Macc 4:33-34):[15] we hear, for example, of successful Jewish protests following Onias' subsequent assassination at the hands of Menelaos' "hired gun." Not only did the revered conservative Onias evidently consider Antioch a suitable haven of refuge, but it is also quite clear that substantial numbers at least of the more cosmopolitan inhabitants of Jerusalem regarded the citizenship of Antioch as a highly desirable prize since the second century BC. Indeed Jason's administration in Palestine apparently made strenuous efforts to have even the population of Jerusalem enrolled as citizens of Antioch (2 Macc 4:9-10, 19).[16] And while the author of 2 Maccabees clearly does not share Jason's enthusiasm for this course of action, prominent Jews of different persuasions continued to consider Antioch an attractive place in which to live and work. A large number of Jews took up residence in the city and in many cases became citizens there (cf. also Josephus, *J.W.* 7.3.3 §44; *Ap.* 2.4 §39). Indeed, Antioch continued for several centuries to serve as a place of residence for important religious leaders; even in the Amoraic period famous Rabbis like Simlai and Isaac Nappaḥa are sometimes cited as teaching in the city.[17] In the first century, the highly visible signs of Herod the Great's recent munificence towards Antioch may well have boosted the Jewish community's prestige.[18]

The Jewish settlement (or settlements[19]) at Antioch was evidently younger than the ones in Alexandria and in a number of other

---

15   Note, however, the observation of Kolb 1996: 101 that Daphne itself shows few signs of urbanisation prior to the third century AD. See further his pp. 102-103 on the attractions of Daphne.

16   Similarly Downey 1961: 109-10; Kraeling 1932: 141; cf. more cautiously Barclay 1996: 245. The situation is somewhat complicated by the Seleucid foundation or re-foundation of several other "Antiochs," including e.g. at Hippos, Dan, and Gadara; the re-named Dan also had another "Daphne" at the nearby springs. Josephus does not help matters by locating a place called "Ulatha" near both the Syrian and the Danite Antioch (e.g. *Ant.* 15.10.3 §360; 17.2.1 §24). See further Avi-Yonah 1966: 51; 1976: 29, 107; Marcus and Wikren 1963: 8. 383 n. (f).

17   E.g. R. Simlai, *y. Qid.* 3.15, 64d; R. Isaac Nappaḥa, *b. Ket.* 88a, *b. ʿArak.* 22b; in the fourth century note also R. Jonah and R. Yose before the Roman governor Ursicinus in Antioch in *y. Ber.* 5.1, 9a.

18   So also Kraeling 1932: 147.

19   Kraeling 1932: 143 thinks by the first century there were no less than three Jewish communities around Antioch: in the city, at Daphne, and in the agricultural plain where rice was grown (*t. Dem.* 2.1; *y. Dem.* 2.1, 22d11-12).

Diaspora cities. In the first century it was probably numerically smaller than that of Alexandria, too, although it was nevertheless very large. Precise figures are very hard to come by: Kraeling's figure of 45,000 Antiochene Jews in the early empire was admittedly speculative and has come in for criticism.[20] Nevertheless, with Hengel and Schwemer 1997 we can in my view still agree that, on the justifiable assumption of at least 300,000 inhabitants (rather than merely citizens),[21] a total of 30,000–50,000 Jews seems entirely reasonable.[22] We must therefore assume a substantial and highly influential Jewish community.

There are many signs that the Jewish community in Antioch had by the first century become highly successful and well to do, and that it continued to be so for a considerable period of time. Although the rule of Caligula occasioned considerable suffering in Antioch and Alexandria alike, the larger economic context of Jewish life in the Syrian capital remained very pleasant and prosperous. Thus in the Second Temple period the Antiochene Jews evidently sent large contributions to Jerusalem; their importance to the welfare of Jerusalem is spelled out in a famous passage in Josephus (*J.W.* 7.3.3 §43-45):

> The Jewish race, densely interspersed among the native populations of every portion of the world, is particularly numerous in Syria, where intermingling is due to the proximity of the two countries. But it was at Antioch that they specially congregated . . . . The Jewish colony grew in numbers, and their richly designed and costly offerings formed a splendid ornament to the Temple.

Josephus further reports of one exceedingly wealthy Babylonian Jew named Zamaris, who in the last decade of the first century BC seized upon the plain of Antioch as the best place to settle with his family of 100 and his private army of 500 mounted archers.[23] Even after the fall of the Temple, the wealth of Antioch remained legendary in rabbinic circles—the spices of Antioch were later said to be as good

---

[20] Kraeling 1932: 136; see Kolb 1996: 110.

[21] These estimates admittedly vary immensely, from 100,000 to 500,000 people, although the latter figure is perhaps more appropriate to the fourth century than the first. As an example of a more conservative estimate, Feissel 1985: 44 n. 51 follows Liebeschuetz in supposing that the figure may have been nearer 150,000 than 300,000; similarly Kolb 1996: 101.

[22] Hengel and Schwemer 1997: 189; cf. Riesner 1994: 98.

[23] Josephus, *Ant.* 17.2.1 §24. Herod later prevailed on him to move to Batanea.

as cash (*b. Ket.* 67a). Just as the Jerusalem church considered Antioch a good place to ask for famine relief, so we are told in the Talmud that second-century rabbis were still travelling there to request support for the poor scholars of Palestine.[24]

One of the most significant archaeological finds from Antioch is the large number of outstanding floor mosaics, which were clearly an important status symbol and fashion statement among the better off. "The excavations have shown that in the whole area there was not a single better-class house without mosaic pavements decorating its entrance, halls, dining rooms, corridors and sometimes the bottoms of its pools."[25] We have no reason to think that wealthy Jews would not have owned such houses. The early Christian community in Antioch, too, evidently included a number of relatively well-to-do people, as can be seen not only from its ability to send famine relief to Jerusalem (Acts 11:29-30) but also from members like Menahem of the court of Herod Antipas (Acts 13:1).[26] These mosaics tell an eloquent story of Antioch's opulence, enjoyment of life and interest in moral philosophy as a popular topic for dinnertime conversation.[27]

Antioch, then, was of very considerable socio-economic importance for Jews in the Land of Israel; indeed it had come to be thought of as the "great city" *par excellence*, as can be nicely demonstrated not

---

24   See the mission to Antioch of Rabbis Eliezer, Joshua and ʿAqiba: *y. Hor.* 3.7, 48a; par. *Lev. Rab.* 5.4 (on Lev 4:3); *Deut. Rab.* 4.8 (on Deut 12:20); cf. Acts 11:27-30.

25   Cimok 1995: 8.

26   Cf. Meeks and Wilken 1978: 15; Downey 1961: 283-84. Note also that Barnabas, a Levite from Cyprus who was previously part of the church in Jerusalem, had sold a field in support of the church there (Acts 4:36-37). There is also a tradition that Theophilus made his large house available for the use of the church in Antioch (*Ps.-Clem. Rec.* 10:71). Eusebius (*Eccl. Hist.* 3.4.2) records a tradition according to which Luke, too, was a native of Antioch.

27   See Downey 1961: 209-10. The mosaics manifest great popular interest in moral and philosophical themes: we may note the personifications and abstractions of figures suggesting time, power, renewal, the acquisition and use of wealth, pleasure, life, salvation, enjoyment, *megalopsychia*, *amerimnia*, memory and friendship (thus one finds naturally unfriendly animals depicted together, as in Isaiah 11). Downey writes, "This collection of abstractions, found in one place, is almost unique in the Graeco-Roman world, and it brings before us, in a way literature could not, the interests of the people of Antioch and their curiosities and their speculations." See also Levi 1944: 312-14.

only from Josephus (*J.W.* 7.3.3 §43, cited above) but also from a number of Palestinian *baraitot*.[28]

It can be argued that, from the Tobiad all the way to the Amoraic period, Antioch and other parts of Syria consistently enjoyed a considerably higher profile in Palestinian Jewish texts than did Alexandria[29] or indeed any other part of the ancient world (except perhaps Babylonia, in the later period). In keeping with Josephus' assertions about Syria as being most densely populated with Jews, the extant Second Temple and rabbinic writings refer rather more frequently to Jews in Antioch and Syria than to the larger metropolis of Alexandria and the million or so Jews who lived in Egypt. This may no doubt be influenced by the easier overland routes and Roman administrative links between Palestine and Syria. Nevertheless, as I hope to show, such considerations alone do not account for the status of Syria from the Palestinian Jewish point of view.

Jews and Gentiles in Antioch

In any discussion of first-century Antioch, therefore, it is useful to bear in mind that the Jews of that city were both more numerous and more prosperous than the Jews of Jerusalem. Their relations with the Gentile majority, moreover, appear to have been comparatively unencumbered by political scruples. At least in peaceful times, the predominant religious climate of the city among both Jews and pagans appears to have been one of relative tolerance.[30] Indeed there is good evidence that Jewish relations with many Gentiles, including Gentile Christians, must often have been tolerably good: that, any rate, is clearly the flip-side of episcopal efforts from Ignatius to Chrysostom to dissuade the Christian faithful of Antioch from their continuing involvement with the local synagogue.[31]

---

[28]   Antioch was the largest city most Palestinian Jews could imagine; a stock phrase is "even if it is a great city like Antioch": *t. ʿErub.* 3.13; *b. ʿErub.* 61b; *y. ʿErub.* 5.5, 22d; *y. Taʿan.* 3.5, 66d; also *Num. Rab.* 2.9 (on Num 2:2).

[29]   For Palestinian Jewish views of Alexandria see now Schäfer 1998.

[30]   See Norris 1990: 2372-73. Note, too, Josephus' comment (*J.W.* 2.18.5 §479) that Antioch, Apamea and Sidon were spared the inter-ethnic violence that engulfed so many cities at the beginning of the first Jewish revolt in AD 66.

[31]   Even Ignatius, although deeply opposed to Gentile Judaizing, was far less hostile to Jewish Christians: "it is better to hear Christianity from the circumcised than Judaism from the uncircumcised" (*Phld.* 6:1). Cf. also Meeks and Wilken 1978: 18: "Moreover, if such a separation did take place around 70, it certainly did

Josephus claims, moreover, that very substantial numbers (πολὺ πλῆθος) of Greeks had become sympathisers of the splendidly fur‐nished central synagogue, and that they enjoyed a measure of social integration with the Jewish population (κἀκείνους τρόπῳ τινὶ μοῖραν αὐτῶν πεποίηντο).[32] Once again this may explain why all the evidence suggests that the impetus for Jewish Christians to dissociate from meal fellowship with Gentiles originated in Jerusalem and not in the Jewish community of Antioch.[33]

This itself must raise questions for the continuing proliferation in New Testament studies of the "all or nothing" assumption that obser‐vant Jews never ate with Gentiles and that those who surrendered this strict separation "ceased to be Jews."[34] To seek proof of a formal Jewish prohibition of commensality in anti-Semitic pagan authors' claims about Judaism, as many scholars do, is clearly to take the

---

not mean the once-for-all isolation of the Judaeo-Christians from gentile Christians nor of Jews from Christians. The active influence of Judaism upon Christianity in Antioch was perennial until Christian leaders succeeded at last in driving the Jews from the city in the seventh century." It is highly likely that this state of affairs was not restricted to Antioch. Note Jerome's comment in writing to Augustine (*Ep.* 112.13): "until this day there is among the Jews throughout all the synagogues of the Orient (*per totas Orientis synagogas*) the so-called heresy of the Minim, which is condemned by the Pharisees even until now; popularly they are known as the Nazarenes, who believe in Christ, the Son of God," etc.

[32]   *J.W.* 7.3.3 §45. Note similarly *J.W.* 2.18.2 §463: Judaising Gentiles were ubiquitous in Syria and were regarded as "mixed up" or "assimilated" (μεμιγμένον) with the Jews. (Smith 1987: 66, 182 n. 33, rightly criticises Thackeray [in the Loeb Classical Library] for rendering this term as "neutrals"; Smith's own preference for "persons of mixed stock," however, seems to me more speculative, as the context makes no reference to intermarriage.) Elsewhere, Josephus claims that all but a few of the women of Damascus had submitted to the Jewish religion (*J.W.* 2.20.2 §559-561).

[33]   It is of course possible, as Prof. Horbury suggests to me, that "those from James" may have come in response to conservative Jewish alarms raised in Antioch; but neither Luke nor Paul alludes to such a course of events.

[34]   So e.g. Esler 1987: 73-86, reiterated in idem 1998: 94-97. Dunn 1993: 119 rightly warns against monolithic views, and Barclay 1996 provides a more apposite (if still somewhat compartmental) paradigm for understanding the spectrum of Jewish belief and practice in the Diaspora. (Note, however, that Barclay offers little insight on the Palestinian view of the matter: in over 500 pages his book does not contain a single reference to the Mishnah, and only three from the Dead Sea Scrolls.)

bulldozer approach.[35] The twentieth century should have taught us that anecdotal gossip and popular prejudice rarely furnish reliable evidence of a given ethnic community's real beliefs and intentions. Outright rejection of the Torah is only one of a wide range of possible scenarios for Jews eating with Gentiles—as is the case to this day. As even the earliest evidence from Daniel (1:3-17), Judith, and the *Letter of Aristeas* (181-184) shows, a good many Jews clearly *did* eat in the company of Gentiles and/or accept food supplied by them, without thereby surrendering their Jewishness or their respect for the Torah.[36]

Attitudes to this question evidently varied a good deal, depending on one's halakhic stance and perhaps one's geographic location. Observant Jews might adopt one of the following four positions: they could either

(1) refuse all table fellowship with Gentiles and refuse to enter a Gentile house,

(2) invite Gentiles to their house and prepare a Jewish meal,

(3) take their own food to a Gentile's house, or indeed

(4) dine with Gentiles on the explicit or implicit understanding that food they would eat was neither prohibited in the Torah nor tainted with idolatry.

This latter policy could, for example, be refined in the request to be given only vegetarian or other specified kinds of food—an option which even Paul explicitly legitimates in Rom 14:1–15:6.[37] Options (2), (3), and (4), moreover, would all be compatible with a shared

---

35   Cf. more cautiously Barclay 1996: 436-37: "It is impossible to understand how such complaints could be raised in different locations and across the centuries (from the first century BCE to the late second century CE) unless Jewish separatism at meals was commonly practised."

36   Cf. also Tobit 1:11. See further Sanders 1990a: 272-83; Tomson 1990: 230-36; Rajak 1992 *passim*. Sanders (1990a: 282) points out quite rightly that there is no reason to think cooking vessels used to prepare food for Jews were thought unclean if they had previously contained Gentile food. There is no established first-century halakhah for indirect impurity derived at two removes in this fashion (*contra* Esler 1987: 85-86, 1998: 98), just as the special arrangements for the shared meal in *Letter of Aristeas* say nothing about vessels. In relation to this document, Esler's argument is sustainable only by special pleading: he suggests that both the banquet manager Dorotheus and every one of his servants must have been Jews (1998: 113-14). Sanders seems more likely to be right in stating that meal fellowship in this case is feasible because, in effect, Ptolemy eats food acceptable to Jews (1990b: 178).

37   Esler's (1998) complete silence on Rom 14:1–15:6 speaks eloquently.

Eucharist involving bread and wine.[38]

Within early rabbinic tradition, R. Eliezer ben Hyrcanus may be the best known Tannaitic exponent credited with the "hard-line" assumption that Gentile intent is always idolatrous (*m. Hul.* 2:7).[39] It is probably the case that Gentiles were not normally thought subject to acquired ritual impurity.[40] Nevertheless, given the widespread Jewish conviction about the impurity of idolatry, it is clearly hard-line views about Gentile intentions which would most obviously incline conservative Palestinian Jews to consider it wholly "unlawful" (Acts 10:28: ἀθέμιτον) for Jews to enter a Gentile's house and to eat with them (Acts 10:28; 11:2: συνεσθίειν).[41] The same position is reflected in the book of *Jubilees* (22:16), which was very popular among the Qumran sectarians; and Josephus confirms that the Essenes invariably bathed after contact with foreigners (*J.W.* 2.8.10 §150).

At first sight a similar trend appears to dominate many of the stipulations in Mishnah *ʿAbodah Zarah*.[42] Even here, however, *m. ʿAbod. Zar.* 5:5 explicitly takes for granted the scenario of 'an Israelite eating with a Gentile at a table' (cf. *m. Ber.* 7:1); and Rabbi Meir is here also credited with a more open approach to the question of how an observant Jew might nevertheless eat with Gentiles.[43] Rabban Gamaliel of course is famously said to have frequented the baths of Aphrodite (*m. ʿAbod. Zar.* 3:4); other regulations in the same tractate permit Gentile women to serve as wet-nurses for Jewish children (*m. ʿAbod. Zar.* 2:1). At the same time, it is worth remembering that the stricter Mishnaic rules are attributed predominantly to the late first and second-century Judaean and Galilean rabbis; to the extent that such attributions are reliable, these views may well be coloured by the nationalistic fervour of their time, and are not necessarily representative of first-century Greek-speaking Jews at Antioch.

---

[38]   Esler 1998: 100, 107-108 assumes eucharistic fellowship with Gentiles to have been categorically ruled out for Jews.

[39]   On Eliezer ben Hyrcanus see Neusner 1973; Gilat 1984; and others cited in Stemberger 1996: 70.

[40]   See the documentation in Klawans 1995.

[41]   See also *t. ʿAbod. Zar.* 4.6: R. Shimon b. Eleazar prohibits dining in a Gentile's house even when taking one's own food and servants.

[42]   So e.g. Esler 1998: 104-105.

[43]   For further documentation see Tomson 1990: 232-33.

New Testament scholars still widely assume that the halakhah on Jew-Gentile table fellowship can be straightforwardly identified as either one thing or another. In fact, however, there was clearly a fairly broad spectrum both of halakhic opinion and of practice, both in Palestine and in the Diaspora.[44] It should in any case be self-evident that the large numbers of Gentile sympathisers in the Diaspora would be impossible to conceive without some measure of association and commensality.[45] Although some level of concern for the purity of foods is very widespread, outright refusal of all meal fellowship with all Gentiles is a rare and unusual counsel in Diaspora circles, as E. P. Sanders has shown: even *Joseph and Aseneth*, which at one point affirms such a position (7:1), seems to remain inconsistent on this matter (cf. 20:8).[46] Philip Esler's forceful and somewhat contrived denial of widespread commensality seems unreasonable, as has also been suggested by E. P. Sanders, B. Holmberg, and others.[47]

This is not of course to deny that Antiochene Jews continued to have significant halakhic reservations about unrestricted intercourse with Gentiles. Thus their worries about the oil freely supplied in the city's baths are entirely in keeping with first-century Palestinian perspectives (and we are told the city's officials accommodated this concern by offering them financial compensation instead).[48] Similarly, the possible association of 4 Maccabees and the Hasmonean martyr tradition with Antioch[49] suggests a clear sense of loyalty to the Torah and the ancestral traditions. This alone, of course, does not dictate separation from Gentiles in practice.

One of the Antioch mosaics offers a particularly charming illustration of how a Jewish "à la carte" approach might be imagined to work in practice.[50] A second-century house contained a mosaic depicting a

---

44   Barclay 1996 provides in many ways a more nuanced account of the spread of Jewish diaspora practice.

45   Cf. Feldman 1993: 45-83 *passim*.

46   Sanders 1990a: 275.

47   Sanders 1990a: 279-83; 1990b; Cohen 1989; Dunn 1993: 119-21; Holmberg 1998; also Hill 1992: 118-25, on Esler 1987: 73-86; cf. 1998.

48   Josephus, *Ant.* 12.3.1 §120; cf. John of Gischala's policy at Caesarea, *Vita* 13 §74-75 = *J.W.* 2.21.2 §591-592. See further Sanders 1990a: 272-83; Tomson 1990: 168-76; Goodman 1990.

49   See on this subject Hengel and Schwemer 1997: 195-96.

50   I am indebted to Downey 1961: 212-13 for the following analysis; see also Norris 1991, Lassus 1984: 366, and Cimok 1995, *inter alia*.

small cold supper buffet. The courses are depicted in sequence; the table is decorated with a garland of flowers, and the food is served on silver dishes. Round flat loaves of bread are scattered about. The hors-d'oeuvre consists of boiled eggs in egg-cups with spoons, cold salted pigs' feet, and artichokes. Apparently there were cucumbers and other vegetables as well. This was followed by a fish served on a rectangular plate, a ham with a wine cup, then wild fowl. Finally there would have been a course of fruit (not preserved on the mosaic) followed by a round layer cake. In a context where a Gentile host could respect his guests' preference not to eat ham or participate in the customary libations, there were no obvious reasons why Jews should not eat with him.

Just as some, and probably many, Jews at Antioch worked and traded alongside Gentiles and frequented the theatre, gymnasia and circus games with Gentiles,[51] so many of the same people must have eaten with Gentiles, without ceasing to be Jews. As we noted earlier, it is telling that objections to the Jewish Christian practice of meal fellowship with Gentiles arose in Jerusalem and not in the Jewish community of Antioch. Among the large number of Jews in Antioch there were a good many who showed a relative latitude in their halakhic observance, and for all their sympathies with Jerusalem were probably *not* naturally inclined to nationalism of the purist sort. Some Antiochene Jews apparently belonged to the Blues, one of the two major circus fan clubs.[52] It was a squabble between the Blues and the Greens that degenerated into a pogrom against Jews under Caligula in the year 39-40; this may well have been related to the simultaneous anti-Jewish riots in Alexandria and the unrest in Jerusalem over Caligula's policies towards the Temple. Crises in Judaea could rally Jewish sympathies in Antioch in support of Jerusalem, and precipitate significant tensions with Gentiles—though it is also important to note Josephus' explicit statement that this was *not* the case at the beginning of the Jewish Revolt of 66–70 (*J.W.* 2.18.5 §479).

---

[51]   For a summary of the diaspora evidence see e.g. Feldman 1993: 59-63 and *passim*.

[52]   Schenk 1931: 188 documents Caligula's preference for the Greens; it is also worth noting that the violence against Jews appears to arise as a consequence of the Blues' publicly insulting the Greens in the theatre (Malalas 10:244.20-25). Cf. further Hengel and Schwemer 1997: 184-85.

Antioch from the Perspective of the Land of Israel

In light of this rather limited but suggestive evidence, we can now turn to ask what sort of image of Jewish Antioch may have prevailed in first-century Jerusalem. It is fairly clear from a variety of sources that Syria had a somewhat doubtful status in relation to the Holy Land, being neither altogether part of it nor clearly abroad.[53] Aharoni rightly points out that while the Mediterranean, the Jordan, the Desert and the Wadi el-Arish provide natural boundaries to the West, East and South, the Holy Land's only natural boundaries in the North are the Taurus and Amanus mountain ranges.[54] As promised to Abraham and Moses and said to have been conquered by David, the Holy Land extended to the North and East of Lebanon all the way to the Taurus Mountains and the River Euphrates.[55] This same vision of the Land had been more explicitly re-affirmed at the time of Ezekiel (Ezek 47:15-17; 48:1).

The Northernmost point in many of these cases is said to be Lebo-Hamath, a place of uncertain identification which in the Biblical text usually marks the boundary of the Land.[56] At the dedication of the Temple Solomon had celebrated in the company of "all Israel, the great congregation [קָהָל גָּדוֹל; LXX: ἐκκλησία μεγάλη], from Lebo-Hamath to the Wadi of Egypt."[57] The same definition of the land occurs as early as Amos 6:14. What is more, the Deuteronomic history preserves evidence that after the political loss of these

---

53 See Neubauer 1868: 292ff.; Neaman 1971: 88-103 *passim*.

54 Aharoni 1979: 65.

55 Gen 15:18; Exod 23:31; Num 13:21; 34:7-9; Deut 1:7-8; 11:24; (34:1-3); Josh 1:4; 1 Kgs 4:21, 24; 2 Chr 9:26. Note also that the Davidic census explicitly included Kadesh and Sidon (2 Sam 24:6-7). On Ituraea see also Freyne 1988:169, 193, who rightly dismisses earlier suggestions (e.g. Schürer 1890: 1.293; Schürer and Vermes 1979: 2.7-10 that the Judaised "Ituraeans" of Josephus, *Ant* 13.11.3 §318 must be Galileans (cf. Josephus' careful delineation in *J.W.* 3.3.1 §35-40 of Galilee as *bordering* on Tyre and its dependent territories). *Pace* Freyne (1988: 169), however, their conqueror was not in fact Alexander Jannaeus but Aristobulus.

56 Num 13:21; 34:8; Josh 13:5; Judg 3:3; 1 Kgs 8:65; 2 Kgs 14:25; 1 Chr 13:5; 2 Chr 7:8; Ezek 47:15, 20; 48:1; Amos 6:14.

57 See the parallel in 2 Chr 7:8. Cf. also 1 Chr 13:5: David assembled (NB LXX ἐξεκκλησίασεν) "all Israel" from the Shihor of Egypt to Lebo-Hamath in order to bring back the ark of the covenant. For the influence on early Christianity of Septuagintal conceptions of the "congregation" (ἐκκλησία) of Israel, see Horbury 1997.

boundaries the restoration of the original Holy Land was still understood to remain a divine command: thus the otherwise objectionable
king Jeroboam II is praised for restoring the boundaries "according
to the word of the LORD . . . by his servant Jonah son of Amittai, the
prophet" (2 Kgs 14:25-28).[58] Another text worth mentioning is
Obadiah's assignment to returning exiles of the coastline up to
Zarephath near Sidon (Obad 20), which of course is the scene for an
important story about Elijah.[59] In the Second Temple period, this
sort of utopian perspective continues, for example, in the Qumran
Genesis Apocryphon, in which the land promised to Abraham
predictably extends to the Euphrates. This latter document explicitly
names several cities well to the North of Galilee[60] and locates the
Northern border at "the mountain of the Bull" (טור תורא), probably
the "Taurus" or "Taurus Amanus" range which later features
similarly in Targumic and rabbinic texts (see below).[61]

Politically, various Jewish conquests may reflect this ideological
tendency to describe the Holy Land in the maximal dimensions
envisioned in the Biblical record. So for example it is worth noting
the Hasmonean proclivity to project a Jewish presence in Syrian
lands wherever a power vacuum lent itself to such adventures.
Jonathan Maccabeus, we are told, despatched 3,000 Jewish auxiliary
troops to put down a mutiny in Antioch against the Seleucid king
Demetrius II—even if doubtless such aid may in part have been a
bargaining chip designed to curry political favours in return.[62]
Similarly, following the destruction of the Samaritan Temple and the

---

58   "He restored the border of Israel from Lebo-hamath as far as the Sea of the
Arabah, according to the word of the LORD, the God of Israel, which he spoke by
his servant Jonah son of Amittai, the prophet, who was from Gath-hepher . . . He
recovered for Israel Damascus and Hamath, which had belonged to Judah . . . ."
Solomon had earlier conquered "Hamath-zobah" and built storage towers there,
according to 2 Chr 8:3-4; but this could be Hamath, a town further South on the
river Orontes.

59   Note however, Luke 4:25-27, which clearly assumes that both Damascus
and Zarephath lie outside the land of Israel.

60   See 1QapGen 21:11-12; note Gebal (Byblos) and Qadesh (near Emesa).

61   For this interpretation cf. e. g. Alexander 1974: 206, 249, who follows
Honigman in assuming that "Taurus/Tauros" in Latin and Greek may itself simply
be a transliteration of an underlying Aramaic תורא. See further Weinfeld 1993: 208.

62   1 Maccabees 11:43-51; cf. Josephus, *Ant.* 13.5.3 §135-142. Bikerman [=
Bickerman(n)] 1938: 71-72 sees this Jewish action as "concession politique de leur
part, récompensée par des privilèges royaux."

conquest of Idumaea in the South by John Hyrcanus in 129 BC, in 104 his successor Aristobulus invaded Ituraea to the North of Galilee.[63] In both cases we are told that the inhabitants were permitted to remain "in the land" (ἐν τῇ χώρᾳ) only if they were circumcised and lived by the laws of the Jews—a practice that, for all its Machiavellian political benefits, seems certain to be related at least in part to an idea of the restoration of Jewish land. The coherence of politics and ideology is nicely illustrated by the Jewish historian Eupolemus, writing in the Hasmonean period, who describes the conquests of David as explicitly including Idumaea, Ituraea, Tyre as well as Commagene by the Euphrates.[64]

Herod the Great is another interesting case in point, if undoubtedly less driven by Jewish religious devotion. A hint of Roman readiness to recognise Jewish claims on "Greater Palestine" may be present in the fact that the provincial administration evidently allowed the Jewish king Herod considerable political leeway in Syria. Josephus in fact claims that when for a brief period Herod threw his support behind Julius Caesar's assassin Cassius, the latter recognised Herod's strategic importance by giving him a force of cavalry and infantry— and assigning him responsibility for all of Syria (Συρίας ἁπάσης ἐπιμελητὴν καθιστᾶσιν).[65] Augustus, we are told, took a compara-

---

[63]   Josephus, *Ant.* 13.9.1 §257-258, 13.11.3 §318; cf. 13.15.4 §397: Pella in Transjordan was demolished by Alexander Jannaeus because its inhabitants would not embrace the Jewish way of life (τὰ πάτρια τῶν Ἰουδαίων ἔθη).

We should perhaps note in passing a *baraita* attested in *b. Sot.* 33a (cf. *Cant. Rab.* 8:13 §1) to the effect that "Yoḥanan the High Priest" once heard a *bat qôl* come out of the Holy of Holies and say (NB in Aramaic), "The young men who went out to war have gained a victory at Antioch" (נצחו טליא דאזלו לאגחא קרבא לאנטוכיא). This looks like a garbled reference to John Hyrcanus, whom Josephus reports as having heard a voice in the Temple assuring him that his sons had just defeated Antiochus Cyzicenus in battle at Samaria (*Ant.* 13.10.2–3 §275-282).

[64]   Eupolemus quoted in Eusebius, *Praep. Ev.* 9.30.3-4; cf. Fallon 1985, Holladay 1992.

[65]   *J.W.* 1.11.4 §225 (note that in *Ant.* 14.11.4 §280 the assignment is only of Coele-Syria). It may even be worth noting that Herod the Great, though hardly impelled by conservative Jewish regard for the holiness of the Land, seems in his numerous campaigns to have pursued territorial gains throughout the biblical land of Israel, but not outside it. It would be interesting in this regard to debate the status of his campaign in 38 BC to relieve Mark Antony at Samosata in Commagene, in the extreme north-eastern corner of Syria between the Euphrates and the Taurus mountains (Josephus, *Ant.* 14.15.8–9 §439-447; *J.W.* 1.16.7 §321-322). Note, on the

ble view, instructing the procurators of Syria to obtain Herod's approval for all their policies (*Ant.* 15.10.3 §360). After Herod's death, the Romans allotted to various of his Jewish relatives the care of parts of Syria that lay well to the North of what might plausibly be claimed as political Palestine.[66] Finally, we should perhaps at least mention the chronicler Malalas' astonishing tale (10:245) of 30,000 men being despatched from Tiberias under the Jewish Priest Phineas to pillage Antioch in revenge for the anti-Jewish pogrom there in AD 39–40. This account is frequently, and probably rightly, dismissed as straining historical credulity a good deal too far.[67] At the same time, it could be worth just one more thought at least from the geographic perspective: leaving aside the historical improbabilities, an action of this kind might make a certain amount of *ideological* sense if Antioch is regarded as part of the biblical Holy Land.[68]

More interesting still are the Palestinian Targums on the Pentateuch, which, despite their uncertain final date, are widely agreed to reflect a good many popular homiletical traditions of the first and second-century synagogue.[69] Several of these Targumim explicitly envision the border at Antioch, which they identify with the biblical

---

other hand, Herod's many munificent gifts to cities well outside the Land (*J.W.* 1.21.11–12 §422-428); and his expedition to aid Marcus Agrippa's campaign on the Black Sea in 14 BC (*Ant.* 16.2.2 §16-23).

[66]   E.g. *Ant.* 19.8.1 §338: Chalcis was ruled by Herod Agrippa II, who was later given extensive lands to the North and East of Galilee (Batanea, Trachonitis, Gaulanitis and north as far as Abilene: *Ant.* 20.7.1 §138; *J.W.* 2.12.8 §247; cf. *Life* 11 §52). His daughter was given in marriage to king Azizus of Emesa (on the Orontes river), after the latter agreed to be circumcised (*Ant.* 20.7.1 §139); other descendants of Herod were assigned Cetis in Cilicia and even Armenia (*Ant.* 18.5.4 §140).

[67]   So e.g. quite cautiously Schenk 1931: 188-92; followed by Hengel and Schwemer 1997: 184-86 and others.

[68]   Hengel and Schwemer 1997: 432 n. 954 suggest somewhat implausibly that the High Priest in question is Phanni (Phanasus), who was appointed by the zealots at the beginning of the Jewish War (*J.W.* 4.3.8 §155; *Ant.* 20.10.1 §227). It is certainly true that reprisals to relieve Jews in Palestinian and Syrian towns were launched in the early weeks of the war (*J.W.* 2.18.1 §458-460). The main problem with Hengel's identification would seem to be that Josephus specifically refers to Antioch as being (with Apamea and Sidon) one of the only *undisturbed* towns at the beginning of the Revolt (*J.W.* 2.18.5 §479).

[69]   See e.g. Kaufman 1994, 1997; Hayward 1989; Gleßmer 1995.

Lebo-Hamath.[70] Similarly, "Riblah" at Num 34:11 becomes "Daphne," thereby further highlighting the significant standing of Antioch's posh suburb in Palestinian Jewish consciousness. Another piece of evidence in support of this perspective may possibly be present in much later rabbinic references to Pappus and Lulianus, apparently two martyrs of the revolt under Trajan, who were said to have set up banks "from Acco to Antioch" to supply the needs of those immigrating from "the Exile" (גולה לעולי, *Gen. Rab.* 64.10 [on Gen 26:28]), a term typically applied to Babylonia.[71] Since Acco itself was even in the first century arguably part of the Holy Land,[72] and Antioch wealthy enough not to need other people's loans, these are presumably banks set up in aid of those newly arrived in the biblical promised land. One might compare the wealthy Jewish aristocrat mentioned earlier, who arrived in the Land from Babylonia with his large clan and private army and decided to settle in the plain of Syrian Antioch before being induced by Herod to help colonise Transjordan instead.[73] A later midrash envisions that in the messianic age the exiles returning from the Diaspora would burst into song when they reached the top of Mt. Taurus Amanus (*Cant. Rab.* 4:8 §2).

The Rabbis still frequently assume a border at Amanah, a

---

[70] *Frag. Tg.* and *Tg. Neof.* Num. 34:8; *Tg. Ps.-J.* Num. 13:21 ("up to the roads into Antioch," possibly implying that Antioch itself is outside, as Alexander 1974: 183 thinks; or perhaps it is merely an attempt to interpret the phrase לבוא in "Lebo-Hamath"). *Num. Rab.* 10.3 (on Num 6:2) similarly identifies the Hamath of Amos 6:2 (cf. 6:14) as "Hamath of Antioch"; cf. *Lev. Rab.* 5.3 (on Lev 4:3); *Yalqut* to Amos (p. 545). Indeed, as Alexander rightly points out, "The identification of *Hamath* with *Antioch* is standard in early Jewish texts" (1974: 207; cf. *ibid.* pp. 181, 187).

[71] On Pappus and Lulianus see now Horbury 1999, to whom I am indebted. Lulianus is described in *Sifra Behuqqotay* 5.2 on Lev 26:19 as "the Alexandrian" (לוליינוס אלכסנדרי), quite possibly a reference to the Syrian Alexandria (modern Iskenderun, Turkey: cf. Strabo, *Geogr.* 676; Ptolemy 5.14.2), on the coast 40km North of Antioch, across the Syrian Gates (Pass of Beilan) and not far from the entrance to the Cilician plain.

[72] See, however, the doubts expressed in the Amoraic period, e.g. in *y. Šeb.* 6.1, 36c (R. Aḥa b. Jacob); cf. already *m. Giṭ.* 1:2 (R. Judah bar Ilai regards Acco as outside the land for the halakhah of divorce bills, R. Meir as inside the Land).

[73] Note also that Pappus and Lulianus' interest in fostering Jewish return and settlement in the Land may go hand in hand with their being martyred at Laodicea-on-Sea (modern Al-Ladhiqiya in Syria, a little way South of Antioch).

mountain whose sole biblical mention occurs in a list of northern mountains in the Song of Songs (4:8).[74] The precise location of this site is difficult to determine, and has generated a certain amount of debate.[75] Both Targumic and rabbinic sources typically locate it at Mount Amanus just Northwest of Antioch. This is a range that marks the border between Syria and Cilicia and forms a Southern extension of the Taurus mountains,[76] although it has occasionally been suggested that the "Taurus" of the rabbinic phrase "Taurus Amanus" could itself be a part of the Amanus range (perhaps near the pass known as Beilan or the "Syrian Gates").[77] Even Avlas of Cilicia (אוולס דקלקי) is explicitly said to mark the border in several potentially early passages;[78] if this is to be identified with the so-called "Cilician Gates" (Πύλαι Κιλίκιαι) rather than somewhere

---

[74]   See Neubauer 1868: 5-10. See above on *m. Šeb.* 6:1 (cf. 9:2) and *m. Ḥal.* 4:8; also *t. Ḥal.* 2.11; *y. Šeb.* 6.2, 36c; *b. Giṭ.* 8a.

It is an interesting bit of *Wirkungsgeschichte* to note that an early eighteenth-century splinter group of the Württemberg pietist movement emigrated to Iowa in 1842 and founded a community called Amana. Among their various ventures was the Amana Society, whose commercial initiatives later led to the popular Amana brand of refrigerators, cookers and air conditioners (see http://www.amana.com).

[75]   This is due not least to the fact that while Mount Hor marks the *Northern* boundary according to Num 34:7, another mountain of that name is in Num 20:22-28 said to be the site on which Aaron dies, "on the border of the land of *Edom*" (v. 23; cf. Num 33:37-39; Deut 32:50). The fourteenth-century Jewish traveller Estori ha-Parḥi (c. 1282–c. 1357) identified it as *Jebel-el-Akhra* just North of today's Syrian-Turkish border, and barely 20 miles South of Antioch. See Ha-Parchi 1897: chap. 11, ed. Luncz p. 250; cf. Neubauer 1868: 8, although he (mistakenly?) cites chap. 2 of the Berlin edition.

[76]   For the position of Mount Amanus see e.g. Strabo, *Geography* 14.5.18. The same location seems already to be presupposed in the book of *Jubilees* (8:21; 9:4); cf. Alexander 1982: 208. See further Alexander 1974: 204, who also plausibly suggests on the basis of *Exod. Rab.* 23.5 (on Exod 15:1) and *Cant. Rab.* 4:8 §2 that the identification with the biblical Mt. Amanah was based on the similarity of sound. Other texts that locate the Northern border at Mount Amanus include *m. Ḥal.* 4:8; *m. Šeb.* 4:1; *t. Ter.* 2.12; *t. Ḥal.* 2.11; *y. Ḥal.* 4.7, 60a.

[77]   So e.g. Alexander 1974: 205, following Honigman. See also n. 79 below.

[78] *Tg. Ps.-J., Neof.* and *Frag. Tg.* on Num 34:8; contrast *t. Šeb.* 4.11 (where Avlas appears to be nearer Galilee). Josephus suggests that the area from "Amanus and Taurus" outward is inhabited by the sons of Japheth (*Ant.* 1.6.1 §122) and Ham (1.6.2 §130), thus suggesting that Mount Amanus is regarded as a significant boundary for Shem as well.

nearer the pass of Beilan,[79] the ideal Land of Israel might on that reckoning be thought to include even the Cilician plain and with it, for example, the city of Tarsus. It is worth noting that during Paul's lifetime this area did in fact form an integral part of the integrated Roman province of Syria, and became incorporated into the new province of Cilicia only under Vespasian in AD 72; a province of "Syria and Cilicia" is probably presupposed in Gal 1:21 and Acts 15:23, 41.[80]

On the whole, however, rabbinic literature tends to greater ambiguity and caution in its definition of the Land.[81] Judaism may well have tended to a more pragmatic view after the catastrophic wars against Rome, being chastened by the need to recognise that the true dimensions of the land of the Jews were in reality and for the foreseeable future always going to remain very much smaller. A similar tendency towards greater realism may be in evidence in Josephus: his apparently more modest contemporary estimation of the Land not only suits his apologetic purpose but coincides with what may have been a late first-century rabbinic shift of perspective, as we shall see in a moment.[82] Such a note of political pragmatism, at

---

[79]   See e.g. Jastrow *s.v.* אבלס (p. 7); Treidler 1975: 287-88. McNamara 1995: 10-11 leaves the matter wide open: the Avlas de-Qilqi is either the pass of Beilan at the Syrian Gates (as Alexander 1974: 208 supposes), or the plain of Cilicia beyond that pass, or even the narrow stretch of sea between Cyprus and Cilicia known as the "Cilician trench [αὐλών]" in Pliny, *Nat. Hist.* 5.130 (cf. similarly Neubauer 1868: 431 n. 4). See also Josephus, *Ant.* 13.15.4 §397: if Κιλίκων αὐλών in that passage is not a mistake, there may have been a similarly named city in Transjordan (but Alexander 1974: 208 not implausibly follows Schalit in emending to Ἀλυκὸς αὐλών, i.e. "Valley of Salt").

[80]   See Bing 1992: 1024; Hemer 1989: 172, 179; Riesner 1994: 236. Note especially the evidence of Codex Sinaiticus in all three passages, which presupposes a province called Συρία καὶ Κιλικία (in Acts 15:41 this is also supported, *inter alia*, by Alexandrinus and the Majority Text).

[81]   Neubauer 1868: 6 writes, "Quelques rabbins veulent que les frontières de la Palestine indiquées dans la Bible, soient considerées comme frontières réelles, quand il s'agit de l'exercice des devoirs religieux; d'autres restreignent beaucoup plus la signification de 'Terre d'Israél'." What he fails to identify is the apparent change in the prevailing opinion during the early Tannaitic period.

[82]   Josephus foregoes a detailed description of the Land, and appears to skip Numbers 33–36 from his running account of the wilderness events in *Ant.* 4.7.3 §171-172. Although he relates that the Hebrew spies explored the land of Canaan all the way North to Hamath, in keeping with Num 13:21, he assigns no contempo-

any rate, would make sense of the fact that later texts (and e.g. the Babylonian Targum Onkelos) usually restrict the size of the Land to more realistic dimensions.[83] Later *halakhot* more commonly assume that Antioch and Syria are outside the Land.[84]

Without undue reliance on precise rabbinic attributions, for our purposes it is worth thinking seriously about the Mishnah's explicit suggestion that around the end of the first century the official halakhic treatment of Syria and Antioch changed from an original "Greater Israel" position to a more realistic estimation of the Holy Land. Mishnah *Hallah* 4:7-8 records a discussion between two famous rabbis of the second Tannaitic generation, Rabban Gamaliel II and Rabbi Eliezer. The latter affirms that Syrian land bought from Gentiles must be treated like Eretz Israel for the purposes of both tithes and the Sabbath year law, while Rabban Gamaliel disagrees and proposes instead a three-zone rule that identifies the Northern limits of the Land at Kezib (= Akhzib), just South of today's border with Lebanon at Rosh ha-Nikra, a line that is explicitly justified in the light of post-exilic realities.[85] Syria on this view is an ambiguous

---

rary name to this place (but see *Ant.* 1.6.2 §138: Hamath = Epiphaneia, in N. Syria). Weinfeld 1993: 214-16 notes a shift in Josephus towards cities and the Temple on the one hand, and a spiritualisation of Land theology on the other.

[83] Even *Tg. Ps.-J.* Numbers 34 shows signs of such redaction, as Neubauer 1868: 430 already noted; cf. further Alexander 1974: 207 and McNamara and Clarke 1995 *ad loc.* Several of the more outlying areas are moved nearer to the land: Tiberias, for example, takes the place of Antioch in v. 8 and a line nearer Damascus is envisioned in v. 10.

[84] So explicitly *b. Git.* 44b (cf. Neubauer 1868: 8-9); and note e.g. the differing halakhah for the sale of slaves (*y. Git.* 4.6, 46a), divorce certificates (*m. Git.* 1:2, Rabbi Judah bar Ilai (mid-second cent.): even Acco and Ashkelon count as outside the Land), and the fruit of young trees (*m. ʿOr.* 3:9: doubtful ʿOrla-fruit is forbidden in Eretz Israel but permitted in Syria).

Note also the tradition (e.g. in *y. Šeqal.* 6.2, 50a; *y. Sanh.* 10.7, 29c) of an exile at Daphne = Riblah, associated with the story of 2 Kgs 25:6 and Jer 39:5; 52:10-30.

[85] *Sipre Deut.* §51 (on Deut 11:24); cf. e.g. *t. Šeb.* 4.6, 11; *t. Hal.* 2.6; *y. Dem.* 2.1, 22d; *y. Šeb.* 6.2, 36c; so also the Rehov Inscription, line 13. See Sussmann 1981: 152 and cf. Safrai 1983: 209; Neusner 1973: 2.176-77 rates the attribution to Eliezer as merely "fair" tradition. Note further the comparable dispute between the third-generation Tannaite R. Yose (b. Halafta) and R. Eleazar b. Yose on whether the biblical boundaries are reckoned to belong to the Land: the former denies and the latter affirms this (*t. Maʿaś. Š.* 2.15). Elsewhere, R. Eleazar b. Yose is similarly credited with the view that the territories on the boundaries of the Land are equivalent to Eretz Israel (*t. B. Qam.* 8.19). In the Amoraic period it may be

halakhic zone between the Diaspora and the land of Israel proper.[86] The Mishnah laconically notes that after a period of compromise Rabban Gamaliel's view eventually prevailed. It is certainly confirmed in a famous *baraita* also found in the inscription from the synagogue at Reḥov in Galilee.[87] Even in these more pragmatic texts, of course, the halakhah for the Sabbath year and dough offerings still recognises at least an ambiguous zone from Akhzib to the Euphrates and Amanah, which is not actually treated as Diaspora. The more modest perspective is evidently a counsel of practical expediency rather than a clear change of principle.[88] In the same context of tractate *Ḥallah*, we find the statement that at the time of the Temple the offering of first fruits brought by one Ariston from Apamea was accepted on the principle that "he who owns land in Syria is like one who owns land in the outskirts of Jerusalem."[89] Even under the

worth comparing the somewhat different dispute in *y. Dem.* 2.1, 22c between R. Eleazar (b. Pedat) and R. Yoḥanan (b. Nappaḥa), as to whether the majority even of the more modestly defined *Eretz Israel* is in the hand of Israelites or in the hand of Gentiles.

[86]   Cf. similarly *m. Šeb.* 6:1; *m. Dem.* 1:3; see also *m. Šeqal.* 3:4 on the halakhah for *terumah* and *m. ʿAbod. Zar.* 1:8 for the lease or sale of land to Gentiles.

[87]   See Sussmann 1981; Stemberger 1996: 37 and the references cited in n. 85 above. Note, however, that the inscription (like its rabbinic parallels) lists "doubtful cities" in the regions of Tyre, Naveh and Transjordan—suggesting that there were cities in these regions that for purposes of the Sabbath year halakhah counted as part of the Land.

[88]   Similarly, it is worth noting R. Yoḥanan's rejection in *y. Sanh.* 3.2, 21a of the idea that the law court in Tiberias has a higher authority than that in Antioch. Cf. further the definition offered by Safrai 1983: 209: "The Land of Israel was defined as the land upon which Israel lived in the context of its being the Promised Land, free of idolatry, not worked on the Sabbath or the Sabbatical Year."

[89]   *M. Ḥal.* 4:11; cf. *b. Giṭ.* 8a; contrast *m. Ḥal.* 4:10 on Alexandria. An ossuary discovered in the Kidron valley in 1990 mentions one Ariston of Apamea (ארסטון אפמי), apparently a proselyte also called Judah (יהודה הגיור), who had moved to Jerusalem (see Ilan 1992: 150-55). Ilan remains cautious on the identification of this man with the one in the Mishnah passage; but the possibility is certainly not remote. "Apamea" also features in *Tg. Ps.-J.* Num 34:10. I remain unpersuaded of Alexander's argument (1974: 212-13; cf. p. 215) that Paneas/ Caesarea Philippi is meant here: "Paneas" is separately mentioned in v. 11 as being further South. Commenting on Ezekiel 47, Jerome separately attests this tradition (Alexander 1974: 217 calls it a "mis-reading") of the border at *Syrian* Apamea; see n. 92 below.

developed three-zone model, for example, the mid-second-century rabbis of the Mishnah agree that one may not sell land to Gentiles either in Palestine or in Syria (*m. ᶜAbod. Zar.* 1:8).[90]

Thus, although no systematic view emerges, we may say that one important perspective in the earlier rabbinic sources is reflected in the Tosefta's bald assertion that "everything from the Taurus Amanus downwards is the land of Israel."[91] And for all the halakhic moderation of Rabban Gamaliel and the "official" Talmudic line, Jerome informs us that (some) Palestinian Jews still held this view around the year 400.[92]

This notion of Antioch as part of the Holy Land of course sounds quite preposterously remote from what one would normally regard as Jewish Palestine—which is perhaps why New Testament scholars seem not to have seriously considered such a possibility.[93] Mental maps, however, usually speak more eloquently about people's true perceptions than political ones. (I was disturbed when I first came to Britain to discover that Vancouver, once at the centre of my world maps and worldview, is at the very end of the world on British maps.) At a time of heightened messianic expectations for the restoration of the city and the land, it is not unreasonable to suspect that the utopian dimensions of the biblical promises would once again come alive in the hopes of observant Jews, just as they had previously done at the time of Ezekiel.[94]

---

90   R. Aqiba is similarly reported as saying that in Syria Jews may not sow, plow or weed during the Sabbath year (*t. Šeb.* 4.12); and even R. Gamaliel II required only one batch of dough offering in Syria as in Palestine (*t. Ḥal.* 2.5). Cf. further Safrai 1983: 210-11; and note the Reḥov synagogue inscription cited above. Cf. also *m. Yad.* 4:3 on Egypt, Babylon, Ammon and Moab as clearly *outside* the Land and subject to quite different halakhic rules. On the general issue, note further Safrai 1983: 207-209 and *passim*; also Weinfeld 1983 on Transjordan.

91   See e.g. *t. Ḥal.* 2.11; *y. Šeb.* 6.2, 36c; *b. Giṭ.* 8a.

92   Jerome, *Comm. on Ezek* 47:15-17 (CCL 75.721); *Quaest. in Gen.* 10:18 (CCL 72.14). A well-attested variant of Num 34:11 in the Vulgate places Riblah *contra fontem daphnim*, "opposite the spring of Daphnis." Cf. Alexander 1974: 216; McNamara 1995: 9-10.

93   Thus, among recent authors, even the opposing positions of Esler 1998: 106, Sanders 1990b: 172; Tomson 1990: 228-29; Bauckham 1995: 423 etc. all assume that Antioch is outside the Land.

94   On the ideological function of such utopian texts within the Old Testament, see also Kallai 1983: 76-79; Smend 1983: 96-99 and *passim*; Weinfeld 1993: 52-75, 99-120.

Quite plausibly, therefore, many first-century Palestinian Jews regarded Antioch as the gateway from the Exile to the Holy Land, and thus fraught with a considerable symbolic significance. For religious Jews concerned about the redemption of the Twelve Tribes, Antioch's status as a large metropolis inside the biblical Promised Land might well carry special halakhic sensitivities.

FOUR THESES ON JAMES THE JUST AND ANTIOCH

With the foregoing observations in mind, I wish to propose four brief but controversial theses for discussion, in the hope that debate on these may help to narrow down the interpretative options regarding James' intervention. My starting point will be an attempt to take both Acts and Galatians more or less at face value in light of what has been said so far, acknowledging tensions and contradictions wherever necessary but without resorting either to grand harmonies or to grand polarities and conflict theories. It will also be useful to bear in mind that our main interest here is confined to James rather than Paul or Peter; the latter would require separate studies.

1. The Mission from James is solely addressed to Jews and not to Gentiles; it must be carefully distinguished from Jewish and Judaizing opposition to Paul.

The phenomenon of Jewish embassies and letters of instruction from Palestine is well established and may on the Christian side be represented in the Epistles of James and Jude, as well as in several stories in Acts.[95] In keeping with this tradition, the Jacobean mission probably came in the form of a reasoned request for solidarity rather than an authoritative demand for compliance.[96] Paul's report, along with the evidence of comparable Jewish embassies from

---

[95] Just as Rabban Gamaliel wrote to the Jewish communities in the South, in upper and lower Galilee and in Babylonia, so James arguably writes to the "Twelve Tribes in the Diaspora" in the New Testament Epistle that bears his name. (Similarly, the address of 1 Peter may conceivably denote Christians in those areas of "the Diaspora" that lie just beyond the ideal boundaries of the Promised Land.) See *t. Sanh.* 2.6; *b. Sanh.* 11a, etc. and cf. recently Niebuhr 1998; Taatz 1991; Bauckham 1995: 423-25. In the third and fourth centuries there seems to be considerable evidence of authoritative instructions to the Diaspora being sent by the Patriarch of Palestine in Tiberias: see Feldman 1993: 71-72 and note Libanius' letter to Priscianus (LCL No. 131) in AD 364.

[96] *Pace* N. Taylor 1992: 129-30.

Jerusalem, makes it likely that James' intervention will have been in the form of an earnest appeal.

All the evidence, therefore, suggests that the "men from James" (Gal 2:12: τινας ἀπὸ 'Ιακώβου) genuinely represented him and were not pretenders or impostors. More importantly, they and their mission must be carefully distinguished from Paul's opponents in Galatia and elsewhere, including in Galatians the false brethren (2:4: ψευδαδελφοί; cf. 2 Cor 11:26), the agitator (5:10: ὁ ταράσσων), the troublemakers (5:12: οἱ ἀναστατοῦντες) and those who fear Jewish persecution and therefore undergo and promote circumcision (6:12-13; note οἱ περιτεμνόμενοι). The same is true *a fortiori* for the super-apostles of 2 Corinthians (11:5-13: ὑπερλίαν ἀπόστολοι; cf. 12:11). In all these cases, the Pauline opponents are people who make a direct approach to *Gentiles* in order to persuade them to be circumcised. In none of them is there any mention of table fellowship or of the name of James.[97] The opponents and agitators are far more likely related to the unauthorised Jerusalem Christians mentioned even in the Apostolic Decree of Acts 15:24 (cf. 15:1-2): they are people "whom we did not send," but who have gone out among the Gentile Christians and "said things to disturb you and unsettle your minds."[98]

By contrast, the men from James address themselves solely to Jewish Christians; and this would of course be the only appropriate stance in keeping with the Jerusalem agreement as reported in Gal 2:7-9. James appeals to the constituency for which he feels responsible, and on a topic of particular relevance to Jewish life in the Holy Land. (See also below.) His emissaries therefore cannot be Judaizers,

---

[97]   So also Pratscher 1987: 71-72. In this regard it is perhaps worth noting once again the old chestnut of F. C. Baur (followed by W. Lütgert, W. Schmithals and others), who supposed that the "Christ party" at Corinth (1 Cor 1:12) were those who stressed close links with the original followers of Jesus at Jerusalem. There is no evidence for this position in the context; if it were true, we would certainly expect ἐγὼ δὲ 'Ιησοῦ. The case against this view is well summarised in Schrage 1991: 146-48, who more plausibly suspects a case of Pauline irony.

[98]   Barrett 1998: 741 hangs on to the view that these people were men genuinely commissioned, who nevertheless "may have gone beyond their brief." More likely, given what both Luke and Paul actually do say about James in Acts 15, Galatians 2 and elsewhere, is that they were people who were precisely *not* charged by James but nevertheless claimed to address the Gentiles as official spokesmen of the Jerusalem church. The difference is subtle but important.

as is still often presupposed.[99]

Correspondingly, James' embassy did not oppose the Gentile mission. Nothing indicates that James made any effort to renege on the Jerusalem agreement (Gal 2:9) to recognise a separate mission to the Gentiles. Nor was his intervention in any sense designed to promote the circumcision of Gentiles. There is no evidence from Galatians, Acts or any New Testament texts that James advocated this. Indeed it is worth noting that even the Apostolic Decree actually presupposes the *rejection* of any idea that Gentiles must be circumcised; it is logically impossible to affirm both the Decree and Gentile circumcision at the same time. Even in Galatians, this bitterest and most polemical of his letters, it is not James whom Paul accuses of "forcing Gentiles to Judaize," but Peter: Paul's main complaint is not that James advocates separate Jewish and Gentile Christian communities, but that Peter first accepts and then rejects table fellowship.

Another important corollary, therefore, is that despite frequent assertions to the contrary, the mission from James was not in any straightforward sense about food or about Gentile carelessness in matters of purity or idolatry. Had the problem been merely the purity of the food consumed at common meals, this could have been easily rectified. We should in that case have expected a conditional or partial withdrawal from commensality, such as making it dependent on Gentile compliance with principles of the kind enunciated in the Apostolic Decree. What we find instead is a complete withdrawal by the entire Jewish membership of the church at Antioch, with the exception of Paul. The decision appears to be to reject not certain kinds of food but any and all commensality *per se*. The problem, in other words, was not the food but the company.[100] This we saw above to be a fairly hard-line stance, which would not perhaps have been widely held outside the Jewish heartland.

This in turn means that the request from James did *not* concern anything like an imposition of the Apostolic Decree.[101] Indeed it is best interpreted without reference to that document. The "Decree" enunciates widely agreed Jewish principles for Gentile behaviour, which almost certainly represent common ground between Paul and

---

[99] So rightly Pratscher 1987: 81 and n. 132, with documentation.

[100] Cf. Bernheim 1997: 177.

[101] *Contra* Catchpole 1977: 442 and many others.

Peter.[102] Regardless of that particular point, however, these principles are clearly irrelevant to the problem as it presents itself in Antioch. Neither the Jacobean mission nor the Apostolic Decree is fundamentally about food; but the former is concerned about *Jewish* behaviour and the latter about *Gentile* behaviour.[103] (Galatians 2 in fact does not even claim that James' intervention explicitly opposed table fellowship, but rather that this was what the Antiochene church concluded.) In any case, Paul in Galatians 2 does not object to anything remotely relevant to the principles enunciated in the Decree. What is more, he himself goes on just a few years later to offer explicit support to the idea that Jewish-Gentile meal fellowship must allow Jewish believers to abstain from meat or wine (Rom 14:1–15:6).[104]

2. James' motivation was in part political.

It remains unclear whether James' concerns about the church at Antioch were primarily political or primarily religious. Most likely both elements were present, and closely interrelated. There is in any case enough evidence of *political* pressure on the Jerusalem church to suggest that the politically motivated plea for solidarity must have been at least part of the reason for James' embassy to Antioch.[105] This was a measure not so much of cowardice but of *realpolitik* in the Jerusalem of the 40s. Just as the wording of Mark 13 may well reflect something of the Jerusalemite alarm at Caligula's intended abomination of desolation in the Temple,[106] so we may assume that in the aftermath of that assault and in the subsequent pro-establishment persecution under Agrippa the Jerusalem church survived only because of its visible support for the Jewish national institutions.

Luke deliberately parallels the 'trials' of Jesus and of Stephen, and implies that Stephen's execution and the subsequent persecution of his followers were due to his radical critique of the Temple in explicit appeal to Jesus. These events could have occurred in the mid-30s,

---

[102] Cf. e.g. Dunn 1993: 124; Bockmuehl 1995; also Borgen 1988.

[103] Cf. Bauckham 1995: 438, 462.

[104] See also n. 37 above. Cf. Wehnert 1997: 139-41, 271, who offers the suggestive, but in my view ultimately unpersuasive, argument that Paul later changed his mind on the Apostolic Decree.

[105] So e.g. Jewett 1971; Pratscher 1987: 85; Dunn 1983: 183-86; Hengel and Schwemer 1997: 255-45 and *passim*.

[106] See Theissen 1992: 151-65.

while Caiaphas was still in office, as the *Pseudo-Clementine Recognitions* suppose (e.g. 1:71).[107] Although the Twelve survived that persecution, it may well be that in the aftermath of Caligula the nationalist hand had been strengthened by a sympathetic Agrippa to the point where the position of the original disciples had become untenable. As the closest followers of a man associated with threats against the Temple, they were obvious targets for persecution: James the son of Zebedee was killed in this context, and the popularity of that measure encouraged Agrippa to turn his attention next to Peter (Acts 12:2-4). Peter escaped, but had to leave the city and arrived before long in Antioch.

Writing to Thessalonica in AD 50 (1 Thess 2:14-17), Paul shows himself aware of recent persecutions of the Palestinian Jewish church, which he explicitly sets in parallel to the opposition suffered by Jesus. In addition to the events of AD 43–44, it is worth noting the remarkably precise suggestion in Malalas (10:247) to the effect that a further significant Jewish persecution of the apostles and their followers took place in AD 48 ("in the eighth year of Claudius"), i.e. during the time of Ventidius Cumanus' bloody tenure as procurator (AD 48–52).[108] While the nature of the evidence makes confirmation of this suggestion impossible, very recent persecution of this kind is certainly plausible and would lend a vivid colour to the proceedings at Antioch.[109] Galatians 6:12 may be another case in point, with its apparent background of Jewish persecution "for the cross of Christ." This would be all the more significant if, as on balance I think likely, Galatians must be dated considerably earlier than the usual assumption of AD 54 or 57, quite possibly in the near aftermath of the Antioch incident itself.[110]

---

[107] Some have supposed the possibility of High Priestly action during the interregnum after Pilate's deposition in AD 36, comparable to the execution of James the Just under Annas the son of Annas (*Ant.* 20.9.1 §200-203). See also the discussion in Riesner 1994: 52-56.

[108] *Ant.* 20.5.2–6.3 §103-136; *J.W.* 2.12.1-7 §223-245. Hengel and Schwemer 1997: 241 point out that AD 48–49 was probably a Sabbath year, which would have accentuated the famine and added to public tensions.

[109] For a positive estimation of Malalas' note see Riesner 1994: 175; cf. Schenk 1931: 200-201.

[110] Paul's angry account suggests that his memory of these events is still quite vivid; his reproachful description of Peter here contrasts notably with the far more respectful picture in 1 Corinthians. Paul also seems to look back on the foundation

It is also important to bear in mind that the Jerusalem church may have been concerned about the mobility of their enemies: just as the accusations of Paul's adversaries followed him from the Diaspora all the way to Jerusalem (e.g. Acts 21:21, 27-28), so also scandalous reports about practices in the Antiochene church could easily travel to Jerusalem and be used against a church under persecution there.

All this makes highly plausible an appeal to Christians in Antioch for an exercise of consideration and solidarity in their possibly fairly recent[111] practice of freely associating with uncircumcised Gentiles. It also lends dramatic definition to Paul's statements about those, including Peter, who manifest "fear of the circumcision" (Gal 2:12; cf. 6:12). Far from being a fear of the authority of James,[112] this may well be motivated by the concrete circumstances in Judaea and Jerusalem of the 40s and 50s, where only a thoroughly Jewish mission could hope to be tolerated. In these circumstances, any politically defensible integration of Gentiles, especially within the biblical Land, might only be possible by "requiring them to live as Jews" (cf. Gal 2:14: τὰ ἔθνη ἀναγκάζεις Ἰουδαΐζειν)—a point of view to which James appeals, and to which Peter gives way.

3. James' religious motivation can be construed in light of the teaching of Jesus.

In trying to fathom James' possible reservations about an integrated church of Jews and Gentiles, it is relevant to bear in mind Jesus' own apparent avoidance of Gentiles and Gentile cities in Galilee, as well as his pre-Easter command to the disciples to go nowhere "among the Gentiles" (Matt 10:5). This prohibition is evidently

---

of the (South) Galatian churches in AD 47-48 as relatively recent: he declares himself astonished that the Galatians have "so quickly" deserted the gospel (1:6) at a time when they should still have in mind the visual image of the apostle's demonstration of Christ (3:1). The reference to the beginning of his mission to Galatia at 4:13 (τὸ πρότερον) cannot be taken as evidence that Paul had visited more than once. The apparent de-emphasis of Galatians on Israel's salvation history and covenantal theology, much noted in recent scholarship (see e.g. Longenecker 1998: 5-23, 174-79), may well have suited the polemical context in which Paul found himself having to justify his Gentile mission apart from Jerusalem and Antioch. Even if this were true for Galatians, however, Romans shows that, upon calmer reflection, Paul's reaction did not last.

[111] Dunn 1993: 117, citing Burton, suggests that the freer meal fellowship may itself be the result of the Jerusalem council.

[112] So again recently Painter 1997: 69.

ethnic rather than geographic in intent. Jesus himself is depicted as happily travelling to the region of Tyre and Sidon (where he stayed in a [presumably Jewish] house; Mark 7:24), to Gaulanitis, the Decapolis and Samaria, all of which represent part of the idealised dimensions of the biblical Holy Land as assigned to the nine-and-a-half lost tribes. In describing the disciples who came to follow Jesus, the gospel tradition characterises the new people as representing all parts of the biblical land of Israel: "a great multitude from Galilee followed; also from Judaea and Jerusalem and Idumaea and from beyond the Jordan and from about Tyre and Sidon a great multitude, hearing all that he did, came to him" (Mark 3:7-8). The drastic and surprising nature of Jesus' stance is particularly well illustrated in Matthew by his response to the Syro-Phoenician woman who comes to him well inside the Roman province of Syria, only to be told, "I was sent only to the lost sheep of the house of Israel" (Matt 15:24).[113]

This geographic dimension of his mission to the lost sheep of the house of Israel may well form an important corollary to Jesus' obvious programmatic interest in the Twelve Phylarchs and the Twelve Tribes.[114] As Sanders and others have shown,[115] Jesus' ministry can be properly understood as a Jewish restoration movement; the restoration of the twelve tribes was widely expected to be part of the eschatological work of Elijah or the Messiah; according to the *Psalms of Solomon*, for example, God would in the messianic period gather his people "and divide them according to the tribes on the land."[116] The appointment of the twelve disciples deliberately reflects this notion of a restoration of all Israel: they are the ones who "will sit on twelve thrones, judging the twelve tribes of Israel" (Matt 19:28 par. Luke 22:30). Their mission appears in part to be territorially defined: they will not have gone through all the

---

[113] All this would seem to suggest the need for a more differentiated reading of the evidence than that offered by Davies 1974: 336-65. It could be worth speculating whether the theme of baptism in the Jordan might for John have had connotations of the second Exodus (as perhaps it later did for Theudas: *Ant.* 20.5.1 §97-99), whereas Jesus' ministry focused on the arrival of the Kingdom in the Land itself.

[114] See Horbury 1986.

[115] See Sanders 1985, 1993.

[116] *Pss. Sol.* 17:28-31, 50; cf. e.g. Sir 36:11; 48:10 (Elijah); 4 Ezra 13:39-40 (Messiah); 1QM 2:1-3; and of course passages like Ezek 47:13; Isa 49:6. See further documentation in Horbury 1986; Sanders 1985: 95-98.

towns of Israel before the Son of Man comes (Matt 10:23).[117] Both
Matthew and Luke offer tantalisingly brief but explicit glimpses of
an interest in the land of the Northern tribes, where Jesus lives and
travels;[118] and in a potentially anti-zealot logion of Matthean
redaction we find that it is the humble who will "inherit the Land"
(Matt 5:5).

James' rise to power had coincided with the disappearance of the
Apostles from Jerusalem. Although listed in the early tradition of 1
Corinthians 15 as an original witness of the resurrection, James
became prominent just at the same time as the apostolic power base
in Jerusalem was eroded by persecution. In particular, it seems clear
that the three years from the death of Caligula in 41 to the death of
Agrippa in 44 brought about a sustained persecution of the original
Apostles, including the execution of James the son of Zebedee and
the removal of Peter from Jerusalem (Acts 12:1-17). This in turn
apparently precipitated a major shift in the leadership of the
Jerusalem church, as a result of which it appears that the "Twelve"
gave way to the "Pillars" and to James and the Elders as the central
authority.[119] Peter and John clearly still belonged to the "Pillars" at
the time of the Antioch incident, though not, it seems, for very much
longer:[120] significantly, James appears together with Peter and John
in Gal 2:7-9, but by himself in 2:12. Peter's arrival in Antioch in Gal
2:11 will mark the end of his leadership in Jerusalem, probably in
AD 43 or 44.[121] James and those who remained were faithful to the

---

[117] In this respect one may also with to reconsider Jesus' recruitment of Simon
the Zealot (and possibly Judas Iscariot along similar lines?), as one who might well
be sympathetic to a land-based restoration theology. Another influence on Jesus
may be the potential Land symbolism implied in his baptism in the Jordan.

[118] Jesus' home is in the "land of Israel" (Matt 2:20-21: γῆ Ἰσραήλ), and his
ministry is in the land of Zebulon and Naphtali (Matt 4:13-15: γῆ Ζαβουλὼν καὶ γῆ
Νεφθαλίμ). The Lukan infancy narrative appears to assign importance to Anna's
belonging to the tribe of Asher (see recently Bauckham 1997, although he suspects
a connection more specifically with the Median Diaspora).

[119] So also Pratscher 1987: 68; Bauckham 1995: 427ff.; Hengel and Schwemer
1998: 244-45.

[120] Hengel and Schwemer 1998: 244-45, 253 and nn. 1266, 1327 point out
that the Apostles are mentioned for the last time in relation to the Decree: Acts 15:2,
4, 6, 22-23; 16:4.

[121] Cf. Bauckham 1995: 440-41: ". . . the persecution of Agrippa I (AD 43 or
44) was the point at which the Twelve ceased to be the leadership of the Jerusalem
church."

vision of national redemption in Jerusalem; Hegesippus describes James as a Nazirite who prayed continually in the Temple to ask forgiveness for the people (Eusebius, *Eccl. Hist.* 2.23.5-7).

James' request, or at least the Antioch church's reception of his request, may be usefully understood in the light of this emphasis in the ministry of Jesus, and against a geographic background in which Antioch was seen as part of the Promised Land. The Messiah's ministry was understood to be carried out for the Twelve Tribes of Israel by the twelve Phylarchs.[122] And the new mission to the Gentiles should not be conducted in such a way as to compromise Jesus' mission to Israel—a point that could carry particular weight within the Scriptural borders of the Twelve Tribes. The mission to the house of Israel in the Land of Israel is a matter that the Jerusalem agreement had left firmly within the jurisdiction of the Pillars (Gal 2:9). This might also explain why James intervenes in Antioch but not, for example, in Alexandria, Corinth or Rome.

Two additional corollaries are worth noting. First, despite our earlier remarks it is interesting to observe the geographic dimension even of the Apostolic Decree, which fits squarely with this view of affairs in Jerusalem. As reported in Acts 15, this document is addressed in the first instance to *Gentile* believers "in Antioch, Syria, and Cilicia"—areas which on the argument here presented are either part of the ideal Holy Land or at any rate immediately contiguous with it.[123] This certainly confirms that the Decree cannot have been the subject of the mission from James. At the same time, however, it is highly significant that the stipulations of the decree are taken precisely from those passages of the Pentateuch that legislate for Gentiles living in the land of Israel. Richard Bauckham has effectively demonstrated that the prohibitions of the decree are precisely those that in Leviticus 17–18 apply to *Gentiles* living "in the midst of" (בתוך) the house of Israel.[124]

And secondly, it could be that Paul understood his task in no less geographic terms than did James. Even the pre-Christian Paul's

---

[122] Cf. Horbury 1986; Bauckham 1995: 423.

[123] Note, however, that Paul and Barnabas are depicted in Acts 16:1-4 as taking the decree beyond Cilia into Galatia: to Derbe, Lystra and Iconium. In 21:25 James evidently assumes that the Decree applies to *all* Gentile believers.

[124] Bauckham 1995: 459-61; see also the Targumic background as highlighted by Wehnert 1997: 219-38, and cf. Bockmuehl 1995.

intervention in Damascus may be subject, *ceteris imparibus*, to comparable reasoning about the Land. Both cities were just inside the Scriptural *Eretz Israel*, as is reasonably clear also from the status of Damascus in the Dead Sea Scrolls.[125] For a self-declared nationalist ("zealot," indeed) like Saul of Tarsus,[126] the integrity of polity and practice was essential if observant Jewish life in the Land was not to be compromised. Outside the Land, practices like the Sabbath year, tithes or purity were possible at best in a very partial manner: Jews arriving in the Land from abroad, for example, were by definition unclean just as Gentile land was unclean.[127] Within the Land, however, a life by the Biblical purity laws was feasible and appropriate caution could be exercised. James and Saul of Tarsus had very different methods and reasons for their intervention in the Jewish Christian communities in Antioch and Damascus; but both were arguably motivated by their concern for national redemption.

Despite brief mentions in Acts 15:41 and Gal 1:21 we have no reason to think that Paul ever regarded any areas of Palestine, Syria or Cilicia to be specifically his mission field. He seems to found no churches there; and despite his claim in Rom 15:19 to have begun his ministry "from Jerusalem," there is little or no evidence of extended activity in these regions. Apart from Antioch, Paul shows remarkably little interest in the churches in any of the other Gentile cities in the Land of Israel.[128] At the same time, as Rainer Riesner has recently argued, it may be that Paul operated with a geographical understanding of the Gentile world that derived from the prophecy of Isa 66:19, interpreted to denote a Gentile mission field beginning with Tarsus and arching from there via Asia Minor through the

---

125 "The land of Damascus" is outside "the land of Judah" but is not obviously in "exile" or outside Israel. See e.g. CD 6:5 par. 4QD^a 3 ii 20-21; 4QD^d 2:12.

126 See Phil 3:5-6; Gal 1:13-14; cf. Rom 10:2. The "zealot" dimension of the pre-Christian Paul is explored e.g. in J. Taylor 1998; cf. Hengel 1991: 69-71 and *passim*.

127 Cf. e.g. Safrai 1983: 206-207; Klawans 1995; Tomson 1990: 228-29 following G. Alon.

128 Note Acts 16:1 (Syria and Cilicia); 18:22 (Caesarea), 21:3-9 (Tyre, Acco, Caesarea), though these all seem to be passing visits to churches Paul did not found. It could be worth speculating if this is why Paul's letters to Asia Minor, Greece and Rome remain silent about the Decree, without contradicting its substance.

Greek islands to Spain (הָאִיִּים הָרְחֹקִים: "the distant islands").[129]

4. The differences between James and Paul were primarily halakhic rather than theological, and had been exacerbated by the Jerusalem Council.

Nothing in Luke or Paul suggests that James had fundamental theological or soteriological disagreements with Paul, or that his mission was anti-Pauline in intent. Indeed, Paul's rebuke of Peter in Gal 2:14-21(?) stresses common ground far more than differences. It would admittedly be worth re-examining James 2 in this connection, but its polemics can best be understood as addressing the way in which an Antiochene or Pauline type of soteriology had been abused in certain circles.

At the same time, there were clearly genuine halakhic differences between James and Paul. While the influence of Jesus may be primary, I would venture the suggestion that James is closer to a number of positions attributed to R. Eliezer ben Hyrcanus, both about the halakhah of *Eretz Israel* and about the extent to which one could trust Gentiles not to commit idolatry.[130] If James did regard Antioch as part of the Land, issues of purity would matter more literally there than in the Diaspora, where purity concerns were difficult to enforce consistently.[131] Although Gentiles might not attract impurity in relation to the biblical laws about food or corpse impurity,[132] they and their land were regarded as effectively impure by virtue of being tainted with idolatry and the associated

---

[129] Riesner 1994: 213-25. See also Scott 1995: 151-59 and *passim* on the influence of Genesis 10 in defining Paul's view of his mission field; he is one of the few scholars to recognise that a potential dispute over the boundaries of the Land might be involved, although he does not explore this further (note pp. 158-59). Others have in the past proposed a straightforwardly territorial interpretation of the Jerusalem agreement, but this is rightly dismissed in Murphy-O'Connor 1996: 142-43. On Spain as the end of the world, see Neubauer 1868: 417.

[130] In this connection it is interesting to note the rabbinic tradition of R. Eliezer's conversation with Jacob of Kefar Sikhnin about a logion of Jesus, in *t. Ḥul.* 2.24.

[131] Cf. Safrai 1983: 207: "Full Jewish life can only be practiced in Israel, not only because of the precepts which could only be fulfilled there, but because those who dwell in foreign lands live in perpetual defilement, with no possibility of acheiving [*sic*] purification."

[132] Cf. Klawans 1995.

immorality.[133] By contrast, the churches of Antioch and the Pauline mission presumed the intention of Gentiles to be free from idolatry unless expressly stated otherwise. Even Paul, of course, instructs his churches not to eat with Christian idolaters (1 Cor 5:11: συνεσθίειν) or to consume meat in cases where the supplier's idolatrous intention is explicit (1 Cor 10:28-29[134]). It seems plausible that Paul would also have differed from James on the applicability of *Eretz Israel* halakhah in Antioch.

There is no evidence to support the frequent assumption especially in German scholarship that the Jewish Christians at Antioch church had simply abandoned Jewish observance in the interest of a "law-free" Gentile mission.[135] As Dunn rightly points out, the phrase "to live like a Gentile" in Gal 2:11 is an intra-Jewish taunt, relative to what it means to "live like a Jew," and it does *not* imply a complete abandonment of all Jewish observance.[136]

The Jerusalem Council may well have created or at least aggravated this problem in the first place. Whether or not the Council produced the Apostolic Decree (and unlike many scholars I think this remains entirely plausible), the proceedings of Acts 15 and Gal 2:1-10 fully validated a Gentile Christian mission. What they did not do was to address the resultant problems of polity and fellowship. Paul's vision of Jews and Gentiles united by faith in Christ derived from Deutero-Isaiah and followed a halakhah in keeping with that

---

133 See Tomson 1990: 222-36; Klawans 1997; Safrai 1983: 206-207, following G. Alon.

134 On the halakhic function of the term συνείδησις in 1 Corinthians 10, see Tomson 1990: 208-16; cf. also Bockmuehl 1995: 97-98.

135 So again recently Hengel and Schwemer 1997: 197, according to whom the church at Antioch had no significant contact with synagogues, circumcision and ritual commandments having lost their significance. (The authors do not tell us how they know any of this.) Even Jewish Christians "will at first have circumcised their own children, simply to avoid the charge of apostasy . . . . However, in common with Gentile Christians they will have dispensed with the observance of ritual regulations, while following them in dealing with Jews who observed the law strictly." The only justification offered is the dubious assurance that "this basic attitude again goes back to the preaching of Jesus, for whom the commandment to love pushed the ritual law into the background" (p. 198, although they acknowledge that "critical of the law" might more appropriately characterise Paul's position than "law-free"). On the latter claim regarding issues, see Bockmuehl 1996, 1998; also Bauckham 1998.

136 Dunn 1993: 128 in criticism of H. D. Betz.

ecclesiology, according to which "all the nations" would be gathered in the last days (Isa 66:18-21).[137] Based perhaps on Jesus' own pattern of table fellowship (Rom 14:14), Paul and the Antiochene church had evidently come to adopt a relatively liberal purity halakhah that could accommodate the Gentiles. James' vision of the Gentiles, by contrast, derived from Amos 9, if Acts 15 can be believed.[138] For him, the messianic redemption would indeed find its eschatological corollary in the Gentiles seeking the Lord (Acts 15:17; LXX Amos 9:12), but this carried no necessary implications for any sort of integrated polity.

At the end of the day, there is perhaps nonetheless reason to think that halakhic differences with James were held at bay for the sake of the one gospel: what Paul rejects as reprehensible is not the conduct of James but that of Peter.

CONCLUSION

We have found evidence that religious and political considerations may have forced James' hand in his intervention at Antioch. It seems worth exploring the possibility that both the Jerusalem agreement and the subsequent dispute at Antioch may have had a territorial dimension. James is seen to interfere only here, but nowhere else in the areas of the Pauline mission, and neither in Galatians nor in Acts do we hear that James had reservations about Jewish-Gentile meal fellowship in any part of the Diaspora proper. James' action is consistent with the *political* desire if possible to secure a *modus vivendi* for the church in Jerusalem, and with a widely attested *religious* perspective in which Antioch would be understood in terms of the biblical dimensions of the Land promised to the Twelve Tribes, who had been the focus of Jesus' mission to Israel. This remains of course no more than a hypothesis, but it is one that may well account for the situation better than many of the more commonly proposed explanations.

James' intervention, Peter's accommodation and Paul's rigid refusal despite being in a minority of one, may each in its own way

---

[137] The formulation of N. Taylor 1992: 135 may be insufficiently precise: "Paul took his stand on principle in a matter on which James, Peter, and Barnabas exercised pragmatism rather than dogma."

[138] Acts 15:16-17: note the definitive discussion of this passage in Bauckham 1996.

have contributed to the emergence of a separate group publicly
known as *Christianoi*—Gentile believers in Christ whose public
image could no longer be most obviously identified in association
either with pagan cults or as sympathisers of the Jewish community.[139] Christianity may well owe its subsequent survival to the fact
that it followed neither the Petrine and Jacobean nor indeed the
Pauline stance at Antioch, but embraced both the former and the
latter together as the apostolic foundation of the Church.[140]

BIBLIOGRAPHY OF WORKS CITED

Adamson, James B. 1989. *James: The Man and His Message*. Grand Rapids:
    Eerdmans.

Aharoni, Yohanan. 1979. *The Land of the Bible: A Historical Geography*. Trans &
    ed. A. F. Rainey. 2nd ed. London: Burns & Oates.

Alexander, Philip S. 1974. *The Toponymy of the Targumim with Special
    Reference to the Table of Nations and the Borders of the Holy Land*. D. Phil.
    Oxford.

Alexander, Philip S. 1982. "Notes on the 'Imago Mundi' of the Book of Jubilees."
    JJS 33: 197-213.

Avi-Yonah, Michael. 1966. *The Holy Land from the Persian to the Arab Conquests
    (536 BC to AD 640): A Historical Geography*. Grand Rapids: Baker.

Avi-Yonah, Michael. 1976. *Gazetteer of Roman Palestine*. Qedem 5. Jerusalem:
    Institute of Archaeology/CARTA.

Barclay, John M. G. 1996. *Jews in the Mediterranean Diaspora from Alexander to*

---

[139] Hengel and Schwemer 1997: 183 suggest that the emergence of a separate
Gentile identity at Antioch may have been facilitated by the population's hardening
anti-Jewish attitudes in the years 39-40, coinciding with Paul's arrival from Tarsus
in the company of Barnabas. The same would presumably again be the case in 48,
if Malalas 10:245 is right. Whether or not Hengel is right on this point, any
politically motivated Gentile desire to distance themselves from the Jewish community after AD 40 might well have been reinforced for existing or prospective Gentile
Christians by the events of Gal 2:12-13. (It remains the case, of course, that the
evidence for strained Gentile Christian relations with the Jewish community at
Antioch in the first and second centuries is very slender indeed.)

   Knox 1925: 196 thinks, somewhat speculatively, that the decision to evangelise
the Gentile world from Antioch was itself a direct result of the controversy in that
city.

[140] Cf. Holtz 1986: 357. Despite Antioch, it was only Marcionite or Jewish
Christian extremists who denied the "catholic" belief that Peter and Paul later jointly
laid the foundation of the church at Rome (so e.g. Irenaeus, *Haer.* 3.1.1; 3.3.1; cf.
already *1 Clem.* 5:1-6).

Trajan (323 BCE – 117 CE). Edinburgh: T. & T. Clark.

Barrett, Charles Kingsley. 1997. "Christocentricity at Antioch." In *Jesus Christus als die Mitte der Schrift: Studien zur Hermeneutik des Evangeliums*, 303-39. BZNW 86. Ed. C. Landmesser et al. Berlin and New York: de Gruyter.

Barrett, Charles Kingsley. 1998. *A Critical and Exegetical Commentary on the Acts of the Apostles*. Vol. 2. Edinburgh: T. & T. Clark.

Bauckham, Richard. 1995. "James and the Jerusalem Church." In *The Book of Acts in Its Palestinian Setting*, 415-80. Ed. R. Bauckham. Grand Rapids: Eerdmans; Carlisle: Paternoster.

Bauckham, Richard. 1996. "James and the Gentiles (Acts 15.13-21)." In *History Literature, and Society in the Book of Acts* [punctuation *sic*], 154-84. Ed. B. Witherington. Cambridge: Cambridge University Press.

Bauckham, Richard. 1997. "Anna of the Tribe of Asher (Luke 2:36-38)." *RevB* 104: 161-91.

Bauckham, Richard. 1998. "The Scrupulous Priest and the Good Samaritan: Jesus' Parabolic Interpretation of the Law of Moses." *NTS* 44: 475-89.

Bernheim, Pierre-Antoine. 1996. *Jacques, Frère de Jésus*. Paris: Éditions Noêsis. ET: *James, Brother of Jesus*. London: SCM Press, 1997.

Bickerman, E. J. 1938. *Institutions des Séleucides*. Paris: Geuthner.

Bing, J. Daniel. 1992. "Cilicia." *ABD* 1: 1022-24.

Bockmuehl, Markus. 1996. "Halakhah and Ethics in the Jesus Tradition." In *Early Christian Thought in its Jewish Context*, 264-78. Ed. J. Barclay and J. Sweet. Cambridge: Cambridge University Press.

Bockmuehl, Markus. 1998. "Let the Dead Bury their Dead" (Matt. 8:22/Luke 9:62): Jesus and the Halakhah." *JTS* 49: 553-81.

Borgen, Peder. 1988. "Catalogues of Vices, the Apostolic Decree, and the Jerusalem Meeting." In *The Social World of Formative Christianity and Judaism*, 126-41. Ed. J. Neusner et al. Philadelphia: Fortress.

Brown, Raymond E. and Meier, John P. 1983. *Antioch and Rome*. New York: Paulist.

Catchpole, David R. 1977. "Paul, James and the Apostolic Decree." *NTS* 23: 428-44.

Cimok, Fatih, ed. 1995. *Antioch Mosaics*. Istanbul: A Turizm Yayinlari.

Cohen, Shaye J. D. 1989. "Crossing the Boundary and Becoming a Jew." *HTR* 82: 13-33.

Davies, W. D. 1974. *The Gospel and the Land: Early Christianity and Jewish Territorial Doctrine*. Berkeley and London: University of California.

Downey, Glanville. 1952. "Greek and Latin Inscriptions." In *Antioch on-the-Orontes*, vol. 2: *The Excavations 1933–1936*, 148-65. Ed. R. Stillwell. Princeton: Princeton University Press; London: Oxford University Press; The Hague:

Martinus Nijhoff.

Downey, Glanville. 1961. *A History of Antioch in Syria: from Seleucus to the Arab conquest*. Princeton: Princeton University Press.

Dunn, James D. G. 1983. "The incident at Antioch (Gal 2:11-18)." *JSNT* 18: 3-57.

Dunn, James D. G. 1993. *The Epistle to the Galatians*. BNTC. London: A. & C. Black.

Esler, Philip S. 1987. *Community and Gospel in Luke-Acts: The Social and Political Motivations of Lucan Theology*. SNTSMS 57. Cambridge: University Press.

Esler, Philip S. 1998. *Galatians*. New Testament Readings. London and New York: Routledge.

Fallon, F. 1985. "Eupolemus: A New Translation and Introduction." In *The Old Testament Pseudepigrapha*, 2: 861-72. Ed. J. H. Charlesworth. Garden City: Doubleday.

Feissel, Denis. 1985. "Deux listes de quartiers d'Antioche astreints au creusement d'un canal (73–74 après J.-C.)." *Syria* 62: 77-103.

Feldman, Louis H. 1993. *Jew and Gentile in the Ancient World: Attitudes and Interactions from Alexander to Justinian*. Princeton: Princeton University Press.

Freyne, Séan. 1988. *Galilee, Jesus and the Gospels: Literary Approaches and Historical Investigations*. Philadelphia: Fortress.

Gilat, Itzchak D. 1984. *Rabbi Eliezer ben Hyrcanus: A Scholar Outcast*. Ramat-Gan: Bar-Ilan University Press.

Gleßmer, Uwe. 1995. *Einleitung in die Targume zum Pentateuch*. TSAJ 48. Tübingen: Mohr (Siebeck).

Goodman, Martin. 1990. "Kosher Olive Oil in Antiquity." In *A Tribute to Geza Vermes: Essays on Jewish and Christian Literature and History*, 227-45. Ed. P. R. Davies and R. T. White. JSOTSup 100. Sheffield: JSOT Press.

Grainger, John D. 1990. *The Cities of Seleucid Syria*. Oxford: Clarendon.

Ha-Parchi, Estori. 1897-99. *Caftor va-pherach: Contient toutes les lois religieuses concernant la Terre-Sainte, la topographie de tout le pays et ses divisions, etc.* (Hebrew). Ed. A. M. Luncz. 2 vols. Jerusalem: Luncz.

Hahn, F. and Müller, P. 1998. "Der Jakobusbrief." *TRu* 63: 1-73.

Hayward, Robert. 1989. "The Date of Targum Pseudo-Jonathan: Some Comments." *JJS* 40: 7-30.

Hengel, Martin and Schwemer, Anna Maria. 1998. *Paulus zwischen Damaskus und Antiochien*. WUNT 108. Tübingen: Mohr (Siebeck).

Hengel, Martin and Schwemer, Anna Maria. 1997. *Paul Between Damascus and Antioch*. Trans. J. Bowden. London: SCM Press.

Hill, Craig C. 1992. *Hellenists and Hebrews: Reappraising Division Within the Earliest Church*. Minneapolis: Fortress.

Holladay, Carl R. 1992. "Eupolemus." *ABD* 2: 671-72.

Holmberg, Bengt. 1998. "Jewish *Versus* Christian Identity in the Early Church?" *RevBib* 105: 397-425.

Holtz, Traugott. 1986. "Der antiochenische Zwischenfall (Galater 2:11-14)." *NTS* 32: 344-61.

Horbury, William. 1986. "The Twelve and the Phylarchs." *NTS* 32: 503-27.

Horbury, William. 1997. "Septuagintal and New Testament Conceptions of the Church." In *A Vision for the Church: Studies in Early Christian Ecclesiology in Honour of J. P. M. Sweet*, 1-17. Ed. M. Bockmuehl and M. B. Thompson. Edinburgh: T. & T. Clark.

Horbury, William. 1999. "Pappus and Lulianus in Jewish Resistance to Rome." Forthcoming in the *Proceedings of the 1998 Congress of the European Association for Jewish Studies at Toledo*, ed. A. Saénz-Badillos.

Ilan, Tal. 1992. "New Ossuary Inscriptions from Jerusalem." *Scripta Classica Israelica* 11: 149-59.

Jeffreys, Elizabeth et al. 1986. *The Chronicle of John Malalas: A Translation.* Byzantina Australiensia 4. Melbourne: Australian Association for Byzantine Studies.

Jewett, Robert. 1971. "The Agitators and the Galatian Congregations." *NTS* 17: 198-212.

Kallai, Zecharia. 1983. "The Reality of the Land and the Bible." In *Das Land Israel in biblischer Zeit: Jerusalem-Symposium 1981 der Hebräischen Universität und der Georg-August-Universität*, 76-90. Ed. G. Strecker. Göttinger Theologische Arbeiten 25. Göttingen: Vandenhoeck & Ruprecht.

Kaufman, Stephen A. 1994. "Dating the Language of the Palestinian Targums and their Use in the Study of First Century CE Texts." In *The Aramaic Bible: Targums in their historical context*, 118-141. Ed. D. R. G. Beattie and M. J. McNamara. JSOTSup 166. Sheffield: JSOT Press.

Kaufman, Stephen A. 1997. "On Methodology in the Study of the Targums and their Chronology." In *New Testament Text and Language*, 267-274. Ed S. E. Porter and C. A. Evans. BibSem 44. Sheffield: Sheffield Academic Press.

Kieffer, René. 1982. *Foi et justification à Antioche: Interprétation d'un conflit (Ga 2, 14-21).* Lectio Divina 111. Paris: Cerf.

Klawans, Jonathan. 1995. "Notions of Gentile Impurity in Ancient Judaism." *AJS Review* 20: 285-312.

Klawans, Jonathan. 1997. "The Impurity of Immorality in Ancient Judaism." *JJS* 48: 1-16.

Knox, Wilfred L. 1925. *St Paul and the Church of Jerusalem.* Cambridge: Cambridge University Press.

Kolb, Frank. 1996. "Antiochia in der frühen Kaiserzeit." In *Geschichte—Tradition—Reflexion: Festschrift für Martin Hengel zum 70. Geburtstag*, 2. 97-

118. Ed. H. Cancik et al. Tübingen: Mohr (Siebeck).

Kraeling, Carl H. 1932. "The Jewish Community at Antioch." *JBL* 51: 130-60.

Lassus, Jean. 1977. "La ville d'Antioche à l'époque romaine d'après l'archéologie." *ANRW* II.8: 54-102.

Lassus, Jean. 1984. "Sur les Maisons d'Antioche." In *Apamée de Syrie. Bilan des recherches archéologiques 1973–1979: Aspects de l'architecture domestique d'Apamée*, 361-75. Fouilles d'Apamée de Syrie: Miscellanea, Fasc. 13. Ed. J. Balty. Brussels: Centre Belge de recherches archéologiques à Apamée de Syrie.

Levi, Doro. 1944. "Aion." *Hesperia* 13: 269-314.

Longenecker, Bruce W. 1998. *The Triumph of Abraham's God: The Transformation of Identity in Galatians*. Edinburgh: T. & T. Clark.

Marcus, Ralph and Wikren, Allen. 1963. *Josephus*. Vol. 8: *Jewish Antiquities, Books XV–XVII*. LCL 410. Cambridge: Harvard University Press; London: Heinemann.

McNamara, Martin, trans. 1995. *Targum Neofiti I: Numbers*. And Clarke, E. G., trans. *Targum Pseudo-Jonathan: Numbers*. ArBib 4. Edinburgh: T. & T. Clark.

Meeks, Wayne A. and Wilken, Robert A. 1978. *Jews and Christians in Antioch in the First Four Centuries of the Common Era*. Missoula: Scholars.

Millar, Fergus. 1993. *The Roman Near East: 31 BC – AD 337*. Cambridge and London: Harvard University Press.

Murphy-O'Connor, Jerome. 1996. *Paul: A Critical Life*. Oxford: Clarendon.

Neaman, Pinchas. 1971-72. *Encyclopedia of Talmudical Geography*. 2 vols. Tel Aviv: Ts'ats'ik.

Neubauer, Adolphe. 1868. *La Géographie du Talmud*. Paris: Michel Lévy.

Neusner, Jacob. 1973. *Eliezer ben Hyrcanus: The Tradition and the Man*. SJLA 4. 2 vols. Leiden: Brill.

Niebuhr, Karl-Wilhelm. 1998. "Der Jakobusbrief im Licht frühjüdischer Diasporabriefe." *NTS* 44: 420-43.

Norris, Frederick W. 1990. "Antioch as Religious Center: I. Paganism before Constantine." *ANRW* II.18.4: 2322-79.

Norris, Frederick W. 1991. "Artifacts from Antioch." In *Social history of the Matthean community*, 248-58. Ed. D. Balch. Minneapolis: Fortress.

Painter, John. 1997. *Just James: The Brother of Jesus in History and Tradition*. Columbia: University of South Carolina Press.

Pratscher, Wilhelm. 1987. *Der Herrenbruder Jakobus und die Jakobustradition*. FRLANT 139. Göttingen: Vandenhoeck & Ruprecht.

Rajak, Tessa. 1992. "The Jewish Community and Its Boundaries." In *The Jews Among Pagans and Christians in the Roman Empire*, 9-28. Ed. J. Lieu et al. London and New York: Routledge.

Riesner, Rainer. 1994. *Die Frühzeit des Apostels Paulus: Studien zur Chronologie,*

Missionsstrategie und Theologie. WUNT 71. Tübingen: Mohr (Siebeck). [ET *Paul's Early Period: Chronology, Mission Strategy, Theology.* Trans. D. Stott. Grand Rapids: Eerdmans, 1998.]

Safrai, Shmuel. 1983. "The Land of Israel in Tannaitic Halacha." In *Das Land Israel in biblischer Zeit: Jerusalem-Symposium 1981 der Hebräischen Universität und der Georg-August-Universität*, 201-15. Ed. G. Strecker. Göttinger Theologische Arbeiten 25. Göttingen: Vandenhoeck & Ruprecht.

Sanders, E. P. 1993. *The Historical Figure of Jesus.* London: Allen Lane/Penguin.

Sanders, E. P. 1985. *Jesus and Judaism.* London: SCM Press.

Sanders, E. P. 1990a. *Jewish Law from Jesus to the Mishnah: Five Studies.* London: SCM Press; Philadelphia: Trinity Press International.

Sanders, E. P. 1990b. "Jewish Association with Gentiles and Galatians 2:11-14." In *The Conversation Continues: Studies in Paul & John in Honor of J. Louis Martyn*, 170-88. Ed. R. T. Fortna and B. R. Gaventa. Nashville: Abingdon.

Schäfer, Peter. 1998. "From Jerusalem the Great to Alexandria the Small: The Relationship between Palestine and Egypt in the Graeco-Roman Period." In *The Talmud Yerushalmi and Graeco-Roman Culture.* Ed. P. Schäfer et al. TSAJ 71. Tübingen: Mohr (Siebeck).

Schenk, Alexander Graf von Stauffenberg. 1931. *Die römische Kaisergeschichte bei Malalas: Griechischer Text der Bücher IX–XII und Untersuchungen.* Stuttgart: Kohlhammer.

Schrage, Wolfgang. 1991. *Der erste Brief an die Korinther.* Vol. 1: *1Kor 1,1–6,1.* EKKNT 7.1. Zurich and Brunswick: Benziger; Neukirchen-Vluyn: Neukirchener.

Schürer, Emil. 1890. *A History of the Jewish People in the Time of Jesus Christ.* Trans. J. Macpherson. 5 vols. Edinburgh: T. & T. Clark.

Schürer, Emil. 1979. *The History of the Jewish People in the Age of Jesus Christ (175 B. C.-A. D. 135).* Rev. & ed. G. Vermes et al. Vol. 2. Edinburgh: T. & T. Clark. [Schürer/Vermes]

Schwartz, Daniel R. 1996. "Temple or City: What did Hellenistic Jews See in Jerusalem?" In *The Centrality of Jerusalem: Historical Perspectives*, 114-27. Ed. M. Poorthuis and Ch. Safrai. Kampen: Kok Pharos.

Scott, James M. 1995. *Paul and the Nations: The Old Testament and Jewish Background of Paul's Mission to the Nations with Special Reference to the Destination of Galatians.* WUNT 84. Tübingen: Mohr (Siebeck).

Smend, Rudolf. 1983. "Das uneroberte Land." In *Das Land Israel in biblischer Zeit: Jerusalem-Symposium 1981 der Hebräischen Universität und der Georg-August-Universität*, 91-102. Ed. G. Strecker. Göttinger Theologische Arbeiten 25. Göttingen: Vandenhoeck & Ruprecht.

Smith, Morton. 1987. *Palestinian Parties and Politics that Shaped the Old Testament.* 2nd ed. London: SCM Press.

Stemberger, Günter. 1996. *Introduction to the Talmud and Midrash.* Trans. and ed.

M. Bockmuehl. 2nd ed. Edinburgh: T. & T. Clark.

Sussmann, J. 1981. "The Inscription in the Synagogue at Reḥob." In *Ancient Syngagogues Revealed*, 146-53. Jerusalem: Israel Exploration Society.

Taatz, Irene. 1991. *Frühjüdische Briefe: Die paulinischen Briefe im Rahmen der offiziellen religiösen Briefe des Frühjudentums*. NTOA 16. Fribourg: Universitätsverlag; Göttingen: Vandenhoeck & Ruprecht.

Taylor, Justin. 1994. "Why were the Disciples first called 'Christians' at Antioch? (Acts 11,26)?" *RB* 101: 75-94.

Taylor, Justin. 1998. "Why Did Paul Persecute the Church?" In *Tolerance and Intolerance in Early Judaism and Christianity*, 99-120. Ed. G. N. Stanton and G. G. Stroumsa. Cambridge: University Press.

Taylor, Nicholas. 1992. *Paul, Antioch and Jerusalem: a study in relationships and authority in earliest Christianity*. JSNTSup 66. Sheffield: JSOT Press.

Theissen, Gerd. 1992. *The Gospels in Context: Social and Political History in the Synoptic Tradition*. Trans. L. M. Maloney. Edinburgh: T. & T. Clark.

Tomson, Peter J. 1990. *Paul and the Jewish Law: Halakha in the Letters of the Apostle to the Gentiles*. CRINT 3.1. Assen and Maastricht: Van Gorcum; Minneapolis: Fortress.

Treidler, Hans. 1975. "Amanos." *Der Kleine Pauly* 1. 287-88.

Waage, Dorothy. 1952. *Antioch on-the-Orontes*, vol. 4.2: *Greek, Roman, Byzantine and Crusaders' Coins*. Princeton: Princeton University Press; London: Oxford University Press; The Hague: Martinus Nijhoff.

Wallace, Richard and Williams, Wynne. 1998. *The Three Worlds of Paul of Tarsus*. London: Routledge.

Wechsler, Andreas. 1991. *Geschichtsbild und Apostelstreit: Eine forschungsgeschichtliche und exegetische Studie über den antiochenischen Zwischenfall (Gal 2,11-14)*. BZNW 62. Berlin and New York: de Gruyter.

Wehnert, Jürgen. 1997. *Die Reinheit des 'christlichen Gottesvolkes' aus Juden und Heiden*. FRLANT 173. Göttingen: Vandenhoeck & Ruprecht.

Weinfeld, Moshe. 1983. "The Extent of the Promised Land – the Status of Transjordan." In *Das Land Israel in biblischer Zeit: Jerusalem-Symposium 1981 der Hebräischen Universität und der Georg-August-Universität*, 59-75. Ed. G. Strecker. Göttinger Theologische Arbeiten 25. Göttingen: Vandenhoeck & Ruprecht.

Weinfeld, Moshe. 1993. *The Promise of the Land: The Inheritance of the Land of Canaan by the Israelites*. Taubman Lectures in Jewish Studies 3. Berkeley: University of California Press.

FOR WHAT OFFENCE WAS JAMES PUT TO DEATH?

Richard Bauckham

1. INTRODUCTION

This chapter is an attempt to answer a single, straightforward historical question: For what legal offence was James the brother of Jesus, leader of the Jerusalem church, tried by the High Priest's council and condemned to death by stoning? Amid much discussion of the death of James, this question seems to have been discussed only briefly and inconclusively. Yet, as this paper attempts to show, careful consideration of the evidence can yield a reasonably probable answer to the question.

We are fortunate in having several ancient accounts of the death of James. That of Josephus (*Ant.* 20.9.1 §199-203) is commonly acknowledged to be the most historically reliable. Though a few scholars have held this passage to be a Christian interpolation,[1] the vast majority have considered it to be authentic.[2] While Josephus' own purposes[3] no doubt determine what he has chosen to include and

---

[1] Most recently T. Rajak, *Josephus: The Historian and His Society* (Philadelphia: Fortress, 1983) 131 n. 73. L. H. Feldman ("A Selective Critical Bibliography of Josephus," in L. H. Feldman and G. Hata [ed.], *Josephus, the Bible and History* [Detroit: Wayne State University Press, 1989] 434) responds to her arguments.

[2] See the summaries of many scholars' works in L. H. Feldman, *Josephus and Modern Scholarship (1937-1980)* (Berlin and New York: de Gruyter, 1984) 704-7.

[3] Cf. S. Mason, *Josephus and the New Testament* (Peabody: Hendrickson, 1992) 176-77. When J. Painter (*Just James: The Brother of Jesus in History and Tradition* [Columbia: University of South Carolina Press, 1997] 138) comments that Josephus' "leaning towards the Pharisees scarcely needs to be argued," he shows his ignorance of Mason's important work, arguing that Josephus generally denigrates the Pharisees, as he does the Sadducees: see S. Mason, *Flavius Josephus on the Pharisees: A Compositon-Critical Study* (SPB 39; Leiden: Brill, 1991); idem, *Josephus and the New Testament*, 131-43. Although the account of the death of James puts the Pharisees in a good light, by contrast with Ananus II and the Sadducees, they are anonymous, identifiable to the informed reader but not to others.

what he knew but has not reported, there is no reason to doubt the accuracy of the account so far as it goes.

It is otherwise with the Christian accounts of the death of James, of which the most important are in Hegesippus, as quoted by Eusebius,[4] and the *Second Apocalypse of James* (CG V,4) from Nag Hammadi. These undoubtedly contain legendary elements, and scholarly judgments as to the possibility of recovering historically reliable material from them have varied widely. This question of historical value is inescapably connected with the question of the literary relationships between the various Christian accounts, which is also disputed. Thus, before we can address the topic indicated in the title of this chapter, we must consider the literary relationships among the Christian accounts of the death of James (section 2). The main result of this study will be to show that Hegesippus and the *Second Apocalypse of James* are dependent on a common Jewish Christian source. We must then examine the way in which the tradition about the death of James embodied in this Jewish Christian source developed (section 3). To some extent it will be possible to identify primary and secondary elements in the accounts, pointing to an original core tradition which has been subsequently elaborated. This may represent a core of reliable historical memory within the legendary narratives it has generated. Finally, in section 4 of the paper, we shall address the question: For what legal offence was James tried by the High Priest's council and condemned to death by stoning? The argument will proceed from the historically more secure evidence of Josephus, drawing conclusions which can then be seen to be coherent with the most plausibly reliable elements in the Christian tradition of the death of James. These can then be used, with due caution, to make the conclusions more specific.

---

4   I assume that Eusebius has faithfully reproduced the text of Hegesippus which he knew. This is argued, against the views of E. Schwartz and H. J. Lawlor, by F. S. Jones, "The Martyrdom of James in Hegesippus, Clement of Alexandria, and Christian Apocrypha, Including Nag Hammadi: A Study of Textual Relations," in D. J. Lull (ed.), *Society of Biblical Literature 1990 Seminar Papers* (SBLSP 29; Atlanta: Scholars Press, 1990) 323-27; and cf. also R. Bauckham, *Jude and the Relatives of Jesus in the Early Church* (Edinburgh: T. & T. Clark, 1990) 80. W. Pratscher (*Der Herrenbruder Jakobus und die Jakobustradition* [FRLANT 139; Göttingen: Vandenhoeck & Ruprecht, 1987] 104-6) proposes only minor interpolations by Eusebius in Hegesippus' text.

2. A JEWISH CHRISTIAN SOURCE COMMON TO HEGESIPPUS AND THE SECOND APOCALYPSE OF JAMES

Alongside the many differences between the accounts of the death of James in these two very different works, there are also striking points of correspondence. Though not of equal weight, the following ten such points of correspondence must bear the weight of a case for literary relationship:

Hegesippus (*apud* Eusebius, *Hist. Eccl.* 2.23.8-18)

Second Apocalypse of James [5]

(1) Who is the gate of Jesus? (8, 12)	through you those who wish to enter in will open the good door. And they turn about, that they may walk in the way which (leads) before this door, and follow you and enter, [and you] accompany them inside . . . (55:6-13)
(2) As many as came to believe did so through James (9)	through you those who wish to enter in will open the good door . . . You are an illuminator and redeemer of those who are mine (55:11, 17-18)
(3) Therefore stand on the pinnacle of the Temple (11) [They] made James stand on the pinnacle of the Temple (12)	they found him standing by the pinnacle of the Temple (61:20-22)
(4) that your words may be audible to all the people, for because of the Passover all the tribes, with the nations (Gentiles) also, have come together (11)	He used to speak these words while the multitude of the peoples was sitting (45:18-20)
(5) Oh, oh, even the just one has gone astray (15)	(O you) who have gone astray! (62:7)
(6) And they fulfilled the Scripture written in Isaiah, "Let us take away the just one, for he is useless to us" (15)	Well then let us kill this man, that he may be removed[6] from our midst! For he will be of no use to us at all! (61:16-19)

---

5   The translation quoted here is that of W.-P. Funk in W. Schneemelcher and R. McL. Wilson (eds.), *New Testament Apocrypha*, vol. 1 (rev. ed., Cambridge: James Clarke; Louisville: Westminster/John Knox Press, 1991) 333-40.

6   It is very notable that *2 Apoc. Jas* here reflects the unique rendering of Isa

(7) [they] threw down the Just one (16)   they cast him down (61:25-26)

(8) Let us stone James the Just (16)   Come! Let us stone the Just (61:13-14)

(9) they began to stone him since the   But [when] they [looked upon him],
fall had not killed him (16)   they observed [that he was still alive(?).
                                        Then] they arose (?) [and went down,]
                                        seized him and [abused] him, dragging
                                        him on the ground. They stretched him
                                        out, rolled a stone on his abdomen
                                        (61:26-62:4)

(10) I beseech you, Lord, God, Father   My God and Father (62:16)
(16)

These close correspondences have usually been explained by the use of a common source,[7] but Jones has questioned the need for this hypothesis, arguing that the relationship is sufficiently explained by the dependence of the *Second Apocalypse of James* on Hegesippus.[8] However, the following three reasons require that we postulate, not a direct literary relationship, but a common source:

(1) According to Hegesippus it is "the scribes and Pharisees" who oppose James and put him to death (10, 12, 14), whereas according to the *Second Apocalypse of James* it is the priests. The former is a reminiscence of the Gospels, but the latter is more probably original,[9] being closer to Josephus' report.

Hegesippus' account of the death of James in fact begins by referring to the Jews who discussed "the gate of Jesus" with James and some of whom believed, as "certain persons from the seven sects among the people" (8), i.e. the seven Jewish sects that Hegesippus listed earlier in his work (*apud* Eusebius, *Hist. Eccl.* 4.22.7). He then says that these sects "did not believe in either resurrection or in one who shall come to reward each person according to their deeds" (9). Of the seven sects listed by Hegesippus, this was in fact true only of the Sadducees. It looks, therefore, as though the account on which

3:10 in Hegesippus (ἄρωμεν) (LXX has δήσωμεν).

   [7]   See the list of scholars taking this view in Jones, "The Martyrdom of James," 331 n. 44.

   [8]   Jones, "The Martyrdom of James," 331-33; cf. the comments on Jones's arguments in Painter, *Just James*, 121-22, 130-31, 179-81.

   [9]   This would be confirmed by *Clem. Rec.* 1.70.4-8, if this passage is dependent on the same account, as has often been argued.

Hegesippus drew referred at this point specifically to the Sadducees as James' interlocutors. This would also make good sense of Hegesippus' next statement that "many even of the rulers [ἀρχοντων] believed" (a reminiscence of John 12:42). Because of this, "there was a tumult of the Jews [meaning, here, as in John, the Jewish authorities?] and the scribes and the Pharisees," who assemble and approach James (10). This group then becomes, in Hegesippus, simply "the scribes and the Pharisees" (12, 14), who put James to death. It may well be that Hegesippus' source continued to speak mainly of the Sadducean chief priests, as the ruling group of Jews, and that it is Hegesippus who has shifted the focus to the scribes and Pharisees. This would bring the common source, at this point better reflected by the *Second Apocalypse of James*, significantly close to Josephus.

(2) In two respects the account of James' death in the *Second Apocalypse of James* conforms to Jewish practice in judicial stoning more closely than that in Hegesippus:[10] (a) In the *Apocalypse* the decision to stone James is taken before he is thrown down from the pinnacle. This conforms to the Jewish procedure: someone condemned to be stoned was first thrown down from a high place. If this did not kill him, he was stoned. This was the procedure according to the Mishna (*Sanh.* 6:4; cf. *b. Sanh.* 45a), while its use in the late Second Temple period is confirmed by Luke 4:29.[11] By contrast, the account in Hegesippus could be read to mean that a first attempt to kill James was made by throwing him down and only when he was found to be still alive was a decision to stone him taken. (b) According to the Mishna, if the condemned person was not killed by the fall, "the second witness took the stone and threw it [literally: placed it] on his heart (= chest). If he died thereby, he (= the second witness) had done his duty. But if not, he (= the condemned) is stoned by all Israel" (*m. Sanh.* 6:4).[12] The account in the *Apocalypse*

---

10   I. Gruenwald ("Halakhic Material in Codex Gnosticus V,4: *The Second Apocalypse of James?*," in *From Apocalypticism to Gnosticism* [Beiträge zur Erforschung des alten Testaments und des antiken Judentums 14; Frankfurt: Lang, 1988] 279-94) makes these two points and also attempts to see further details in the account in the *Second Apocalypse of James* as reflecting authentic practice.

11   See e.g. J. Nolland, *Luke 1–9:20* (WBC 35A; Dallas: Word, 1989) 201; and cf. D. Neale, "Was Jesus a *Mesith?* Public Response to Jesus and his Ministry," *TynBul* 41 (1993) 99-100.

12   Translation from Gruenwald, "Halakhic Material," 285. The procedure is

of James evidently reflects something like this procedure: "They stretched him out (and) rolled [literally: placed] a stone on his abdomen . . . . Again they raised him up, since he was (still) alive" (62:3-9). Hegesippus lacks these details. It is much easier to believe that a source common to Hegesippus and the *Second Apocalypse of James* was informed about the proper procedure in stoning than that these details were added to the account of Hegesippus by the author of the *Apocalypse*, who shows no other sign of familiarity with Jewish practice.

(3) As we shall see in section 3 below, the story of the death of James in Hegesippus has been strongly influenced by an exegesis of Psalm 118. Some of the most significant material derived from Psalm 118 is missing in the *Second Apocalypse of James*, but it also reflects Psalm 118 in ways that are not preserved in Hegesippus. Most notable of these is the reference to "the mighty cornerstone" (61:22-23; cf. Ps 118:22).

These three considerations, in conjunction with the ten points of significant correspondence between the two accounts, are sufficient to require the hypothesis of a source common to Hegesippus and the *Second Apocalypse of James*. From Hegesippus' undoubted dependence on Palestinian Jewish Christian traditions[13] we can presume the source to come from Jewish Christian circles of the early second century.

A difference between the two accounts is that Hegesippus' account has many close verbal allusions to the Gospels (10: John 12:42; Luke 20:21; 11, 12: Matt 4:5 = Luke 4:9; 13: Matt 20:17; 26:64; 14: Matt 21:9, 15; 16: Luke 23:34).[14] All these are missing from the *Second Apocalypse of James*, except for the reference to "the pinnacle of the Temple" (61:21-22). It is possible that Hegesippus is responsible for adding these reminiscences of the Gospels to the material he drew from the common source. On the other hand, most of them occur in relation to the fact that in Hegesippus' account James' preaching to the people is highly successful and to the dialogue between James and his enemies which follows from that. This whole theme is missing

---

explained, probably correctly, as exegetical in origin in *b. Sanh.* 43a.

[13]   Bauckham, *Jude and the Relatives of Jesus*, 80.

[14]   Dependence on Acts 7 is also frequently asserted, but there seem to be no similarities to Acts 7 which cannot be better explained as borrowings from the Gospels.

from the *Apocalypse*, where, on the contrary, the people are not persuaded (61:4) and there is no dialogue between James and those who put him to death. Gnostic theology (with its belief in the salvation of a small elite; cf. 51:15-19; 55:16-20) may be responsible for this difference, as also for the omission of James' dying prayer for the forgiveness of his enemies. Fortunately, it is not of great importance for our purposes to determine whether the Gospel allusions are due to Hegesippus himself or were in his source.

We must briefly raise the issue of the literary relationships between, on the one hand, Hegesippus, the *Second Apocalypse of James*, and their common source, and, on the other hand, the accounts of James' death in Josephus and in Clement of Alexandria (*apud* Eusebius, *Hist. Eccl.* 2.1.5). Since Josephus refers only to stoning as the means of death, while Clement speaks of James' being thrown from the pinnacle of the Temple and battered to death with a fuller's club, but not of stoning, it has been supposed that the Christian account, to which Clement, Hegesippus and the *Second Apocalypse of James* are indebted, originally had no reference to stoning, which was introduced secondarily under the influence of Josephus.[15] But such an hypothesis is quite unnecessary in the light of the fact that throwing the condemned person down from a high place was an integral element in the procedure of execution by stoning.[16] It is quite intelligible that Clement's very brief summary of the events should include only the first and last actions in the killing of James as narrated by Hegesippus, and there is no good reason to doubt that it is on Hegesippus' account as we have it in Eusebius that Clement is dependent.[17] There is no need to postulate either an earlier version of Hegesippus' own text or an original version of the source common to Hegesippus and the *Second Apocalypse of James* which lacked the stoning, and so nor is there any need to postulate dependence on Josephus at any stage. Josephus and the Christian tradition which we

---

15   The latest scholar to express a version of this view is Painter, *Just James*, 116, 129, 141.

16   G. Lüdemann (*Opposition to Paul in Jewish Christianity* [Minneapolis: Fortress, 1989] 173) objects that the high place prescribed for stoning cannot be the pinnacle of the Temple. Of course, the pinnacle of the Temple would not normally have been used for the stoning procedure, but it is perfectly intelligible that it should be considered as used in this way in the highly legendary account of stoning which we find in the Christian tradition of the martyrdom of James.

17   So Jones, "The Martyrdom of James," 328.

have in two forms (Hegesippus and the *Second Apocalypse of James*) are completely independent accounts of the death of James. The one element they have in common (that he was executed by stoning) shows that the Christian tradition, like Josephus, had some access to historical fact.

Finally, *Clementine Recognitions* 1:27-71 has also often been seen as dependent on some version of the common source which lies behind Hegesippus and the *Second Apocalypse of James*.[18] The resemblances[19] are in fact rather minimal, insufficient in my view to prove a literary relationship. But in any case, full account must be taken of the fact that *Clementine Recognitions* 1:66-71 does not describe the death of James but a failed attempt on the life of James. The author may well have borrowed some elements in this from an account of the death of James which he knew, but if so he borrowed them as aids to his own narration of what he certainly regarded as a quite different event. It is therefore impossible to use this passage to reconstruct the account of the death of James which he knew. Any differences from the versions of the Christian tradition of James' death which we know can be readily ascribed to the Clementine author's reuse of the material for his own purposes. Whatever the relationship of this passage to accounts of the death of James might be, it is likely to be of very little help in reconstructing the tradition of such accounts.

3. THE DEVELOPMENT OF THE LEGEND

Our investigation of the making of the account of James in the common source reflected most fully in Hegesippus can usefully start with the one of the points which has long puzzled scholars, the name Oblias. Hegesippus writes: "because of his excessive righteousness [James] was called 'the Righteous [ὁ δίκαιος]' and Oblias ['Ωβλίας], which is, in Greek, 'Rampart of the People (περιοχὴ τοῦ λαοῦ),' and 'Righteousness (δικαιοσύνη),' as the prophets show concerning him" (*apud* Eusebius, *Hist. Eccl.* 2.23.7). Of these three titles, the first is

---

[18]   Jones ("The Martyrdom of James," 328 n. 33) lists those who have taken this view, while 329 n. 34 lists those who think the Clementine passage dependent on Hegesippus, the view which Jones himself takes; and cf. Painter, *Just James*, 197-98.

[19]   See the list in Jones, "The Martyrdom of James," 329-30.

well known,[20] and the third is clearly a variation of the first (no doubt introduced to enable the discovery of prophetic references to James in the Hebrew Bible), but the second is obscure. Most scholars have rightly supposed that the unintelligible 'Ωβλίας must be a corrupt form of a Semitic word or words, but the many attempts[21] to identify this word or phrase have, in my view, been unsuccessful. None has provided a wholly satisfactory explanation which does justice to what Hegesippus says the term means in Greek.

I have argued in detail elsewhere[22] that the term Oblias and its interpretation should be seen in the context of the early church's understanding of itself as the eschatological Temple. Like the Qumran community, which also understood itself as a Temple, the first Christians could describe themselves and their leaders as various parts of the structure of the Temple building. Christians in general were the stones of which the Temple is constructed (1 Pet 2:5; Hermas, *Vis.* 3; *Sim.* 9); the apostles and Christian prophets were the foundation (Eph 2:20); Peter was the rock on which the Temple is built (Matt 16:18); Jesus Christ was the foundation (1 Cor 3:11) or the cornerstone/keystone (Eph 2:20; 1 Pet 2:4, 6-7). That this kind of imagery goes back to the early Jerusalem church can be seen from the designation of James, Peter and John as pillars (Gal 2:9), i.e. supports on which the messianic Temple building rests.[23] We should note that in many cases specific references to these architectural facets of the eschatological Temple were found in scripture, as also

---

20   *Gos. Hebr.* §7; *Gos. Thom.* §12; *1 Apoc. Jas* 32:2-3; *2 Apoc. Jas* 44:14; 59:22; 60:12; 61:14.

21   H. J. Schoeps, "Jacobus ὁ δίκαιος καὶ ὠβλίας," in Schoeps, *Aus frühchristliche Zeit* (Tübingen: Mohr [Siebeck], 1950) 120-25; C. C. Torrey, "James the Just, and his Name 'Oblias,'" *JBL* 63 (1944) 93-98; H. Sahlin, "Noch einmal Jacobus 'Oblias,'" *Bib* 28 (1947) 152-53; C. K. Barrett, "Paul and the 'Pillar' Apostles," in J. N. Sevenster and W. C. van Unnik (eds.), *Studia Paulina* (J. de Zwaan Festschrift; Haarlem: Bohn, 1953) 15 n. 2; K. Baltzer and H. Köster, "Die Bezeichnung des Jakobus als 'Ωβλίας," *ZNW* 46 (1955) 141-42; S. Gero, "'Ωβλίας Reconsidered," *Mus* 88 (1975) 435-40; Pratscher, *Der Herrenbruder Jakobus,* 116-18.

22   Bauckham, "James and the Jerusalem Church," in R. Bauckham (ed.), *The Book of Acts in its Palestinian Setting* (Carlisle: Paternoster; Grand Rapids: Eerdmans, 1995) 441-50.

23   This is argued in detail in Bauckham, "James and the Jerusalem Church," 442-48.

happened at Qumran:[24] stones (Isa 54:11), foundations (Isa 54:11), cornerstone (Isa 28:16; Ps 118:22; both quoted in 1 Pet 2:6-7), and pillars (Prov 9:1).

That James was called "Rampart of the People" would fit well into such a sphere of imagery. In fact we can find the source of this description in Isa 54:11-12, the key prophetic passage describing the architectural features of the eschatological Zion. (Probably both at Qumran and in early Christianity it was read as referring to the Temple, rather than the city, or to the two without distinction.) In v. 12, the word גבול, which elsewhere usually means boundary or territory, refers to the surrounding wall of the city or Temple. It is rendered in the LXX as περίβολος, while in Tob 13:16 and Revelation 21 τεῖχος is used.[25] περιοχή would be a very suitable translation. Transferred from its context in Isa 54:12 to be used as a title for James, גבולך (your wall) would become גבל־עם (wall of the people). It is not difficult to see how this could become 'Ωβλίας in Greek (the final ς being an assimilation to Greek name endings).

This explanation takes seriously Hegesippus' reference to the prophets, which should probably be taken to refer to all three designations of James as designations by which he is named in the prophecies of the Hebrew Bible. A reference to James as "the righteous one" was found in Isa 3:10, as we can tell from our passage in Hegesippus (15; cf. 2 Apoc. Jas 61:14-19), and probably in other texts. A reference to James as "righteousness" was probably found in Isa 54:14, which would make James the means by which God builds the eschatological Zion, and/or Isa 28:17 (which continues from v. 16, the favourite early Christian text about Christ as the cornerstone of the messianic Temple), which would make James the plumb-line which God uses to build the new Temple. As we shall see below, "righteousness" in Ps 118:19, and Zadok, read as "righteousness," in Ezek 44:15, read as references to James, probably help to account for the exegesis that underlies Hegesippus' text.

Why should James have been identified as the "rampart" of Isa 54:12? The protective surrounding wall of the eschatological Zion was of considerable importance (cf. Jos. Asen. 15:7, 16; 19:6; Rev 21:12, 17-18). Moreover, of the various architectural features

---

[24]   See especially 4QpIsa[d] commenting on Isa 54:11-12.

[25]   In the parallel to Eusebius, Hist. Eccl. 2.23.7, in Epiphanius, Haer. 78.7.7, Oblias is said to mean τεῖχος.

mentioned in Isa 54:11-12, it is the only one which occurs in the singular. It was therefore appropriate to describe the unique position James came to hold at the head of the mother-church in Jerusalem. From the preceding context in Hegesippus (6), we can see that it was in his role as intercessor in prayer that James was thought to protect the people, forming a protective wall around them. No doubt after his death, this thought was connected with a pun on the term גְּבֶל־עָם ('Ωβλιας). Through James' constant prayer for the people, as their גבול (wall), his knees became like those of a גמל (camel). However, we can also see in Hegesippus how the original meaning of his title "Rampart of the People," as part of the concept of the church as the messianic Temple, was transformed in legendary development to bear another significance. Impressed by the way the Jewish revolt and the fall of Jerusalem followed swiftly on James' death, later Jewish Christians supposed that it had been James' constant prayer for the forgiveness of the Jewish people which restrained the divine judgment[26] until Jerusalem's guilt reached its high point in putting James to death and depriving itself of the power of his intercession. Thus "Rampart of the People" came to be understood as referring to his protective function in relation to the Jewish people (cf. Eusebius, *Hist. Eccl.* 3.7.8), not the messianic people of God imaged as the new Temple.

Identifying "Rampart of the People" as originally a reference to a feature of the eschatological Temple, a reference already submerged in the tradition Hegesippus reported, can also provide the clue to another feature of Hegesippus' account of James which has always been found puzzling.[27] The narrative of James' death begins when some people "enquired of him who was the gate of Jesus, and he said that he was the Saviour" (ἐπυνθάνοντο αὐτοῦ τίς ἡ θύρα Ἰησοῦ, καὶ ἔλεγον τοῦτον εἶναι τὸν σωτῆρα) (8). The use of τοῦτον in James' answer requires that the question be translated, not "what is the gate of Jesus?" but "who is the gate of Jesus?" It is repeated later: "tell us who is the gate of Jesus" (12). The odd formulation becomes more intelligible if we remember that the architectural features of the messianic Temple were taken, in early Christianity, to represent

---

26   Compare the anticipated result of the death of Moses, who interceded for Israel every hour, in *T. Moses* 11:16-17.

27   For other explanations of "the gate of Jesus," see Pratscher, *Der Herren-bruder Jakobus*, 113 n. 34; E. Bammel, *Jesu Nachfolger* (Studia Delitschiana 3/1; Heidelberg: L. Schneider, 1988) 39.

persons. The question presupposes reference to a gate or door to the Temple: James is asked to explain who this represents. Isaiah 54:12 refers to gates of the eschatological Zion, but our text seems to require a reference to a single gate. This can be found in Ps 118:20. This is the psalm which in v. 22 refers to the rejected stone that becomes the keystone or cornerstone, a statement which early Christians understood to mean that Jesus became the cornerstone of the new Temple (1 Pet 2:7; cf. Mark 12:10). It is not at all surprising that the gate to which the adjacent v. 20 refers should also be interpreted as an element in the architecture of the messianic Temple. This verse reads: "This is the gate of YHWH; the righteous shall enter through it."[28] We can easily imagine an account, a little garbled in Hegesippus' version, in which James is asked about this "gate of the LORD" through which the righteous shall enter the messianic Temple, i.e. become members of the messianic Israel of the last days. James interprets "the LORD" as Jesus, and explains that the gate is Jesus in his role as the Saviour (cf. Ps 118:21) granting entrance into the Temple. It is possible that the *Second Apocalypse of James* preserves a little more of James' exposition of the gate, albeit in gnosticized form:

> through you those who wish to enter in will open the good door. And they turn about (on the path they have so far followed?), that they may (henceforth) walk in the way which (leads) before this door, and follow you and enter, [and you] accompany them inside and give to each one the reward that falls to his share (55:6-14).

Since the psalm says that "the righteous shall enter through it," James the Righteous One is appropriately the one who enters first so that others may follow him.

So far we have discovered plausible explanations of two very puzzling features of Hegesippus' account by finding their background in early Christianity's metaphorical understanding of the eschatological Temple. But whereas the eschatological Temple nowhere appears on the surface of Hegesippus' account, the physical Temple in Jerusalem is prominent, as the location of James' prayer, his preaching, his martyrdom and his burial. The narrative in the *Second Apocalypse of James* is also located in the Temple, and makes

---

28 The use of θύρα in Hegesippus, rather than πύλη (LXX Ps 117:20), probably indicates that the Hebrew text of the psalm, rather than the Greek, lies behind the account Hegesippus follows.

its own contact with Psalm 118 when it says that priests, intent on killing James, "found him standing by the pinnacle of the Temple, beside the mighty cornerstone" (61:20-23). Here the cornerstone is not an image of Jesus Christ in his relation to the eschatological Temple (as in 1 Pet 2:7), but a literal part of the Temple building, the spot from which James is thrown down to his death. Here, as in other instances we shall notice shortly, Psalm 118 has been used as a source for describing the events of James' death. But in this procedure the Temple to which Psalm 118 refers is not the eschatological Temple metaphorically understood, but the literal Temple in which James preached and was put to death.

In this transition from metaphorical to literal Temple imagery I suggest we have an instance of a common phenomenon in ancient storytelling. M. R. Lefkowitz, in her study of the lives of the Greek poets, showed how the authors of these lives produced biographical stories about the poets by taking metaphorical references literally. For example, Pindar's reference to his song as "like a bee" (*Pyth.* 10.45) was the source of an anecdote in which a bee builds a honeycomb in his mouth.[29] Jewish exegetes did the same with texts of the Hebrew Bible. For example, God's command to Abraham to leave his "father's house" (Gen 12:1) is understood literally in the *Apocalypse of Abraham*'s story about Abraham's escape from the fire: he is commanded to leave his father Terah's dwelling house and does so just as fire from heaven falls to consume it (*Apoc. Abr.* 8:4-6). Similarly, the author of the *Acts of Paul* took Paul's apparently metaphorical statements about fighting with wild animals at Ephesus (1 Cor 15:32) and being rescued from the mouth of the lion (2 Tim 4:17), and created a story of Paul's encounter with an actual lion in the amphitheatre of Ephesus.[30] These analogies help us to postulate how old traditions about James and the Jerusalem church imaged as the eschatological Temple, gave rise, through appropriate biblical

---

[29]   M. R. Lefkowitz, *The Lives of the Greek Poets* (London: Duckworth, 1981) 59, 155-56.

[30]   R. Bauckham, "The Acts of Paul as a Sequel to Acts," in B. C. Winter and A. D. Clarke (eds.), *The Book of Acts in Its Ancient Literary Setting* (Grand Rapids: Eerdmans; Carlisle: Paternoster Press, 1993) 125-27. A. Hilhorst ("Biblical Metaphors Taken Literally," in T. Baarda, A. Hilhorst, G. P. Luttikhuizen and A. S. van der Woude [eds.], *Text and Testimony* [A. F. J. Klijn Festschrift; Kampen: J. H. Kok, 1988] 123-29) discusses other Jewish and Christian examples of the phenomenon.

exegesis, to an account in which the physical Temple building in Jerusalem plays a major role in James' story. To understand the development of this account from biblical exegesis, we should also remember the key that Hegesippus has given us: that the prophets call James "the Righteous One" and "Righteousness." Finally, we should expect, as often in early Christian interpretation of the Hebrew Bible, that the Jewish exegetical principle of *gezerâ šawâ* (according to which passages in which the same words occur can be used to interpret each other) will be important.

We begin with the way Psalm 118 has generated much of the story of James' death in the common source on which Hegesippus and the *Second Apocalypse of James* depend. Perhaps because of the use of Ps 118:20-22 that we have already discussed, perhaps also because of the references to "righteousness" and "the righteous" in vv. 19-20, James was understood to be the speaker in the whole psalm. This has generated elements of the story as follows:

(1) Ps 118:13: "I was pushed hard so that I fell":
cf. Hegesippus 14-16; *2 Apoc. Jas* 61:23-26.

(2) Ps 118:10: "All nations surrounded me":
cf. Hegesippus 11: "all the tribes, with the nations also, have come together"; *2 Apoc. Jas* 45:19: "the multitude of the peoples."

(3) Ps 118:25: "Save us, we beseech you [= Hosanna], Yhwh":
cf. Hegesippus 14: "Hosanna to the son of David" (cf. Matt 21:9, 15).

(4) Ps 118:22: "the stone . . . the head of the corner":
cf. *2 Apoc. Jas* 61:21-23: "standing by the pinnacle of the Temple, beside the mighty cornerstone"; Hegesippus 11, 12: "the pinnacle of the Temple" (cf. Matt 4:5; Luke 4:9).

(5) Ps 118:28: "You are my God, and I will give thanks to you":
cf. *2 Apoc. Jas* 62:16: "My God and Father . . ."

(6) Ps 118:8-9, 14, 17-18, 21, 27a seem to be echoed in James' prayer in *2 Apoc. Jas* 62:16–63:29, which must therefore preserve material from a prayer in the common source, even though it has been strongly gnosticized by the author of the *Second Apocalypse of James*.

(7) Ps 118:15: "The voice of joy and salvation in the tents of the righteous."

This can be connected by *gezerâ šawâ* with Jer 35:7, 10 ("tents"), with the result that "the tents of the righteous" are "the tents of the Rechabites." The Rechabites, like James in Hegesippus, abstained from wine (Jer 35:6, 14), and in Jeremiah 35 they represent those who are faithful to God by contrast with the people of Jerusalem on whom judgment is threatened (35:17). They are therefore suitably associated with James, and called "the righteous" in Ps 118:15, just as James himself is "the Righteous one." Jewish exegesis understood the promise to the Rechabites in Jer 35:19, that "Jonadab son of Rechab shall not lack a descendant to stand before me for ever," to mean that the Rechabites would be priests, since the phrase "to stand before me" (עמד לפני) elsewhere means "to minister as priests in the Temple" (Deut 10:8; 2 Chr 29:11; Ezek 44:15).[31] These exegetical connexions explain the otherwise inexplicable appearance of "one of the priests of the sons of Rechab, the son of the Rechabim, of whom Jeremiah the prophet bore witness" in Hegesippus' narrative of the death of James (17).[32]

(8) The dating of Hegesippus' narrative at Passover (10) may be explained by Psalm 118, since, although this psalm played an important part in the ritual of the Feast of Tabernacles, the Gospels connect it with Jesus' entry into Jerusalem at Passover time (Matt 21:9; Mark 11:9-10; Luke 19:38; John 12:13, quoting Ps 118:25-26).

(9) Finally, Psalm 118 probably also provides the starting-point for the description of James as a Nazirite who alone was allowed to enter the Temple sanctuary, with which Hegesippus' account of James begins. Psalm 118:19 reads:

> Open to me [i.e. James] the gates of "Righteousness" [= James] that I may enter through them . . .

This can be connected with Ezek 44:15-17, according to which "the sons of Zadok" (צדק = "Righteousness" = James?) "shall enter my sanctuary" and "enter the gates of the inner court," wearing no wool but linen. Of these priests it is also required that they do not shave their heads (44:20) or drink wine (44:21). These requirements

---

31   *Sipre Num.* §78 (on Num 10:29-36); *Tg.* Jer 35:19. See C. H. Knights, "Jethro Merited that his Descendants should Sit in the Chamber of Hewn Stone," *JJS* 41 (1990) 247-53; F. Manns, "Une tradition judéo-chrétienne rapporté par Eusebius de Césarée," *Cristianesimo nella Storia* 15 (1994) 145-48.

32   In the parallel passage in Epiphanius, *Haer.* 78:14, Simeon son of Clopas (James' cousin and successor as bishop of Jerusalem) appears in place of this Rechabite priest. The most likely explanation of this is not that Epiphanius preserves a more original text of Hegesippus, as H. J. Lawlor (*Eusebiana* [Oxford: Oxford University Press, 1917] 7), for example, thought, but that Epiphanius could make no sense of the reference to a Rechabite priest, and substituted the person in Jerusalem at the time who was most likely to speak in support of James at the time of his death.

correlate with some of the requirements made of Nazirites, according to Num 6:2-5 and Judg 13:4-14. Exegetical links between these three passages—Ezekiel 44, Numbers 6 and Judges 13—account for most of Hegesippus' opening description of James the ascetic intercessor:

Hegesippus	Ezekiel 44	Numbers 6	Judges 13
holy from mother's womb			5, 7
did not drink wine or strong drink	21[33]	3	4, 7, 14
did not eat flesh			(4, 7, 14)[34]
no razor went on his head	20	5	5
did not anoint himself with oil			
did not go to the baths			
did not wear wool but linen	17		

Evidently, to the features derived from scriptural exegesis have been added some standard elements of ascetic practice. Abstaining from wine was often combined with abstention from meat, as a kind of mild fasting (abstention from luxury in food and drink) which could be sustained indefinitely, sometimes as a form of mourning (e.g. Dan 10:3; *t. Sot.* 15.11-15; Philo, *Vit. Cont.* 37.73; 4 Ezra 9:23-26; 12:51; *T. Reub.* 1:10; *T. Judah* 15:4).[35] Abstention from anointing oneself with oil is similarly associated with mourning (Isa 61:3; Dan 10:3), but another reason for avoiding it was that it was particularly easily subject to impurity (Josephus, *J.W.* 2.8.3 §123; CD 12:15-17). Though apparently not attested elsewhere for Jews, abstention from bathing (the baths here are not the those for ritual purification, but the public baths for washing and relaxing) was a common ascetic practice. Like abstention from wine and meat, it was a case of avoiding luxury.

Thus the list of practices of holiness may have been expanded in the course of transmission, with standard elements of asceticism added to those elements derived from exegesis of Ezekiel, Numbers

---

[33]   For priests not drinking wine when entering the Temple, see also Lev 10:9; Pseudo-Hecataeus, *apud* Josephus, *Against Apion* 1.22 §199.

[34]   According to these verses, the Nazirite is not to eat anything *unclean.*

[35]   The *Gospel of the Ebionites* changes the text of Matt 3:4 in order to make John a vegetarian, perhaps interpreting John's Nazirite status (Luke 1:15) to require , abstention from meat as well as wine, in the same way as the account of James in Hegesippus does.

and Judges. But postulating the exegetical connexions suggested above as the source of the account of James in Hegesippus has the considerable advantage of explaining the extraordinary assertion that he alone was allowed to enter the sanctuary (Hegesippus 6). Ezekiel 44 is explicitly concerned with discriminating between those excluded from the sanctuary and those who alone may enter, the sons of Zadok, if they observe the requirements of abstention from wool, razors and wine (44:5, 9, 16). In the Greek of Eusebius, it is the holy place (τὰ ἅγια) and the Temple (ναός) which James alone was allowed to enter. The Latin and the Syriac correct this to "the holy of holies," which many modern scholars have assumed must be intended. In that case, James would be portrayed as the High Priest. From any knowledge of what occurred in the Temple or even of what the Torah prescribed, it would be incomprehensible that James alone could be admitted to the Temple building, the holy place, which all priests could enter. But the account in Hegesippus, dating from long after the destruction of the Jerusalem Temple, was concerned not with historical plausibility, but with exegetical deductions. James alone fulfilled the conditions Ezekiel 44 lays down for entering the gates of the inner court of the Temple, as James himself in Ps 118:19 says that he does!

But perhaps a further explanation is possible. Since Ezekiel 44 concerns the eschatological Temple, it may be that the application to James originally belonged to the metaphorical understanding of the Temple as the messianic Israel. James was the new Zadok who alone entered the inner court when he offered the sacrifices of intercessory prayer for his people. Only when this metaphorical understanding was transmuted into a literal account did the extraordinary notion that James and James alone was allowed into the sanctuary of the Herodian Temple result.

Two elements of the narrative of James' death in Hegesippus that are not connected with Psalm 118 remain to be considered. One is the quotation of Isa 3:10, the other the notion that James was finally killed with a blow from a fuller's club. The text form of the quotation from Isa 3:10 (Hegesippus 16) has never been adequately explained.[36] It differs considerably from the MT and in this

---

[36]   In this connexion reference is often made to Wis 2:12 (ἐνεδρεύσωμεν τὸν δίκαιον, ὅτι δύσχρηστος ἡμῖν ἐστιν), which is presumably dependent on LXX Isa 3:10. But to suppose that Hegesippus (or his source) had this text in mind explains nothing that is not better explained by his knowledge of LXX Isa 3:10.

resembles the Septuagint, but it also presupposes a Hebrew text different from that which the Septuagint follows:

MT   (etc.) ... אמרו צדיק כי טוב

LXX   εἰπόντες Δήσωμεν τὸν δίκαιον, ὅτι δύσχρηστος ἡμῖν
            ἐστιν· τοίνυν τὰ γενήματα τῶν ἔργων αὐτῶν φάγονται

Hegesippus ἄρωμεν τὸν δίκαιον, ὅτι δύσχρηστος ἡμῖν ἐστιν· τοίνυν τὰ
            γενήματα τῶν ἔργων αὐτῶν φάγονται

The difference between Δήσωμεν (LXX) and ἄρωμεν (Hegesippus) must derive from variant readings of the first verb in the Hebrew (MT: אמר; LXX: אסר; Hegesippus: אסף). For MT's אמרו, LXX must have read נאסר, and Hegesippus (or his source) נאסף. But Hegesippus' version of the rest of the verse is identical with the Septuagint. So he (or his source) must have been following the Septuagint, but also had access to a Hebrew text which supplied him with the variant ἄρωμεν. Δήσωμεν ("let us bind") would have spoiled the correspondence between the prophecy and its claimed fulfilment in the death of James. So Hegesippus (or his source) has resorted to a technique characteristic of both the Qumran Pesharim and early Christian citation of prophetic scripture: choice or creation of a text form that suits the interpretation to be placed on the text.[37] (Sometimes the variant text may be chosen among existing variants known to the exegete, sometimes created by the exegete, deliberately altering the Hebrew text by the change of a letter or two to suit the desired meaning.) Hegesippus (or his source) is evidently working with the Hebrew text as well as the Greek version, something which must have been natural for a Palestinian Jew writing in Greek, though scholars rarely allow for it.

Thus, in this quotation of Scripture, we are once again in touch with detailed prophetic exegesis of the kind which had been practised in Palestinian Jewish Christianity from the beginning.[38] The rele-

---

[37]   G. J. Brooke, *Exegesis at Qumran: 4QFlorilegium in its Jewish Context* (JSOTSup 29; Sheffield: JSOT Press, 1985) 111-12, 288-89; M. P. Horgan, *Pesharim: Qumran Interpretations of Biblical Books* (CBQMS 8; Washington: Catholic Biblical Association, 1979) 245 n. 69; E. E. Ellis, *Paul's Use of the Old Testament* (Edinburgh: Oliver & Boyd, 1957) 139-47; idem, *Prophecy and Hermeneutic in Early Christianity* (WUNT 18; Tübingen: Mohr [Siebeck], 1978) 152, 175-80.

[38]   Cf. the discussion of Jude's exegesis in Bauckham, *Jude and the Relatives of Jesus*, 179-234.

vance of this particular text did not lie solely in its reference to "the righteous one," readily understood as James, but also in its context in Isaiah's prophecy of the judgment and destruction of Jerusalem, just as Jeremiah's encounter with the Rechabites is connected with his prophecy of the judgment of the city. Isaiah 3:10 in its context expresses the link between the martyrdom of James and the fall of Jerusalem which the common source used by Hegesippus and the *Second Apocalypse of James* stressed. Palestinian Jewish Christians read the whole of Isaiah 1–5 with reference to the fall of Jerusalem in 70 CE. It was surely they who first understood Isa 1:8 and 2:3[39] with reference to their own headquarters, the mother church on the southern part of the western hill of Jerusalem, where James himself had presided and which had survived the destruction of the city, a lone synagogue "like a booth in a vineyard" (Isa 1:8; cf. 5:1-7). Plausibly, it was they who first called this southern part of the western hill, outside the walls of Aelia Capitolina, "mount Zion" precisely because of their application of these prophecies to the Jerusalem church. As with the literalistic reading of Temple imagery in Hegesippus' account of the death of James, so also the Zion of Isaiah's prophecies became the geographical location of the Jerusalem church as well as the messianic community centred there.

In Hegesippus' account James is finally killed with a blow from a fuller's club. (Whether this should be seen as an added brutality, or as a mercifully quicker death than the slow agony of being stoned to death, is not clear.) It could, of course, be a genuine historical reminiscence. If it has, as we might suspect after our study of the influence of Psalm 118 on the narrative, an exegetical source, this has not yet been discovered. But one other form of explanation is also possible. The *Ascension of Isaiah* describes how Isaiah was sawn in half with a wooden saw (5:1), an event which an angel predicts to him, when he is ascending to heaven, in this way: "you are destined in the lot of the Lord, the lot of the tree, to come here [i.e. to heaven after death]" (8:12). The meaning is that Isaiah's fate is to be the same as the Lord's, i.e. Jesus Christ's. Not only would both be put to death, but the instrument of their death would in both cases be

---

39   For these texts in Eusebius and Cyril of Jerusalem, see P. W. L. Walker, *Holy City, Holy Places?* (Oxford: Clarendon Press, 1990) chap. 9. For Epiphanius' quotation of Isa 1:8, relaying local Jerusalem church tradition, see J. Murphy-O'Connor, "The Cenacle–Topographical Setting for Acts 2:44-45," in Bauckham (ed.), *The Book of Acts*, 307-8.

wooden ("the tree"). The function of the club in Hegesippus could be similar, completing the parallels between Jesus and James which run through the account. Since James was known to have been stoned, the use of an instrument of wood had to be additional to the stoning. The information that it was a fuller who clubbed James with the instrument he used to beat the clothes is then a narrative device to explain how a wooden club should have been available in the crowd.

Finally, is it now possible to identify an original core of tradition from which the account developed in the—mainly exegetical—ways we have described. We have suggested that the two instances of Temple imagery used metaphorically for the Christian community— James as "rampart of the people" and the discussion of "the gate of Jesus"—predate the references to the literal Temple, which have developed from the use of Psalm 118, already linked with James' death through the metaphorical use of the "gate of Jesus" image (Ps 118:20), but now treated as an account of the death of James in the Temple building. Tentatively, we may suggest that, in the core tradition, James' christological interpretation of "the gate of YHWH" (Ps 118:20) led to his judicial execution by stoning. It remains to consider, in the next section, whether this possibly authentically historical core of the tradition coheres with the conclusions that can be drawn from Josephus' more reliably historical information.

4. FOR WHAT OFFENCE WAS JAMES PUT TO DEATH?

That James was stoned to death is the one point on which Josephus and our witnesses to the Christian tradition about the death of James agree. According to Josephus, the High Priest Ananus (Annas) II convened a council and accused James and some others of transgressing the law (παρανομησάντων), for which they were condemned and stoned to death (*Ant.* 20.9.1 §200). Josephus does not specify the offence of which James and the others were accused, and we cannot be sure that it was the same in each case. However, it is clear that James was condemned for an offence for which the High Priest and his council believed that the Torah prescribed execution by stoning.[40]

---

40 R. P. Martin (*James* [WBC 48; Waco: Word, 1988] lxiii) denies that Josephus can mean that James was charged with transgression of the Torah, since the Pharisees would not then have objected, but he concedes that the stoning of James "at least indicates that Ananus was invoking the Sadducean penal code." He fails to see that "the Sadducean penal code" was simply the Sadducean interpretation

It is important to notice that the stoning of James was a matter of judicial sentence. Stoning to death could occur as the spontaneous action of a mob enraged against an individual (1 Sam 30:6; 1 Kgs 12:18; cf. Josephus, *Ant.* 16.11.7 §394), since it was a form of killing for which weapons could usually be found immediately at hand. This seems to be what happened in the only other accounts of stoning in the Second Temple period recorded by Josephus besides that of James and his companions: the stoning of Onias (Honi the Circle-drawer) (*Ant.* 14.2.1 §22-24) and the attempted stoning of Menaḥem the son of Judas the Galilean (*J.W.* 2.17.9 §445). However, it is possible in both these cases that the crowd had a specific legal offence in mind, which Josephus' narrative does not make apparent. They would then be comparable with John 8:59 and 10:31-33, where the attempted stoning of Jesus by the Jewish leaders is a matter of judicial execution for the crime of blasphemy. Formal trial is evidently not required, since those who undertake to stone him have themselves witnessed the crime. Only one other stoning occurs in a narrative set in the Second Temple period: that of Stephen in Acts 7. This resembles the case of James in that Stephen is arraigned before the High Priest's council (Acts 6:12, 15; 7:1). But it is more like the Synoptic Gospels' accounts of the trial of Jesus in that Stephen is not convicted of the charges initially brought against him (6:13-14), but condemned for his own words, understood as blasphemous, when members of the council themselves hear them (7:55-57; cf. Mark 14:62-64). Following Jewish legal procedure (Deut 17:7; cf. John 8:7), the witnesses themselves begin the stoning (Acts 7:58). At this point the account seems to contradict the probable implication of Josephus' account of the execution of James, corroborated by the Gospel accounts of the trial and death of Jesus: that only the Roman governor had the right to execute.[41] The correct solution to this difficulty is probably not that Stephen's death was the result of mere mob violence, since it is the members of the High Priest's council who seize Stephen and embark on stoning him. But the case may be similar to those in the Fourth Gospel (8:59; 10:31-33): witnessing the

---

of the Torah, and that the Pharisees' objection can readily be understood in terms of a difference between Pharisaic and Sadducean interpretations of the Torah.

[41] See E. P. Sanders, *Judaism: Practice and Belief 63 BCE – 66 CE* (London: SCM Press, 1992) 540-41 n. 40, for a sensible recent endorsement of this view, which has, of course, been much disputed.

crime themselves, the members of the court are stirred to immediate implementation of the penalty the Torah demands. Their zeal leads them to ignore the need to refer the matter to the governor.

In Josephus' account of the death of James, the High Priest is evidently concerned in a more premeditated way to avoid the constraint on his powers constituted by the governor's prerogative. Presumably the governor would not have been likely to accept his case for these executions. So he takes advantage of an interregnum between Roman governors. However, it is inconceivable that he should not have acted according to the Torah as he understood it. James must have been convicted of a crime for which the Torah was understood to prescribe execution by stoning. This is in any case clear from Josephus who, despite his generally unfavourable view of Ananus II in this passage, says that James and his companions were accused of transgressing the law (*Ant.* 20.9.1 §200). Our inquiry now concerns the crime of which James was accused. We are not concerned with Ananus' *motives* for wanting James executed, which may or may not have been connected with the legal charge brought against James. Too many discussions of James' death confuse these two issues and thereby evade the question: For what offence, according to the Torah, was James condemned to be stoned to death?

The Torah explicitly prescribes stoning for the following offences: giving offspring to Molech (Lev 20:2),[42] being a medium or wizard (Lev 20:27), blasphemy (Lev 24:13-23), breaking the Sabbath (Num 15:32-36), secretly enticing to the worship of other gods (Deut 13:11[10]), idolatry (Deut 17:2-7),[43] disobedience by a son to parents (Deut 21:18-21), premarital intercourse by a woman subsequently married (Deut 22:20-21), adultery by and with a betrothed woman (Deut 22:23-27). Apart from the case of an apostate city, all of whose inhabitants are to be put to the sword (Deut 13:13-16[12-15]), only one other form of capital punishment, burning, is specifically prescribed in two cases: for intercourse with both a woman and her daughter (Lev 20:14) and for prostitution by a daughter of a priest (Lev 21:9; but cf. also Gen 38:24-26). The execution of a murderer by an avenger of blood (Num 35:19, 21) must be presumed to be by sword or dagger, but the method is not stated.[44] Strangulation, which

---

42   *Jubilees* 30:7-11 interprets this to mean giving a daughter or sister in marriage to a Gentile husband.

43   This law is quite closely reproduced in 11QT 55:15-21.

44   *m. Sanh.* 9:1 treats this case and that of the apostate city as execution by

was the penalty for certain crimes according to the Mishna (*Sanh.* 11:1), is not mentioned in the Torah, where hanging is not a method of execution but the exposure of an already dead corpse (Deut 21:22).

In many cases of capital punishment, the method is not prescribed explicitly in the Torah. It would then be a matter of halakhah, and so is very likely to have been debated in the Second Temple period. In the Mishna tractate Sanhedrin, all cases of capital punishment required by the Torah are allocated a method, one of the four which it recognizes: stoning, burning, strangulation and beheading. To the list of crimes for which stoning is the punishment, it adds: three cases of incest (Lev 20:11-12), male homosexual intercourse (Lev 20:13), bestiality by men and by women (Lev 20:15-16; Exod 22:19), cursing father or mother (Lev 20:9; Exod 21:17), leading people astray to other gods (Deut 13:14[13]), and sorcery (Deut 18:10; Exod 22:18) (*m. Sanh.* 7:4–8:5). The crimes for which strangulation is the penalty are: striking father or mother (Exod 21:15), kidnapping an Israelite (Deut 24:7; Exod 21:16), rebellion by an elder against the decision of the court (Deut 17:8-13), false prophecy (i.e. prophesying in YHWH's name what he has not commanded: Deut 18:20b-22), prophecy in the name of false gods (Deut 18:20a), adultery (Lev 18:20; Deut 22:22), and false witness against a daughter of a priest and her lover (a debatable instance of Deut 19:19) (*m. Sanh.* 11:1-6). The crimes meriting burning to death are not increased, while those meriting beheading (culpable murder, and the apostasy of a whole city: *m. Sanh.* 9:1; 10:4-5) are those which the Torah states or implies incur death by the sword (Deut 13:13-16[12-15]; Num 35:19, 21).

These provisions of the Mishna cannot be presumed to date from the Second Temple period, still less to have been operative in the judgments of the High Priest's council. However, they do correspond to Josephus' comment that the Pharisees are "naturally lenient [ἐπιεικῶς] in the matter of punishments" (*Ant.* 13.10.6 §294), and so may represent at least the general tendency of Second Temple Pharisaic halakhah with regard to capital punishment. Of the two most severe punishments, burning and stoning,[45] burning is restric-

---

beheading.

[45] The Mishna reports disagreement between the Sages and R. Simeon as to whether the order of severity is stoning, burning, beheading, strangling, or

ted to those crimes to which the Torah itself explicitly applies it, while the list of crimes incurring stoning is extended only to include the most heinous of sexual transgressions and crimes virtually equivalent to others for which the Torah itself prescribes stoning. Other crimes for which the form of execution is not specified in the Torah are all treated as incurring the less severe punishment of strangulation. These include adultery, which (from comparison of Deut 22:20-21, 22, and 23-24) would be much more naturally supposed to incur stoning (and cf. Ezek 16:40; 23:47). Indeed, the *pericope adulterae* (John 8:4-5) shows that at least some people in the late Second Temple period thought Deut 22:22 requires the stoning of a woman caught in the act of adultery. In what follows we shall not treat the material in Mishna Sanhedrin as direct historical evidence for the Second Temple period, but we shall treat it as suggestive of the kind of interpretation of the Torah which could have been practised—by Pharisees or others—in the late Second Temple period.

Josephus introduces his account of the "rash" act of Ananus II in convening the council to try James and others by explaining that Ananus "followed the school of the Sadducees" and reminding his readers of his earlier contrast between the Sadducees and the Pharisees on the issue of severity in punishments (*Ant.* 13.10.6 §294), though he does not here name the Pharisees: "the Sadducees . . . are more cruel (ὠμοί) than all the Jews in the matter of judgments" (*Ant.* 20.9.1 §199). When he goes on to say that "those of the inhabitants of the city who were considered the most lenient [ἐπιεικέστατοι] and also accurate [ἀκριβεῖς] with respect to the laws were deeply offended by this" (20.9.1 §201), undoubtedly meaning Pharisees,[46] Josephus must be implying that they objected to the harshness of the punishment inflicted.[47] A difference in interpretation of the law between Sadducees and Pharisees must be at stake.[48] Josephus does

---

burning, stoning, strangling, beheading (*m. Sanh.* 7:1; 9:3). In either case, burning and stoning are more severe than beheading and strangling.

46   Cf. *J.W.* 1.5.2 §110; 2.8.14 §162; *Ant.* 17.2.4 §41; *Vita* 38 §191, as well as *Ant.* 13.10.6 §294, quoted above.

47   It is less likely that they insisted on more rigorous procedures of proof than the High Priest. In *Ant.* 13.10.6 §294, Josephus seems to be commenting on the kind of punishments they favoured, rather than their caution in reaching and sustaining a verdict.

48   This is recognized by P.-A. Bernheim, *James, Brother of Jesus* (London:

not go into detail because, as in his more formal accounts of the differences between the Jewish "schools," he does not expect his Gentile readers to be interested in halakhah. Moreover, in relation to the execution of James, Josephus has a further motive for not discussing the charge in detail. He did not wish to refer to items of Christian belief, for Jewish Christianity is a topic he conspicuously avoids throughout his work, even in this reference to James.

What could be the crime for which James was condemned, under Sadducean halakhah, to be stoned, but for which the Pharisees considered this too severe a penalty? While it is not impossible that James was accused of adultery or incest, it is highly probable that a plausible charge was connected in some way with his Christian allegiance and his highly public role as head of the Jerusalem church. There seem to be only two possible charges which could account for the difference between Sadducees and Pharisees over his punishment. One is that he was charged with blasphemy. In this case, it is beyond dispute that the Torah itself prescribes stoning (Lev 24:10-23), but it is quite possible that Sadducees and Pharisees differed over the definition of blasphemy,[49] the Sadducees defining it more broadly, the Pharisees more narrowly. The latter would be more "lenient" in this case by restricting the scope of the crime which incurred stoning. According to the Mishna, the blasphemer "is not culpable unless he pronounces the Name itself" (*m. Sanh.* 7:5), but the New Testament strongly suggests that a wider interpretation of blasphemy was employed by the Temple authorities (Matt 9:3; 26:64-66; Mark 2:7; 14:62-64; Luke 5:21; John 8:59; 10:31-33; Acts 6:11) and that they considered blasphemy in this wider sense punishable by stoning

---

SCM Press, 1997) 249, but he misses the possibility, which we shall develop, that the Pharisees agreed that James' crime merited death, but not that it merited the severe form of capital punishment that stoning was considered to be. Cf. also Mason, *Josephus*, 180-81.

[49]   This topic has been much debated because of its relevance to the Synoptic accounts of the trial of Jesus. For recent discussions, see E. P. Sanders, *Jewish Law from Jesus to the Mishnah* (London: SCM Press, 1990) 57-67; R. E. Brown, *The Death of the Messiah*, vol. 1 (New York: Doubleday, 1994) 520-27, 532-47; D. L. Bock, "The Son of Man Seated at God's Right Hand and the Debate over Jesus' 'Blasphemy'," in J. B. Green and M. Turner (eds.), *Jesus of Nazareth: Lord and Christ* (I. H. Marshall Festschrift; Grand Rapids: Eerdmans; Carlisle: Paternoster, 1994) 181-91.

(John 8:59; 10:31-33; Acts 7:55-58).[50] The view of the Mishna—a plausible interpretation of Lev 24:10-23, especially in view of v. 16[51]—could have been the Pharisaic view in the time of James.

In fact, it is probable that Josephus himself, in the context in which he first explains that, by contrast with the Sadducees, the Pharisees "are naturally lenient in the matter of punishments" (*Ant.* 13.10.6 §294), narrates an example of this difference which concerns the law on blasphemy and its penalty. A Pharisee had slandered (βλασφημία) Hyrcanus I by suggesting that he might be illegitimate and should give up the high priesthood. A Sadducee, a friend of Hyrcanus, urges him to ask the Pharisees what punishment the man deserves, knowing that they would not think the crime worthy of the death penalty. The Pharisees, not considering this a case of blasphemy for which the Torah prescribes death, recommend flogging as sufficient (*Ant.* 13.10.5–6 §289-295). Hyrcanus, in thinking the crime worthy of death, probably relies on a different interpretation of the law, supplied by his Sadducee friend. According to this interpretation, the penalty for blasphemy prescribed in Lev 24:10-23 can be applied also to the crimes described in Exod 22:28 ("You shall not revile God, or curse a leader of your people"), since the passages are linked by common use of the verb קלל (Piel: to revile, to bring into contempt). Thus slandering the High Priest, God's representative, constitutes a form of blasphemy and incurs stoning.[52] We need not suppose that Ananus II accused James of blasphemy in this sense. But if Exod 22:28 is brought into connexion with Lev 24:10-23 as defining the crime of blasphemy for which stoning is prescribed, then the crime is not restricted to cases in which the Name is uttered, but extends to any speech which can be construed as dishonouring God or bringing God into contempt. Claims made about Jesus by James, similar to those attributed to Jesus (Matt 26:64-66; Mark 14:62-64) and Stephen (Acts 7:55-58), could thus have been construed as blasphemous by the High Priest and his council, guided by Sadducean halakhah, but not according to a narrower interpretation

---

50   Whether or not these passages are historically reliable, they are certainly evidence for the view that in Jewish law blasphemy in a quite wide sense was punishable by death, and show that this view was widely held in early Christianity.

51   LXX Lev 24: 11, 16, seems to be evidence of the currency at an early date of the interpretation found in the Mishna.

52   If this Sadducean interpretation of the law were well-known, it would add significant overtones to Acts 23:2-5.

of the law advanced by Pharisees.

The alternative possibility is that James was charged under the laws of Deuteronomy 13, which concern those who lead people to worship other gods. There seem to be three categories. The first (vv. 2-6[1-5]) is a prophet or seer ("a dreamer of dreams") who promises portents that take place, and says, "Let us follow other gods" (vv. 2-3[1-2]). He is not a false prophet in the sense condemned in Deut 18:20b-22: a prophet who speaks in the name of YHWH words which YHWH has not commanded and whose predictions do not prove true. The predictions of the prophet of Deuteronomy 13 are fulfilled, and so his encouragement to apostasy from YHWH is the more insidious. A good indication of the way this passage was understood in the late Second Temple period is the account in Pseudo-Philo's *Biblical Antiquities* of the non-biblical character Aod the Midianite magician (chap. 34). Like the prophet of Deuteronomy 13, Aod is a means by which God tests Israel's loyalty to himself (Deut 13:4-5[3-4]; *LAB* 34:5). Aod promises to show the people the sun by night and uses magic to do so. They suppose this portent to show the power of the gods of the Midianites, and so are led astray (*implanatus est*) into serving other gods (34:4-5). The episode is clearly modeled on Deut 13:2-6[1-5], and shows that the prophet to which it refers could be understood, not as giving true prophecies in YHWH's name or performing true miracles by YHWH's power before then preaching apostasy,[53] but as a pretended prophet who works miracles by magic in order to lead Israel into apostasy. Understood in this way, the passage fits remarkably well the Jewish charge against Jesus, as reported by Justin (*Dial.* 69.7; cf. 108.2): "a magician and a deceiver of the people,"[54] and as later reported in rabbinic literature: "he practised sorcery and beguiled [היסית] and led Israel astray [הידיח]" (*b. Sanh.* 43a). According to this rabbinic passage Jesus was stoned to death, a view which must have arisen from the assumption that someone guilty by the law of Deuteronomy 13 must have been executed by the method there prescribed (13:11[10]).[55] Evidence in

---

53   This is how G. Brin ("The Laws of the Prophets in the Sect of the Judean Desert: Studies in 4Q375," *JSP* 10 [1992] 19-51) supposes that Deut 13:2-6(1-5) was understood in 4Q375 (which summarizes the passage in 1 i 4-5). I do not find the argument wholly convincing, but for our purposes it is sufficient to note that *LAB* 34 attests a different interpretation.

54   Cf. also *T. Levi* 16:3.

55   The further statement that Jesus was hanged is probably not a reminiscence

the Gospels can also be adduced in support of the view that Jesus was seen by some during his ministry[56] and after his death (Matt 27:63-64; John 7:12, 47) as one who led Israel astray and was guilty under the law of Deuteronomy 13.

While Jesus could have been seen in this way, it is not likely that James, who is not reported to have prophesied or worked miracles, could be categorized with the prophet condemned in Deut 13:2-6(1-5). But the rest of Deuteronomy 13 appears to speak of those who lead people to worship other gods but have none of the features specific to prophets or seers. Verses 6-10(7-11) concern the person who "secretly entices you [יְסִיתְךָ] . . . saying, 'Let us go worship other gods'" (13:5[6]). Such a person is to be stoned to death (13:10-11[9-10]). Rabbinic literature calls this person the *mēsît* (מסית, from סות, as in Deut 13:5[6]: יְסִיתְךָ). Then vv. 11-19(10-18) prescribe what is to be done with a whole town that apostatizes to other gods. Here those "who led the inhabitants of the town astray [יַדִּיחוּ], saying, 'Let us go and worship other gods'" (13:14[13]) are mentioned only incidentally, and so their punishment is not prescribed, unless it is assumed that they are slaughtered along with the inhabitants of the town. But rabbinic literature treated such deceivers of the people as another category of criminal, called the *maddiaḥ* (מדיח, from נדח, as in Deut 13:14[13]: יַדִּיחוּ). But these terms—*mēsît* and *maddiaḥ*—are not necessarily exclusive to the second and third categories in Deuteronomy 13 respectively: the deceiving prophet, as well as the deceiver of a whole town, is said to lead astray (נדח: Deut 13:6[5]), while the verb סות (Hiphil: "to entice") can be used of the deceiving prophet (*b. Sanh.* 43a) and of the one who deceives a whole town (*m. Sanh.* 10:4).

Deuteronomy 13 leaves plenty of scope for differing interpretations. It appears to distinguish the prophet who openly entices to apostasy (vv. 2-6[1-5]) from the person who "secretly entices" (vv. 6-10[7-11]) and who is not, presumably, a prophet.[57] The former

---

of the fact that Jesus died by crucifixion, but a conclusion from the general rule that criminals executed by stoning—or at least blasphemers and idolaters—were subsequently hanged (*m. Sanh.* 6:4, a rule deduced from Deut 21:22; cf. Josephus, *Ant.* 4.3.12 §202).

56   See the evidence adduced by Neale, "Was Jesus a *Mesith*?," 89-101. Reference to *LAB* 34 and its consonance with *b. Sanh.* 43a would have enabled him to fit the hostile interpretation of Jesus' exorcisms (Mark 3:22) into the same picture.

57   *m. Sanh.* 7:10 makes this explicit: "an ordinary person who entices another

must be put to death (13:6[5]), but only for the latter is stoning explicitly prescribed (13:10-11[9-10]). It could easily be argued that the two crimes are equivalent—seducing people into the worship of other gods—and therefore that stoning is intended in both cases. This could be supported by the fact that the expression, "So you shall purge the evil from your midst" (13:6[5]) is elsewhere used in cases where execution is explicitly by stoning (Deut 17:7; 21:21; 22:21, 24) as well as in other cases where the mode of execution is not specified (Deut 17:12; 19:19; 22:22; 24:7).[58] On the other hand, the special emphasis on showing no pity to the person who "secretly entices," even if this is a close relative or friend (13:7-9[6-8]),[59] could be supposed to indicate that stoning is a more severe penalty for this case, suggesting a less severe form of execution for the deceiving prophet.

The third category, the person who leads a whole town astray, is even more problematic, mainly because Deuteronomy is at this point interested in the town that is led astray rather than in those who lead it astray. While certainly people who lead a town astray do not entice "secretly," and so must be distinguished from the second category, they are not clearly distinct from the deceiving prophet. If they are understood to be ordinary people, not prophets, then they form a distinct third category, whose punishment is left unmentioned. Suppose they attempt to seduce a whole town but fail? They will not then be slaughtered with the rest of the town's inhabitants, but they must surely be punished? Their punishment can hardly be less than death, but it might or might not be stoning. They may be treated as analogous to the one who secretly entices, or to the deceiving prophet, if the latter is taken to deserve a death less severe than stoning.

In the rabbinic literature, we can see how the three categories can be both assimilated and distinguished, and the question of the form of punishment due to the deceiving prophet and the one who deceives a town answered in different ways. The *baraita* about Jesus, quoted

---

ordinary person."

[58]   All these are treated in *m. Sanh.* 11 as instances where the penalty is strangulation, but at least one (Deut 22:22) was, as we have seen, treated elsewhere (John 8:4-5) as indicating stoning.

[59]   For the way rabbinic literature therefore treats the *mēsît* with extraordinary severity, as an exception to the kind of clemency and concern for fair treatment applied to other accused persons, see J. Schwartz, "Peter and Ben Stada in Lydda," in Bauckham (ed.), *The Book of Acts*, 400-403.

above from *b. Sanh.* 43a, clearly, by its reference to sorcery, puts
Jesus in the category of the deceiving prophet, but uses verbs from
Deuteronomy's accounts of both the deceiving prophet or the one
who deceives a town (נדח, used in Deut 13:6[5] and 13:14[13])) and
of the one who entices secretly (סות),[60] and has Jesus executed by
stoning, the punishment of the one who entices secretly, according to
Deuteronomy. Mishna *Sanhedrin* treats both the *mēsît* and the
maddiaḥ as liable to death by stoning (7:4, 10), but it is unclear how
it treats the deceiving prophet, who is not listed as a distinct category
of criminal in its lists of those liable to the various punishments. It is
possible that the deceiving prophet and the one who leads astray a
whole town are identified, since נדח is used of both (Deut 13:6[5];
13:14[13]). It is more likely that the deceiving prophet is identified
with the false prophet of Deut 18:20a, who speaks in the name of
other gods, or with the false prophet of Deut 18:20b-22, both of
whom are listed among those whose punishment is death by
strangulation (*m. Sanh.* 11:1). In that case, the Mishna extends the
punishment by stoning from the *mēsît* to include also the *maddiaḥ*,
but not the deceiving prophet, whose execution takes a less severe
form. The Babylonian Talmud's comments on *m. Sanh.* 7:10 record
two other rabbinic views: that all three categories in Deuteronomy
13 incur death by stoning, and that only the *mēsît* is to be stoned,
while the deceiving prophet and the *maddiaḥ* are both to die by
strangulation (*b. Sanh.* 67a).

These rabbinic views cannot tell us directly what was thought in
the late Second Temple period, but they illustrate the sort of halakhic
differences that could easily have existed at that time. If James were
accused of leading people astray into apostasy, through his preaching
about Jesus, then he is most likely to have been considered a
maddiaḥ, one who (potentially) leads astray a whole town. As the
well-known leader of the Christian community in Jerusalem, he
could not plausibly be considered a *mēsît*, working secretively to
entice individuals to apostasy, and, as we have already noticed, the
lack of any tradition of miracles or prophecy attributed to him,
makes the charge of being a deceiving prophet unlikely. But, as a
maddiaḥ, the form his punishment should take could be easily open
to dispute. It could well be that Sadducean halakhah prescribed

---

60   It is possible that John 18:20-21 rebuts the charge of *secret* enticing to
apostasy, based on Deut 13:7(6).

stoning, by analogy with the case of the *mēsît*, while Pharisees, concerned to confine stoning as far as possible to cases where the Torah explicitly prescribed it, argued that the *maddiaḥ* should be executed in a less savage way.

Our attempt to explain Josephus' account of the death of James has therefore left us with two plausible possibilities: that he was executed as a blasphemer or as a *maddiaḥ*. (Of course, it is possible that he was convicted of both crimes.) Both possibilities have the advantage of coherence with the policies of the Temple authorities towards Jesus and the Jerusalem church at an earlier stage in its history. At least according to the Synoptic accounts, Ananus II's own brother-in-law Caiaphas and his council found James' own brother Jesus worthy of execution for blasphemy. Caiaphas also presided over the council meeting which led to the stoning of Stephen for blasphemy, according to Acts 7. (It is not too fanciful to see here a family tradition, in the high priestly house of Annas, of determined opposition to Jesus and the movement that revered him as Messiah. See also Acts 4–5, with the reference to Annas as well as Caiaphas in 4:5. It is likely that another son of Annas, Matthias [Josephus, *Ant.* 19.6.4 §316, 19.8.1 §342], was High Priest at the time of Agrippa I's action against the leaders of the Jerusalem church [Acts 12:1-4] and may well have played a role in instigating this.) But, as we have noticed, there is also reason to suppose that Jesus was regarded as guilty of the crime of leading the people astray, as defined in Deuteronomy 13, even if this was not the charge on which he was finally condemned in the High Priest's council.

Finally, we should consider whether either of the possible charges against James finds support in the Christian tradition about his death which lies behind the accounts of Hegesippus and the *Second Apocalypse of James*. According to Hegesippus, when James was asked by the scribes and the Pharisees to "tell us who is the gate of Jesus?," he replied: "Why do you ask me about the Son of Man? He is seated in heaven on the right hand of the Great Power, and he will come on the clouds of heaven" (*Hist. Eccl.* 2.23.12-13). It was precisely this claim that Jesus will be or is at the right hand of God which is considered blasphemous by the High Priest and his council in the cases of Jesus himself (Matt 26:64-66; Mark 14:62-64)[61] and

---

61   In my view of this much debated issue, the blasphemy consists in the claim to participate in God's unique sovereignty over the cosmos, which sitting at God's

Stephen (Acts 7:55-58). The charge of blasphemy does not appear in Hegesippus' account, but these words of James lead the scribes and the Pharisees to declare that "even the just one has gone astray" and to throw him down from the pinnacle (14-15). However, the words Hegesippus attributes to James are very close to those of Jesus in Matt 26:64, and must constitute one of the borrowings from the Gospel passion narratives which are characteristic of Hegesippus' account (cf. 10: John 12:42; Luke 20:21; 11, 12: Matt 4:5 = Luke 4:9; 13: Matt 20:17; 14: Matt 21:9, 15; 16: Luke 23:34). They cannot be considered historical. Perhaps they substitute for other words attributed to James at this point in an earlier form of the account, but if so we cannot tell whether such words were such as could be construed as blasphemous. It is perhaps significant that the borrowing from Matt 26:64 has not brought with it an echo of the accusation of blasphemy which is the immediate response to Jesus' words in Matt 26:65.

Another striking feature of Hegesippus' account is the fourfold occurrence of the passive of the verb πλανάω, meaning "to be led astray," or simply "to go astray." The scribes and the Pharisees comment that whole people "has gone astray [ἐπλανήθη] to Jesus, as though he were the Messiah" (10), and ask James to persuade the people "not to go astray [πλανᾶσθαι] about Jesus" (11). When James is on the pinnacle of the Temple, they again say that "the people is going astray [πλανᾶται] after Jesus who was crucified" (12). Finally, they use the verb of James himself: "Oh, oh, even the just one has gone astray [ἐπλανήθη]" (15). This final statement also occurs in the *Second Apocalypse of James*: "(O you) who have gone astray" (62:7). In both cases it looks like a statement of the crime for which James is being executed. It must have featured in the common source.

The meaning of πλανᾶσθαι here is not that of turning aside from the right way of ethical conduct, but that of apostasy from the God of Israel. The people have gone astray "to" (εἰς) or "after" (ὀπίσω) Jesus (10, 12), as though Jesus were a false god. The closest parallels to this usage in the New Testament are in the predictions of false messiahs and prophets who will lead people astray (Matt 24:4-5, 11, 24; Mark 13:5-6, 22; Luke 21:8), but these passages themselves reflect the deceiving prophet of Deuteronomy 13. In enticing people

---

right hand on his heavenly throne symbolizes. Such a claim, if untrue, is blasphemous.

to follow and serve other gods, he is said to have spoken "apostasy (or turning aside: סרה) from YHWH your God . . . to turn you from (הדיחך) the way in which YHWH your God commanded you to walk" (13:6[5]). The key verb (נדח Hiphil) is also used of the *maddiaḥ* in v. 14(13): it is the activity from which the term *maddiaḥ* derived in the rabbinic terminology. Though the Septuagint does not use πλανάω to translate נדח in these verses of chap. 13, it does in Deut 4:19; 22:1; 30:17. Of these 22:1 is a literal use, but 4:19 and 30:17 speak of being led astray to worship other gods. The Septuagint does use πλανῆσαι to translate סרה (apostasy, going astray) in Deut 13:8(5), and πλανάω translates the cognate verb סור in Deut 11:28, where the sense is that of going astray to worship other gods. Thus, of the six occurrences of πλανάω in LXX Deuteronomy, four refer to apostasy from the God of Israel to false gods (4:19; 13:5; 11:28; 30:17). The verb is well suited to describe the activity of the deceiving prophet and the *maddiaḥ* of Deuteronomy 13. In Pseudo-Philo's account of Aod the magician, which we have seen to be based on Deuteronomy 13, the Latin version twice uses the verb *implano* (34:5), no doubt reflecting πλανάω in its Greek *Vorlage*.

In the accounts of James' death, his enemies do not say that he has led the people astray, but that he has gone astray. This is intelligible in the *Second Apocalypse of James*, where the people have not been persuaded, but is odd in Hegesippus, where the people have in fact been led astray by James. The scribes and the Pharisees ask James to speak to the people to persuade them not to continue straying after Jesus, "for the whole people and we all obey you" (11). Perhaps they are ignorant of the fact that, according to Hegesippus, it is James himself who has led the people to believe in Jesus, or perhaps their request is a ruse to get James to incriminate himself in their hearing and in a fully public context. In any case, the result of what James does say, in the hearing of the crowd, is that many of them openly confess Jesus (14). Clearly James' own confession of Jesus has led the people astray to Jesus. Thus we should expect the statement of his crime, voiced by the scribes and the Pharisees as they go to effect his death, to be that he has led the people astray, rather than simply that he also has gone astray. In the latter case he would be no more guilty than the crowds; all would incur stoning as idolaters. It seems likely that, here as in some other places, the sense of the original account has been partly lost in successive versions, and that the verb πλανάω originally featured in the account because it was as a *maddiaḥ* that he was put to death.

Another point at which the true significance of an element in the account has been obscured in Hegesippus' version is the question put to James: "Who is the gate of Jesus?" (8, 12). As we have seen this is probably part of the earliest core of this tradition about the death of James, since it uses an aspect of the Temple building, taken from Psalm 118, metaphorically rather than with reference to the existing Temple building. It refers to Ps 118:20: "This is the gate of YHWH; the righteous shall enter through it." The exegesis ascribed to James must have understood YHWH in the text to be Jesus, as is not infrequently the case in early Christian exegesis of the Hebrew Bible. The gate of YHWH/Jesus is Jesus himself as the gate of the eschatological Temple, the one through whom the righteous (with James the Righteous at their head) enter the presence of God in the midst of his people, the messianically renewed Israel. Some such exegesis of Ps 118:20, expounded in James' preaching, could well have been understood to associate Jesus so closely with YHWH as to be evidence that James was leading the people into apostasy. It is possible that we have here a rather distant report of the evidence actually used at James' trial to prove him to be a *maddiah*.

JESUS AND JAMES
MARTYRS OF THE TEMPLE

Craig A. Evans

The Temple and Psalm 118 point to significant common ground shared by Jesus and James. A careful probing of these traditions may clarify the nature of their respective ministries and the factors that brought both into deadly conflict with the Jerusalem Temple establishment.

THE DEATHS OF JESUS AND JAMES

According to the four New Testament Gospels, Jesus engaged in controversy with the ruling priests, a controversy which included a demonstration in the Temple precincts, and was subsequently handed over to the Roman governor, who executed him as "king of the Jews."[1] The essence of this sequence is independently attested in the so-called *Testimonium Flavianum* (Josephus, *Ant.* 18.3.3 §63-64), the authentic part of which reads:

> At this time there appeared Jesus, a wise man. For he was a doer of amazing deeds, a teacher of persons who receive truth with pleasure. He won over many Jews and many of the Greeks. And when Pilate condemned him to the cross—the leading men among us [τῶν πρώτων ἀνδρῶν παρ' ἡμῖν] having accused him—those who loved him from the first did not cease to do so. And to the present the tribe of Christians, named after this person, has not disappeared.[2]

---

[1]   The *titulus* and its reference to Jesus as "king of Jews" (Mark 15:26) enjoy wide acceptance by critical scholars. There is literary evidence of such posting of an inscription that refers to the crime (Lat. *causa poenae* = αἰτία in Mark 15:26; Matt 27:37) and/or the name of the victim (cf. Suetonius, *Caligula* 32.2 and *Domitian* 10.1; Dio Cassius 73.16.5). In one case the victim carried a placard around the Forum before his crucifixion (Dio Cassius 54.3.6-7). According to Eusebius one of the Christian martyrs was led around an amphitheatre carrying a placard "on which was written in Latin, 'This is Attalus, the Christian'" (*Hist. Eccl.* 5.1.44; cf. John 19:20: "it was written in Hebrew, Latin, and Greek").

[2]   For a compelling defense of the authenticity of this part of the *Testimonium*, see J. P. Meier, "Jesus in Josephus: A Modest Proposal," *CBQ* 52 (1990) 76-103.

There is good reason to believe that the "leading men among us" (lit. "first men among us") are in this context the ruling priests, just as the New Testament Gospels relate.[3] Jesus encounters opposition from the ruling priests, is handed over to the Roman authorities, who then put him to death. The juridical process that unfolds is parallel at many points to that which overtook Jesus ben Ananias some thirty years later (*J.W.* 6.5.3 §300-309).[4]

Although different at points, the fate that overtook James, the brother of Jesus, is similar. Again Josephus (*Ant.* 20.9.1 §197-203) provides the following account:

> And now Caesar, upon hearing the death of Festus, sent Albinus into Judea, as procurator. But the king (Agrippa) deprived Joseph of the high priesthood, and bestowed the succession to that dignity on the son of Ananus, who was also himself called Ananus. Now the report goes that this eldest Ananus proved a most fortunate man; for he had five sons who had all performed the office of a High Priest to God, and who had himself enjoyed that dignity a long time formerly, which had never happened to any other of our High Priests. But this younger Ananus, who, as we have told you already, took the high priesthood, was a bold man in his temper, and very insolent; he was also of the sect of the Sadducees, who are very rigid in judging offenders, above all the rest of the Jews, as we have already observed; when, therefore, Ananus was of this disposition, he thought he

---

3   The author of Luke-Acts refers to Israel's leaders as the "first of the people": "And he was teaching daily in the Temple. The chief priests and the scribes and the principal men of the people [οἱ πρῶτοι τοῦ λαοῦ] were seeking to destroy him" (Luke 19:47). Luke links these "first" ones with "the ruling priests and the scribes." More importantly, elsewhere Josephus refers to ruling priests as the "first men": "There came to (Ezra) certain men who accused some of the common people as well as Levites and priests of having violated the constitution and broken the laws of the country . . . No sooner did he hear this than he rent his clothes for grief . . . because the first men among the people [τοὺς πρώτους τοῦ λαοῦ] were guilty of this charge" (*Ant.* 11.5.3 §140-141). Here, the "first men" are synonymous with the Levites and priests. In a text closer to the one that concerns us, Josephus describes Vitellius' movement against Aretas: "Since he had started to lead his army through the land of Judea, the Jews of the highest standing [ἄνδρες οἱ πρῶτοι] went to meet him and entreated him not to march through their land. For, they said, it was contrary to their tradition to allow images . . . to be brought upon their soil" (*Ant.* 18.5.3 §121). These "first men" who are concerned that Roman icons not be allowed to pass through Judea were in all probability religious leaders.

4   The parallels are delineated in C. A. Evans, "Jesus and the 'Cave of Robbers': Toward a Jewish Context for the Temple Action," *BBR* 3 (1993) 93-110, esp. 105-107.

had now a proper opportunity (to exercise his authority). Festus was now dead, and Albinus was but upon the road; so he assembled the Sanhedrin of judges [συνέδριον κριτῶν], and brought before them the brother of Jesus, who was called Christ, whose name was James, and some others, (or, some of his companions); and when he had formed an accusation against them as breakers of the law [παρανομήσαντες], he delivered them to be stoned. But as for those who seemed the most equitable of the citizens, and such as were the most uneasy at the breach of the laws, they disliked what was done; they also sent to the king (Agrippa), desiring him to send to Ananus that he should act so no more, for what he had already done was not to be justified; nay, some of them went also to meet Albinus, as he was upon his journey from Alexandria, and informed him that it was not lawful for Ananus to assemble a Sanhedrin without his consent. Whereupon Albinus complied with what they said, and wrote in anger to Ananus, and threatened that he would bring him to punishment for what he had done; on which king Agrippa took the high priesthood from him, when he had ruled but three months, and made Jesus, the son of Damneus, High Priest.[5]

Jesus had been accused of blasphemy, while James later was accused of being a lawbreaker. Both were condemned by High Priests—High Priests who were related by marriage. Jesus was handed over to the Roman governor, who complied with the wishes of the ruling priests, while James was executed without the approval of the Roman authority. We may presume that neither Festus nor Albinus would have approved. In the case of Jesus, Pilate saw warrant in execution, for a serious political charge could be made (i.e. "king of the Jews"). In the case of James, however, evidently no such compelling case could be made. If it could have been, one would have thought that Ananus would not have acted so rashly. Evidently he realized that apart from a grave charge against James, the type of charge that would have been taken very seriously by Rome, execution was doubtful. We should remember that Roman governors had no interest in meddling in purely religious matters. One thinks of the position adopted by the Proconsul Gallio, at least as it is depicted in Acts: "If it were a matter of crime or serious

---

5   According to Eusebius (*Hist. Eccl.* 2.23.4-18), Josephus also said: "And these things happened to the Jews to avenge James the Just, who was the brother of Jesus the so-called Christ, for the Jews killed him in spite of his great righteousness." This passage is found nowhere in the MSS of the works of Josephus. The tone is Christian and exudes a whiff of anti-Judaism. It is probably based on Josephus' comment regarding the fate of Herod Antipas' army after the execution of John the Baptist (cf. *Ant.* 18.5.2 §116-117).

villainy, I would be justified in accepting the complaint of you Jews; but since it is a matter of questions about words and names and your own law, see to it yourselves; I refuse to be a judge of these things" (Acts 18:14-15). There is no reason to believe that under ordinary circumstances the policies of Pilate in the time of Jesus or of either Festus or Albinus in the time of James would have been significantly different.

It is also interesting to observe the dynamics in Acts 21–23. When Paul arrives in Jerusalem, he meets James who impresses upon him the necessity to convince all of his fidelity to the Law (21:17-25). Paul agrees (21:26), but his opponents create a stir when they accuse him of bringing a Gentile into the Temple precincts (21:27-28). Paul is arrested (21:30-36) and eventually brought before the ruling priests and Sanhedrin (22:30–23:10). What is overlooked in all of this drama is the precarious position in which James probably found himself. His association with Paul must have been prejudicial to his security in Jerusalem. Although there is no way of ascertaining it, Paul's visit and the controversy that ensued may very well have contributed to the high priestly opposition toward James and other leaders of the Jewish church.

There is one other interesting parallel between the fate of James and what perhaps threatened to befall Jesus. Howard Clark Kee directs our attention to Jesus' saying, in which others describe him as a "glutton and drunkard": "the Son of man came eating and drinking, and they say, 'Behold, a glutton and a drunkard, a friend of tax collectors and sinners!'" (Matt 11:19 = Luke 7:34).[6] Kee appeals to *m. Sanh.* 7:4 ("These are they that are to be stoned: . . . he that beguiles [others to idolatry], and he that leads [a whole town] astray, and the sorcerer and a stubborn and rebellious son"; cf. 8:1-2) and comments:

> That the issue of community definition is indeed the central concern here is implicit in a crucial phrase, the implications of which have been largely overlooked in exegesis of this passage: namely, the denunciatory designation which Jesus here apparently borrows from his opponents with reference to himself: "a glutton and drunkard." The verbal links of this phrase with Deut 21:20 have been noted and discussed[7] but not adequately

---

[6]   H. C. Kee, "Jesus: A Glutton and Drunkard," in B. Chilton and C. A. Evans (eds.), *Authenticating the Words of Jesus* (NTTS 28.1; Leiden: Brill, 1998) 311-32.

[7]   J. Jeremias, *The Parables of Jesus* (New York: Scribner's, 1963) 160. J.

explored. The fact that the phrase in Q (φάγος καὶ οἰνοπότης) differs sharply from the LXX (συμβολοκοπῶν οἰνοφλυγεῖ) can be used to argue for the authenticity of the saying, since a direct quotation from the LXX, even its wording, would be a likely sign of a later addition to the Q tradition. What has been largely overlooked is the context in which the phrase occurs in Deuteronomy (21:18-21) and the implications which this carries with it for the use of the phrase in the Jesus tradition. The passage in Deuteronomy outlines the procedure for dealing with a "stubborn and rebellious son," who refuses to obey his parents. More is at stake than relations within the family, however. He constitutes a threat to the welfare of the community as a whole, as is evident in the court of appeal to which the case is to be referred and the agents through whom the legally prescribed punishment is to be carried out. The problem is not to be resolved by the parents alone. Instead, the charge against the rebel is to be brought to the town council: to the elders gathered at the town gate. The execution of the rebel is to be by stoning, and is to be carried out by all the adult males of the community.[8]

If Kee is correct in his surmise, then Jesus' saying may hint at threats that had been directed against him during his ministry. The Synoptic tradition tells us nothing about stoning, with the possible exception of the incident in Nazareth where the attempt to throw Jesus from a cliff may have been a prelude to stoning.[9] In the fourth Gospel, however, Jesus is said to have been threatened with stoning (cf. 8:59; 10:31-33; 11:8). Even if these narratives and dialogues are viewed as Johannine creations, they may contain a historical reminiscence that Jesus had in fact been threatened with stoning. If so, then the parallels between James, who was stoned, and Jesus, who was threatened with stoning, are drawn closer.

The important point thus far is that two Galilean brothers—Jesus and James—were put to death either indirectly or directly by two high priestly brothers-in-law—Caiaphas and Ananus. In the case of Jesus, we know that a demonstration and series of criticisms were leveled in the Temple precincts, to which ruling priests reacted

---

A. Fitzmyer (*The Gospel according to Luke I–IX* [AB 24; Garden City: Doubleday, 1981] 681), however, dismisses the proposal of a connection, since the Greek of Q differs from the LXX of Deuteronomy.

8   Kee, "Jesus: A Glutton and Drunkard," 329.

9   J. Nolland, *Luke 1–9:20* (WBC 35A; Dallas: Word, 1989) 201, following J. Blinzler, "The Jewish Punishment of Stoning in the New Testament Period," in E. Bammel (ed.), *The Trial of Jesus* (C. F. D. Moule Festschrift; SBT 13; London: SCM Press, 1970) 147-61, and others.

angrily (Mark 11–12). In the case of James, we are told that he was accused of breaking the Law. Can the critical points of antagonism between brothers Jesus and James, on the one hand, and brothers Caiaphas and Ananus, on the other, be brought into sharper relief? I believe we can understand the underlying causes of this antagonism more clearly if we highlight and scrutinize Temple traditions linked to both Jesus and James.

PSALM 118 AND TEMPLE IMAGERY

Early Christian traditions associate both Jesus and James with the Jerusalem Temple. In the earliest traditions pertaining to Jesus (Mark and Q),[10] Jesus' contact with the Temple is limited to his fateful Passover visit (cf. Mark 11–15). Jesus' entrance into Jerusalem concludes with a visit of the Temple (11:11), after which he demonstrates in the precincts (11:15-18), teaches in the precincts "daily" (14:49; cf. John 18:20), criticizes the ruling priests (chap. 12), predicts the Temple's destruction (13:2), and is accused of threatening to destroy the Temple (14:48). Although we must recognize the presence in Mark of a polemical stance toward the Temple,[11] it is probable that Jesus engaged in many of the things the evangelist describes.[12]

The Temple appears in three Q traditions. In one Jesus refers to the murder of Zechariah son of Berachiah, whom his critics murdered between the sanctuary and the altar [μεταξὺ τοῦ ναοῦ καὶ τοῦ θυσιαστηρίου]" (Matt 23:35). The ending in Luke is a bit different and is judged by some critics as closer to the original form:

---

[10] I am aware that not all of my colleagues who are participating in the James Consultation accept the solution to the Synoptic Problem that is presupposed in this paper. I maintain that no important point in this paper depends on Markan priority and the existence of the hypothetical Q source. The primary dominical tradition, to which I appeal, is found fully and firmly in Matthew.

[11] As ably documented by D. H. Juel, *Messiah and Temple: The Trial of Jesus in the Gospel of Mark* (SBLDS 31; Missoula: Scholars Press, 1977).

[12] On Jesus' critical stance toward the Temple establishment, see C. A. Evans, "Jesus' Action in the Temple and Evidence of Corruption in the First-Century Temple," in D. J. Lull (ed.), *Society of Biblical Literature 1989 Seminar Papers* (SBLSP 28; Atlanta: Scholars Press, 1989) 522-39; idem, "Opposition to the Temple: Jesus and the Dead Sea Scrolls," in J. H. Charlesworth (ed.), *Jesus and the Dead Sea Scrolls* (ABRL 4; New York: Doubleday, 1992) 253-53; H. D. Betz, "Jesus and the Purity of the Temple (Mark 11:15-18): A Comparative Religion Study," *JBL* 116 (1997) 455-72.

"between the sanctuary and the house [μεταξὺ τοῦ θυσιαστηρίου καὶ τοῦ οἴκου]" (Luke 11:51).[13] The editing of this saying, coupled with complaints about rough and murderous treatment of prophets and apostles (as in Luke 11:49), points to the experience of the Church. But the core of the saying, including the reference to the murder of Zechariah "between the sanctuary and the house," is probably genuine dominical tradition.[14] Although the main point has to do with the rejection of God's will, the implication of the last part of the saying seems to have to do with defilement of the Temple. In other words, these persecutors of the prophets have not only committed murder, they have committed murder within the sanctuary itself and thus have defiled the Temple. We should remember the bitter criticism voiced by Josephus against the rebels, whose battle tactics resorted in the slaughter of many Jews who tried to worship and offer sacrifices in the Temple precincts (*J.W.* 4.9.12 §577-578; 5.1.2–3 §7-20). Josephus comments that their actions "converted the sanctuary into a charnel-house of civil war," so that it was necessary for the Romans to purge the Temple with fire (*J.W.* 5.1.3 §19).

The Temple also appears in Q's version of the Temptation, that is, in the second (Matt 4:5)—or third (Luke 4:9)—temptation, where Satan takes Jesus to the "pinacle of the Temple" (πτερύγιον τοῦ ἱεροῦ) and dares him to cast himself down. This tradition may have inspired the later, legendary story of James' being cast down from the pinacle of the Temple and then beaten to death with a fuller's club (cf. Eusebius, *Hist. Eccl.* 2.1.5).

Before turning to the third Q text, it is worth mentioning briefly a few later traditions. We think immediately of the Fourth Gospel, where Jesus visits Jerusalem three, possibly four times. He is depicted as routinely teaching in the Temple precincts (cf. John 2:13-22; 5:1, 14; 7:10, 14, 28; [8:2,] 20, 59; 10:23). And finally, one is reminded of the tale of the boy Jesus who is found by his anxious parents, teaching in the Temple, in his "Father's house" (Luke 2:46-52).

---

13   So D. A. Hagner, *Matthew 14–28* (WBC 33B; Dallas: Word, 1995) 675; cf. R. H. Gundry, *Matthew: A Commentary on His Handbook for a Mixed Church under Persecution* (Grand Rapids: Eerdmans, 1994) 470-72.

14   See the discussion in D. C. Allison and W. D. Davies, *A Critical and Exegetical Commentary on the Gospel according to Saint Matthew.* Volume III: *Commentary on Matthew XIX–XXVIII* (ICC; Edinburgh: T. & T. Clark, 1997) 313-14.

Probably the most important Q tradition, in which Jesus makes reference to the Temple, is the so-called Lamentation over Jerusalem (Matt 23:37-39 = Luke 13:34-35):

Matthew 23:37-39	Luke 13:34-35
Ἰερουσαλὴμ Ἰερουσαλήμ, ἡ ἀποκτείν- ουσα τοὺς προφήτας καὶ λιθοβολοῦσα τοὺς ἀπεσταλμένους πρὸς αὐτήν, ποσάκις ἠθέλησα ἐπισυναγαγεῖν τὰ τέκνα σου, ὃν τρόπον ὄρνις ἐπισυνάγει τὰ νοσσία αὐτῆς ὑπὸ τὰς πτέρυγας, καὶ οὐκ ἠθελήσατε. 38 ἰδοὺ ἀφίεται ὑμῖν ὁ οἶκος ὑμῶν ἔρημος. 39 λέγω γὰρ ὑμῖν, οὐ μή με ἴδητε ἀπ' ἄρτι ἕως ἂν εἴπητε, Εὐλογημένος ὁ ἐρχόμενος ἐν ὀνόματι κυρίου.	Ἰερουσαλὴμ Ἰερουσαλήμ, ἡ ἀποκτείν- ουσα τοὺς προφήτας καὶ λιθοβολοῦσα τοὺς ἀπεσταλμένους πρὸς αὐτήν, ποσάκις ἠθέλησα ἐπισυνάξαι τὰ τέκνα σου ὃν τρόπον ὄρνις τὴν ἑαυτῆς νοσσιὰν ὑπὸ τὰς πτέρυγας, καὶ οὐκ ἠθελήσατε. 35 ἰδοὺ ἀφίεται ὑμῖν ὁ οἶκος ὑμῶν. λέγω [δὲ] ὑμῖν, οὐ μὴ ἴδητέ με ἕως [ἥξει ὅτε] εἴπητε, Εὐλογημένος ὁ ἐρχόμενος ἐν ὀνόματι κυρίου.

The parallel passages read in English, with the allusions to Jeremiah 22 and Psalm 118 in italics:

"O Jerusalem, Jerusalem, killing the prophets and stoning those who are sent to you! How often would I have gathered your children together as a hen gathers her brood under her wings, and you would not! 38 Behold, your *house* is *forsaken* and desolate. 39 For I tell you, you will not see me again, until you say, *'Blessed is he who comes in the name of the Lord!'*"

"O Jerusalem, Jerusalem, killing the prophets and stoning those who are sent to you! How often would I have gathered your children together as a hen gathers her brood under her wings, and you would not! 35 Behold, your *house* is *forsaken*. And I tell you, you will not see me until you say, *'Blessed is he who comes in the name of the Lord!'*"

In my judgment Werner Georg Kümmel argues persuasively that Matt 23:37-39 = Luke 13:34-35 is authentic dominical tradition and that it is consistent with Jesus' vow not to drink wine until he may drink it new in the kingdom of God (Mark 14:25).[15] Although it is not necessary to agree with Kümmel that Jesus must have envisioned a long interval between his death and parousia[16] (I rather suspect that Jesus expected vindication sooner, not later), it does seem probable that Jesus anticipated national repentance, at which time he will be

---

15   W. G. Kümmel, *Promise and Fulfillment: The Eschatological Message of Jesus* (SBT 23; London: SCM Press; Naperville: Allenson, 1957) 79-82. See also I. H. Marshall, *The Gospel of Luke* (NIGTC; Grand Rapids: Eerdmans, 1978) 573-74.

16   Kümmel, *Promise and Fulfillment*, 82: "a considerable period."

received into Jerusalem amidst priestly cries of "Blessed is he who comes in the name of the Lord." Until Jerusalem takes up this cry, national deliverance will be postponed.

For our purposes, the important exegetical question centers on the meaning of "your house" and what it means for it to be left "forsaken." The phrase, ὁ οἶκος ὑμῶν ἔρημος, is probably an allusion to Jer 22:5: ἐὰν δὲ μὴ ποιήσητε τοὺς λόγους τούτους κατ' ἐμαυτοῦ ὤμοσα λέγει κύριος ὅτι εἰς ἐρήμωσιν ἔσται ὁ οἶκος οὗτος,[17] the latter part of which is a close rendition of the Hebrew: כִּי־לְחָרְבָּה יִהְיֶה הַבַּיִת הַזֶּה. The Davidic elements of the wider context of this passage from Jeremiah should not be missed: "For if you will indeed obey this word, then through the gates of this house shall enter kings who sit on the throne of David, riding in chariots and on horses, they, and their servants, and their people. 5 But if you will not heed these words, I swear by myself, says the LORD, that this house shall become a desolation" (Jer 22:4-5). The dominical tradition may also allude to Jer 12:7: ἐγκαταλέλοιπα τὸν οἶκόν μου ἀφῆκα τὴν κληρονομίαν μου, which again renders the Hebrew literally (עָזַבְתִּי אֶת־בֵּיתִי).[18] "House" is the catchword that links these related texts from Jeremiah: God says (in Jer 12:7), "I have forsaken my house," while the words of Jer 22:5 clarify the result of this abandonment: "this house will become a desolation."[19]

The "house" that is left "desolate" probably refers to the Temple,[20] though it may also have a more inclusive reference and thus mean that the city itself, as well as the Temple, is abandoned.[21] Matthew's

---

[17] So J. A. Fitzmyer, *The Gospel according to Luke X–XXIV* (AB 24A; Garden City: Doubleday, 1985) 1033.

[18] Gundry, *Matthew*, 473.

[19] Again, see Gundry, *Matthew*, 473; Marshall, *Luke*, 576.

[20] So Gundry, *Matthew*, 473. W. Grundmann (*Das Evangelium nach Lukas* [THKNT 3; Berlin: Evangelische Verlagsanstalt, 7th ed., 1974] 289) asserts: "Gott wird den Tempel verlassen . . . unter ὁ οἶκος ὑμῶν ist der Tempel zu verstehen, in dem Gott wohnt . . ."

[21] Marshall, *Luke*, 576. Marshall cites *1 Enoch* 89:50-51; *T. Levi* 10:5. F. D. Weinert ("Luke, the Temple, and Jesus' Saying about Jerusalem's Abandoned House (Luke 13:34-35)," *CBQ* 44 [1982] 68-76, here 75-76) concludes that "house" in Luke refers more to Israel's leadership than simply to the Temple. C. F. Evans (*Saint Luke* [London: SCM Press; Philadelphia: Trinity Press International, 1990] 565) makes a good point when he notes that "your house [is] unprecedented for the temple, which is God's house." Perhaps so, but describing the Temple as Jerusalem's (and thus no longer God's) is consistent with the context and is consis-

Jerusalem setting, as opposed to Luke's journey setting, is probably closer to the original context,[22] which is consistent with this interpretation. Jesus' lament is, moreover, consistent with his prediction of the Temple's doom.[23]

The concluding saying is a verbatim quotation of Ps 118(117):26: εὐλογημένος ὁ ἐηρχόμενος ἐν ὀνόματι κυρίου, which in turn is an exact equivalent of the Hebrew's בָּרוּךְ הַבָּא בְּשֵׁם יְהוָה. Given the simplicity of the construction and the exact correspondence between the Hebrew and the Greek, there is no justification for ruling against the authenticity of the saying on the grounds of its agreement with the LXX.[24] The importance of the interpretive tendencies in the Aramaic tradition will be considered shortly.

Traces of Psalm 118 in the Gospel of Mark may now be considered. The first allusion to this text is heard in the cries of the crowd during Jesus' entrance into Jerusalem (Mark 11:9-10):

Ὡσαννά·
Εὐλογημένος ὁ ἐρχόμενος ἐν ὀνόματι κυρίου·
Εὐλογημένη ἡ ἐρχομένη βασιλεία τοῦ πατρὸς ἡμῶν Δαυίδ·
Ὡσαννὰ ἐν τοῖς ὑψίστοις.

Hosanna;
Blessed is he who comes in the name of the Lord;

---

tent too with prophetic anger and sorrow. In favor of "house" as referring to the Temple is the allusion to Ps 118:26, which are words understood to be spoken "from the house of the Lord" (as Evans acknowledges).

22   So also Allison and Davies, *Matthew*, 312.

23   C. H. Dodd, *The Parables of the Kingdom* (London: Nisbet, 1935) 62-63. Jesus is one of many who predicted the Temple's destruction; cf. C. A. Evans, "Predictions of the Destruction of the Herodian Temple in the Pseudepigrapha, Qumran Scrolls, and Related Texts," *JSP* 10 (1992) 89-147; repr. in J. H. Charlesworth (ed.), *Qumran Questions* (BibSem 36; Sheffield: Sheffield Academic Press, 1995) 92-150; D. C. Allison, *Jesus of Nazareth: Millenarian Prophet* (Minneapolis: Fortress, 1998) 98-99.

24   Several have argued for the dominical origin of the saying; cf. H. F. Bayer, *Jesus' Predictions of Vindication and Resurrection: The Provenance, Meaning and Correlation of the Synoptic Predictions* (WUNT 2.20; Tübingen: Mohr [Siebeck], 1986) 45-48; D. R. Catchpole, "Temple Traditions in Q," in W. Horbury (ed.), *Templum Amicitiae: Essays on the Second Temple presented to Ernst Bammel* (JSNTSup 48; Sheffield: JSOT Press, 1991) 305-29, here 327-28. However, J. Nolland (*Luke 9:21–18:34* [WBC 35B; Dallas: Word, 1993] 739) views v. 35b as "a Christian development of vv 34-35a." Allison and Davies (*Matthew*, 314) are undecided.

Blessed is the coming kingdom of our father David;
Hosanna in the highest.

The cries of "hosanna" transliterate הוֹשִׁיעָה נָּא. The LXX translates literally: σῶσον δή. However, the Markan ὡσαννά probably reflects the Aramaic הושע־נא (*hôšaʿ-nāʾ*).[25] The Hebrew text says nothing about the "coming kingdom of our father David." But in the Aramaic, Ps 118:19-27 is explicitly Davidic: "Jesse and his wife" are understood to utter the second part of v. 25, while David himself utters the second part of v. 26: "'They will bless you from the house of the sanctuary of the Lord,' said David."

The second important reference to Psalm 118 is found in the formal quotation that concludes the Parable of the Wicked Vineyard Tenants (Mark 12:1-12). The Markan evangelist provides a verbatim quotation of the LXX (12:10-11; cf. Ps 118:22-23);

Λίθον ὃν ἀπεδοκίμασαν οἱ οἰκοδομοῦντες,
οὗτος ἐγενήθη εἰς κεφαλὴν γωνίας·
παρὰ κυρίου ἐγένετο αὕτη
καὶ ἔστιν θαυμαστὴ ἐν ὀφθαλμοῖς ἡμῶν.

The stone that the builders rejected,
This has become the head of the corner;
From the Lord this has happened
And it is marvelous in our eyes.

Once again we find important coherence with the Aramaic version of this psalm.

טליא שביקו ארדיכליא הות ביני בניא דישי
וזכה לאתמנאה למליך ושולטן.
מן קדם יהוה הות דא אמרו ארדיכליא
היא פרישא קדמנא אמרו בנוי דישי.

The boy that the builders abandoned was among the sons of Jesse
and he is worthy to be appointed king and ruler.
"From before the Lord this came about," said the builders.
"It is marvelous before us," said the sons of Jesse.

The Aramaic טליא ("boy") probably derives from a wordplay involving הָאֶבֶן ("the stone") and הַבֵּן ("the son"). Such a wordplay in Hebrew and reflected in the targumic tradition, but not preserved in the LXX, suggests that the quotation derives from Jesus and not from the Greek-speaking Church (as many interpreters suppose). The linkage between the quotation and the parable, which tells of a

---

25   Allison and Davies, *Matthew*, 124.

rejected son, becomes much closer.[26] The thematic and exegetical coherence between the parable proper (Mark 12:1-9) and the Aramaic paraphrase of Isa 5:1-7, as well as the exegetical coherence between the Aramaic paraphrase of Ps 118:22-23 and its appearance as the concluding Scripture, points to early and probably authentic tradition.[27] George Brooke has recently commented, rightly in my judgment: "The literary context of the parable is thoroughly suitable to its use of scripture; Jesus is portrayed as in the temple, challenging those in charge. Indeed the historical context portrayed suggests that the use of scripture in the pericope as a whole is not the result of the creative work of the early church, but goes back to Jesus himself, to a Jesus who even taught in the temple."[28]

The picture of the "builders" in the Targum is somewhat ambiguous. They are the ones who "abandoned" the boy. Yet, as the Psalm progresses it seems that they come to recognize his worth, as the exchange in v. 26 may imply. As in the Targum, religious authorities were sometimes called "builders." We see this in rabbinic literature,[29] but more importantly we find it in Qumran where it is quite negative.[30] Of special importance is the appearance of Ps 118:22 in

---

[26]   See K. R. Snodgrass, *The Parable of the Wicked Tenants* (WUNT 27; Tübingen: Mohr [Siebeck], 1983) 95-106, 113-18.

[27]   On the Aramaic of Isa 5:1-7 and its relevance for interpreting the Parable of the Wicked Vineyard Tenants, see B. D. Chilton, *A Galilean Rabbi and His Bible: Jesus' Use of the Interpreted Scripture of His Time* (GNS 8; Wilmington: Glazier, 1984). On the coherence of the underlying Aramaic tradition, as well as the similar interpretive tradition attested in 4Q500, see G. J. Brooke, "4Q500 1 and the Use of Scripture in the Parable of the Vineyard," *DSD* 2 (1995) 268-94.

[28]   Brooke, "4Q500 1," 294. It might be added that the allusions to Psalm 118 on the lips of Jesus and his followers are consistent with his occupation of the Temple (so Dodd, *Parables*, 62).

[29]   "R. Yohana said: 'These are scholars, who are engaged all their days in the upbuilding of the world'" (*b. Šabb.* 114a); "[When quoting Isa 54:13], do not read *banayik* ['your children'] but *bonayik* ['your builders']" (*b. Ber.* 64a); Rabbi Zeira called Rabbi Hila a "builder of scholarship [בניה דאוריתא]" (*y. Yoma* 3.5); cf. 1 Cor 3:10: "as a wise master-builder I laid a foundation"; LXX Isa 3:3: "(The Lord will remove from Judah) master-builder and wise lecturer"; Philo, *On Dreams* 2.8: "(Allegory is the) wise master-builder." In both passages the Greek expression is σοφὸς ἀρχιτέκτων.

[30]   "Such men are builders of a rickety wall" (CD 4:19, alluding to Ezek 13:10); ". . . those who build the wall and cover it with whitewash" (CD 8:12); "[God hates the] builders of the wall" (CD 8:18 = 19:31).

Acts 4:11 where the builders are specifically identified as members of the Sanhedrin who oppose the movement that Jesus had founded.[31]

The data thus far adduced may suggest that Psalm 118 was important for Jesus' program, especially with respect to his stance over against the Temple. But the evidence is suggestive only, for it is not enough to draw firm conclusions. However, the presence of a similar scriptural strain in Jacobian traditions may alter this assessment in a significant way. To these traditions we may now turn.

James' association with the Jerusalem Temple, both in his life and in his death, is underscored in early Christian tradition, and indirectly attested in Josephus' account of his death, already mentioned. In Acts 12:17 we have reference to "James and the brothers." The implication here is that James has assumed leadership of the church in Jerusalem (at least with Peter imprisoned). James appears next in Acts 15, where he plays an important mediating role in the dispute over the question of what parts of the Mosaic Law need be observed by Gentile converts. He reappears in Acts 21:18, where his role as leader of the Jerusalem church evidently continues ("to visit James; and all the elders were present").

James' priority among leaders of the early church is attested in 1 Cor 15:7, where in reference to Jesus' Easter appearances, Paul states that "then he appeared to James, then to all the apostles." Here James is secondary to Peter (Cephas) and the "twelve" (the eleven plus Matthias, the replacement?). In Gal 2:9 Paul refers to James as one of the "pillars [στῦλοι]" of the church. "Pillar" here may carry Temple connotations, for στῦλος occurs frequently in the LXX in reference to the pillars, or upright frames, in the Tabernacle (e.g. Exod 26:15-37; 27:10-17; 35:11, 17; 36:36, 38; 38:10-19; 39:33, 40; 40:18). For example, "Moses erected the tabernacle; he laid its bases, and set up its frames, and put in its poles, and raised up its pillars [LXX: στύλους; MT: עַמּוּד]" (Exod 40:18). Solomon commissioned two special pillars of bronze for the Temple (1 Kgs 7:15-22), by one of which the king of Judah later would customarily stand (2 Kgs

---

31 Was Psalm 118 understood messianically as early as the time of Jesus? J. Jeremias thinks so (cf. *The Eucharistic Words of Jesus* [rev. ed., London: SCM Press, 1966] 257-60), but the evidence is meager. For a late, possibly messianic interpretation, see *Esth. Rab.* 7.10 (on Esth 3:6). For the argument that the Aramaic tradition presupposes a messianic understanding of Psalm 118, see B. Gärtner, 'טליא als Messiasbezeichnung," *SEÅ* 18-19 (1953-54) 98-108.

11:14; 23:3). The Babylonians would later plunder these pillars (2 Kgs 25:13-17; Jer 52:17, 20). Pillars will be erected in the eschatological Temple promised in Ezekiel (40:49; 42:6).[32] The New Testament Apocalypse also speaks of a pillar in the new Temple: "He who conquers, I will make him a pillar in the Temple of my God..." (Rev 3:12). C. K. Barrett suspects that Gal 2:9 understands James, Peter (or Cephas), and John as "pillars of the new Temple."[33]

The documentation for designating a human as a "pillar" on which people may be supported is sufficient (and is summarized by Barrett).[34] Note also 1QSa 1:12-13: "At age twenty-five, he is eligible to take his place among the pillars [יסודות] of the holy 13 congregation and to begin serving the congregation."[35]

In post-New Testament literature, James is called "the Just." Some of these traditions include the following:

> Clement of Alexandria, *Hypotyposes* 6 (*apud* Eusebius, *Hist. Eccl.* 2.1.3): "For Peter and James and John after the Ascension of the Savior did not struggle for glory, because they had previously been given honor by the Savior, but chose James the Just as bishop of Jerusalem."

> Clement of Alexandria, *Hypotyposes* 7 (*apud* Eusebius, *Hist. Eccl.* 2.1.4): "After the resurrection the Lord gave the tradition of knowledge to James the Just and John and Peter, these gave it to the other Apostles and the other Apostles to the seventy, of whom Barnabas was one."

> Eusebius, *Hist. Eccl.* 2.1.2: "At that same time also James, who was called the brother of the Lord, inasmuch as the latter too was styled the child of Joseph . . . this same James, to whom the men of old had also given the surname of Just [δίκαιος] for his excellence of virtue, is narrated to have been the first elected to the throne of the bishopric of the Church in Jerusalem."

---

32   See also 11QT 34:15, which speaks of "twelve pillars [עמודים]" in the Temple.

33   C. K. Barrett, "Paul and the 'Pillar' Apostles," in J. N. Sevenster and W. C. van Unnik (eds.), *Studia Paulina: In Honorem Johannis De Zwaan Septuagenarii* (Haarlem: De Erven F. Bohn, 1953) 1-19, here 17. Barrett convincingly argues that Paul grudgingly acknowledges James' pillar status.

34   Barrett, "Paul and the 'Pillar' Apostles," 4. Reflecting the androcentrism of the time, Iphigeneia declares that "male children are the pillars of homes [στῦλοι γὰρ οἴκων]" (Euripides, *Iphigeneia in Tauris* 57).

35   יסוד normally means "foundation," or the pedestal on which a pillar or altar rests. See the discussion in R. Bauckham, "James and the Jerusalem Church," in R. Bauckham (ed.), *The Book of Acts in Its Palestinian Setting* (Grand Rapids: Eerdmans, 1995) 415-80, esp. 443-45.

Eusebius, *Hist. Eccl.* 2.23.12: "So the scribes and Pharisees . . . made James stand on the battlement of the Temple, and they cried out to him and said, 'Oh, Just [δίκαιε] . . .'"

GThom §12: "The disciples said to Jesus: 'We know that you will go away from us. Who is it that shall be great over us?' Jesus said to them: 'Wherever you have come, you will go to James the Just [δίκαιος] for whose sake heaven and earth came into being.'"

It may be that Ps 118:19 ("Open to me the gates of righteousness [שַׁעֲרֵי־צֶדֶק], that I may enter through them . . .") or v. 20 ("This is the gate of the Lord; the righteous shall enter through it") lies behind the Jacobian sobriquet "the Just."[36]

There are other allusions to Psalm 118 in the Jacobian traditions. The curious Hegesippian tradition that speaks of the "gate of Jesus" may also allude to Ps 118:19-20. According to Eusebius:

12 So the scribes and Pharisees . . . made James stand on the battlement of the Temple, and they cried out to him and said, "Oh, Just [δίκαιε], to whom we all owe obedience, since the people are straying [πλανᾶται] after Jesus who was crucified, tell us what is the gate of Jesus [ἡ θύρα τοῦ Ἰησοῦ]?" 13 And he answered with a loud voice, "Why do you ask me concerning the Son of Man? He is sitting in heaven on the right hand of the great power, and he will come on the clouds of heaven." 14 And many were convinced and glorified because of the testimony of James and said, "Hosanna [ὡσαννά] to the son of David." (*Hist. Eccl.* 2.23.12-14)

The final statement, "Hosanna to the son of David," is a citation of Matt 21:9 (= Mark 11:10), which in turn is the already mentioned allusion to Ps 118:25. If Psalm 118 is in view, then perhaps the "gate of Jesus" is an allusion to the "gate of the Lord,"[37] through which the righteous must pass (Ps 118:20). James the Just (or "righteous") has passed through this gate and is now condemned for having led many astray. The Hebrew's זֶה־הַשַּׁעַר לַיהוָה is rendered in the LXX αὕτη ἡ πύλη τοῦ κυρίου (not ἡ θύρα τοῦ κυρίου), but θύρα sometimes translated שַׁעַר (cf. Exod 39:19[40]; Ezek 46:12; Job 5:4; Prov 14:19).[38]

---

36   In Acts 22:14 the Lukan Paul reports that Ananias called Jesus "the Just" (ὁ δίκαιον). See the discussion in R. Bauckham's chapter in this book ("For What Offence Was James Put to Death?" 210).

37   Again, Bauckham's chapter in this book is pertinent ("For What Offence Was James Put to Death?" 209-218).

38   Bauckham ("For What Offence Was James Put to Death?" 218) has concluded in his chapter that "in the core tradition, James' christological interpretation

With regard to the intriguing tradition found in *2 Apoc. James* 60:2–63:30, C. W. Hedrick comments: "It is obvious that the author of the *Second Apocalypse of James* made extensive use of Jewish-Christian tradition. Such is particularly clear with regard to the account of the martyrdom of James, which is quite similar to the account in the *Memoirs* of Hegesippus."[39] The relevant material reads as follows:

> "And play your trumpets, your flutes, and your harps [of this house]. The Lord has taken you captive from the Lord, having closed your ears, that they may not hear the sound of my word. Yet you [will be able to pay] heed in your hearts, [and] you will call me 'the Just One.' Therefore, I tell you: Behold, I gave you your house, which you say that God has made. Did he who dwells in it promise to give you an inheritance through it? This (house) I shall doom to destruction and derision of those who are in ignorance. For behold, those who judge deliberate . . ."

> [On] that day all the [people] and the crowd were disturbed, and they showed that they had not been persuaded. And he arose and went forth speaking in this [manner]. And he entered (again) on that same day and spoke a few hours. And I was with the priests and revealed nothing of the relationship, since all of them were saying with one voice, "Come, let us stone the Just One." And they arose, saying, "Yes, let us kill this man, that he may be taken from our midst. For he will be of no use to us."

> And they were there and found him standing beside the columns of the Temple beside the mighty corner stone. And they decided to throw him down from the height, and they cast him down. And . . . they seized him and [struck] him as they dragged him upon the ground. They stretched him out, and placed a stone on his abdomen. They all placed their feet on him, saying, "You have erred!"

> Again they raised him up, since he was alive, and made him dig a hole. They made him stand in it. After having covered him up to his abdomen, they stoned him in this manner.

---

of 'the gate of YHWH' (Ps 118:20) led to his judicial execution by stoning."

[39] C. W. Hedrick, "The Second Apocalypse of James (V, *4*)," in J. M. Robinson (ed.), *The Nag Hammadi Library* (Leiden: Brill; San Francisco: Harper & Row, 1977) 249. F. S. Jones ("The Martyrdom of James in Hegesippus, Clement of Alexandria, and Christian Apocrypha, Including Nag Hammadi: A Study of Textual Relations," in D. J. Lull [ed.], *Society of Biblical Literature 1990 Seminar Papers* [SBLSP 29; Atlanta: Scholars, 1990] 322-35, here 327) has concluded that Hegesippus' account underlies Eusebius and *2 Apoc. James*. He further believes that there is no good reason for not accepting Eusebius' quotations as essentially reliable. He also believes that Epiphanius drew on Eusebius.

And he stretched out his hands and said this prayer—not that (one) which it is his custom to say: "My God and my Father . . . Save me from an evil death! Bring me from a tomb alive . . . Save me from evil affliction! But now is the [time] and the hour. O Holy [Spirit], send [me] salvation . . ."

The significant elements are the close association with the Temple, criticism of it, prediction of its doom, and James' martyrdom "beside the columns of the Temple beside the mighty corner stone" (61:21-23).

What is fascinating here are the links between Jesus and James provided by Ps 118:19-27. These links are enhanced when the Targum is taken into consideration, especially the explicit Davidism. That both brothers, Jesus and James, should be done away by Caiaphas and his brother-in-law Ananus is surely more than mere coincidence. A Davidic element, perhaps captured best by the interpretive tradition that grew up alongside Psalm 118, complete with devotion to the Temple (which Psalm 118 presupposes) and probable criticism of Temple polity (which in turn implies a criticism of the ruling priests), seems to be the thread that runs throughout.

The line of continuity between Jesus and brother James, the leader of the Jerusalem church,[40] supports the contention that Jesus and James may very well have advanced the same agenda over against the Temple establishment, and both suffered the same fate at the hands of essentially the same people. In the case of Jesus, of course, due process (in the eyes of Rome) was followed. In the case of James, it was not, with the result that Ananus was removed from office. I believe that the central thesis of this paper is borne out: Comparison of the Temple activities (and fates) of Jesus and James, along with careful scrutiny of links with Psalm 118, should help us understand better both figures. The subsequent, partially-parallel career of James moves us to view the activities of his brother Jesus in terms of the Jewish Temple and teachings that his contemporaries understood as holding serious implications for this sacred institution. For this reason we must eschew recent faddish scholarship that minimizes the role of the Temple in the life and ministry of Jesus.

---

[40] M. Hengel, "Jacobus der Herrenbruder—der erste 'Papst'?" in E. Grässer and O. Merk (eds.), *Glaube und Eschatologie: Festschrift für W.G. Kümmel zum 80. Geburtstag* (Tübingen: Mohr [Siebeck], 1985) 71-104. James was leader, but not "pope" (pp. 103-104).

CONCLUSIONS AND QUESTIONS

Bruce Chilton

Our consultation on James took place over the course of three days, on the basis of papers which had been distributed beforehand. That procedure enabled participants to give abbreviated, oral versions of their contributions for the purposes of discussion. Each presentation was discussed, both by the invited contributors and by those who joined us for the consultation. The growth of the entire discipline of biblical criticism over the past few decades has been widely noted, and not altogether welcomed. Reservations have been expressed both by religious scholars who are concerned with a theological reading of the Scriptures, a reading which sometimes seems to have been lost in the shuffle of competing approaches, and by academic scholars who have observed that growth has brought with it a balkanization of approaches, so that coherent insight into the production of the texts and their meanings has been difficult to achieve.[1] The purpose of our consultation was both to enhance our knowledge of James and to address the perceived confusion over what it is we do when we engage in biblical exegesis together.

Our progress was to some extent possible because we joined in an occasion in which we could actually listen to one another, and did so. Civil exchange and searching criticism[2] have often fallen victim in the sudden growth of our discipline and the evolution of large institutional structures that do not facilitate the intense, common engagements which are often necessary for scholarship to prosper. But at a deeper level, the participants appreciated our consultation because it provided an occasion to relate approaches to one another which are often kept separate. Literary, historical, cultural, religious, and theological perspectives were all brought to bear in our discussions, and fitted into a common focus.

That focus is topically defined as James, of course, but "James" in

---

[1]   See Markus Bockmuehl, "'To be or not to be': the Possible Futures of New Testament Scholarship," *SJT* 51 (1998) 271-306.

[2]   Among scholars, either both are present, or neither.

a particular sense. Throughout our discussions, we found James to be an influence within our texts—appreciable by all our perspectives—owing to the practices that were associated with him, and to the issues and questions those practices occasioned. Of all those practices, none stands out more clearly than that of the Nazirite vow. In this concluding essay, I wish to suggest that the breadth of this practice within primitive Christianity has been underestimated, and that James' deep influence is perhaps best measured by the extent to which other prominent teachers fell in with his program.

THE NATURE OF PAUL'S VOW AS PORTRAYED IN ACTS

In Acts 18:18, Paul is said to shave his head in Cenchraea, because he had a vow (κειράμενος ἐν Κεγχρεαῖς τὴν κεφαλήν, εἶχεν γὰρ εὐχήν). The reference to the cutting of hair naturally associates Paul's practice with the Nazirite vow, because a Nazirite was held to have completed his vow at the time he shaved his hair and offered it at the altar (see Num 6:18). As set out in Numbers 6, a Nazirite was to let his hair and (if at issue) beard grow for the time of his vow, abstain completely from grapes, and avoid approaching any dead body. At the close of the period of the vow, he was to shave his head, and offer his hair in proximity to the altar (so Num 6:18). The end of this time of being holy, the LORD's property, is marked by enabling the Nazirite to drink wine again (6:20).

Although the identification of the vow may seem straightforward, such a simple reading is immediately complicated by any attempt to read Acts 18 within the terms of reference of Numbers 6. After all, Num 6:18 is quite specific that the Nazirite is to shave his head at the opening at the tent of appointment and put it on the fire under the sacrifice of sharings. The reading would seem to suggest that the vow could only be fulfilled by shaving one's head at the threshold of the sanctuary and by placing one's hair on the fire in the sanctuary. That has caused commentators to be cautious about equating Paul's vow and Nazirite practice.

The text of Numbers itself, however, should encourage us to be cautious about our caution. Numbers 6:2 opens with the explicit statement that a man or a woman might undertake the vow. Evidently, the Nazirite practice of woman would not have included their admission into the sanctuary, where the presence of women was regularly prohibited and the presence of men was not infrequently prohibited, so that the presentation of the hair in the that place must have been by means of a surrogate.

Indeed, Mishnah conceives of Nazirite vows as being undertaken by slaves, as well as Israelites, so that a strict association with the sanctuary would have been untenable (*Nazir* 9:1). Such vows in regard to hair alone were held in Mishnah to equate to a Nazirite vow (*Nazir* 1:1); the opening of the tractate is also emphatic that a precise pronunciation of the term *nazir* was not necessary to engage the full requirements of the vow. So whatever Paul or Acts thought of his vow from his own perspective, many would have seen him as falling in with the program of what is referred to in the Mishnah, and some would have seen him as obligated by the prevailing custom.

In his careful evaluation of Paul's practice, Maas Boertien has crafted a skillful association between Acts 18:18 and Acts 21:23-26, where Paul is convinced to undertake the expenses of four Nazirites.[3] The reference to their shaving their heads makes the association with Numbers 6 evident, especially since the context within the Temple makes the identification with a Nazirite vow straightforward. Boertien's overall argument is that Paul had has hair shorn in Cenchraea to fulfill the temporal requirements of his vow, and then took part in an offering in the Temple to fulfill the sacrificial requirements of his vow. To make out that case, Bortien must show that the moment of cutting of the hair and the moment of sacrifice could in fact be dissociated from one another.

Particularly, in regard to hair, he must answer the question: if Paul's vow were as a Nazirite, what would he have done with the hair he had cut? After all, one was holy, to the LORD, all the days that one vowed (Num 6:5, 13), by virtue of that uncut hair. Two institutions enable Bortien to reply to that question.

First, within the terms of reference of Numbers 6 itself, the problem of what we might call the missing hair is addressed in the Mishnah. When a Nazirite's head is rendered impure by the sudden death of one near to him, he shaves on the seventh day, the day of purification (Num 6:9), and then he offers at the opening of the tent of appointment on the eighth day (Num 6:10). The priest takes these offerings as a sacrifice for sin and a whole sacrifice, and makes

---

3 The discussion appears in M. Boertien, *Nazir (Nasiräer). Text, übersetung und Erklärung nebst einem textkitischen Anhang: Die Mischna* (Berlin: de Gruyter, 1971) 28-29, 71-72, 90-95.

appeasement; the Nazirite's head is consecrated again (Num 6:11), and the vow starts all over again (Num 6:12). Numbers accounts for everything but the hair which was has been cut in view of impurity. *M. Tem.* 7:4 provides the answer: such hair is buried, in an evident analogy to the blood of a slaughtered animal, which is poured into the ground when it is not poured out in sacrifice.

But cutting hair in view of purity is obviously different from cutting one's hair to fulfill the vow, which is what Paul is portrayed as doing in Acts 18:18. That is why the second institution is crucial to Bortien's analysis. *M. Nazir* 3:6 attributes to beth Shammai the regulation of those who undertake Nazirite vows outside of Israel: when they fulfill the requirement of time abroad, they are to serve out an additional thirty days in the land of Israel. Implicitly, the hair is cut outside Israel, and the offering is accomplished in the Temple.[4] The only question left open by Mishnah is whether an additional period is really necessary, and how long it should be.[5] The fact of the temporal fulfillment of Nazirite vows abroad is taken for granted.

The case of hair shorn abroad in fulfillment of the vow is analogous to hair shorn in view of contamination. In both cases, shearing is performed under conditions of impurity. *M. Nazir* 6:8 stipulates that the sacrificial offering of the hair by the Nazirite is to be carried out, even when he has been shorn outside of Jerusalem, but that the "shearing of impurity" is not to be offered.[6] But that still leaves the Nazirite from abroad with the problem of missing hair: what is he to offer? Beth Shammai solves the problem by providing for an additional month to grow some more. But what of those who proceed directly to the sacrificial moment specified by Numbers 6?

Bortien addresses that question by referring to the practice of association within a Nazirite offering. *M. Nazir* 2:5 sets out an at first sight complicated arrangement, which addresses what to do when a Nazirite pledges himself to bring both his own hair offering and the hair offering of another Nazirite. Under those circumstances, the recommendation is to make this offering with a fellow, to economize on the costs involved. After all, each Nazirite was to offer three animals and grain with oil and the accompanying wine (so Num

---

4   See Boertien, *Nazir*, 90-91.
5   In this case, beth Hillel appears to be more stringent, requiring that the entire period of the vow should be repeated.
6   See Boertien, *Nazir*, 93.

6:14-15): the expense involved was considerable. So one could make a commitment to double one's pledge, while paying only as if for oneself. In this way, even a person of relatively modest means—by taking on the expenses of Nazirites—could imitate the prosperous piety of Alexander Jannaeus (see *Gen. Rab.* 91.3 [on Gen 42:4-5]; and in *y. Naz.* 54b, 5f, and *b. Ber.* 11a-b) and Agrippa I (*Ant.* 19.6.1 §293-294).

Boertien brings all of these elements together in order to account for Paul's practice as narrated in Acts. Paul first completed his Nazirite vow outside Israel (Acts 18:18) and then, after his arrival in Jerusalem, offered the sacrifices of dedication in association with other Nazirites (Acts 21:23-26).[7] In this regard, he calls particular attention to Acts 21:26, where Paul observes a period of seven days of purification before he completes the offering. That corresponds to the seven days stipulated in Numbers (6:9-10) for cases in which a Nazirite has encountered impurity. In effect, residence outside of Israel was itself treated as an instance of impurity.[8]

The question of Paul's vow in Acts 18:18 has been dogged by the problem that, although some relationship to Numbers 6 seems to be implicit, Paul is not near enough to the Temple to accord with the requirements of the Nazirite vow. Bortien resolved that problem, by showing that the issue of Nazirites outside of Israel was addressed in the Mishnah. He was aware that Mishnah could not be assumed to be contemporaneous with the New Testament, and in fact attributed this section of the tractate *Nazir* to Yudah ben Ilai, the Tannah of the second century. Whether or not that association is fully tenable, the assumption within the tractate that such vows can be effectuated, much as in the case of the vow of *Qorbana*.[9]

Beyond that, however, Bortien seems to press Acts into the mold of the Mishnah. *Nazir* 2:5 assumes that, at the time one pledged, one might agree to take on the expenses of someone else. Acts clearly separates Paul's own vow (18:18) from the suggestion of James and the elders, that Paul should—as a public display of piety—demonstrate his fidelity to the Torah (Acts 21:24). Paul and his companion arrive in Jerusalem and are confronted by James and the elders'

---

7   Boertien, *Nazir*, 72.
8   So Boertien, *Nazir*, 92 (citing *m. Nazir* 7:3).
9   Mishnah envisages a man saying, "Qorban be any benefit my wife gets from me, for she stole me purse" (*m. Ned.* 3:2).

report to them that Paul's reputation in Jerusalem is that he is telling Jews in the Diaspora to forsake Moses, and especially to stop circumcising their children (Acts 21:17-21). Paul is then told to take on the expense of four men who had taken a vow, entering the Temple with them to offer sacrifice (Acts 21:22-26). The indications of time in Acts simply do not allow for Paul to accord with the halakhah of beth Shammai; he delays one week, not one month. Further, James' attempt to have Paul correspond to the halakhah on a more liberal understanding is a failure according to the narrative in Acts: once in Jerusalem, Acts portrays Paul as received joyfully (21:17), and then as proceeding to follow the advice given him the following day (21:26). That advice, of course, had disastrous consequences. Paul's entry into the Temple caused a riot, because it was supposed he was bringing Greeks in. As a result, he was arrested by a Roman officer (Acts 21:27–22:30), and so began the long, legal contention which resulted ultimately in his death. Even Acts has to admit that there was some substance in the accusation of the "Jews from Asia": they had seen Paul in the city, not with a quartet of Nazirites, but with a Greek from Ephesus (Acts 21:27-29). And when Paul defends himself before Felix, his own protestation of innocence is not framed in terms of his own or others' Nazirite vow, but in terms of his bringing alms and offerings, the occasion of his having purified himself (Acts 24:17-19).

Acts, in other words, agrees substantially with Paul's own statement of his program in regard to the Temple: the priestly service of preaching the gospel is to lead to the presentation of the offering of the Gentiles (Rom 15:16). The tangible generosity of congregations in Greece is a matter of pride for Paul, and he boasts that, "having sealed this fruit," he will return "with the fullness of Christ's blessing" (Rom 15:25-29). Openly boastful though he is at this stage (so Rom 15:17), Paul is also cautious: he urges his Roman supporters to pray that he might escape the unpersuaded in Judah, and that his service for the saints in Jerusalem might be an acceptable offering (15:30-33).

And then, having mentioned both his sacrificial offering in Jerusalem and his fear of some in Judah, Paul goes on in the present text of Romans to recommend Phoebe to the Romans, the servant of the congregation among the Cenchraeans, whom Paul describes as an aid of many, including himself (Rom 16:1). The Romans are asked to accept her, and to aid her "in whatever matter in which she has need of you." Romans 16 opens with a famously long list of Paul's associates and helpers, but Phoebe is the only person who is commended in this way. She is called a servant (διάκονος, the same term used of Christ in 15:8) just after Paul has referred to his own collection as service (διακονία, in Rom 15:31), and has referred to his own activity as serving (Rom 15:25).

The importance of these links is attenuated, of course, if one follows the argument that chap. 16 is an addition to the original letter, perhaps initially destined for Ephesus. Pierre Benoit has nonetheless come to the conclusion that Phoebe is the bearer of the letter, and that the salutations are designed to underscore Paul's familiarity with those known to the congregation(s) in Rome.[10] If the reference to Phoebe and the congregation in Cenchraea is Pauline, then we can correlate the itinerary of Acts with Paul's implicit itinerary. If, on the other hand, the chapter is an appendix, then it reflects a later correlation of the two itineraries. Either way, Cenchraea turns up as a linking moment between Paul's activity among the Gentiles and what is about to happen in Jerusalem.

The Cenchraean moment is a time when Paul is well aware of enmity in Judah, and he is disquieted by it. His response is to align himself as best he can with the most powerful Christian group in Jerusalem, the one associated with James. That, indeed, is the best explanation for Paul's willingness to take on a Nazirite vow, and to take on the expenses of other Nazirites. As cited by Eusebius (see *Eccl. Hist.* 2.23.1-18),[11] Hegesippus characterizes James, Jesus' brother, as the person who exercised immediate control of the church in Jerusalem. Although Peter had initially gathered a group of Jesus' followers in Jerusalem, his interests and activities further afield left the way open for James to become the natural head of the community there. That change, and political changes in Jerusalem itself, made the Temple the effective center of the local community of Jesus' followers. James practiced a careful and idiosyncratic purity in the interests of worship in the Temple. He abstained from wine and animal flesh, did not cut his hair or beard, and forsook oil

---

10   See *La Bible de Jérusalem* (Paris: Les éditions du Cerf, 1977) 619-20.

11   Florence Morgan Gillman suggests that Hegesippus' source is the *Acts of the Apostles* used among the Ebionites, a Christian group which sought also to follow the Torah. She connects their veneration of James to the praise given him in *GThom* §12.

and frequent bathing. According to Hegesippus, those special practices gave him access even to the sanctuary. These practices of holiness are for the most part consistent with the requirements made of those undertaking a Nazirite vow. The additional notice, that James avoided oil, is consistent with the especial concern for purity among Nazirites. They were to avoid any contact with death (Num 6:6-12), and the avoidance of all uncleanness—which is incompatible with sanctity—follows naturally. Josephus also attributes the avoidance of oil to the Essenes (*J.W.* 2.8.3 §123), and the reason seems plain: oil, as a fluid pressed from fruit, was considered to absorb impurity to such an extent that extreme care in its preparation was vital.[12] Absent complete assurance, abstinence was a wise policy. James vegetarianism also comports with a concern to avoid contact with any kind of corpse. Finally, although Hegesippus' assertion that James could actually enter the sanctuary seems exaggerated, his acceptance of a Nazirite regime, such as Acts 21 explicitly associates him with, would account for such a remembrance of him, in that Nazirites were to be presented in the vicinity of the sanctuary.

James' characteristic theology is in fact confirmed in the passage which relates Paul's agreement to take on the expenses of the Nazirites (Acts 21:23-25). James and the elders urge Paul to associate himself with the four Nazirites to show that he himself keeps the law; in that vein, they tell Paul (what he has in Acts supposedly agreed with) that they have instructed believing Gentiles to abstain from food sacrificed to idols, from blood, from strangled products, and from fornication. These basic tenets of purity are highlighted in Acts 15, which represents the settlement of a controversy concerning the very identity of belief in Jesus. The account in Acts 15 is romanticized; one sees much less of the tension and controversy which Paul attests. But once allowance has been made for the tendency in Acts to portray the ancient Church as a body at harmonious unity, the nature and force of James' position become clear.

The two issues in dispute, circumcision and purity, are dealt with in Acts 15 as if they were the agenda of a single meeting of leaders in Jerusalem. (Paul in Galatians 2 more accurately describes the meeting he had with the leaders as distinct from a later decision to

---

12   See Josephus, *J.W.* 2.21.2 §590-594; *m. Menaḥ.* 8:3-5 and the whole of *Makhshirin*. The point of departure for the concern is Lev 11:34.

return to the question of purity.) The first item on the agenda is settled by having Peter declare that, since God gave his holy spirit to Gentiles who believed, no attempt should be made to add requirements such as circumcision to them (Acts 15:6-11). Paul could scarcely have said it better himself; and that is consistent with the version of Paulinism represented in Acts.

The second item on the agenda is settled on James' authority, not Peter's, and the outcome is not in line with Paul's thought. James first confirms the position of Peter, but he states the position in a very different way: "Symeon has related how God first visited the Gentiles, to take a people in his name" (Acts 15:14). James' perspective here is not that all who believe are Israel (the Pauline definition), but that in addition to Israel God has established a people in his name. How the new people are to be regarded in relation to Israel is a question which is implicit in the statement, and James goes on to answer it. James develops the relationship between those taken from the Gentiles and Israel in two ways. The first method is the use of Scripture, while the second is a requirement of purity. The logic of them both inevitably involves a rejection of Paul's position (along the lines laid out in Galatians 2).

The use of Scripture, like the argument itself, is quite unlike Paul's.[13] James claims that "with this (that is, his statement of Peter's position) the words of the prophets agree, just as it is written" (Acts 15:15), and he goes on to cite from the book of Amos. The form of James' interpretation is an immediate indication of a substantial difference from Paul. As James has it, there is actual agreement between Symeon and the words of the prophets, as two people might agree. The continuity of Christian experience with Scripture is marked as a greater concern than within Paul's interpretation, and James expects that continuity to be verbal, a matter of agreement with the prophets' words, not merely with possible ways of looking at what they mean.

The citation from Amos (9:11-12) comports well with James' concern that the position of the Church agree with the principal vocabulary of the prophets (Acts 15:16-17):

> After this I will come back and restore the tent of David which has fallen,

---

[13] For a treatment of this issue, see Chilton, "The Brother of Jesus and the Interpretation of Scripture," in L. V. Rutgers, P. W. van der Horst, et al. (eds.), *The Use of Sacred Books in the Ancient World* (Leuven: Peeters, 1998) 29-48.

and rebuild its ruins and set it up anew, that the rest of men may seek the
Lord, and all the Gentiles upon whom my name is called . . . .

In the argument of James as represented here, what the belief of
Gentiles achieves is, not the redefinition of Israel (as in Paul's
thought), but the restoration of the house of David. The argument is
possible because Davidic genealogy of Jesus—and, therefore, of his
brother James—is assumed.

In a recent conference at Trinity Western University, John J.
Collins referred to the two citations of Amos 9:11 which are attested
at Qumran.[14] He relied on his findings in an earlier work that the
two exegeses are quite different from one another, and from James'
exegesis.[15] For reasons of context, I would be inclined to describe
the relationship among the interpretations as complementary. The
more recently identified usage (in 4Q174 3:10-13, a florilegium) is
the more straightforward, in that the image of the restoration of the
hut of David is associated with the promise to the David in 2 Sam
7:13-14 and with the Davidic "branch" (cf. Isa 11:1-10), all taken in
a messianic sense.[16] Given the expectation of a son of David as
messianic king (see *Pss. Sol.* 17:21-43), such an application of the
passage in Amos, whether at Qumran or by James, is hardly strange.
On the other hand, it is striking at first sight that the passage in
Amos—particularly, "the fallen hut of David"—is applied in the
Damascus Document (CD 7:15-17), not to a messianic figure, but to
the law which is restored. Now the book of Amos itself makes
Judah's contempt for the Torah for pivotal issue (Amos 2:4), and
calls for a program of seeking the Lord and his ways (Amos 5:6-15),
so it is perhaps not surprising that "the seeker of the law" is
predicted to restore it in the *Damascus Document*. So Collins sees the
reading of the Florilegium as messianic, and that of the *Damascus*

---

[14]   See Craig A. Evans and Peter W. Flint (eds), *Eschatology, Messianism, and the Dead Sea Scrolls* (Grand Rapids: Eerdmans, 1997) 151. For an accessible and interesting presentation of the texts in English, see Michael Wise, Martin Abegg, and Edward Cook (eds.), *The Dead Sea Scrolls: A New Translation* (San Francisco: Harper, 1996).

[15]   See John J. Collins, *The Scepter and the Star. The Messiahs of the Dead Sea Scrolls and other Ancient Literature* (ABRL; New York: Doubleday, 1995). He develops his reading of the difference between this interpretation and that contained in the *Damascus Document* on pp. 64-65, following the lead of Joseph A. Fitzmyer.

[16]   Collins, *Scepter and Star*, 61.

Document as relating to the Torah. Still, CD 7:15-20 directly refers to the "books of the Torah" as "the huts of the king," interpreted by means of the "fallen hut of David." Evidently, there is a correspondence between the power of the messiah and the establishment of the Torah, as is further suggested by the association with the seeker of the law *not only here*, in the *Damascus Document*, but also in the Florilegium. A contextual reading of the two passages demonstrates a dual focus, on messiah and Torah in each case, which is so in Acts as well. The texts stand in a complementary relationship. The possibility of influence on James' interpretation of Amos as presented in Acts 15 may not be discounted.

An account of James' preaching in the Temple is given by Hegesippus (see Eusebius, *Hist. Eccl.* 2.23). James there represents Jesus as the son of man who is to come from heaven to judge the world. Those who agree cry out, "Hosanna to the Son of David!" Hegesippus shows that James' view of his brother came to be that he was related to David (as was the family generally) and was also a heavenly figure ("the son of man") who was coming to judge the world. When Acts and Hegesippus are taken together, they indicate that James contended Jesus was restoring the house of David because he was the agent of final judgment, and was being accepted as such by Gentiles.

But on James' view, Gentiles remain Gentiles; they are not to be identified with Israel. His position was not anti-Pauline, at least not at first. His focus was on Jesus' role as the ultimate arbiter within the Davidic line, and there was never any question in his mind but that the Temple was the natural place to worship God and acknowledge Jesus. Embracing the Temple as central meant for James, as it meant for everyone associated with worship there, maintaining the purity which it was understood that God required in his house. Purity involved excluding Gentiles from the interior courts of the Temple, where Israel was involved in sacrifice. The line of demarcation between Israel and non-Israel was no invention within the circle of James, but a natural result of seeing Jesus as the triumphant branch of the house of David.

Gentile belief in Jesus was therefore in James' understanding a vindication of his Davidic triumph, but it did not involve a fundamental change in the status of Gentiles vis-à -vis Israel. That characterization of the Gentiles, developed by means of the reference to Amos, enables James to proceed to his requirement of their recognition of purity. He first states that "I determine not to trouble those of the Gentiles who turn to God" (15:19) as if he were simply repeating the policy of Peter in regard to circumcision. (The implicit authority of that "I" contrasts sharply with the usual portrayal in Acts of apostolic decision as communal.) But he then continues that is determination is also "to write to them to abstain from the pollutions of the idols, and from fornication, and from what is strangled, and from blood" (15:20).

The rules set out by James tend naturally to separate believing Gentiles from their ambient environment. They are to refrain from feasts in honor of the gods and from foods sacrificed to idols in the course of being butchered and sold. (The notional devotion of animals in the market to one god or another was a common practice in the Hellenistic world.) They are to observe stricter limits than usual on the type of sexual activity they might engage with, and with whom. (Gross promiscuity need not be at issue here; marriage with cousins is also included within the likely area of concern. That was fashionable in the Hellenistic world, and proscribed in the book of Leviticus [see chap. 18 and 20:17-21]). They are to avoid the flesh of animals which had been strangled instead of bled, and they are not to consume blood itself. The proscription of blood, of course, was basic within Judaism. And strangling an animal (as distinct from cutting its throat) increased the availability of blood in the meat. Such strictures are consistent with James' initial observation, that God had taken a people from the Gentiles (15:14); they were to be similar to Israel in their distinction from the Hellenistic world at large.

The motive behind the rules is not separation in itself, however. James links them to the fact that the Mosaic legislation regarding purity is well and widely known (15:21):

> For Moses from early generations has had those preaching him city by city,
> being read in the synagogues every Sabbath.

Because the law is well known, James insists that believers, even Gentile believers, are not to live in flagrant violation of what Moses enjoined. As a result of James' insistence, the meeting in Jerusalem decides to send envoys and a letter to Antioch, in order to require Gentiles to honor the prohibitions set out by James (Acts 15:22-35).

The same chapter of Leviticus which commands, "love your neighbor as yourself" (19:18) also forbids blood to be eaten (19:26) and fornication (19:29 see also 18:6-30). The canonical (but second-hand) letter of James calls the commandment of love "the royal law"

(Jas 2:8), acknowledging that Jesus had accorded it privilege by citing it alongside the commandment to love God as the two greatest commandments (see Mark 12:28-32). In Acts James himself, while accepting that Gentiles cannot be required to keep the whole law, insists that they should acknowledge it, by observing basic requirements concerning fornication and blood and idolatry.

It is of interest that Leviticus forbids the eating of blood by sojourners as well as Israelites, and associates that prohibition with how animals are to be killed for the purpose of eating (17:10-16). Moreover, a principle of exclusivity in sacrifice is trenchantly maintained: anyone, whether of Israel or a sojourner dwelling among them, who offers a sacrifice which is not brought to the LORD's honor in the Temple is to be cut off from the people (17:8-9). In other words, the prohibitions of James, involving sacrifice, fornication, strangled meat produce, and blood, all derive easily from the very context in Leviticus from which the commandment to love is derived. They are elementary, and involve interest in what Gentiles as well as Israelites do.

James' prohibitions are designed to show that believing Gentiles honor the law which is commonly read, without in any way changing their status as Gentiles. Thereby, the tent of David is erected again, in the midst of Gentiles who show their awareness of the restoration by means of their respect for the Torah. The interpretation attributed to James involves an application of Davidic vocabulary to Jesus, as is consistent with the claim of Jesus' family to Davidic ancestry. The transfer of Davidic promises to Jesus is accomplished within an acceptance of the terms of reference of the Scripture generally: to embrace David is to embrace Moses. There is no trace in James' interpretation of the Pauline gambit, setting one biblical principle (justification in the manner of Abraham) against another (obedience in the manner of Moses). Where Paul divided the Scripture against itself in order to maintain the integrity of a single fellowship of Jews and Gentiles, James insisted upon the integrity of Scripture, even at the cost of separating Christians from one another. In both cases, the interpretation of Scripture was also—at the same moment as the sacred text was apprehended—a matter of social policy.

The twin pillars of James' practice, then, were Gentile recognition of the Torah on the one hand and Nazirite purity on the other hand. Paul's insistence was on the single offering to be accomplished in

Jerusalem by means of his own ministry, where Christ would realize his identity as the ἰσλαστήριον (Rom 3:25), the definitive place of appeasement. Once he arrived in Jerusalem, Paul attempted to square the circle of his own theology, by taking on the Nazirite sponsorship suggested to him by James and others from the ample funds available to him. But his own thought, as well as the statement attributed to Paul in Acts 24:17, precludes the inference that Paul was in Jerusalem as a simple Nazirite. His service of alms and offerings was indeed for the saints, but it was also on behalf of the nations. Within Paul's own thinking, he could personally accept the Nazirite discipline, and Acts 18:18 suggests he even anticipated doing so. But his repute in Jerusalem assured that his attempt at compromise would be mistaken as a deliberate affront, with predictable results.

SEQUEL: THE END OF THE NAZIRITE VOW

In his treatment of the subject in the present volume, Jacob Neusner shows that there was, in the structure of the Mishnah, a direct conflict between the world of the now defunct Temple and the world of the household:[17]

> The special vow of the Nazirite, like the vow in general, draws in its wake consequences for the life of the family of which that individual that takes the vow is (by definition) a key member: the householder, his wife, children, and slaves. Not drinking wine, not shaving the head, not contracting corpse-uncleanness are matters that are personal and impinge upon the household; they do not pertain in any weighty way to public life, on the one side, or to relations between the people, Israel, and God, on the other. The Nazirite cannot attend to the deceased, cannot drink wine with the family, and subjects himself to his own rule when it comes to his appearance. As is the priest to the family of Israel, so is the Nazirite to the household of Israel, a particular classification of persons, distinguished in consequential and practical ways as to nourishment and comportment.

Because Mishnah structures an imaginative revolution, in which the domain of the Temple is transposed into the world of the household, the matter of vows is of particular importance to its overall presentation, and Neusner is here able to show how that transposition is achieved. Indeed, the issue is even starker within Mishnah than might be expected, because all grape products, not just wine, are prohibited

---

17   J. Neusner, "Vow-Taking, the Nazirites, and the Law: Does James' Advice to Paul Accord with Halakhah?" 67.

to the Nazirite (Num 6:3-4).

The tractate *Nazir* is situated "in the division on the family ['Women'], even though it bears upon men as much as upon women." Topically, there is a rationale for this organization:[18]

> That is because the right of the husband to annul his wife's vows extends to the Nazirite vow that she may take. That is surely the formal reason that justifies situating the tractate where it is.

The Nazirite vow in the Bible entails both personal restrictions and public, sacrificial devotion. The destruction of the Temple rendered the latter impossible, but the obligation of the former remained, at least in theory. It was incumbent on those who framed the Mishnah to demonstrate, in terms of the halakhah, why vowing is—in Neusner's words—"a disreputable use of the holy."[19] Absent the Temple, a reason other than the accidental fact of its destruction needed to be developed to obviate the taking of vows:[20]

> But because the halakhah begins and ends with the conviction that language is power, the halakhah also takes account of the sanctifying effect of even language stupidly used. That is the message of the halakhah, and it is only through the halakhah at hand that sages could set forth the message they had in mind concerning the exploitation and abuse of the power of language. It is a disreputable use of the holy. And language is holy because language gives form and effect to intentionality—the very issue of the halakhah at hand!

Although the Nazirite vow had become impossible in the public space of the Temple, for the Mishnah its personal character had in any case fallen into disrepute.

Neusner's analysis enables us at last to see why the Mishnah entertains surreal instances of vow taking. A husband who believes his wife is stealing says, "Qorban be any benefit my wife gets from me, because she stole my purse!" (*m. Ned.* 3:2). A guest who can drink no more wine exclaims, "I am a nazirite from it!" (*m. Nazir* 2:3). In each of those cases—and in many more like them—Mishnah takes up the fateful question: what then? Indeed, those two cases form the paradigm instances for Neusner:[21]

> So sages' statement through the halakhah of Nedarim-Nazir is clear. Vows

---

[18]   Neusner, "Vow-Taking," 67.
[19]   Neusner, "Vow-Taking," 77.
[20]   Neusner, "Vow-Taking," 77.
[21]   Neusner, "Vow-Taking," 77-78.

are a means used on earth by weak or subordinated person to coerce the more powerful person by invoking the power of Heaven. They are taken under emotional duress and express impatience and frustration. They are not to be predicted. They do not follow a period of sober reflection. They take on importance principally in two relationships, [1] between friends (e.g. host and guest), [2] between husband and wife. They come into play at crucial, dangerous points, because they disrupt the crucial relationships that define life, particularly within the household: marriage, on the one side, friendly hospitality, on the other. They jar and explode. By admitting into human relationships the power of intentionality, they render the predictable —what is governed by regularities—into a source of uncertainty, for who in the end will penetrate what lies deep in the heart, as Jeremiah reflected, which is beyond fathoming? But language brings to the surface, in a statement of will best left unsaid, what lurks in the depths, and the result, Heaven's immediate engagement, is not to be gainsaid. That is why vows form a source of danger. What should be stable if life is to go on is made capricious. So far as marriage is concerned, vows rip open the fabric of sacred relationships.

The power of Neusner's analysis resides in its capacity to explain why the Mishnaic tractate so rigorously discuss practices which, given the destruction of the Temple, can not be followed. By logical surgery, pressing the *reductio ad absurdum* to surreal conclusions, vowing is made to seem foolish.

The irony here is not lost on Neusner, who goes on the compare the stance of Mishnah to that of the Gospels:[22]

Jesus said exactly the same thing in the Sermon on the Mount.

He accordingly finds that, if James advised Paul to take on a Nazirite vow, whether personally or as a sponsor, he "will not have found agreement among the rabbis of the Mishnah represented by the halakhah of the Mishnah, Tosefta, Yerushalmi, and Bavli."[23] But that, I would suggest, is for the same reason that Matthew's Jesus is so global in his rejection of both oaths (Matt 5:33-37) and of vows (Matt 15:3-9[24]), two distinct categories which are conflated: in the era after the destruction of the Temple, institutions dependent upon

---

22   Neusner, "Vow-taking," 82.

23   Neusner, "Vow-taking," 81-82.

24   This teaching concerning the Temple is most plausibly related to the circle of James, see B. Chilton, "A Generative Exegesis of Mark 7:1-23," *The Journal of Higher Criticism* 3.1 (1996) 18-37.

that center need to be transformed.

A consideration of Bortien's exegesis of Mishnah and Neusner's enables us more fully to appreciate Paul's last actions in the Temple than we could without them. With Bortien, we can see that what Paul engaged in, publicly and emphatically, was naturally associated with the Nazirite vow. At the same time, we also must allow greater distance between Paul's vow and the stipulations of Mishnah than Bortien would allow. Paul was principally concerned with what he called the offering of the nations, and was willing to defer to Nazirite practice, to become "to those under law as under law" himself as part of his wider practice of becoming all things to all people (1 Cor 9:19-23). With Neusner, we can see that in the wake of the destruction of the Temple both Mishnah and Matthew came to view vows (and even oaths, in Matthew's case) with the utmost skepticism. At the same time, we must also allow that James, Jesus' brother, was still a partisan of the Nazirite vow in his brother's name, that he convinced Paul of its propriety, and that his view of the purity of the Gentiles and the holiness of Israel was the closest thing to a consensus in the pluralism of primitive Christianity.

Our consultation has opened the prospect of James' pragmatic influence within Christianity at its most primitive and formative stage. Paul's conformity to the program of the Nazirite vow is perhaps the most striking testimony to that influence. Comparison with Paul obviously has a place on our agenda of prospective work. At the same time, to proceed immediately to such a comparison seemed hasty to the members of our consultation. The destruction of the Temple and the end of the practice of the Nazirite vow, within the same decade as James' death, brought profound changes to both Judaism and Christianity, changes which eventually permitted Paulinism—a radical minority in Paul's own time—to emerge at or near the center of the Christian movement. The dominance of that perspective is perhaps the principal reason for which the study of James is now an exercise in recovery. Indeed, the influence of Paul became so great, it casts a shadow retrospectively on the figure of Peter, as well. James and Peter can perhaps best emerge from that shadow together, and our anticipation is that the next occasion of our consultation should address of the questions of their mutual relations and distinctive programs of practice.

INDEX OF ANCIENT LITERATURE

55:6-14	210	2.1.5	205, 239
55:6-13	201	2.23	261
55:11	201	2.23.1-18	8, 257
55:16-20	205	2.23.1-9	115
55:17-18	201	2.23.3-25	34 n. 3
59:22	207 n. 20	2.23.4-18	235 n. 5
60:2–63:30	248	2.23.4-9	55 n. 63
60:12	207 n. 20	2.23.5-7	187
61:4	205	2.23.6	209, 215
61:13-14	202	2.23.7	206, 208 n. 25
61:14-19	208	2.23.8-18	201
61:14	207 n. 20	2.23.8	201
61:16-19	201	2.23.8	202, 209, 231
61:21-23	211	2.23.9	201, 202, 213
61:20-22	201	2.23.10	202, 203, 204, 213, 230
61:21-22	204		
61:21-23	249	2.23.11	201, 204, 212, 230, 231
61:22-23	204		
61:23-26	212	2.23.12-13	229
61:26–62:4	202	2.23.12	201, 202, 203, 204, 209, 230, 231, 247
61:25-26	202		
62:3-9	204		
62:7	201, 230	2.23.13	204, 230
62:16	212	2.23.14-16	212
63:29	212	2.23.14	202, 203, 204, 212, 230, 231
		2.23.15	201, 208, 230
1 Clem. 5:1-6	192 n. 140	2.23.16	202, 204, 230
		2.23.17	2113
Clement of Alexandia		3.4.2	162 n. 26
Hypotyposes 6	246	3.7.8.	209
Hypotyposes 7	246	5.1.44	233 n. 1
		Praeparatio Evangelica	
Epiphanius		9.30.3-4	171 n. 64
Haer. 78.7.7	208 n. 25		
Haer. 78:14	213	Gos. Heb. §7	207 n. 20
Eusebius		Gos. Thom. §12	14, 34 n. 3, 55, 115, 207 n. 20, 247, 257 n. 11
Commentary on the Psalms			
68:8-9	98 n. 31		
Historia Ecclesiastica			
2.1.1-6	9		
2.1.2	246		
2.1.3	246		
2.1.4-5	34 n. 3	Ignatius	
2.1.4	246	Philadephians 6:1	163 n. 31

b. ʿErub. 61b	163 n. 28
b. Giṭ. 8a	174 n. 74, 177 n. 89, 178 n. 91
b. Giṭ. 44b	176 n. 84
b. Ket. 67a	162
b. Ket. 88a	160 n. 17
b. Menaḥ. 70b	157 n. 6
b. Pesaḥ. 35a	157 n. 6
b. Šabb. 114a	244 n. 29
b. Sanh. 11a	179 n. 95
b. Sanh. 43a	204 n. 12, 225, 226, 226 n. 56, 227
b. Sanh. 45a	203
b. Sanh. 67a	228
b. Soṭa 33a	171 n. 63

Midrash

Sipre Deut. §51	176 n. 85
Sipre Num. §78	213 n. 31
Sipra Behuq. 5.2	173 n. 71
Gen. Rab. 64.10	173
Gen. Rab. 91.3	255
Exod. Rab. 23.5	174 n. 76
Lev. Rab. 5.3	173 n. 70
Lev. Rab. 5.4	162 n. 24
Num. Rab. 2.9	163 n. 28
Num. Rab. 10.3	173 n. 70
Deut. Rab. 4.8	162 n. 24
Cant. Rab. 4:8 §2	173, 174 n. 76
Cant. Rab. 8:13 §1	171 n. 63
Esth. Rab. 7.10	245 n. 31
Yalqut to Amos	173 n. 70

Targums
Fragment Targum

Num. 34:8	173 n. 70, 174 n. 78

Neofiti 1

Num. 34:8	173 n. 70, 174 n. 78

Pseudo-Jonathan

Num 13:21	173 n. 70
Num 34	176 n. 83

Num 34:8	174 n. 78, 176 n. 83
Num 34:10	176 n. 83, 177 n. 89
Tg. Ps 118:22-23	243
Tg. Ps 118:26	244
Tg. Qoh 1:18	79
Tg. Qoh 7:9	79
Tg. Qoh 11:10	79

INDEX OF MODERN AUTHORS

INDEX OF SUBJECTS AND FIGURES